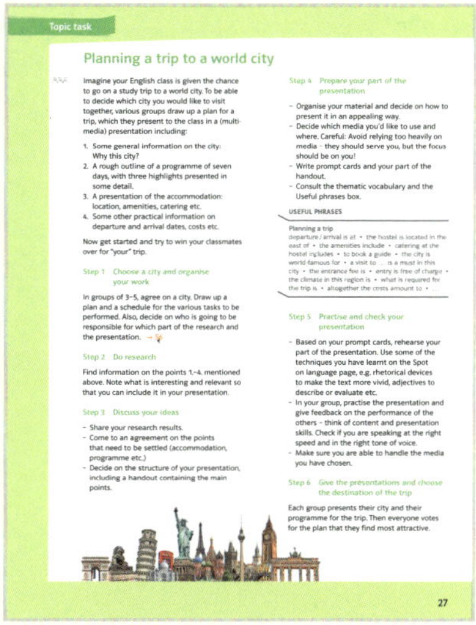

Texts / Optional texts

Vielfältige Textsorten und Medien beleuchten unterschiedliche Aspekte des Themas. Die *Optional texts* enthalten fakultative Materialien zur thematischen Erweiterung / Vertiefung.

Topic task

Handlungsorientierte, projektartige Aufgabe zur Überprüfung und kreativen Umsetzung erlernter Fertigkeiten.

Symbole und Medien

- Partnerarbeit
- Gruppenarbeit
- A 1 Audio
- V 2 Video
- MK Aufgabe mit Schwerpunkt Medienkompetenz
- → S 14 Verweis auf *Skill* im Anhang
- → WB 1/5 Verweis auf Aufgabe im *Workbook*
- → ○ Verweis auf leichtere / zusätzliche Aufgabe im *Practice pool*
- → ● Verweis auf anspruchsvollere Aufgabe im *Practice pool*

Alle Audios, Videos und Dokumente zum Schulbuch sind im **eBook** und in den **Medien zum Schulbuch** verfügbar.

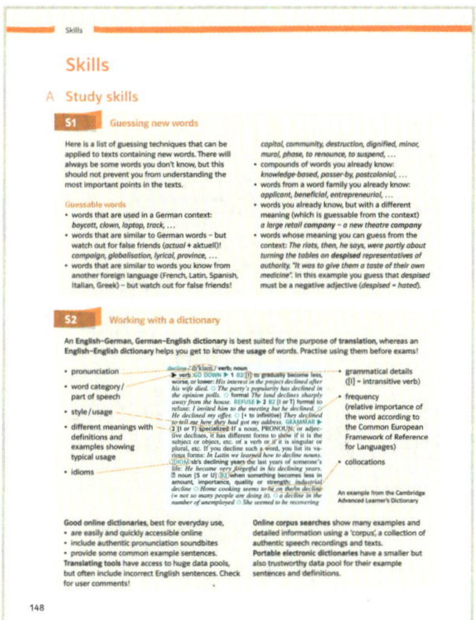

Skills

Alle wichtigen Skills mit Tipps und *Useful phrases*. Inklusive Operatorenliste.

Grammar

Die wichtigsten Grammatikregeln kompakt zusammengefasst.

Thematic vocabulary

Thematischer Wortschatz mit Übungen. *Vocabulary sheets* zu den Lesetexten finden Sie in den **Medien zum Schulbuch**.

Abkürzungen

adj	adjective
adv	adverb
AE	American English
BE	British English
CE	Canadian English
esp	especially
fml	formal
infml	informal
n	noun
pej	pejorative
pl	plural
sg	singular
sb	somebody
sl	slang
sth	something
v	verb
etw.	*etwas*
jmd./jmds.	*jemand/-es*
jmdm./jmdn.	*jemandem/-en*

Green Line Transition
Einführungsphase
für Klasse 11 an Gymnasien in Bayern

Zusatzmaterial für Schülerinnen und Schüler zu diesem Band:

Workbook mit Mediensammlung
978-3-12-834375-4

1. Auflage 1 6 5 4 3 2 | 2027 26 25 24 23

Autorinnen und Autoren: Jennifer Baer-Engel, Göppingen; Louise Carleton-Gertsch, München; Melissa Keller, Iphofen; Vera Kirchhübel, Bietigheim-Bissingen; Jon Marks, Ventnor; Eveline Stuke-Wennemann, Krefeld; Reiner Verspai, Rheinbach; Alison Wooder, Ventnor; unter Mitwirkung von Ronja Roth, Jena sowie Jason Humphreys, Frickenhofen; Cornelia Kaminski, Fulda; Florian Otte, Schwarmstedt
Beratung: Dr. Thomas Becker, Nürnberg; Christel Beck-Zangenberg, Erlangen; Elmar Beyersdörfer, Gräfelfing; Alexander Funk, Bamberg; Wolfgang Funk, Bamberg; Andrea Holler, Dachau; Michael Kleis, Geltendorf; Berit Möckel, Nürnberg; Wolfram Scharrer, Laaber; Nicolas Zehe, Hof

Entstanden in Zusammenarbeit mit dem Projektteam des Verlages.

Externe Redaktion: Anja Treinies, Düsseldorf (Vokabular)
Gestaltung: normaldesign GbR, Schwäbisch Gmünd
Umschlaggestaltung: normaldesign GbR, Schwäbisch Gmünd
Titelbild: 1 stock.adobe.com, Dublin (oneinchpunch); **2** Getty Images Plus, München (Orbon Alija)
Satz: media office GmbH, Kornwestheim
Druck: Mohn Media Mohndruck GmbH, Gütersloh

Printed in Germany
ISBN 978-3-12-834370-9

9 783128 343709

Skills workshop 2 Analysing fictional texts

Visions of the future

Skills

Grammar

Thematic vocabulary

Appendix

Der Verlag orientiert sich bei der Bezeichnung von Minderheiten an Begrifflichkeiten, die sich zum Zeitpunkt des Erscheinens als Selbstbezeichnungen mit breiter Akzeptanz durchgesetzt haben. Dabei respektieren wir ausdrücklich die Belange der Betroffenen und die Vielfalt der Positionen in der Diskussion um korrekte bzw. präferierte Bezeichnungen. Konkret werden in diesem Band beispielsweise die Bezeichnungen „Zulu", „Xhosa" und „Bantu" bzw. „Black South Africans" (South Africa) und „First Nations", „Inuit", „Métis" sowie als Sammelbegriff „Indigenous peoples" (Canada) verwendet. „Indigenous" und „Black" bzw. „Schwarz" werden großgeschrieben; Originaltexte wurden diesbezüglich nicht verändert. Im Hinblick auf geschlechtergerechte Schreibung im Deutschen wird gemäß der aktuellen Empfehlungen des Rats für deutsche Rechtschreibung verfahren. Für den Fall, dass sich der akzeptierte Sprachgebrauch über die Laufzeit des Lehrwerks verändert, weisen wir ausdrücklich darauf hin, dass zu keiner Zeit eine Diskriminierung von Menschen durch die verwendeten Begriffe intendiert war und ist.

1 New York – aspects of a world city

Introduction

1

2

3

MK **1** VISUALS

a) Choose one of the pictures and spontaneously write down the first ten words that come to your mind when you look at it. Compare your lists in class.

b) Describe the photos in detail. After each description define which impression of the city is conveyed. In doing so, consider the atmosphere that is created and the feelings the photos evoke.

c) Locate the three sights on the map at the back of the book. In class, collect what you know about them. Then explain in a short statement which of them you would you like to see if you had just one afternoon in New York.

V1 **2** VIEWING

MK a) Watch the video *Moving through New York* and note down objects and scenes shown.

b) Describe the picture of New York presented in the video. Compare it to that conveyed in the photos: What are the similarities, what are the differences?

c) Explain how the special effects used (time lapse) and the camerawork (distance, angle, movement) help to create a certain image of the city in the video. → S35

d) Discuss whether the photos and / or the video present a realistic picture of New York. Which aspects of the city are missing in both the photos and the video?

3 VOCABULARY Think about city life. Then draw a mind map of its key aspects with a partner.

4 ACROSS CULTURES Describe three photos you would show young people from New York as an introduction to the village / town / city you live in and explain your choice.

5 SPEAKING Find information on one of the sights (e.g. from the photos or the list below) and make a short presentation about it which is meant to win over the students for a visit.

Broadway • Brooklyn Bridge • One World Trade Center • Empire State Building • Fifth Avenue • Grand Central Station • High Line • MoMA • 9/11 Memorial • Rockefeller Center • UN • Wall Street • Chrysler Building …

V2 **6** VIEWING Together with a friend, you are planning a trip to New York. Watch the video about the Governors Ball music festival and take notes on what to expect: type of festival, music genres and other cultural offers and possible troubles. Would you like to attend the festival?

7 VISUALS Describe the cartoons. Then explain their message and comment on them. Which cartoon do you find more effective?
→ O 1 → S38

1

2

Aspects of New York City

The population of New York

First of all, it should be noted that New York is not Manhattan. It actually consists of five parts, called boroughs: The Bronx, Brooklyn, Manhattan, Queens and Staten Island (look at the map at the back of your book.) Each borough has its own character and makes an important contribution to the city.

With about 8.8 million inhabitants (2020), New York is by far the most populous city in the US. And it is very densely populated: The area of the city (778 km²) is half as big as that of London, but it houses roughly the same number of people.

New York is home to people of many different backgrounds. More than 800 languages are spoken there, making it the linguistically most diverse city in the world. English (51 %) and Spanish (25 %) remain the most common languages spoken in NYC. Though many citizens of New York have a wide-ranging ancestry, statistically 30.9 % are white, while 28.3 % are Hispanic, 20.2 % are Black and 15.6 % are Asian.

Diversity is a central feature of the city in other respects, too. People of many different religions call New York their home, with the Jewish community being particularly strong: New York has more Jews than, e.g. Jerusalem. Moreover, the city boasts of one of the largest LGBTQIA+ communities in the world, attracted by the great freedom the city offers.

New Yorkers are said to be sturdy people with a 'can-do spirit'. They have gone through many crises, most recently the Covid pandemic, during which the city was among the hardest hit places worldwide. But as usual in times of trouble, New Yorkers stood together and showed their determination to build back up again, which is said to be part of their nature.

A look at New York's history

Although New York is not the capital of the US, it has an outstanding position, nationally as well as internationally, and some people have even gone so far as to call it 'the capital of the world'. What are the roots of New York's unique reputation?

At the beginning there was no sign of greatness: The first settlers in the region, the Dutch, bought the island of Manhattan from a Native American tribe for $ 24 in 1626. They called the place New Amsterdam, but it was only a small trading post until it was conquered by the English and renamed New York in 1664.

Due to its favourable position on the Atlantic coast, New York quickly grew as a trading centre. After America had declared its independence from Britain in 1776, the number of immigrants from European countries like Britain, Ireland, Germany and Italy increased steadily. New York vastly profited from this influx of hard-working people, as most immigrants entered the US via New York Harbour. At the same time the city attracted migrants from within the US such as former slaves from the more repressive southern states.

It was in this period that, thanks to infrastructure projects and industrialisation, New York became America's largest and economically most powerful city and developed strong ties with places all over the world, making it a "global city". As a result, the metropolis also became a cultural centre, giving birth e.g. to a movement called the Harlem Renaissance, a blossoming of African-American culture.

Immigration also shaped New York's reputation as a global "refuge" for people "yearning to be free" (inscription on the Statue of Liberty). The fact that New York has not lost its power as a symbol of the free world was dramatically demonstrated on 9/11 (11th September 2001), when Islamist terrorists steered two hijacked planes into the Twin Towers of the World Trade Center, killing almost 3,000 people.

1 VOCABULARY Collect words and expressions from the texts on this double page which are useful when talking about urban development. → WB 9/1, 10/4–5

2 COMPREHENSION Make a list of all the reasons given for New York's unique reputation in the first three texts.

New York today – a city of superlatives

Despite such setbacks, New York has retained its prominent position. If the city were a country, it would be number 8 in the world economically. There is no doubt that New York is the number one financial centre in the world. Since World War II, many international organisations have established their headquarters in New York, among them the UN. The metropolis is now an important media hub, a magnet for advertising companies and a major tourist attraction, welcoming more than 30 million visitors every year.

One factor contributing much to New York's unique image worldwide is certainly the architecture of Manhattan – the magnificent skyline is an emblem known worldwide. From the end of the 19th century on, because of the scarcity of land, architects began to construct skyscrapers in Manhattan, such as the Empire State Building (1931) built in the art déco style. Exciting new projects keep being realised, with 2022 seeing the completion of the Steinway Tower, said to be the world's thinnest skyscraper.

Despite fierce competition, New York still is a centre for the arts and for culture in general. The metropolis has a number of spectacular museums, such as the Metropolitan Museum of Art, and the name Broadway is symbolic of the theatre industry. At the same time New York keeps originating new art styles like hip-hop culture and graffiti-writing in the 1970s and 80s.

Challenges of the present and the future

Traffic in NYC is a major concern. The problem is not the transit system – the subway e.g. may be old but it still functions well. It is rather the number of cars producing traffic jams and aggravating air pollution that make life less agreeable. In general, New York's infrastructure and architecture require drastic changes in order to fend off the negative effects of climate change. The other major challenge is a set of interrelated social problems: Although the city is a much safer place than it used to be, the crime rate has been on a constant upward trend since the 2010s. A major root of social unrest is the acute housing crisis: As the city lacks space but attracts more and more rich investors, prices have skyrocketed, meaning that poor people cannot find affordable homes. In general, disparities of wealth and poverty remain central issues to be tackled and it is frustrating to see that people's living conditions and their well-being are still to a certain degree dependent on their ethnic background.

New York university students

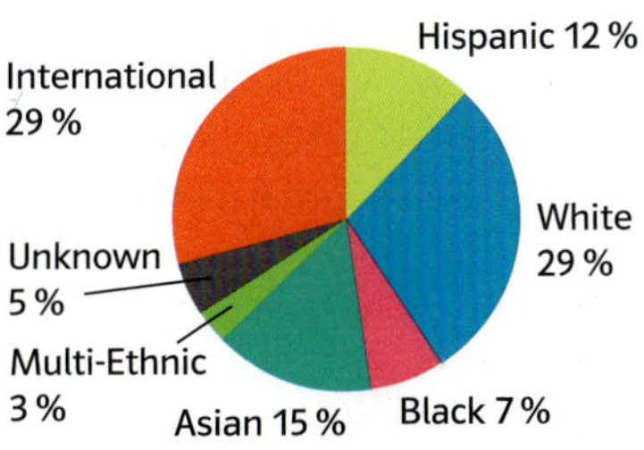

Front line workers in public transit

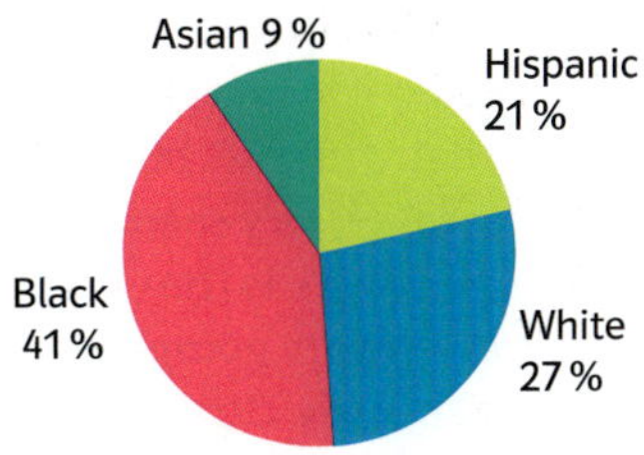

Front line workers in building cleaning services

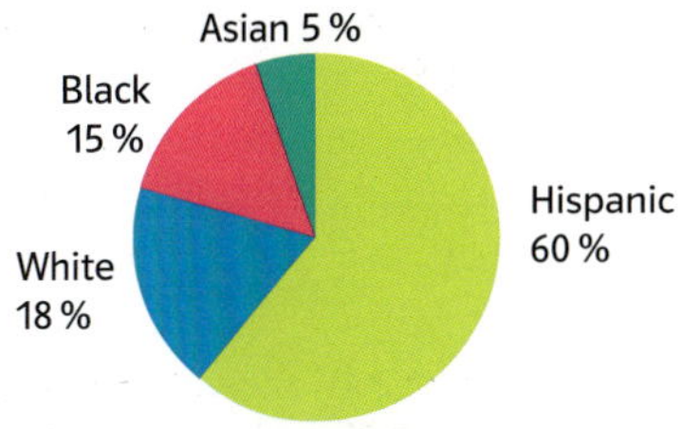

CollegeFactual.com, 2022 (1); U.S. Census Bureau, 2014–2018 (2–3)

3 VISUALS

a) Express the facts visualised in the three charts in words. → ○ 2

b) On the basis of the size of the various ethnic groups in NY (see statistics in the first text), explain what the charts show about the career choices of people from different ethnic backgrounds. → S37

c) Comment on the possible reasons for the different career choices and their consequences. Are these differences a sign of inequality or injustice? → S19

4 EVALUATION Which aspects of city life (safety, diversity, jobs, attractions, architecture, arts and entertainment, housing, traffic and transport, people's character) do you personally regard to be most important? Why? Prepare a short statement and then discuss in class. → ○ 3 → WB 9/3

A Real New Yorkers

Voices of New York

Over six years Craig Taylor spoke to more than 180 New Yorkers about their views on life in the city. Here are some of their opinions.

Gus Powell – a photographer

New York is an incredibly generous place. I'm inherently an optimist. The sidewalks are generous, the light is generous, the people are generous. This is why you can get things done here. There's so many opportunities as a photographer. You go other places and it's like squeezing water from a stone. Whereas here, it just keeps coming and coming and coming. Some days, there ends up being this proprietary moment when you feel like New York, it's all for you. You'll even walk past another photographer and you can tell the way they're holding the camera and the way they're looking at the world and they'll just nod like, *Yeah, This is all for us. This is like Disneyland.*

2 **inherent** by nature
5 **to squeeze** to press
6 **proprietary** when you feel something belongs to you

Zack Arkin – a former cab driver

In order to make it, you've got to connect with people. You gotta be creative, and you gotta go outside the box. If nothing works, you have one second to do something. You've got that one chance. Say it. Do it. [...]

Driving a cab, I used my skill, which was connecting with people in the cab. I would drive Sunday morning. And I'd go up to Harlem on the way up to the churches. In the summertime, hot sweltering heat, I knew my friend was up in the barrio, in Spanish Harlem.

Being in a cab gave us power because you had mobility. You shot through cultures, neighborhoods. You shot through levels. You had a virtual reality.

That's why art is fascinating with the textures. In New York, people are the textures.

Every breath that you take you have to realize that you have an opportunity. And so if you let New York swallow you, you're going to be sorry. It's up to you. You have to help people. But they're going to help you. There's a balance of life, you know. And it always comes back. Never worry about getting repaid. And don't get caught up in the money. Don't get caught up over living in a particular place. You may be living where it is.

Have fun. Who cares if you're on fucking Fifth Avenue in Trump Tower or you're in a fucking tenement. You go meet a girlfriend and you fall in love. People can find love. It's hard. It's a thing that you can't buy. You can't buy New York. You've got to live it. You have to live New York every second. Otherwise, you don't get it. Go out to the burbs.

The thing about New York is the eyeballs. You have to make contact with people in New York. If you don't, they're going to put one over on you. Why do people get robbed in New York? They turn away. Do you notice that? Don't ever turn away from someone. New Yorkers eyeball you, make you stay in the eye.

12 **to go outside the box** *über den Tellerrand schauen*
15 **Harlem** part of Manhattan, centre of African-American culture
18 **to shoot through** *here:* to come into contact with
29 **burbs** *(infml)* suburbs
31 **to put one over on sb** *jmdn. betrügen*

Maggie Parker – a nanny

Your relationship with the city asks you to confront so many gross things about yourself. Envy was a big thing for me. When I came here I didn't have a job. I was working part-time. Being around it, feeling envious, makes you feel gross. You're not in the safety of your own car, or far away from this. It's all next to you. Even if you don't open *Vogue*, you walk by all of the stuff.

I came from higher education, a lot of privilege. I got a car when I turned sixteen and for most of the world that's extreme privilege. We had a pool growing up. You know, wow! Then you come here and you're like *This is a violent amount of wealth.* But it was also helpful because it redefined the term for me. People who are violently wealthy or aggressively wealthy, they don't seem very happy or that proportionately happy.

Everybody around you seems like they have so much purpose, and they're succeeding so much more. They're younger than you, they're better than you, they're cooler than you. Even if I was raised with all the money, that currency of cool I can't manufacture.

47 **currency** *here:* kind, type

Pete Meehan – a cop

What makes New York different is the concentration of people from so many different backgrounds. I don't think it's really a challenge. I think it's a benefit. It's a deal that, to deal with so many different aspects, different languages, different customs.

I remember going into a Japanese lady's house and taking my shoes off before taking her to court for a stolen vehicle. Why wouldn't you? [...]

I remember going into an Orthodox Jewish household. I could not greet the wife and my female partner could not have any contact with the man. And the kosher kitchen and the Sabbath and things of that nature and dealing with it, so many different cultures and so many different cultural aspects – it's awesome. It wasn't a challenge. It was a benefit.

If you work with it, there's nothing that can't be accomplished. And because we deal with everything, I think we can accomplish it. New York City is so huge, other than downhill skiing and maybe desert kite sailing, I don't think there really is an activity that we don't have in the city.

From: Craig Taylor, *New Yorkers*, 2021

56 **kosher** prepared according to rules of Jewish law

57 **Sabbath** in Judaism, day of rest

1 COMPREHENSION With a partner, find a suitable heading for each of the four parts. Compare your ideas in class. → S8

2 COMPREHENSION

a) Say whether the view of New York presented in each text is more positive or negative.
b) Describe the images of New York that the interviewees convey.
c) State the messages each person tries to get across.

3 ANALYSIS

a) The four interviewees have different ways of expressing their views on the city. Try to identify some of the strategies and stylistic devices used in the texts. Look at the tip box for help.
b) Explain the effect of the devices in the concrete context. → S11

TIP

Some common (rhetorical, linguistic and argumentative) devices
enumerations • repetitions • images (metaphors and similes) • personifications • contrasts • questions • short sentences • informal language • imperatives • comparisons, superlatives • examples • personal experiences

A1 **4 LISTENING** Listen to a further voice of New York, a rapper called *'Cook Monsta Da Illest'*, and take notes. Find a suitable heading for this part and do Task 2 above. → ○ 4

5 CREATIVE TASK Think about the place where you live and what life is like there. Then prepare a short statement – similar to the voices of New York – on what you feel and like or dislike about it and share it with the class. Try to make use of some of the devices in the tip box. → ○ 5

B Making a life in the city of dreams

Dreams come true?

A "If I can make it there, I'll make it anywhere."
Frank Sinatra, *Theme from New York, New York*

B "Big lights will inspire you."
Alicia Keys, *Empire State of Mind*

C "It's like a jungle sometimes I wonder how I keep from going under."
Grandmaster Flash and the Furious Five, *The Message*

D "Everybody here wanted somethin' more
Searchin' for a sound we hadn't heard before."
Taylor Swift and Ryan Tedder, *Welcome To New York*

1 COMPREHENSION Read the quotes and explain which points are made about living and "making it" in New York. Define the rhetorical figures used.

2 VIEWING Find the video *Making a living: Kianee Truvillon* by *Voice of America* online. In a chart, take notes on Kianee's life in New York (general information, flat, career, jobs, money, family, future plans) and then talk about it in class.

It's kind of a funny story

3 BEFORE YOU START
First look at the picture of the Brooklyn Bridge and then locate the bridge on the map at the end of the book. What do you think it is like for young people to walk across the bridge at night? How would you feel? → ● 6

Craig Gilner, the narrator of the story, is an ambitious teenager from Manhattan. In the middle of a party night, he and his friend Aaron decide to walk across the Brooklyn Bridge. Craig is in a good mood and his friend Aaron has just made out with a girl.

We weren't even a tenth of the way up the bridge, but it did look cool. Behind us the walkway extended to City Hall, where the city had sprung for some spotlights to illuminate the dome of the building. It looked like a white pearl nestled between giants like the Woolworth Building, which I learned in English class Ayn Rand had described as a "finger of God," and that was about right – green and white at the top like the world's most decorated mint. To our left were the other bridges of Manhattan, arrayed against each other like alternating sin and cos waves, carrying a smattering of late-night trucks whose tops trailed mist.

2 **City Hall** seat of the NYC government
2 **to spring for sth** *(infml)* to pay for sth
4 **Ayn Rand** American writer and philosopher
6 **to array** to arrange
7 **sin and cos** *Sinus und Cosinus*
7 **smattering** a small amount
8 **to trail** to pull sth behind sth

But to the right was the best view: New York Harbor. Mostly black. The Statue of Liberty was lit up, but it always struck me as a little cheesy, standing out there being all cute. The real action was on the sides: Manhattan had its no-nonsense downtown, where people made money, and on the other side was Brooklyn, sleepy and dark but with a trump card – the container cranes, lit up not for show or government pride but because there was work going on, even at this hour – ships unloading stuff that was famously unchecked for terrorist threats but somehow hadn't blown us up yet. Brooklyn was a port. New York was a port. We got things done. I had gotten things done, too.

Between Brooklyn and Manhattan, miles across the water, we saw the final curtain of New York City – the Verrazano Narrows Bridge. It spanned the opening to the port, a steel-blue pair of upper lips greeting the blackness.

I could do anything anywhere, in all four directions.

"Craig?" Aaron was like.

"What's up."

"What's up with you? You okay?"

"I'm happy," I said.

"Why not?"

"No, I said I'm happy."

"I know. Why not be?"

We came up to the first tower of the bridge, with a plaque proclaiming who had built it; I stopped to read. John Roebling. Aided by bis wife, and then his son. He died during construction. But hey, the Brooklyn Bridge might be here for eight hundred years. I wanted to leave something like that behind. I didn't know how I was going to do it, but I felt like I had taken the first steps.

"The really cool thing about Nia ..." Aaron was saying, and he started to go into anatomical details, things about her that I didn't need to hear; I tuned him out; I knew he was talking to himself. This was what he was happy about. I was happy about different stuff. I was happy because someday I'd be walking across this bridge looking at this city, owning some piece of it, being valuable here.

"Her butt is like – I think her butt shape is where they got the heart logo. ..."

We came to the middle of the bridge. On either side of us the cars hissed past; red on the left and white on the right, the lanes encased by thin metal trussing that stretched out from the walkway.

I had a sudden urge to walk out over the trussing and lean over the water, to declare myself to the world. Once it came into my head, I couldn't push it away.

"I don't know if it was real –" Aaron was saying.

"I want to stand out over the water," I told him.

"What?"

"Come with me. You want to do it?"

He stopped.

"Yeah," he said. "Yeah, I see where you're coming from."

There were pathways built onto the top of the trussing, places for the bridge workers to get out to the cables and repair them. I clambered onto one on the harbor side, the side crowned by the Verrazano, and grabbed the handrails and balanced my feet one in front of the other on a piece of metal about four inches wide. Below me cabs and SUVs hummed by. In front of me was the black of the water and the black of the sky and the cold.

"You're crazy," Aaron said.

I took steps forward. It was easy. Stuff like this always is. The stuff adults tell you not to do is the easiest.

Below me there were three lanes of traffic; I cleared the first, got halfway over the second; then Aaron yelled:

10 **cheesy** *(infml)* romantic, kitschy
19 **to span** to stretch right across sth
29 **plaque** *Gedenktafel*
30 **to aid** to help
35 **to tune sb out** not to listen to sb
39 **butt** *(infml)* *Hintern*
41 **encased** surrounded (for protection)
41 **trussing** construction made of pieces of metal to support sth
52 **to clamber** to climb with difficulty
60 **to clear** to make it to

"What are you going to do out there?!"

"I'm just going to think!" I called back.

"About what?"

I shook my head. I couldn't explain. "It'll only take a minute!"

Aaron turned back.

I moved past the second lane and kept my eyes on the horizon. I didn't move my eyes from it for the last lane, shifting my hands in front of one another in a tight rhythm. I came to the edge of the bridge and was sort of surprised how there wasn't any fence. There wasn't anything to keep you from falling off, just your hands and your will. I gripped the bars at either side – they were freezing – and then sprung my hands open and spread my arms wide and felt the wind whip and tug at me as I leaned myself over the water like ... well, like Christ, I guess.

I closed my eyes and opened them, and the only difference was the feel of the wind on my eyeballs, because when I closed them I could still see the dotted lights perfectly. I threw back my head and yelled. When I was a kid I read these books, the Redwall books, fantasy books about a bunch of warrior mice, and the mice had this war cry that I always thought was cool: "Eulalia."

And like an idiot, that's what I yelled off the Brooklyn Bridge:

"Eulaliaaaaaaaaaaaaaaa!" [...]

After howling off the Brooklyn Bridge, I walked home and felt great.

From: Ned Vizzini, *It's kind of a funny story*, 2010

72 **to whip** *peitschen*
72 **to tug** to pull hard
75 **dotted** *gepunktet*
77 **bunch** *(infml)* a group of

4 COMPREHENSION What are your first reactions to the story? What do you think of Craig and his nightly "walk" on the Brooklyn Bridge?

5 COMPREHENSION Summarise the scene. → S28

6 ANALYSIS Analyse Craig's thoughts and feelings in this scene: → S10
1. Explain his view of New York. For this purpose, interpret some of the stylistic devices the narrator uses to describe his view of the city, especially in ll. 1–20.
2. Outline what Craig thinks and feels before, while and after reading the plaque about John Roebling (ll. 21–42).
3. Examine and comment on the motives for Craig's 'climbing tour' (ll. 43–80).
4. Summarise the results of the analysis by characterising the experience Craig has on the Brooklyn Bridge.

7 EVALUATION What about you? Do you feel an urge to do something 'grand' and leave something "valuable" (l. 38) like Craig does? How important are the aims of a career and of success for you?

8 CREATIVE TASK When Craig comes home, he meets his sister and tells her about his feat. With your partner, imagine the situation and write down their conversation. → S26

C Urban jungle or city of the future?

His name is Raheem

"It's Arabic," he told me. Sometime yesterday morning, Raheem had parked his caravan of three separate shopping carts, each piled six feet high with near-bursting bags of collected cans and bottles, on Eighth Avenue, across the street from where Oliver and I live. You couldn't miss it, really – there was audacity in his taking over the bus lane as if it were his private parking spot – and yet, people streamed by without glancing in his direction. Or maybe he wasn't really there. In the extreme heat and humidity of the day – temperatures over ninety – one might almost think Raheem was a mirage.

I was on my way to a doctor's appointment uptown when I first saw him, asleep on a milk crate, his bags shading him from the sun. I could see the photo in my mind even before I was close enough to take it. I thumbed my camera on and pocketed the lens cap as I raced toward him. I crouched down directly across from him, found his face in the frame, and snapped: 1, 2, 3, 4. I felt like a poacher. I was a poacher: The sleeping man roused, and cried out angrily, "Get the fuck away from me!"

I felt terrible, ashamed. I never do that – never take pictures of people without asking them. It was wrong, and I apologized to the man, who looked like he was silently laying a curse on me. [...]

Returning home later in the afternoon, I saw him still there from a block away. I bought a bottle of water, approached, and gave it to the man. He had hundreds, maybe thousands of empty water bottles, but did he have a full one?

"You getting enough water today?" I asked. I don't know if he remembered or recognized me, but he accepted the water with thanks. Maybe he would just empty it and add it to his collection; I didn't know.

I asked him what he was up to. He told me that he was on his way, eventually, to Duane Reade, the drugstore, where he would turn in his bags and get money in return. He told me there isn't a Recycling Center in Manhattan, as there is in the Bronx, and the drugstores won't take everything at once, so you have to go to one after the other after the other.

"Do you have something to eat? A place to sleep tonight?"

He nodded, again very matter-of-fact; he wasn't worried about that. This was when I asked his name and he told me it was Raheem. I later learned that it means "merciful."

I said my name is Billy. I told him I'd like to give him something to help him out. He had not asked me for a dime, after all. I didn't want to offend him again. "Is that cool?"

Raheem nodded. I gave him $ 20.

"Peace and love, and hallelujah," he said quietly, sincerely, like a prayer, "blessings to you." When I asked, he said it was okay if I took his picture now, and I took a few more.

I asked him how long he'd been on the streets and he told me sixteen years. Anyway, finding food and a place to sleep weren't a problem – that's the least of it, he implied. The problem is the police, who harass him, tell him to get his junk out of the street, or even worse, he said, "These people here now with $ 120 million apartments – they say, 'Get away from my building! Why don't you just throw all that shit in the garbage? I'm gonna call the cops!' And they do! Fuckers. And then I have to deal with the cops again."

He murmured, "The Village was a lot friendlier when it was entirely gay."

This made me chuckle, and I said I'll bet it was, I wish I'd lived here then.

"They think I don't know the law. I know the law. I know my rights. I'm not doing anything illegal. I'm not a junkie. I have every right to do this," he said. He looked over at the bags and bags of what most of us would call garbage. "This is my work!" he said with real feeling. "My work!"

In that moment, I suddenly saw every person on the streets of New York who collected bottles and cans from garbage bins and turned-over trash cans differently –

4 **audacity** *Dreistigkeit*

6 **humidity** amount of water in the air

10 **lens cap** *Objektivdeckel*

12 **poacher** sb who hunts and kills animals illegally

13 **to rouse** to wake up and move

16 **to lay a curse on sb** *jmdn. verfluchen*

23 **to be up to sth** *(infml)* to plan to do

34 **blessings to you** *viel Glück und Segen*

37 **the least of it** *here:* the easiest thing

42 **the Village** Greenwich Village, part of Manhattan

all the elderly tiny Asian women, sometimes whole families, Peruvian, African, some with bags balanced on poles carried on their shoulders: They were making work for themselves, performing a job most of us were too lazy or busy or wealthy to even think about.

But Raheem wasn't finished speaking. "I say to those guys, the ones who own the buildings, 'What are YOU doing? I'm saving the Earth! What are you doing for this planet?'"

From: Bill Hayes, *Insomniac City*, 2017

1 EVALUATION Collect six objects and / or places from the text that are important for Raheem and then make a list of the six most important objects and places in your everyday life. Compare the lists and comment on them.

2 COMPREHENSION
Sum up what happens to photographer Bill Hayes one day, including what he learns about Raheem's life and work.

3 ANALYSIS → ○ 7

a) Analyse Raheem's character. Pay special attention to what he says about other people and about himself and his life. Talk about the stereotype one has of homeless people and explain whether Raheem fits this stereotype or not.

b) Analyse the narrator's feelings and thoughts in the different parts of the scene. Pay special attention to what Hayes does and the way he talks to Raheem (interaction). Include an interpretation of the two images he uses at the beginning ("mirage", "poacher") and of the headline "His name is Raheem". → S11, 13–14

4 SPEAKING Raheem does more for the planet than other people. Discuss this statement. Do not only think of his 'work', but also consider his way of life in general, compared to that of 'normal' people.

5 CREATIVE TASK Raheem is resting on his milk crate in front of a posh high-rise again when a rich inhabitant comes out of the building, walks up to him and addresses him. He is obviously annoyed. Write down their dialogue. → S25–26

FACT FILE

- Homelessness in NYC has increased by 13 % in 10 years and has reached the highest levels since the 1930s, according to an organisation called Coalition for the Homeless. In March 2022, about 49,000 homeless people were sleeping in NYC's shelters, among them more than 15,000 children.
- In NYC all homeless people have a right to a shelter. But many of them prefer to live on the streets because the living conditions in the shelters are appalling due to frequent violence, lack of hygiene and flats being in a state of disrepair.
- The primary cause of homelessness is the lack of affordable housing. Investors buy up houses in poor neighbourhoods and renovate them to attract wealthy tenants, thus driving out the poor. This process is called 'gentrification'.
- Ethnic minorities are disproportionately affected by homelessness: In 2021, of the families with children in shelters 52.8 % were Black, 41.2 % Hispanic, and 2.6 % white, according to the NYC Department of Homelessness Services.

6 VIEWING Find the documentary *Poor in New York – Survival and the city* by *Deutsche Welle* online. Take notes on the three people (Sixta, Bridget, Mike) and then talk about their problems, activities and feelings.

I've seen a future without cars, and it's amazing → WB 54–55/1–3

As coronavirus lockdowns crept across the globe this winter and spring, an unusual sound fell over the world's metropolises: the hush of streets that were suddenly, blessedly free of cars. City dwellers reported hearing bird song, wind and the rustling of leaves.

You could smell the absence of cars, too. From New York to Los Angeles to New Delhi, air pollution plummeted, and the soupy, exhaust-choked haze over the world's dirtiest cities lifted to reveal brilliant blue skies.

Cars took a break from killing people, too. About 10 pedestrians die on New York City's streets in an ordinary month. Under lockdown, the city went a record two months without a single pedestrian fatality. [...]

As the roads became freer of cars, they grew full of possibility. Rollerblading and skateboarding have come back into fashion. Sales of bicycles and electric bikes have skyrocketed.

But there is a catch: Cities are beginning to cautiously open back up again, and people are wondering how they're going to get in to work. Many are worried about the spread of the virus on public transit. Are cars our only option? How will we find space for all of them?

In much of Manhattan, the average speed of traffic before the pandemic had fallen to 7 miles per hour. In Midtown, it was less than 5 m.p.h. That's only slightly faster than walking and slower than riding a bike. Will traffic soon be worse than ever?

Not if we choose another path.

Rather than stumble back into car dependency, cities can begin to undo their worst mistake: giving up so much of their land to the automobile. [...]

A few weeks ago, I began talking to Vishaan Chakrabarti, a former New York City urban-planning official and the founder of Practice for Architecture and Urbanism, a Manhattan-based architecture firm. Like other urbanists, Chakrabarti believes that the pandemic has created an opportunity for New York and other cities to reduce their reliance on cars.

Manhattan, already one of the most car-free places in the country, is the best place to start. Chakrabarti's firm, known as PAU, had been working on an intricate proposal to show what it might look and feel like to live in a city liberated from cars, to show how much better life in New York might be with one simple change: Most cars would be banished from Manhattan. [...]

You already know what's terrible about cars: They're dirty. They're dangerous. They're expensive to buy and maintain, and environmentally hazardous to produce and operate. Automobiles kill around 90,000 Americans every year – about 40,000 in car accidents, and an estimated 50,000 more from long-term exposure to air pollution emitted by cars.

But Chakrabarti is among a group of urbanists who've been calling attention to a less-discussed problem with cars. Automobiles are not just dangerous and bad for the environment; they are also profoundly wasteful of the land around us, taking up way too much physical space to transport too few people. It's geometry.

In most American cities, wherever you look, you will see a landscape constructed primarily for the movement and storage of automobiles, not for the enjoyment of people: endless wide boulevards and freeways for cars to move swiftly; each road lined with parking spaces for cars at rest; retail establishments ringed with spots for cars; houses built around garages for cars; and a gas station, for cars to feed, on every other corner. [...]

How would people get around in a Manhattan without private cars?

Mostly on foot, by bus or by subway; often on a bicycle, e-bike, scooter, or some future light, battery-powered "micromobility" device (things like one-wheeled,

NYC 2020: Empty streets during lockdown

2 **hush** silence
3 **blessedly** fortunately
6 **to plummet** to fall suddenly or quickly
6 **exhaust-choked** filled with waste gas from car engines
6 **haze** air that is difficult to see through
14 **a catch** *(infml)* a hidden disadvantage
22 **to stumble** to walk unsteadily
30 **intricate** complex
37 **exposure to** *Belastung durch*
46 **ringed with** *here:* surrounded by

52 **in a pinch** if absolutely necessary
52 **Uber** mobility service allowing users to book private cars
59 **intractable** very difficult
62 **contagion** *ansteckende Krankheit*
62 **to thrive on** to profit from

self-balancing skateboards); and sometimes, in a pinch, in a taxi or Uber. [...]

Under PAU's plan, road traffic in a car-free Manhattan would fall by about 60 percent. The absence of cars would allow pedestrians, buses and bikes to race across New York at unheard-of speeds. Today, a bus trip from uptown to downtown – for instance, from Harlem to City Hall – takes an hour and 48 minutes. With the sort of rapid bus system PAU imagines, and without cars in the way, the same trek would take 35 minutes. [...]

At the moment, many of the most intractable challenges faced by America's urban centers stem from the same cause – a lack of accessible physical space. We live in a time of epidemic homelessness. There's a national housing affordability crisis caused by an extreme shortage of places to live. And now there's a contagion that thrives on indoor overcrowding.

Given these threats, how can American cities continue to justify wasting such enormous tracts of land on death machines?

Farhad Manjoo, in: *The New York Times*, 2021

7 **VOCABULARY** Scan the text and note down words and expressions from the word field of traffic and arrange them in a mind map. → S1

8 **COMPREHENSION** First describe the negative effects the number of private cars in cities like New York has. Then outline the solution proposed by the author and the advantages it has according to him.

9 **ANALYSIS** Analyse how the author tries to make his article interesting and to convince the readers of his proposal. Pay special attention to:
1. words with positive or negative connotations and emotive/evaluating words
2. contrasts and comparisons
3. facts and figures
4. questions and short sentences
5. metaphors and enumerations → S10–11

10 **EVALUATION** In many big cities, authorities are trying to reduce the number of cars as much as possible. Do you agree with this policy? Suggest and discuss other ways of fighting traffic problems in big cities.

11 **CREATIVE TASK** Write a letter to the editor of the *New York Times* and comment on the author's ideas and proposals. → S21

MK **12** **SPEAKING** Choose a world city like London, Paris, Berlin, Singapore, Mexico City, Lagos, Beijing, etc. and research information on the use of private cars and traffic in general. Report to the class. Use visual material in the form of statistics or charts. → O 8

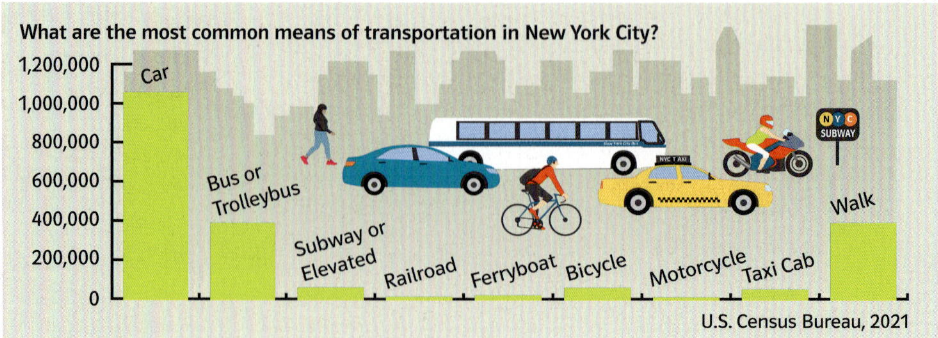

Darum ist New York nicht die genialste Stadt der Welt

13 MEDIATION The New York City Tourist Office has launched an online enquiry into why the city's reputation as a magnet for foreign tourists has suffered lately. Write an email to the office highlighting the negative aspects of the city mentioned in the article by Annette Schimanski as well as those illustrated in the photos. → S39

Die enormen Kontraste

In Manhattan glänzen die Wolkenkratzer um die Wette und auf dem *Times Square* versuchen die Leuchtreklamen zum Shoppen zu animieren, doch nur wenige Blocks entfernt stapelt sich der Müll auf der Straße, tropft der Regen durch die Decke auf die U-Bahn-Schienen und billige Lichterketten blinken wie wild an den Fenstern sämtlicher Cafés und Restaurants. Es ist erstaunlich zu sehen, wie das Land, das sich selbst stets an der Weltspitze sieht, tatsächlich aussieht. Über den Gehwegen verläuft ein unübersichtlicher Salat aus Stromkabeln, die sich von einem schiefen Strommast zum nächsten hangeln. Die Autos donnern über Schlaglöcher in den Straßen. Eine zunächst hübsch erscheinende Wohngegend endet abrupt in einem Brachland aus Müll, Dreck und Bauruinen. Die Busse wirken veraltet und würden in Deutschland keinesfalls den TÜV bestehen. Das Wasser wird mit Chlor gereinigt – und das ist deutlich zu schmecken. Man fühlt sich ein wenig an Zustände in Entwicklungsländern erinnert, nicht aber an die USA.

Das fehlende Umweltbewusstsein

In Deutschland wurden die kostenlosen Plastiktüten abgeschafft, Kaffeebecher sollen weniger werden und man hat ein schlechtes Gewissen, wenn man doch mal in Plastik eingepacktes Gemüse kauft. Nicht so in den USA. Alles wird grundsätzlich zum Mitnehmen verpackt – der Kuchen im Café kommt in eine kleine Tüte, der Kaffee in den Becher und das, obwohl man im Laden bleiben möchte. In einem schicken französischen Café wurde mir die Quiche am Tisch in einer Plastikschachtel mit Plastikgabel gereicht. Für das Getränk gab es immer einzeln verpackte Strohhalme und zu Pancakes Cent-große Butterstücke, die ebenfalls einzeln in Plastik verpackt sind. Da wundern einen die Berge an Müll, die sich in den Straßen auftürmen, nicht mehr.

Das chaotische Stadtbild

Auch wenn man noch nie in New York war: Den Central Park kennen viele aus Hollywood-Filmen – er ist ein beliebter Drehort der Stadt. Oft sieht man die Protagonisten in dem riesigen Park sitzen und gedankenverloren in die Skyline blicken. Im Film sieht das wunderschön aus. Die Skyline, die den Süden des Central Parks tatsächlich einrahmt, ist ernüchternd chaotisch. Es herrscht eine Dichte an Wolkenkratzern, die so gar nicht zueinander passen wollen. Jedes Gebäude scheint einen anderen Stil zu bedienen und ist in den seltensten Fällen eine Reaktion auf die umliegenden Bauten.

Es ergibt sich ein wildes Stadtbild, das ohne jegliches städtebauliches Konzept entstanden zu sein scheint. Als hätte jeder Bauherr auf seinem Grundstück das umgesetzt, wonach ihm war und nicht das, was möglicherweise das Beste für die Stadt gewesen wäre. Im Süden Manhattans hingegen, wo sich ein weiteres dichtes Wolkenkratzer-Gebiet befindet, ist ein klareres, in sich stimmiges Stadtbild zu erkennen.

Annette Schimanski, *Travelbook* Webseite, 2018

Arguing convincingly

Language skills can be very useful to explain your point of view or to convince others. Try out strategies like avoiding common words, using rhetorical devices or emphasising ideas.

1 Olivia's mom Sandra would like to move to Manhattan in order to take on a new job, but her dad Tom has doubts. Olivia would love to live in Manhattan and tries to convince him. Read Olivia's dialogue part and replace common words like *good, great* etc. with a word from the list:

awe-inspiring • convenient • excellent • ideal • marvellous • once-in-a-lifetime • perfect • spectacular • valuable

Well, Dad, you know that the job with *Jones & Lawensky* is a great chance for Mom. It'll never come again. We could rent an apartment close to Central Park, which is the best place to walk the dog. The view of the park is just great. There are many schools which offer great courses and a good preparation for college. Granddad and Grandma will often come to see us. They love the city's great sights. Remember when we visited the 9/11 memorial together. It was such a good experience. And it would be nice to see our friends who already live in New York without having to travel by car. To me, the move to Manhattan seems to be a very good opportunity for all of us.

2 Sandra speaks to Tom too. Express the points she is making more forcefully by using the rhetorical device indicated in brackets.

1. For an artist like you, New York is the ideal place to go. I am sure many people will want to see and buy your work. *(exaggeration)*
2. Don't worry about the children. For them, making new friends will be very easy. *(simile)*
3. And just imagine: Within a five-minute walk there are all kinds of restaurants. *(enumeration)*
4. I know how much you love baseball and the Yankee Stadium. I'm afraid you'll be there very often. *(metaphor / exaggeration)*
5. It is true that New York used to be a dangerous place. But now it is very safe. *(comparison / simile)*
6. If friends come to stay, we could show them New York's sights. *(enumeration)*
7. In our apartment on 34th floor, you can hardly hear the noise of the city. In fact it is very quiet there. *(comparison / simile)*

3 Tom explains to Sandra why he has doubts about moving. Make his statements more convincing by using the constructions below to emphasise the marked ideas.

TIP

Possibilities to emphasise certain ideas:
1. The pronouns **"myself"**, **"yourself"**, etc.: *The village **itself** is not what keeps me here.*
2. Cleft sentences, i.e. "It is / was … who / that …", "What … is / are …": ***It is** seeing my parents **that** I would miss most. / **What** I would like to see **is** the skyscrapers.*
3. Emphatic "do" to stress a verb: *I may not talk to my parents every day, but I **do** love them being around.*

1. The number of cars in big cities really annoys me.
2. The kids may not love the countryside. But they enjoy the freedom to roam around here.
3. You are right. The apartment is ideal for us but we would not be able to pay for it. We would have to ask my parents.
4. You know that I love going out, but I cannot stand the masses of people.
5. I am not joking, the amount of garbage and dirt in New York really puts me off.
6. I feel we would leave my parents alone here. They would have to do all the work.
7. I don't mind the noise so much. I am worried about safety.
8. The prospect of living in the city scares me but I see what the move means to you.

4 Sandra and Tom have decided to move to New York and want to sell their car. Olivia (who's 16) and her brother Noah (aged 14) disagree whether that is a good idea. With your partner, write the teenagers' dialogue using some of the methods of arguing convincingly. → WB 9/2

D World cities, global cities, diverse cities

Cities of choice – global city ranking → WB 12/7–8

1 BEFORE YOU START In your opinion, what would be the best city to live in? What makes a city a good place to live in? How can one find out or measure which city is the "best"?

Cities of choice – global city ranking

Rank	City	Country	Total score (max. 100)	Quality of life	Economic opportunities	Social capital	Interaction with authorities	Speed of change
1	London	UK	65.7	68	69	77	65	35
2	New York	USA	64.9	65	71	74	66	45
3	Helsinki	Finland	60.2	67	64	55	64	34
4	Copenhagen	Denmark	59.8	64	57	56	56	52
5	Abu Dhabi	UAE	59.4	50	78	61	71	73
6	Madrid	Spain	59.3	60	43	74	48	54
...								
26	Paris	France	49.7	56	55	57	45	10
27	Montreal	Canada	49.5	53	49	37	73	41
28	Delhi	India	49.2	30	36	81	35	94
29–30	Berlin	Germany	48.7	52	47	57	39	29
29–30	Vancouver	Canada	48.7	57	45	32	62	39
...								
42	Hong Kong	China	33.0	33	38	18	52	41
43	São Paulo	Brazil	28.4	25	5	40	10	58
44	Rio De Janeiro	Brazil	22.5	15	1	44	5	54
45	Santiago	Chile	20.8	15	12	26	31	44

The colours reflect the place of the city in the respective category:

very high | high | average | low | very low

BCG Henderson Institute: Cities of choice, 2021

2 VISUALS

a) Describe the table and say what information it provides. → S37

b) Explain the five different categories and what they (probably) mean.

c) Talk about and compare the scores / positions of the cities. Say which results surprise you and give possible reasons.

MK **3 SPEAKING** Go online, find other city rankings and report on them. Compare the results and, if possible, also the criteria used to establish the ranking.

FACT FILE

World cities, global cities, diverse cities

"World city" and "global city" are often treated as synonyms, as both refer to any large city that enjoys a reputation for its internationality. Sometimes though, the term global city, coined by sociologist Saskia Sassen, is used in a narrower sense: It designates a city that has attracted a large number of international companies and acts as a command centre of the globalised world economy. Such cities often develop a high degree of independence from the region around them.

The first global city in this sense of the word was London in the 19th century. Due to its position as the capital of the British Empire, it established strong economic and political ties with its colonies in all corners of the earth, thus becoming the heart of international finance and trade.

As a result of their international connectedness, global cities are usually also diverse cities, meaning that the number of inhabitants from different foreign countries who have made the cities their home is relatively high.

London's DNA has always been diversity, not its 'Englishness'

A few years ago I was in Dehradun, a bustling city in India's mountainous north. A man at a colourful fruit stand began to chat to me, and was visibly startled by the accent of the boy opposite him. He asked me where I was from, suspecting I was not local. I could have given any number of answers but the word "London" slipped out. It seemed the simplest way to explain how I could look like him, speak his language (poorly), and yet be a native of another place entirely.

My comfort with an inclusive and distinct London identity is not shared by all. Last month an American columnist visited London and called it "New York with better scones". She pointed out that a lot of things in big cities around the world are becoming the same: ride-sharing, smart hotels, slick, expensive cocktails in upmarket former industrial zones. Globalisation and multinational companies have indeed produced similarities but Western travellers who come to foreign cities only to use the same things are not without blame.

More dangerous is the claim that recent immigration and globalisation have somehow stripped London of its culture. Some conservatives claim that one rarely hears English in the streets, or that London has imported people and customs that fundamentally threaten its singular identity. John Cleese, of Monty Python fame and now a resident of the Caribbean island of Nevis, wrote last month that "London [is] not really an English city any more". This requiem is only the latest of many. The 2011 census revealed the capital to be the first major UK region with a minority of white Britons, setting off hysterical claims of the death of English London.

Complaints of this type focus on globalisation and migration, to suggest the city has changed beyond recognition. Yet those who mourn the death of a quintessentially "English" London tend to have two things in common: they rarely live in London, and they misunderstand that a Londoner is not simply an Englishman or a Briton.

London has never been a purely English city. In its first 1,000 years it was founded by Romans, razed by Celts, settled by the Anglo-Saxons, and ruled by Normans. From the start London was outward-looking and its lifeblood was international exchange. [...]

London was forged by its surroundings: England, Europe, and the world.

From this heritage emerges a large and civic identity for Londoners, rather than a more narrowly, often ethnically, defined Englishness. The Centre for London found in 2018 that only half of Londoners strongly identified as "English", with more opting for "British" and even more simply for "Londoner". [...]

Londoners are largely comfortable with multiple identities. The 70 per cent non-British London School of Economics, where I studied, is testament to Londoners' ease with difference: a Haitian student of philosophy can be as much a Londoner as someone who can trace his ancestry to Samuel Pepys, or this boy born in St Mary's Hospital to Indian parents 22 years ago. Of course London's diversity is not only through chic international restaurants and successful minority figures. To deny the challenges of segregation, communication, poverty and racism would be ignorant. Some people do feel afraid, isolated or lost.

Yet these problems are authentically London. To say it isn't an English city "any more" suggests a misunderstanding, or whitewashing, of its history. [...]

In past and present, Londoners, Britons and the English live side by side, embracing seemingly contradictory identities and sharing heritage, culture and social challenges. Statistics about demographic change are misleading – London was never a purely English city and it belongs to no single label. Sorry, but things weren't better before.

It is said that cities are laboratories of modernity. Back in Dehradun, my new friend observed me with fresh interest. Perhaps he was studying me for evidence of my exoticism. Or perhaps he understood that I, along with eight million others, am heir to the most ambitious experiment of them all.

Arjun Neil Alim, in: *The Evening Standard*, 2019

17 **Monty Python** famous group of British comedians
19 **requiem** a Christian ceremony for sb who has died
21 **to set off** to make sb start to do sth
23 **to mourn** to be sad about sb's death
23 **quintessential** very typical
27 **to raze** to destroy completely
35 **testament to** proof of

4 VOCABULARY Use the text and create a word bank on cultural identity and diversity.

5 COMPREHENSION

a) According to the author, what do many people criticise about the route many big cities in general and London in particular have taken in recent years?

b) What is the author's view of London's "Englishness"?

6 ANALYSIS Analyse the argumentative and rhetorical strategies the author uses to convince readers of his view of London and its diversity. → ○ 9

7 EVALUATION As far as life in a city is concerned: Is diversity something positive or something negative (for you)? Think of aspects like shopping, sights, festivities, restaurants on the one hand and people on the other hand. Discuss.

8 LISTENING Find the podcast "The Notting Hill Carnival" from the series *Fierce City: A London History Podcast* (Episode 6) online. Listen to the first part (00:00–04:00) and take notes on the historical roots of the carnival. → S34

Notting Hill Carnival

MK **9** VIEWING

a) Find the trailer to the film *Rocks* (2020) online. Describe what life is like for the Black British teenage girl called "Rocks".

b) Does the trailer succeed in making you want to watch the film? Why (not)?

10 ACROSS CULTURES Choose a world city and find out about its diverse population. Search for information about the different ethnic groups like living conditions, career choices, cultural and economic contributions to the city etc. Compare your results.

Can global cities still thrive after the Covid-19 crisis? → WB 11/6

We spoke to Tom Walker, a fund manager specialising in global cities, to find out what the future holds for global cities and what impact Covid-19 has had around the world.

Are global cities at risk of decline if people move away to rural areas?

Tom Walker: "If everyone leaves a city, it will lose the huge benefits that are derived when people cluster together to collaborate and exchange information. We have seen this before, perhaps Detroit is the best example of a city losing its appeal. When the car industry, the dominant employer, faltered, people moved away, and the city went into decline.

Today, we are not seeing the pandemic force people to move away from cities. The media is focussing on the people who are moving "away" from the city and not on those who are moving to the city, especially younger people. So far, the data is telling us that those that are moving away are not moving very far, only to the suburbs. People understand that they cannot be too far from the city, both from a professional and personal point of view."

How has the pandemic affected global cities?

Tom Walker: "Historically, any city-focussed crisis has always led to an acceleration of changes that were inevitable. For example, outbreaks of cholera in Victorian London led to the development of sewers and improved sanitation. The Great Fire of London led to the creation of fire-proof bricks. Covid-19 will be no exception.

Fast forward to today's crisis and it has accelerated the trends of working from home and the adoption of e-commerce, both of which were already afoot before the Covid-19 crisis. However, one of the key points to understand is that the pandemic has had, and will have, very different impacts on different cities.

fund manager sb who manages and invests money for a financial organisation

In parts of Asia, such as Shanghai, Beijing, Tokyo or Sydney, generally the pandemic was well managed. In these cities, life has returned to normal with little desire to work from home in any dramatic fashion. In contrast, cities in countries that did not handle the crisis so well, such as Paris, London and New York, will see a much stronger demand for working from home. There will be no uniform impact on cities, as ever each city, culture and region will react differently to the pandemic."

So, what changes could occur?

Tom Walker: "Trends that may have taken a number of years, if not decades, to occur have now been accelerated. The clearest trend is the reduction in demand for office space. As per my earlier comment, this will be more significant in Europe and the US in comparison to Asia.

There will be more demand for logistics space, in and around cities, to serve the ever-growing e-commerce demand. There is also a chance that cities become younger; the older demographic may now decide they do not want to live in such close proximity to many people. A younger city could be hugely beneficial from a productivity perspective. Younger people are often more dynamic, open minded and entrepreneurial. This could significantly boost economic growth."

How will the trend of working from home affect global cities?

Tom Walker: "The trend for working from home is here to stay and this will result in a reduction in demand for office space. We expect this to be most significant in cities in Europe and the US such as, London, Paris, New York and San Francisco. This should allow redundant office space be repurposed as another use such as residential, schools, hospitals or even data centres."

Will working from home vary by city?

Tom Walker: "Absolutely, Asia will be far less impacted by the working from home trend. Generally, people in Asia have shorter commute times and live in smaller residential accommodation. Those cities with the longest commute times and poor transport infrastructure will be most impacted. In cities where people have long commutes, such as in London, Paris and New York, people will likely work from home more frequently."

Mark Herlihy et al, *The Schroders Wealth Management* website, 2021

31 **as per my earlier comment** as I said before
35 **demographic** a part of the population who are of the same age
38 **entrepreneurial** active (in business)
43 **to repurpose sth** to find a new use for sth

11 VOCABULARY Scan the text and note down words and expressions that are helpful when talking about modern trends in cities. → ● 10 → S8

12 COMPREHENSION Describe the effects the pandemic has had and will have on global cities, as outlined by the interviewee.

13 SPEAKING Discuss the negative and positive effects of working or studying from home for individuals and cities. You may refer to your personal experiences during the pandemic. → S31, 33

14 EVALUATION Living in a world city: Is it an option for you? Outline your views and refer to some of the issues discussed in the topic.

Detroit

Shanghai

Sydney

Planning a trip to a world city

Imagine your English class is given the chance to go on a study trip to a world city. To be able to decide which city you would like to visit together, various groups draw up a plan for a trip, which they present to the class in a (multi-media) presentation including:

1. Some general information on the city: Why this city?
2. A rough outline of a programme of seven days, with three highlights presented in some detail.
3. A presentation of the accommodation: location, amenities, catering etc.
4. Some other practical information on departure and arrival dates, costs etc.

Now get started and try to win your classmates over for "your" trip.

Step 1 Choose a city and organise your work

In groups of 3–5, agree on a city. Draw up a plan and a schedule for the various tasks to be performed. Also, decide on who is going to be responsible for which part of the research and the presentation. → S6

Step 2 Do research

Find information on the points 1.–4. mentioned above. Note what is interesting and relevant so that you can include it in your presentation.

Step 3 Discuss your ideas

- Share your research results.
- Come to an agreement on the points that need to be settled (accommodation, programme etc.)
- Decide on the structure of your presentation, including a handout containing the main points.

Step 4 Prepare your part of the presentation

- Organise your material and decide on how to present it in an appealing way.
- Decide which media you'd like to use and where. Careful: Avoid relying too heavily on media – they should serve you, but the focus should be on you!
- Write prompt cards and your part of the handout.
- Consult the thematic vocabulary and the Useful phrases box.

USEFUL PHRASES

Planning a trip
departure / arrival is at • the hostel is located in the east of • the amenities include • catering at the hostel includes • to book a guide • the city is world-famous for • a visit to … is a must in this city • the entrance fee is • entry is free of charge • the climate in this region is • what is required for the trip is • altogether the costs amount to • …

Step 5 Practise and check your presentation

- Based on your prompt cards, rehearse your part of the presentation. Use some of the techniques you have learnt on the Spot on language page, e.g. rhetorical devices to make the text more vivid, adjectives to describe or evaluate etc.
- In your group, practise the presentation and give feedback on the performance of the others – think of content and presentation skills. Check if you are speaking at the right speed and in the right tone of voice.
- Make sure you are able to handle the media you have chosen.

Step 6 Give the presentations and choose the destination of the trip

Each group presents their city and their programme for the trip. Then everyone votes for the plan that they find most attractive.

Skills workshop 1
Listening and viewing skills

Step 1 The five phases of listening comprehension

A Preparation
- Read the task / introduction carefully.
- Find out what the subject of the podcast or talk is.
- Find some clues as to the structure, the intention, the participants (see B).
- Think about which words, expressions and ideas you are going to hear.

B First listening: Listening for gist
The aim of the first listening round is to arrive at a general understanding of the text. Do not listen for details but stay focused and try to find answers to the following questions:

1. What is the main message or point of the speaker / interviewee / text?
2. What type of text is it (monologue, dialogue, interview, discussion, ...)?
3. Who are the participants and what do we get to know about them?
4. What is the structure of the text? Which different parts does it fall into (pros and cons, chronological order as in a story, enumeration of aspects, ...)?
5. What is the main intention (inform, educate, convince, instruct, warn, ...)?

C Break
- In the short break, note down all information relevant to the task.
- If possible, plan how to note the information in a systematic way (e.g. pros and cons).
- Prepare for the second listening: Identify the "blind spots" you need to concentrate on.

D Second listening: Listening for details
Listen and take notes at the same time.

E Final phase: Completion of notes
Complete your notes, arrange or rearrange them.

A2 **1** LISTENING Listen to the beginning of the interview *The world's healthiest building* with Mattias Goldmann, who is an expert working for Sweco, a Swedish organisation planning sustainable communities.

1. Go through the points noted under A. Collect words that you expect to hear.
2. Listen a first time and answer the questions in B during the break (C).
3. Listen a second time and take notes on Goldmann's ideas about the characteristics of healthy buildings and why they matter.
4. Share your notes with a partner and then explain Goldmann's ideas in class.
5. According to Goldmann's criteria, is your school a healthy building? Discuss.

A3 **2** LISTENING Listen to the beginning of the interview *Healthy cities for the next generation* with Andreas Gyllenhammar, the head of sustainability at Sweco. Go through the phases A–E, then summarise Gyllenhammar's ideas concerning a healthy city and finally comment on them.

Step 2 Analysing videos: The basics

Understanding a video involves the same five phases as a listening exercise. In addition, it includes an analysis of the visual elements and of further auditory elements:

1. visual information that is presented in the single pictures or "shots"
2. colour and light
3. the camera distance: close to or far away from the object?
4. the camera angle: from above, below or at eye-level?
5. the movement of the camera
6. the usage of special effects (e.g. slow motion or blurred picture)
7. the way shots are connected and follow each other
8. the background music / soundtrack

Chicago, USA

Singapore, Singapore

Tokyo, Japan

3 VISUALS

a) Let's train for a video analysis with one of these photos. Choose one and note all the words that come to mind when you look at it.

b) Describe the photo in detail. Include the formal elements 1–4 and 6.

c) Explain what impression of the city the photo conveys. In doing so, examine how the object chosen, the use of colour and light, the camera distance, camera angle and special effects contribute to this impression.

Step 3 Analysing TED talks and documentaries

V3 **4 VIEWING**

a) Watch the beginning of the TED talk *How we can design timeless cities for our collective future* by Vishaan Chakrabarti. Go through phases A–E outlined above and note what Chakrabarti says about modern cities and why it matters how they are designed. Then exchange your ideas in class.

b) In a second step, concentrate on the three visual elements of this talk:

> the speaker's gestures and facial expressions • photos • visual aids / animations

Examine the role these elements play in the TED talk. For this purpose, take a closer look at some of them and pause e.g. at 00:40, 00:50, 01:50, 02:06, 02:21 and 02:45.

c) Comment on Chakrabarti's negative view of modern cities. → S19

TIP

TED talks are short presentations of an interesting issue and often present new insights. They are usually given by one person and accompanied by a number of visual aids.

5 VIEWING

a) Find the TED talk by Kotchakorn Voraakhom entitled *How to transform sinking cities into landscapes that fight floods* online. Describe the problem the city of Bangkok faces (00:00–05:30) and then outline the project that Voraakhom initiated in her hometown to deal with it (05:30–09:15).

b) Analyse the visual components of the talk and how they help to make her message clear.

V4 **6 VIEWING**

a) Briefly describe Adria Gomila's job and the project he realised during the pandemic.

b) Describe the image of Barcelona created in this documentary and analyse how the following aspects contribute to this effect:

> choice of pictures / shots • camerawork • special effects • music / soundtrack

c) Is a bike-friendly city a more liveable and a more sustainable city? Discuss.

TIP

Documentaries present factual material in a concise way and are intended to educate people. They often do not show any "narrator" at all, but contain a large number of photos, shots and other visual elements.

7 VIEWING

a) Find the documentary *Creating sustainable cities* by *Going Green* online and then talk about the five key aspects of sustainable cities and the cities presented.

b) Explain how the following elements make the documentary effective and convincing:

> choice of pictures • visual aids • colour and light • camerawork • special effects • music

c) Write a comment: Which idea do you find most interesting / important? Which city do you find most appealing?

2 Colonial legacies
Introduction

1
A street in Simon's Town, South Africa

2
The Gateway of India at the port of Mumbai

3
An official building in Nairobi, Kenya

4
King Charles III visits Canada

HDI[1] rankings of the United Kingdom and some former British colonies (2019)

8	Australia	58	Bahamas, Barbados	130	Namibia	150	Zimbabwe
13	United Kingdom	62	Malaysia	131	India	161	Nigeria
14	New Zealand	67	Trinidad and Tobago	138	Ghana	168	Tanzania
16	Canada	100	Botswana	143	Kenya	174	Malawi
17	United States	114	South Africa	146	Zambia	189	Niger

UNDP Human Development Report, 2021

[1] **The United Nations' Human Development Index (HDI)** considers the level of health, education and income in a country to provide a measure of human development, listed from 1 (highest) to 189 (lowest).

1 VISUALS

a) Describe and compare the photos and share your knowledge about the countries they were taken in. Which elements in the photos show links with Britain? → ○ 1 → S38

b) Give historical reasons for the figures in the following fact file and explain their effects on the world today.

FACT FILE

English as a world language
English is the main language and / or one of the official languages in 59 countries. It is widely used as a language of government and / or education in 16 more. The population of these countries combined is approximately 1.8 billion.

2 COMPREHENSION Point out what the following fact file says about Britain's post-imperial relationship with its former empire. → ○ 2, ● 3

FACT FILE

Multicultural Britain
Inhabitants of British colonies had come to Britain from the earliest days of the empire, but only in small numbers. The British Nationality Act 1948 gave the right to live in the UK to anyone who had been born in a British colony or a Commonwealth state (a former colony that maintained connections with Britain). The main motive was to maintain close political relationships with those countries after the end of the British Empire. From then until the law changed in 1971, many people from countries with British colonial histories such as India, Pakistan, Nigeria and Jamaica emigrated to the UK, mostly building new lives in London and other large cities. This is one of the main reasons why the UK is a strongly multicultural society today, especially in its major cities.

3 ANALYSIS Read the quotes, sum up what they say about the British Empire and how they make their point. It may be helpful to find out more about the people who said them.

"In recent times, European nations, with the use of gunpowder and other technical improvements in warfare, controlled practically the whole world. One, the British Empire, brought under one government a quarter of the earth and its inhabitants.

John Boyd Orr (1880–1971), first Director-General of the UN Food and Agriculture Organisation (FAO)

The sun never sets on the British Empire.

Popular saying from the 19th to the mid 20th centuries

The story of the British Empire helps to explain the roots of most British people: white, black, and Asian.

Sadiq Khan, elected Mayor of London in 2016 and 2021

We are here because you were there.

Ambalavaner Sivanandan (1923–2018), British writer and activist born in Sri Lanka

[...] what we call 'empire' spans 400 years in time and thousands of miles in space; every continent on Earth was directly affected by it.

Kwasi Kwarteng, British Member of Parliament first elected in 2010"

4 EVALUATION

a) Assess the HDI rankings on the previous page and what they tell you about the post-colonial development of the countries in the list.

MK b) Choose one of the countries ranked between 1 and 20 and one between 100 and 189. Find out more about their resources, their economic and political situations and try to explain the reasons for the difference in ranking.

The British Empire and its former colonies

Key events in the history of the British Empire

1583 The start of the 'First' British Empire

Queen Elizabeth I (1533–1603) authorises attempts to start British colonies on the east coast of North America. The next year Sir Walter Raleigh sends an expedition to found the Roanoke Colony. The colony only lasts for two years, but permanent colonies soon follow. Conflicts with the Indigenous population begin due to the settlers claiming more and more land. In the course of the following centuries, the majority of Native Americans is killed, the rest is forced to move to reservations.

1600 The founding of the East India Company

A group of merchants and explorers get royal permission to found a company to trade with India and beyond. The trade brings spices, tea and other exotic goods to Britain, and is hugely profitable. The company becomes extremely powerful, and effectively takes control of much of the Indian subcontinent. This eventually leads to full British colonisation.

17th–19th centuries The transatlantic slave trade

Millions of people become enslaved in Africa and are shipped from the west coast to British and other European colonies in North and South America. Loaded with sugar, cotton and other goods produced by slave labour, the ships then sail to Europe, where the goods are sold. The ships complete the 'trade triangle' by sailing back to Africa with goods to exchange with slave traders. The huge profits from the 'triangular trade' help to fund the expansion of the empire. Rivalries with other colonial powers develop.

1775–1783 The American War of Independence

Britain loses its biggest colony, British America (later: the USA), and refocuses its colonial ambitions towards Asia, Africa and the Pacific. The 'Second' British Empire begins.

1788 The first convicts arrive in Australia

Eleven British ships arrive and a prison colony settlement is established at Sydney Cove. Britain claims much of the continent as its territory. This becomes disastrous for the Aboriginal population, who suffer from violence, disease and eviction from their land.

1815–1914 Britain's 'imperial century'

Around 26 million km² and 400 million people are added to the British Empire, which now spans the globe. India is 'the jewel in the crown', and in 1876 Queen Victoria is also made 'Empress of India'. By the late 19th century, around 30% of the population of Africa is under British rule.

1947 Indian independence

After a long struggle (with Mahatma Gandhi as a figurehead), India achieves independence. Attitudes to colonialism are changing, and over the next two decades most of Britain's remaining colonies also become independent.

1997 The return of Hong Kong

Britain's last major overseas territory is returned to China. The empire has gone, but more than 50 former British colonies maintain links with the UK and with each other through the Commonwealth of Nations, a voluntary political association of states.

MK **1** COMPREHENSION Do research on one of the key events summarised above for a short presentation in class. Find a suitable visual (photo, drawing, diagram, map) to use in your presentation. → S3

2 EVALUATION Assess the colonialist mindset on the basis of what you have just learned. Think of the perspective of colonial powers like Britain on the countries they colonised and the people who lived there before.

3 SPEAKING What do you know about the history and culture of the people in America, Australia, Africa and on the Indian subcontinent before they were colonised? Discuss the effects of colonisation on their societies. → WB 13/2 → S31, 33

Case study: South Africa

Pre-colonial era

Some of the earliest known modern humans existed in southern Africa around 250,000 years ago. One of numerous sophisticated cultures, the 11th to 13th century Kingdom of Mapungubwe (in the north of present-day South Africa) became a prosperous trading centre with links throughout southern Africa and to India and China. At the beginning of the colonial era, the Zulu Kingdom was a major power in the region.

Colonial era

Coastal areas of what is now South Africa were colonised by the Dutch from 1652 onwards. In the early 1800s, the British took control and many Dutch-speaking colonists (Boers) migrated inland. In the second half of the 19th century, large gold and diamond fields were discovered. The British went to war against African peoples including the Zulu and the Xhosa and also (in 1880 and again in 1899) the Boers. South Africa became a self-governing white-ruled part of the British Empire in 1910 and a white-ruled republic in 1961. Apartheid – a brutal system of racial segregation – began in 1948 and continued until 1991. White minority rule continued until Nelson Mandela was elected president in 1994.

Post-colonial status

South Africa is a member of the Commonwealth of Nations. It is a republic whose head of state and head of government is the president. There are still a lot of social, economic and political issues which have not been solved since the end of apartheid. In 2022, South Africa's population is about 80.9 % Black, 8.8 % "Coloured" (with diverse genetic background), 7.8 % white and 2.6 % Asian, the median age being 28 years. It is also the country with the highest economic inequality in the world.

Case study: Canada

Pre-colonial era

Humans probably first migrated into what is now Canada around 15,000 years ago. Hundreds of cultures developed, each with its own distinct language, art and traditions. Even today, there are over 600 Indigenous peoples (First Nations, Métis and Inuit).

Colonial era

Different parts of what is now Canada were first colonised by the British and the French in the first half of the 17th century. At first Indigenous peoples and Europeans coexisted peacefully and often cooperated, but conflicts over land and huge numbers of deaths from European diseases had terrible effects on the Indigenous population. After several wars against First Nations and the French, most of what is now Canada came under British rule in 1763. Separate provinces joined to form a new country called Canada in 1867. It became increasingly self-governing from then onwards, but did not become fully independent until 1982.

Post-colonial status

Canada is a member of the Commonwealth of Nations. It is a constitutional monarchy and a parliamentary democracy whose head of state is the British monarch represented by the governor general and whose head of government is the Canadian prime minister. There are still a lot of social and political issues which have not been solved since the end of the government's efforts to assimilate First Nations, Métis and Inuit.

4 COMPREHENSION Outline the similarities and differences between the histories of South Africa and Canada.

5 VOCABULARY Collect words and expressions connected with colonialism and make a mind map. → WB 13/1

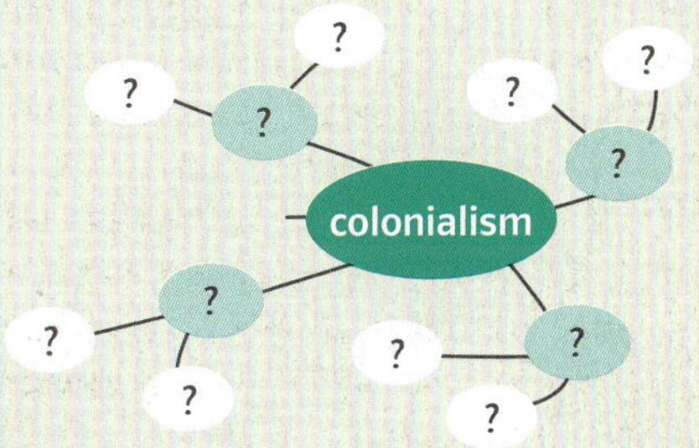

MK **6** CREATIVE TASK Do research and make a brief case study like the ones above for another former British colony, e.g. Australia, New Zealand, Jamaica or Hong Kong.

A South Africa: The Rainbow Nation

The many faces of South Africa

1 BEFORE YOU START

a) Guess why South Africa's nickname is "the Rainbow Nation".
b) Create a mind map with ideas about South Africa with your partner.

2 VISUALS

a) In groups of four, deal with one photo each. Describe your photo to the other members. Explain how you would feel if you were in that place, and what you would want to do there. → S38
b) On your own, think of another aspect of South Africa's present or past that could be shown in a photo. Imagine a suitable photo and describe it.

USEFUL PHRASES

diverse society • distribution of wealth • to reduce / remove / redress inequality • to reduce / alleviate unemployment • urban middle class • to create prosperity • to live in shacks

1 Jeep safari, Kruger National Park

2 Open-air concert, Johannesburg

3 Beach promenade, Camps Bay, Cape Town

4 Khayelitsha Township, Cape Town

3 ACROSS CULTURES Find population statistics of South Africa and Germany online and compare the two countries. Identify and comment on the most important challenges for each one.

MK **4 CREATIVE TASK** Do research on the ideas you have talked about in Tasks 1 and 2, adding pieces of information you find important. Imagine living in South Africa. Use your findings either to make an advertisement / commercial to attract tourists to South Africa or to write a short comment criticising the situation in South Africa and suggesting what should be improved. → S3, 9, 19

A free spirit

Trevor Noah is a South African comedian, TV host and political commentator who lives in the US and hosted *The Daily Show*, a satirical news programme, from 2015 to 2022. His book *Born A Crime: Stories from a South African Childhood* explores South African history, culture and politics. Since his mother is Xhosa and his father Swiss-German, he belongs to the group labelled "coloured" during apartheid.

In the early 1980s, the South African government began making minor reforms in an attempt to quell international protest over the atrocities and human rights abuses of apartheid. Among those reforms was the token hiring of black workers in low-level white-collar jobs. Like typists. Through an employment agency she [my mom] got a job as a secretary at ICI, a multinational pharmaceutical company in Braamfontein, a suburb of Johannesburg.

When my mom started working, she still lived with my grandmother in Soweto, the township where the government had relocated my family decades before. But my mother was unhappy at home, and when she was twenty-two she ran away to live in downtown Johannesburg. There was only one problem: It was illegal for black people to live there.

The ultimate goal of apartheid was to make South Africa a white country, with every black person relocated to live in black territories. But this so-called white country could not function without black labor to produce its wealth, which meant black people had to be allowed to live near white areas in the townships, government-planned ghettos built to house black workers, like Soweto. The township was where you lived, but your status as a laborer was the only thing that permitted you to stay there. [...]

To leave the township for work in the city, or for any other reason, you had to carry a pass with your ID number; otherwise you could be arrested. There was also a curfew: After a certain hour, blacks had to be back home in the township or risk arrest. My mother didn't care. She was determined to never go home again. So she stayed in town, hiding and sleeping in public restrooms until she learned the rules of navigating the city from the other black women who had contrived to live there: prostitutes.

Many of the prostitutes in town were Xhosa. They spoke my mother's language and showed her how to survive. They taught her how to dress up in a pair of maid's overalls to move around the city without being questioned. They also introduced her to white men who were willing to rent out flats in town. A lot of these men were foreigners, Germans and Portuguese who didn't care about the law and were happy to sign a lease giving a prostitute a place to live and work in exchange for a steady piece on the side. My mom wasn't interested in any such arrangement, but thanks to her job she did have money to pay rent. She met a German fellow through one of her prostitute friends, and he agreed to let her a flat in his name. She moved in and bought a bunch of maid's overalls to wear. She was caught and arrested many times, for not having her ID on the way home from work, for being in a white area after hours. She would scrape together the money, pay the fine, and go right back about her business.

My mom's secret flat was in a neighborhood called Hillbrow. Down the corridor was a tall, brown-haired, brown-eyed Swiss / German expat named Robert. As a former trading colony, South Africa has always had a large expatriate community. People find their way here. Tons of Germans. Lots of Dutch. Hillbrow at the time was the Greenwich Village of South Africa. It was a thriving scene, cosmopolitan and liberal. There were galleries and Underground theaters where artists and performers dared to speak up and criticize the government in front of integrated crowds. There were restaurants and nightclubs, a lot of them foreign-owned, that served a mixed clientele, black people who hated the status quo and white people who simply thought it

2 **to quell** to put down, to stop
2 **atrocity** *Gräueltat, Grausamkeit*
4 **white-collar** office work
24 **to contrive** to make sth happen, especially by using clever or dishonest methods
30 **piece on the side** *(infml) here:* a person to sleep with while abroad, without worrying that the partner or spouse finds out
39 **expatriate** sb who lives in a country that is not their place of birth

ridiculous. These people would have secret get-togethers, too, usually in someone's flat or in empty basements that had been converted into clubs. Integration by its nature was a political act, but the get-togethers themselves weren't political at all. People would meet up and hang out, have parties. My mom threw herself into that scene. She was always out at some club, some party, dancing, meeting people. She was a regular at the Hillbrow Tower, one of the tallest buildings in Africa at that time. It had a nightclub with a rotating dance floor on the top floor. It was an exhilarating time but still dangerous. Sometimes the restaurants and clubs would get shut down, sometimes not. Sometimes the performers and patrons would get arrested, sometimes not. It was a roll of the dice. My mother never knew whom to trust, who might turn her in to the police. Neighbors would report on one another. The girlfriends of the white men in my mom's block of flats had every reason to report a black woman – a prostitute, no doubt – living among them. And you must remember that black people worked for the government as well. As far as her white neighbors knew, my mom could have been a spy posing as a prostitute posing as a maid, sent into Hillbrow to inform on whites who were breaking the law. That's how a police state works – everyone thinks everyone else is the police.

From: Trevor Noah, *Born a crime*, 2016

54 **roll of the dice** *(idiom)* used to say that sth can have either a good or a bad result

5 VOCABULARY
Collect useful vocabulary from the text and note it down with suitable collocations to talk about apartheid in South Africa. Discuss the pros and cons of finding collocations in a printed dictionary compared to online resources. → ○ 4

6 ANALYSIS
a) Characterise Trevor Noah's mother and explain how she managed to avoid some of the limitations of apartheid.
b) Analyse how the author characterises his mother and how he presents the reality of apartheid. → ● 5 → S13, 14

7 EVALUATION Comment on the quality of the text and how successfully it brings about its message.

8 SPEAKING Work in groups. Find out about one of these laws and its effect on Black South Africans. Present the information in class.

Prohibition of Mixed Marriages Act (1949) • Group Areas Act (1950) • Population Registration Act (1950) • Abolition of Passes Act (1952) • Separate Amenities Act (1953) • Bantu Education Act (1953)

V5 **9 VIEWING**
a) Watch the extract from an interview with Trevor Noah. What impression do you get of him?
b) Watch the clip again and take notes on the following aspects:
1. the concept of 'race'
2. apartheid, its aims, how it was designed and what made it effective
3. the classification of people
4. how racism still works in modern day society
5. privilege
c) Go back to the statements that make the audience laugh and explain why.

10 EVALUATION Use the knowledge you have gained to point out how apartheid worked in a short presentation or an explainer video.

I am prepared to die → WB 15–16/4–5

At his trial in 1964, Nelson Mandela gave a three-hour speech explaining the injustices of apartheid and the reasons for his activities in opposing it. This has become known as the "I am prepared to die" speech. It is considered to be one of the great speeches of modern history, and a key event in the history of South African democracy. Below is the closing part.

VIP FILE

Nelson Rolihlahla Mandela (1918 – 2013) was the first Black president of South Africa (1994 – 1998). In his youth, he trained as a lawyer and became a leading figure in the African National Congress (ANC), an organisation which opposed apartheid and white minority rule. In 1964 he was imprisoned and spent the next 18 years at the prison on Robben Island, where he suffered inhuman treatment during the first years. He was finally released from prison in 1990 as part of South Africa's transition to democracy.

Africans want to be paid a living wage. Africans want to perform work which they are capable of doing, and not work which the Government declares them to be capable of. Africans want to be allowed to live where they obtain work, and not be endorsed out of an area because they were not born there. Africans want to be allowed to own land in places where they work, and not to be obliged to live in rented houses which they can never call their own. Africans want to be part of the general population, and not confined to living in their own ghettoes. African men want to have their wives and children to live with them where they work, and not be forced into an unnatural existence in men's hostels. African women want to be with their menfolk and not be left permanently widowed in the Reserves. Africans want to be allowed out after eleven o'clock at night and not to be confined to their rooms like little children. Africans want to be allowed to travel in their own country and to seek work where they want to and not where the Labor Bureau tells them to. Africans want a just share in the whole of South Africa; they want security and a stake in society.

Above all, we want equal political rights, because without them our disabilities will be permanent. I know this sounds revolutionary to the whites in this country, because the majority of voters will be Africans. This makes the white man fear democracy.

But this fear cannot be allowed to stand in the way of the only solution which will guarantee racial harmony and freedom for all. It is not true that the enfranchisement of all will result in racial domination. Political division, based on colour, is entirely artificial and, when it disappears, so will the domination of one colour group by another. The ANC has spent half a century fighting against racialism. When it triumphs it will not change that policy.

This then is what the ANC is fighting. Their struggle is a truly national one. It is a struggle of the African people, inspired by their own suffering and their own experience. It is a struggle for the right to live.

During my lifetime I have dedicated myself to this struggle of the African people. I have fought against white domination, and I have fought against black domination. I have cherished the ideal of a democratic and free society in which all persons live together in harmony and with equal opportunities. It is an ideal which I hope to live for and to achieve. But if needs be, it is an ideal for which I am prepared to die.

From: Nelson Mandela, speech at the Rivonia Trial, Pretoria, April 20, 1964

3 **to endorse out** to evict, drive out

19 **enfranchisement** giving sb the right to vote

11 COMPREHENSION Summarise what demands Mandela puts forward and what he says about his and the ANC's intentions. → S28

12 ACROSS CULTURES Compare the aspects Mandela addresses with the German constitution *(Grundgesetz)* and its democratic principles.

13 ANALYSIS Find examples of the following rhetorical devices and say what effect Mandela creates by using them:
1. enumeration
2. anaphora (repetition of a sequence of words at the beginnings of sentences / clauses)
3. contrast
4. repetition of single words for rhetorical effect
5. personalisation → S16

14 EVALUATION Give possible reasons why this is considered to be one of the great speeches of the 20th century. → ○ 6

MK **15** CREATIVE TASK Do research on Nelson Mandela's life. Make a time line with key dates and events and explain why he became South Africa's first president.

A human being is a human being is a human being

Another very influential and popular person who fought against racism and apartheid all his adult life was Desmond Tutu, a South African priest of the Anglican Church. He was Bishop of Johannesburg and then Archbishop of Cape Town between 1985 and 1994, the year apartheid ended. From 1996–1998 he was a member of the Truth and Reconciliation Commission. He was awarded the Nobel Peace Prize for his activism against apartheid in 1984. He died in 2021 at the age of 90.

V6 ▷ **16** MEDIATION
For a presentation in your German history lesson, you want to use a video from 1980 that portrays Desmond Tutu and his activism against apartheid in South Africa.
Write prompt cards in German for your presentation. Deal with the following points:
- what kind of person Tutu was and why he was so popular
- his concept of civil disobedience
- how he addresses the white audience during his lecture and what he intends to achieve by saying "A human being is a human being is a human being" (0:24–0:28)
- what he says about the ideas and people who influenced him

Start your presentation by saying what parts the film consists of and why you found it helpful. → S39

The aftermath of apartheid → WB 14/3

In this extract from *Born a crime*, Trevor Noah explains why the end of apartheid did not end all the problems of non-white people in South Africa.

The genius of apartheid was convincing people who were the overwhelming majority to turn on each other. Apart hate, is what it was. You separate people into groups and make them hate one another so you can run them all.

At the time, black South Africans outnumbered white South Africans nearly five to one, yet we were divided into different tribes with different languages: Zulu, Xhosa, Tswana, Sotho, Venda, Ndebele, Tsonga, Pedi, and more. Long before apartheid existed, these tribal factions clashed and warred with one another. Then white rule used that animosity to divide and conquer. All nonwhites were systematically classified into various groups and subgroups. Then these groups were given differing levels of rights and privileges in order to keep them at odds.

Perhaps the starkest of these divisions was between South Africa's two dominant groups, the Zulu and the Xhosa. The Zulu man is known as the warrior. He is proud. He puts his head down and fights. When the colonial armies invaded, the Zulu charged into battle with nothing but spears and shields against men with guns. The Zulu were slaughtered by the thousands, but they never stopped fighting. The Xhosa, on the other hand, pride themselves on being the thinkers. My mother is Xhosa. Nelson Mandela was Xhosa. The Xhosa waged a long war against the white man as well, but after experiencing the futility of battle against a better-armed foe, many Xhosa chiefs took a more nimble approach. "These white people are here whether we like it or not," they said. "Let's see what tools they possess that can be useful to us. Instead of being resistant to English, let's learn English. We'll understand what the white man is saying, and we can force him to negotiate with us."

The Zulu went to war with the white man. The Xhosa played chess with the white man. For a long time neither was particularly successful, and each blamed the other for a problem neither had created. Bitterness festered. For decades those feelings were held in check by a common enemy. Then apartheid fell, Mandela walked free, and black South Africa went to war with itself.

From: Trevor Noah, *Born a crime*, 2016

17 COMPREHENSION

a) Outline Noah's definition of apartheid and how it affected the different groups of people in South Africa.

b) Summarise how, according to the author, the Zulu and the Xhosa responded to colonisation differently. → S5, 8

18 EVALUATION Interpret what Noah means by "South Africa went to war with itself". Support your answer with research about present-day conflicts in South Africa. → S3, 4

19 SPEAKING Discuss the different strategies the Zulu and the Xhosa adopted when they were confronted with the colonial powers. Think of (and if necessary, research) the ways that Indigenous societies in other countries responded to being colonised and how successful they were.

V7 **20** VIEWING

a) Watch the video and summarise what it is about. → O 7

b) Compare and contrast the opinions of the people who were interviewed and explain how the pictures illustrate their points.

The economy of South Africa

MK **21** BEFORE YOU START Use a dictionary or digital tools to find out and note down the meanings of the following words and phrases:

1. hangover • 2. determinant factor • 3. to end up (somewhere) • 4. factoid • 5. to beget sth • 6. absolute / relative poverty • 7. threshold • 8. social mobility • 9. the powers that be • 10. civil unrest • 11. gated community • 12. precaution • 13. to carjack • 14. proximity • 15. asset • 16. abundance • 17. to squander

V8 **22** VIEWING

a) Watch the report (from 2020) about economic developments in South Africa after the end of apartheid. Decide if the following statements are true or false and correct the false ones.

1. About 98% of South Africans lead lives similar to the ones of upper middle-class Americans.
2. Whether someone will get rich in South Africa is hugely determined by their parents' income.
3. Over 50% of South Africans were living in absolute poverty in 2018, but since then this number has been falling.
4. Thanks to technological progress and globalisation, living conditions in many countries including South Africa are improving.
5. Widespread poverty leads to less productivity because poor people lack access to a good education and to decent food or healthcare.
6. The lack of social mobility in South Africa makes people work even harder.

b) Choose the correct answers. More than one answer may be correct.

1. Political changes like the end of apartheid and Nelson Mandela's election ...
- **a)** helped to stabilise South Africa's economy.
- **b)** led to the phenomenon of capital flight.
- **c)** made the rich, mostly white population move to gated communities.
- **d)** led to rising crime and civil unrest.

2. Crime ...
- **a)** is rising although there are more and more armed guards.
- **b)** is very high, especially in big cities like Johannesburg.
- **c)** is often caused by the fact that the extremely poor and the extremely rich live close to each other.
- **d)** should be accepted if it is the only way of earning money for poor people.

c) Give short answers (just key words) to the following questions.

1. What examples are given to illustrate what capital flight means?
2. Why is capital flight such a huge problem for South Africa?
3. What are South Africa's main advantages (3 items) and what does the country make of these advantages?

23 SPEAKING Find out about South Africa's current economy (distribution of wealth and poverty, unemployment and crime). Compare your results to the situation described in the video and present your findings in class.

24 EVALUATION Comment on the statement from the video: "Wealth builds wealth and poverty builds poverty". Do you think this is true for Germany too? Think of how people become wealthy, and if wealth in society could/should be distributed more equally.

B Canada: Many nations in one

Perspectives on Canada 150

Canada is a big country blessed with a wealth of natural resources and beautiful countryside as well as a rich culture made up of people with Indigenous, colonial and more recent immigrant backgrounds. Its highly-developed economy is stable and it provides jobs in all of the economic sectors. According to recent surveys, it is one of the most liveable places in the world.

The former British colony likes to present itself as a mosaic of different backgrounds and cultures existing side by side, and it was the first country to officially adopt multiculturalism as a policy. In 2021 Mary Simon became the first governor general of Canada with Inuit roots. Internationally Canada has had a very positive image, which prompted U2 singer Bono as well as former U.S. president Barack Obama to state that "the world needs more Canada". In 2017, Canada celebrated its 150th anniversary with a campaign called 'Canada 150', an official logo and song as well as various regional projects and events.

New Canadian citizens celebrating Canada Day in London, Ontario

Bilingual stop sign in front of the Canadian Parliament in Ottawa, Ontario

Downtown Vancouver, British Columbia

Peyto Lake, Banff National Park

1 **BEFORE YOU WATCH** Remember what you know about Canada and say what you would expect to be part of the campaign.

V9 **2** **VIEWING** Who are the speakers and what aspects do they talk about? Take notes.

3 **ANALYSIS** Identify the structure of the video and how it conveys its message. Explain how you might feel about issues mentioned if you were in the situation of the people shown in the video. → S35

MK **4** **EVALUATION** Search online for the video of the official Canada 150 song "Lead You Home". Compare and contrast its message and tone with the first video. Discuss whether or not you think the song should have focused more on the issues described in the first video.

Canada: Indigenous people fished sustainably for 1,000 years before settlers arrived

A First Nations community on Canada's west coast practiced the sustainable harvest of wild salmon for 1,000 years before the system was largely destroyed after the arrival of European settlers, a new study has concluded.

FACT FILE

Colonisation and economic interests The North American continent has been inhabited by Indigenous peoples living on the land in their traditional ways for about 14,000 years. In the 15th century, Britain and France claimed parts of Canada, and after the French and Indian War (1754–1763), Canada became part of the British Empire. From the 17th century to the mid-19th century fur trade was the most important business in Canada, and Europeans worked together closely with Indigenous peoples. The Métis developed as a third distinctive Indigenous group beside First Nations and Inuit. After the decline of the fur trade, other natural resources like coal, oil, gas, gold, timber or fish became economically more important to the Europeans, which resulted in conflicts with the Indigenous peoples about the use of the land and its resources.

2 **weir** a device to trap fish in a river
2 **to spawn** to release eggs
6 **chum salmon** Ketalachs
9 **overwhelming** enormous
9 **even** balanced
15 **to tear, tore, torn down** to pull down
17 **to exacerbate** to make worse
17 **watershed management** *Wasserbewirtschaftung*
20 **to scramble** to struggle
22 **ailing** weak
22 **stock** *here:* population

The Tsleil-Waututh, an Indigenous community [...], were long known to have used large weirs to capture salmon preparing to spawn. New research published on Wednesday shows that the Tsleil-Waututh used sex selection when harvesting spawning salmon, releasing the females to ensure the population would remain healthy for future use.

Archaeologists studied chum salmon bones dating from between 400 BC and AD 1200 from four archeological sites around the Burrard Inlet. In their research, the authors of the study discovered that salmon bones taken from former village sites were overwhelmingly male, instead of an even mix with females.

"People were harvesting the same sort of fish consistently, probably from the same places, for 1,000 years," said Jesse Morin, archeologist for the Tsleil-Waututh Nation and an adjunct professor at the University of British Columbia [...]. "Here we are, 150 years later, 150 years' worth of industrial harvesting, and we've really destroyed these resources." [...]

The [...] weirs were torn down during European colonization, said Morin.

In recent decades, wild salmon populations have collapsed. [...] The crash of salmon – exacerbated by overfishing, poor watershed management and a changing climate – has significant effects on the region's ecosystems. [...]

The Tsleil-Waututh practices highlight the importance of properly managing a fishery as governments scramble to find a way to save the troubled salmon populations. In recent years, members of the Nation have not fished on their [...] territory, despite a treaty right to do so, in order to help rebuild ailing stocks.

Leyland Cecco, in: *The Guardian*, 2021

5 **COMPREHENSION** Decide whether the following statements are true or false.

1. The article reports the findings of a new study by archaeologists in Canada and the conclusions they draw about the Tsleil-Waututh's sustainable way of fishing.
2. The archaeologists examined salmon bones over a period of 1,600 years.
3. They discovered that the Tsleil-Waututh mainly ate female salmon to stay healthy.
4. The practice of catching the male salmon with big weirs is called sex selection.
5. The European settlers destroyed the weirs and introduced industrial fishing.
6. The Tsleil-Waututh have stopped catching salmon because the government introduced a fishing quota some years ago.

6 **EVALUATION** Compare and comment on the Tsleil-Waututh's and the Europeans' attitudes to fishing.

"Like a razor slash across the Mona Lisa"

The following extract is from a story about Dene chief Frank T'seleie and his fight against a projected gas pipeline through the Mackenzie Valley, where the Dene had been granted the right to live in their traditional way. T'seleie was educated at a residential school but kept in touch with his roots. Fearing the negative effects of the project, the Dene went to court over the issue, and the judge, Thomas Berger, made an extensive inquiry. At one hearing with representatives of the gas companies, T'seleie gave a remarkable speech.

"Obviously, Mr. Blair, President of Foothills, and his friend, Mr. Horte, President of Gas Arctic, wants to see us destroyed.

Maybe, Mr. Blair, it is because you do not know us or understand us.

Or maybe money has become so important to you that you are losing your own humanity."

"You are the 20th century General Custer.

You are coming with your troops to slaughter us and steal land that is rightfully ours."

"You are coming to destroy a people that have a history of 30,000 years.

Why? For 20 years of gas. Are you really that insane?"

"You can destroy my nation, Mr. Blair, or you could be a great help to give us our freedom.

What choice do you make, Mr. Blair?

Which choice do you make for your children and mine?"

From: R. van Camp / S. B. Henderson & S. A. Ford, *Like a razor slash*, 2019

7 ANALYSIS Sum up T'seleie's arguments in this part of the speech. Then analyse the rhetorical devices he uses and examine the artwork style. → ○ 8 → S11, S38

8 EVALUATION Do research on the issue and give a short summary of the events. Point out how they are represented in the extract. Interpret the title, too.

9 VIEWING Find a video of Frank T'seleie's speech online and watch it. Consider the reactions of the audience and comment on the speech and its effectiveness. → S16

Canada discovers 751 unmarked graves at former residential school

Paying tribute to victims of the residential school system (Parliament Hill, July 1, 2021)

A First Nation in Canada's Saskatchewan province is treating a now-defunct residential school as a "crime scene" following the discovery of 751 unmarked graves just weeks after a similar discovery in British Columbia prompted a fresh reckoning over the country's colonial past.

Chief Cadmus Delorme of the Cowessess First Nation said that the graves were found on the site of the Marieval Indian residential school [...] after a search with ground-penetrating radar was launched on 2 June.

"This is not a mass grave site. These are unmarked graves," said Delorme at a press conference on Thursday morning, adding that the discovery has "reopened the pain" that many suffered at the school.

From the 19th century, more than 150,000 First Nations children were forced to attend state-funded Christian schools as part of a program to assimilate them into Canadian society. The children were forced to convert to Christianity and not allowed to speak their native languages. Many were beaten and verbally abused, and thousands died from disease, neglect and suicide.

Cowessess First Nation said that the number of unmarked graves at the site is "the most significantly substantial to date in Canada". [...]

"We are seeing the results of the genocide that Canada committed – genocide on our treaty land," said chief Bobby Cameron of the Federation of Sovereign Indigenous Nations. "Canada will be known as a nation that tried to exterminate the First Nations. Now we have evidence."

In 2015, Canada's Truth and Reconciliation Commission described the schools policy as one of "cultural genocide". In recent weeks, there have been growing calls for the Catholic church, which operated many of the schools, to release its records on the institutions.

"Our people deserve more than apologies and sympathies, which we are grateful for. Our people deserve justice," said Cameron. [...]

The grim discovery brings the total of unmarked graves discovered in the past month to about 1,000, with experts predicting more will come as provincial governments announce funding to help Indigenous communities conduct their own searches. [...]

The Canadian government formally apologized in parliament in 2008 and admitted that physical and sexual abuse in the schools was rampant. [...] Indigenous leaders have argued that the legacy of abuse and intergenerational trauma persists today as the root cause of epidemic rates of alcoholism and drug addiction on reservations.

Leyland Cecco, in: *The Guardian*, 2021

3 **reckoning** *Abrechnung*
32 **rampant** *here:* a common problem that was not addressed appropriately

10 **VOCABULARY** Look up unknown words in a dictionary and write them down together with similar or related words and their translations. → S1–2

11 **COMPREHENSION**
a) Outline the event that is reported and the background of it.
b) Summarise the responses of the two chiefs.
c) Describe the next steps the authorities and Indigenous communities are going to take.
d) Examine the perspective of the article.

12 MK **CREATIVE TASK** Work in groups of three to do research on the history of Indigenous peoples in Canada. Choose one of these Indigenous communities and write a fact file on it: First Nations, Métis and Inuit. → S3, 9

13 **SPEAKING** Comment on the idea of the Canadian mosaic, regarding what you know about the way the government has treated the Indigenous peoples in Canada.

Kenny finds his uncle

British Columbia, 1966. Kenny, aged 13, has escaped from a residential school. He has travelled to find his uncle, who is one of the fishermen preparing to head towards Simpson to catch salmon in the Skeena River. A fisherman named Mack stops him and wants to send him back.

"No, no! I'm looking for my uncle. He said I could work on his boat. He's supposed to be here."

The fisherman loosened his grip on Kenny's shoulder but stood between him and the town side of the dock. Kenny looked up at him for the first time, surprised. This guy could even be his uncle, with that shining black, rod-straight hair, gumboots, fisherman's sweater and suspenders.

"Work on his boat?" He shook his head and laughed. "How old are you? Twelve?"

Kenny squared his shoulders and tried to seem tall. "What? Twelve? Heck no, I just turned sixteen. I can work."

"Sixteen?" He laughed again. "You sure as hell ain't no sixteen. What's your uncle's name? Shouldn't you be in school?"

"Clifford. Clifford Bart. He has a big purse seiner." Kenny stood a little taller, trying not to look scared at the thought of being sent back to the school.

"I know Clifford." The fisherman looked at Kenny, as if for the first time taking in the clothes, the immediately identifiable Indian School issue. "Just saw him yesterday. Didn't say a word about you."

"Musta forgot."

"Let's go find him. See what he has to say about all this."

"Oh, umm, all right." Kenny smiled up at the fisherman, his heart pounding.

"He's probably on his boat."

"You could just point the way." Kenny smiled as though his pants were dry and he had real leather shoes or even gumboots. "I can find him."

"No trouble." The fisherman placed a hand, softly this time, on Kenny's shoulder and steered him toward the far end of the dock. "This way."

Kenny hadn't seen so many grown-up Indians since he was taken to the Mission. Both men and women worked the boats, checking the rigging, readying their nets. The sun shone off their slick black hair, tied back or cut short, as they greeted the fisherman and looked curiously at Kenny. A tall, muscular woman straightened, removed one work glove and wiped wisps of hair from her face.

"Who you got there, Mack? Long-lost love child?" She pulled her glove back on, laughing and elbowing her crew mate. [...]

"Well, boy, you're in luck."

Kenny couldn't tell if he meant it or if Mack knew how surprised Clifford would be to see him. The pair walked past three more boats and Kenny figured this one must be it. Had to be. The last slip.

Mack stopped at the prow, looked up and called out, "Clifford! Clifford! You up there?"

"Yeah, yeah. I'm busy here." Each word seemed louder, punctuated by firm steps on the deck, as the speaker made his way from the stern. A large, exasperated dark man leaned over the prow. "Whaddya want? Oh, hi, Mack."

The fisherman nudged Kenny a little toward the boat. "Your new help is here."

Kenny looked up, barely recognizing his mother's brother. "Uncle Clifford!"

"What?" Clifford raised a gloved hand to shield his eyes from the sun. "Who are you?"

"It's me, Kenny. Bella's my mom."

8 **heck** interjection used for showing that you are annoyed or surprised
12 **purse seiner** fishing boat with a large net
26 **rigging** the ropes and chains used for supporting a ship's sails and masts
35 **slip** *Bootsrampe*
36 **prow** front of a ship or boat
38 **stern** rear part of a ship or boat
38 **exasperated** irritated

"What? I'll be right down." Clifford was on the dock in no time, agile and fast for such a big man.

"I found him stowed away on my skiff. Says he works for you. Sixteen, he says."

Mack chuckled. Kenny looked up at him and didn't think Mack found it funny at all.

"Well, he's all yours now, Clifford. I'm heading up Simpson way too." He waved over his shoulder without looking back. "Maybe see you in Rupert."

Kenny sat on the deck. "I can help you. I can work for you. Help you for getting me home."

"Kenny, you're just too young. You can't work for me. C'mon, let me get you some dry clothes."

Kenny followed him below deck and changed into the clothes, rolling up the ankles and sleeves, trying for a better fit.

"I work all the time. I'm strong. I can do it. Just give me a chance."

"You're supposed to be in school. They could throw me in jail just for having you on the boat. I just can't risk it. I'm going to have to take you back."

Kenny followed him back above deck and sat on the deck next to some rigging. "I can't go back. I just can't." Panic rose in him, thinking of Clifford delivering him back to the Mission.

Kenny takes the shirt off his emaciated body and shows his uncle the bruises he got from being beaten at the residential school. Close to tears, he begs him again not to send him back. At first, his uncle can hardly believe what Kenny has gone through. Finally, he talks about how he himself and Kenny's mother grew up.

"You know, me and your mom, we never had to go to the Indian School. Your grandfather made sure of that. He would take us out on his fishing boat every fall for a few days when they were coming to collect the kids. Never wrote our names down anywhere so the government didn't have us on their list." Clifford picked up the shirt and wrapped it around Kenny's shoulders. "We knew it was no good, but not this."

"Why didn't Mom come see me? You could have brought her on the boat." Kenny looked away, feeling the tears pressing at his eyes again.

"We did. The year they took you, we went down during the halibut season. We docked right there at the school. The principal – don't remember his name –"

"Father Levesque."

"Yeah, that's right. He wouldn't let us see you. He said he would send us a letter saying when we could see you and if we came back before then, he would call the police. Your mom never got a letter."

"So you just gave up?" Kenny broke down, sitting in a puddle of khaki, sobbing.

Clifford put his arms around him and rocked him gently. "No, Kenny. Your mom wrote that school every day. She walked to town every day to mail her letters, asking about you. She even wrote to the Indian agent in Terrace. She wrote you letters, too. Sent you money. Even presents at Christmas. That principal never wrote back either."

Kenny rubbed his eyes with the heels of his hands. "I never got any letters, Uncle. Not one. Nothing." The tears started again. "Please don't take me back. Please."

Clifford stood and turned his back to Kenny, taking his work gloves out of his back pocket. "I'm heading up to Simpson tomorrow to pick up a crew. The sockeye are running. We'll be fishing outside of Rupert within a day or two."

"So, I can work for you?" Kenny leapt up, grabbing on to the waist of the too-large pants to keep from losing them. "Okay, what do you want me to do? Just show me once. I'll do a good job."

Clifford laughed. "You are too young! Maybe next year, when you're fourteen, I'll take you out. Show you the ropes. I'm gonna take you to Simpson. To your mom."

"Really?" The thought of his mom worried him. He'd been gone such a long time.

48 **to stow away** to hide in a vehicle, ship, or plane in order to travel without permission

emaciated extremely thin due to serious illness and / or lack of food

71 **halibut** *Heilbutt*

91 **to show sb the ropes** *jmdn einweisen*

"Yeah, really. If that priest wants you back at that school, he can come get you himself." Clifford stood and pointed below deck. "Come on. Let's get you fed up and then we are out of here."

Like a jackrabbit suddenly free from the trap, Kenny ran a full circle around the deck, laughing at the top of his lungs, running finally into his uncle, hugging him for dear life. "You'll see. I'll help you."

Clifford hugged him back. "Now look at me, Kenny. It's been rough for your mom. You were all she had after your dad died. When they took you ... Well, it's been rough."

Kenny looked at him, wondering what this could mean. Just as he was going to ask, the crew started climbing aboard and the fishing boat came to life.

From: Michelle Good, *Five little Indians*, 2020

97 **for dear life** desperately

14 COMPREHENSION Complete these sentences to sum up the information from the text. → S8

1. When Kenny arrives at the dock, he is stopped by …
2. That man looks …
3. Mack laughs because …
4. At the dock there are … who …
5. Kenny's plan is …
6. At first, Clifford wants …
7. When he learns what happened to Kenny at the residential school, …
8. He tells Kenny how his grandfather …
9. When Kenny asks his uncle why his mother never came to visit him, …
10. Clifford also tells Kenny that his mother …
11. Kenny is very happy when …
12. But he is also unsure …

15 ANALYSIS

a) Examine the narrative perspective and the structure of the text. → S14

b) Characterise Kenny and his uncle. Give line numbers to show how the text provides information about their personalities and their emotions. → S13

c) Assess the way the author illustrates what residential schools in Canada did to Indigenous children and their families.

16 SPEAKING

a) Compare your ideas about what you think Kenny's future may hold.

b) *Five Little Indians* won several awards and was nominated for several others. It was a bestseller in Canada. Discuss possible reasons for these things.

17 CREATIVE TASK Write the dialogue between Kenny and his mother when he finally meets her. → ● 9

18 LISTENING Find the interview with the novel's author "Michelle Good on how residential schools fit into our national story" online. Listen to the excerpt (7:38–12:02) and sum up her thoughts on the following points:

1. Prime Minister Trudeau speaking of "a dark and shameful chapter of our country's history" and lowering the flags on federal buildings to half-mast at the discovery of the children's bodies on former residential school ground
2. setting the book after the characters have left residential school
3. the negative effects of residential school on the children
4. the goals of the residential school system → S34 → WB 56–57/1–2

Talking about the past

Alternate history fiction

How would the world be different if Europeans hadn't colonised much of it? The people in the places that were colonised had, of course, been living in highly complex societies for centuries – or millennia – before ships full of white men with guns arrived. What might those cultures be like now if they had been left alone? How might they have developed if their societies hadn't been devastated and their resources hadn't been stolen? Contrary to the imperial philosophy of the time, these civilisations were not 'inferior' – they just had not developed ships and guns. The Maya civilisation of Central America had great stone-built cities when most Europeans were still living in huts.

This 'what if?' has been the topic of a number of fictional works. The Marvel Comics character Black Panther comes from the fictional African state of Wakanda, which was never colonised and has become the world's most technologically advanced country. Several novels have explored how the world might be different if the Black Death in 14th century Europe had killed far more people than it actually did, slowing down or entirely stopping the continent's technological development. Kim Stanley Robinson's *The Years of Rice and Salt* charts the history of a world without European influence from 1405 to 2025. Other books examine what could have happened if one key event in history had been different. *Age of Aztec* by James Lovegrove depicts an alternate reality based on the question of what might have happened if the Aztecs had won a key battle against the Spanish in 16th century Mexico, and had gone on to dominate the world.

While most of these works are primarily for entertainment, they draw attention to a serious issue. Most of the world's poorest countries are former European colonies. It seems almost certain that if they weren't still in the aftermath of colonialism, they would have achieved greater levels of economic development and more equality with the rest of the world.

1 Analyse the examples of tenses referring to the past in the text and explain why they are used. Distinguish between simple and progressive, active and passive forms.

Examples: *The past perfect simple in line 2 ("hadn't colonised") is used in the if-clause, which is part of a mixed conditional sentence. The passive form of the simple past in line 4 ("were colonised") is used to show that the focus … The present perfect in line …*

2 Which of the conditional sentences in the text are not purely type 3 (condition and consequence referring to the past, fulfilling the condition is no longer possible)? Explain.

3 Express the ideas in the pairs of statements given using type 3 sentences. You needn't use exactly the same words.

1. Europe's coastal nations were good at building ships. This allowed them to travel to faraway places.
2. The Chinese invented gunpowder. This invention made it possible for Europeans to develop guns.
3. Many Indigenous peoples at first welcomed the visitors, so starting new colonies in those places was easy.
4. Other European powers had been expanding their territories in Africa from the 1870s. Germany joined the competition and started its own colonies there.

4 Make conditional sentences with the ideas given.

1. Explorers | reach America | we possibly not know potatoes
2. The British | colonise India | English not widely used as a lingua franca
3. The climate | not be tropical in India | pepper not grow so well there
4. North America | not be colonised | …
5. It | be possible to travel back in time | …
6. There be no imperialism | our world be …

C Different perspectives

Two poems

Rudyard Kipling (1865–1936) was a British journalist, novelist and poet born in India. He was also the author of *The Jungle Book* and very popular in the late 19th and early 20th centuries. *The White Man's Burden* was published in 1899 as a message to the US after they took control of the former Spanish colonies of Cuba and the Philippines. The phrase 'white man's burden' came into common use as a result, although Kipling did not invent it. Not everyone shared Kipling's imperialist views, and there were many critical responses to the poem. One was a poem written by H. T. Johnson, an African-American clergyman and magazine editor.

The White Man's Burden (first stanza)

Take up the White Man's burden –
Send forth the best ye breed –
Go bind your sons to exile
To serve your captives' need;
To wait in heavy harness
On fluttered folk and wild –
Your new-caught sullen peoples,
Half devil and half child.

Rudyard Kipling, February 1899

The Black Man's Burden (second stanza)

Pile on the Black Man's Burden
His wail with laughter drown
You've sealed the Red Man's problem,
And will take up the Brown,
In vain ye seek to end it,
With bullets, blood or death
Better by far defend it
With honor's holy breath.

H. T. Johnson, April 1899

1 **burden** a heavy load
3 **to breed** to produce
5 **captive** sb you have caught
6 **to wait on sb** to serve sb
6 **harness** gear used to tie a horse to a cart
7 **fluttered** *here:* unstable, irrational
8 **sullen** uncooperative

3 **wail** crying
4 **to seal** to conclude
4 **'Red man'** was used at the time to describe Native Americans; nowadays it is considered to be offensive
6 **in vain** without success

1 COMPREHENSION

a) Look at both excerpts and sum up the main ideas of each. Think of the perspective, who is addressed and which groups of people are mentioned.

b) Johnson's poem mimics Kipling's use of a style of poetic language that was popular at the time. Rewrite the stanza so that every line is in easy-to-understand English. The new version does not need to rhyme or have the same rhythm. Exchange texts and peer-edit each other's work.

2 ANALYSIS

Analyse and compare how the two excerpts convey their main ideas (form, language and content). Use your knowledge to explain what the white and the Black man's burdens are meant to represent. → S15

3 EVALUATION

Evaluate the attitudes to imperialism expressed in the two poems and how they differ.
OR: Create your own response to Kipling's poem. This could be another poem, a cartoon, a fictitious dialogue with him, a digital storyboard, a video etc. Remember that this is a sensitive issue and make sure your text is respectful towards Indigenous peoples. → ○ 10

Binyavanga Wainaina

How to write about Africa

Always use the word 'Africa' or 'Darkness' or 'Safari' in your title. Subtitles may include the words 'Zanzibar,' 'Masai,' 'Zulu,' 'Zambezi,' 'Congo,' 'Nile,' 'Big,' 'Sky,' 'Shadow,' 'Drum,' 'Sun' or 'Bygone.' Also useful are words such as 'Guerrillas,' 'Timeless,' 'Primordial' and 'Tribal.' [...]

Never have a picture of a well-adjusted African on the cover of your book, or in it, unless that African has won the Nobel Prize. An AK-47, prominent ribs, naked breasts: use these. If you must include an African, make sure you get one in Masai or Zulu or Dogon dress.

In your text, treat Africa as if it were one country. It is hot and dusty with rolling grasslands and huge herds of animals and tall, thin people who are starving. Or it is hot and steamy with very short people who eat primates. Don't get bogged down with precise descriptions. Africa is big: fifty-four countries, 900 million people who are too busy starving and dying and warring and emigrating to read your book. The continent is full of deserts, jungles, highlands, savannahs and many other things, but your reader doesn't care about all that, so keep your descriptions romantic and evocative and unparticular.

Make sure you show how Africans have music and rhythm deep in their souls, and eat things no other humans eat. Do not mention rice and beef and wheat; monkey-brain is an African's cuisine of choice, along with goat, snake, worms and grubs. [...] Make sure you show that you are able to eat such food without flinching, and describe how you learn to enjoy it – because you care.

Your African characters may include naked warriors, loyal servants, diviners and seers, ancient wise men living in hermitic splendour. Or corrupt politicians, inept polygamous travel-guides, and prostitutes you have slept with. The Loyal Servant always behaves like a seven-year-old and needs a firm hand. [...] The Ancient Wise Man always comes from a noble tribe (not the money-grubbing tribes like the Gikuyu, the Igbo or the Shona). He has rheumy eyes and is close to the Earth. [...]

Among your characters you must always include The Starving African, who wanders the refugee camp nearly naked, and waits for the benevolence of the West. Her children have flies on their eyelids and pot bellies, and her breasts are flat and empty. She must look utterly helpless. She can have no past, no history; such diversions ruin the dramatic moment. Moans are good. She must never say anything about herself in the dialogue except to speak of her (unspeakable) suffering. Also be sure to include a warm and motherly woman who has a rolling laugh and who is concerned for your well-being. Just call her Mama. Her children are all delinquent. These characters should buzz around your main hero, making him look good. Your hero can teach them, bathe them, feed them; he carries lots of babies and has seen Death. Your hero is you (if reportage), or a beautiful, tragic international celebrity / aristocrat who now cares for animals (if fiction). [...]

Always end your book with Nelson Mandela saying something about rainbows or renaissances. Because you care.

Binyavanga Wainaina, in: *Granta*, 2005

3 **bygone** *vergangen*
6 **AK-47** a Soviet assault rifle
11 **don't get bogged down** *hier: verzettel dich nicht*
19 **grubs** *Larven, Maden*
23 **splendour** *Pracht*
23 **inept** unskilled or ineffective
35 **delinquent** *straffällig, kriminell*

4 COMPREHENSION | ANALYSIS

a) Sum up the instruction given in each paragraph.
b) Analyse the function of the title and the choice of text type.
c) Discuss who is addressed by the text. Examine the function of the repeated phrase "because you care".
d) Explain the text's actual message. Give examples to support your interpretation. Think of language / tone, rhetorical devices, imagery, examples given. → S10–11
e) Discuss whether the text will cause readers to rethink their attitudes and actions.

Is there only one history?

"Wait a minute! *You* were chasing *me*? I'm sorry, but I remember it a little differently."

"Oh, I don't think it's as bad as all that. In fact, I think we're in the golden age of something which we won't even realise it's the golden age of until many years from now."

> Every word a woman writes changes the story of the world, revises the official version.
>
> Carolyn See, US feminist writer

> It was in the eighteenth century that Indian History started.
>
> From: *1066 and all that* by W. C. Sellar and R. J. Yeatman, British humourists

> Study the historian before you begin to study the facts.
>
> Edward Hallett Carr, British historian

Step 1 Understand the task

a) Analyse the cartoons and the quotes above and point out what they say about history. Discuss the consequences caused by different perspectives on history.

b) Work in pairs. You are each going to write a reference article about the same period in history. Choose from these options:

1. The Middle Ages in Germany
2. The Spanish colonisation of the Americas
3. The Victorian Age in Britain
4. The USA between 1789 and 1865
5. Germany between 1949 and 1990
6. Germany between 1990 and 2020 (from an imaginary future perspective)

Think of different groups of people who experienced the period in question and choose whose point of view you are going to write from.

A: Write your article as somebody who would call it a 'golden age'.

B: Write your article as somebody who would call it a difficult period to live in.

Step 2 Do research and make a plan

MK a) Do research and collect useful information from different sources.

b) Make notes of your ideas and put them in a logical order.

Step 3 Improve your plan

Compare your notes and add more ideas so that they report some of the same topics from both points of view.

Step 4 Write and revise your texts

After writing your first drafts, compare your texts and give each other feedback on content and language. Use the feedback to improve your texts. → S7, 29

Step 5 Present and assess your results

Do a gallery walk. Assess each other's essays. Possible criteria for assessment:

- structuring and presenting the information
- consistent expression of the perspective
- presenting a plausible argument
- language

Skills workshop 2
Analysing fictional texts

Step 1 Getting a first idea

English class in Ghana, 1962

FACT FILE

Asante Empire
The Asante state was a well-organised and wealthy kingdom which lost its independence after several wars to the British in 1901. The given extract from the novel *Homegoing* is set at a boarding school in 1957, shortly before the former Asante state gained its independence from Britain and became the Republic of Ghana.

1 BEFORE YOU READ

a) Look at the photo and imagine it is the students' first day at school after the holidays. Share ideas with your partner: What is the lesson like for the students? How might they feel and what might they expect?

b) The following extract is about a history teacher and one of his classes of students who "learn the white man's book". What do you think this means?

Yaw

It was Yaw's tenth year of teaching at the school. Every year was the same. The new crop of schoolboys would begin to flower the school grounds, their hair freshly cut, their school uniforms freshly pressed. They would bring with them their timetables, their books, what little money their parents or villages had been able to collect for them. They would ask each other whom they had for this or that subject, and when one said Mr. Agyekum, another would tell the story that his elder brother or cousin had heard about the history teacher.

On the first day of the second term, Yaw watched the new students amble in. They were always well-behaved children, these boys, having been handpicked for their brightness or their wealth in order to attend school, learn the white man's book. In the walkways, on the way to his classroom, they would be so boisterous that it was possible to imagine them as they must have been in their villages, wrestling and singing and dancing before they knew what a book was, before their families knew that a book was a thing a child could want – need, even. Then, once they reached the classroom, once the textbooks were placed on their small wooden desks, they would grow quiet, spellbound. They were so quiet on that first day that Yaw could hear the baby birds on his window ledge, begging to be fed.

"What does the board say?" Yaw asked. He taught Form 1 students, fourteen- and fifteen-year-olds mostly, who had already learned to read and write in English in their lower-level classes. When Yaw had first gotten the post, he had argued with the headmaster that he should be able to teach in the boys' regional tongues, but the headmaster had laughed at him. Yaw knew it was a foolish hope. There were too many languages to even try.

Yaw watched them. He could always tell which boy would raise his hand first by the way he pushed forward in his seat and moved his eyes from left to right to see if anyone else would challenge his desire to speak first. This time, a very small boy named Peter raised his hand.

---

19 **boisterous** [ˈbɔɪ.stər.əs] noisy and full of energy   30 **board** blackboard

"It says, 'History is Storytelling,' " Peter answered. He smiled, the pent-up excitement releasing.

" 'History is Storytelling,' " Yaw repeated. He walked down the aisles between the rows of seats, making sure to look each boy in the eye. Once he finished walking and stood in the back of the room, where the boys would have to crane their necks in order to see him, he asked, "Who would like to tell the story of how I got my scar?"

The students began to squirm, their limbs growing limp and wobbly. They looked at each other, coughed, looked away.

"Don't be shy," Yaw said, smiling now, nodding encouragingly. "Peter?" he asked. The boy, who only seconds before had been so happy to speak, began to plead with his eyes. The first day with a new class was always Yaw's favorite.

"Mr. Agyekum, sah?" Peter said.

"What story have you heard? About my scar?" Yaw asked, smiling still, hoping, now, to ease some of the child's growing fear.

Peter cleared his throat and looked at the ground. "They say you were born of fire," he started. "That this is why you are so smart. Because you were lit by fire."

"Anyone else?"

Timidly, a boy named Edem raised bis hand. "They say your mother was fighting evil spirits from Asamando."

Then William: "I heard your father was so sad by the Asante loss that he cursed the gods, and the gods took vengeance."

Another, named Thomas: "I heard you did it to yourself, so that you would have something to talk about on the first day of class."

All of the boys laughed, and Yaw had to stifle his own amusement. Word of his lesson had gotten around, he knew. The older boys told some of the younger ones what to expect from him.

Still he continued, making his way back to the front of the room to look at his students, the bright boys of the uncertain Gold Coast, learning the white book from a scarred man.

"Whose story is correct?" Yaw asked them. They looked around at the boys who had spoken, as though trying to establish their allegiance by holding a gaze, casting a vote by sending a glance.

Finally, once the murmuring subsided, Peter raised his hand. "Mr. Agyekum, we cannot know which story is correct." He looked at the rest of the class, slowly understanding. "We cannot know which story is correct because we were not there."

Yaw nodded. He sat in his chair at the front of the room and looked at all the young men. "This is the problem of history. We cannot know that which we were not there to see and hear and experience for ourselves. We must rely upon the words of others. Those who were there in the olden days, they told stories to the children so that the children would know, so that the children could tell stories to their children. And so on, and so on. But now we come upon the problem of conflicting stories. Kojo Nyarko says that when the warriors came to his village their coats were red, but Kwame Adu says that they were blue. Whose story do we believe, then?"

The boys were silent. They stared at him, waiting.

"We believe the one who has the power. He is the one who gets to write the story. So when you study history, you must always ask yourself, Whose story am I missing? Whose voice was suppressed so that this voice could come forth? Once you have figured that out, you must find that story too. From there, you begin to get a clearer, yet still imperfect, picture."

The room was still. The birds on the ledge were still waiting for their food to come, still crying for their mother. Yaw gave the boys some time to think about what he had said, to respond, but when no one did he continued. "Let us open our textbooks to page –"

One of the students was coughing. Yaw looked up to see William with his hand raised. He nodded at the boy to speak.

"But, Mr. Agyekum, sah, you still have not told us the story of how you got your scar." [...]

Yaw did not touch his scar. Instead, he set his book down carefully and reminded himself to smile. He said, "I was only a baby. All I know is what I've heard."

From: Yaa Gyasi, *Homegoing*, 2016

---

55 **to squirm** *sich winden* 74 **Asamando** the land of the spirits and place of the ancestors; land of the dead
76 **Asante loss** after several wars and uprisings in the 1890s the Asante were defeated by the British
77 **vengeance** revenge 87 **Gold Coast** former British colony in West Africa, now known as the Republic of Ghana
107–109 **Kojo Nyarko / Kwame Adu** characters mentioned in the novel whose status and function remain vague

Step 2 Reading and understanding the text

2 COMPREHENSION

a) State your first reaction. As a student, how would you have felt in Yaw's first history lesson?

TIP

- Read the text a first time to get a general idea of what it is about.
- Read the text a second time and focus on the comprehension task.
- Make notes on the setting, the characters and the plot.

b) Outline what happens in the extract (external action) and the topic(s) discussed in the classroom.

Step 3 Analysing the position of the narrator

The **narrative perspective** describes the position of the narrator and the point of view. The point of view may be **limited** or **omniscient**. Basically, there are three different narrators: a **first-person narrator**, a **third-person limited narrator** and a **third-person omniscient narrator**. → S14

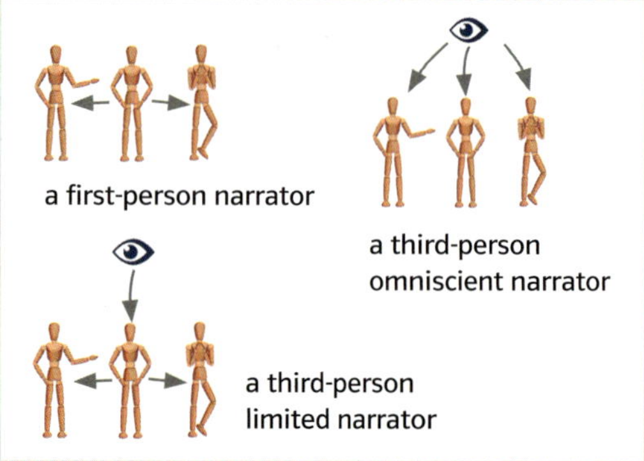

3 ANALYSIS Analyse the narrative perspective and its impact on the reader. Share your examples with your partner.

TIP

For your analysis, it is essential to find passages that are relevant to do the tasks you are given. Highlight or note down important words and phrases. Then draw conclusions from your notes and explain what exactly is revealed or what effect this has on you as a reader. Support your conclusions using quotes from the text.

4 CREATIVE TASK Change the third-person narrator and rewrite the scene from Peter's point of view. → S26

Step 4 Analysing a character

5 CREATIVE TASK Match the following sentences with the character traits they reveal.

respectful and expectant • idealistic and self-confident • experienced and professional

1. "It was Yaw's tenth year of teaching at the school. Every year was the same." (ll. 1–2)
2. "[…] placed on their small wooden desks, they would grow quiet, spellbound." (ll. 25–26)
3. "When Yaw had first gotten the post, he had argued with the headmaster that he should be able to teach in the boys' regional tongues, but the headmaster had laughed at him." (ll. 33–37)

TIP

Direct characterisation The narrator or a character in the story tells the reader directly about a character's look, behaviour, traits or attitude.
Example: *"They [the new students] were always well-behaved children, these boys, having been handpicked for their brightness or their wealth […]"* (ll. 14–16)

Indirect characterisation The reader draws conclusions from the way a character behaves, acts, speaks, interacts with others, and from the body language that is used.
Example: Peter to Mr. Agyekum: *"We cannot know which story is correct because we were not there."* (ll. 96–97)

6 ANALYSIS Read Peter's answer in the tip again and explain what it shows about his character.

7 ANALYSIS Find more examples in the text of direct and indirect characterisation and explain what they tell the reader about the characters.

8 ANALYSIS Write a characterisation of Yaw. Examine his attitude towards his job and his relationship with the students as revealed in ll. 30–136. Take into account:

- the way Yaw communicates with his students,
- the way they respond to what he says,
- the choice of words and stylistic devices. → S11, 13

USEFUL PHRASES

Talking about the attitude towards a job
positive / (very) negative / indifferent • ambitious • eager to do your job properly • very pleased with your job • sympathetic towards the people you work with • good at communicating with others • inspiring • encouraging • enthused • enthusiastic • reluctant / unwilling to do your job

Step 5 Analysing suspense

Suspense is created when the reader becomes excited and has questions because an incident or the development of the plot is not described completely but rather alluded to or the beginning of a conflict is described. The most exciting or important moment is the **climax**. The reader is curious to know how the conflict will be solved and goes on reading to find out more about his or her questions.
Narrative techniques like **scenic presentation** and **foreshadowing** are often used to create suspense. Scenic presentation (showing) shows an event in detail as it occurs. Foreshadowing implies hints about what is going to happen in the future. Often suspense is created in this way as the reader would like to know whether his or her expectations were correct.

9 SPEAKING Decide which of the following sentences you consider most (or least) suspenseful. Discuss your rankings in class.
1. "On the first day of the second term, Yaw watched the new students amble in." (ll. 13–14)
2. "Who would like to tell the story of how I got my scar?" (ll. 53–54)
3. "Whose story is correct?" (ll. 89)

10 ANALYSIS
a) Describe the atmosphere created in lines 13 ("On the first day …") to 97 ("… because we were not there.").

USEFUL PHRASES

Describing the atmosphere
cheerful • tense • gloomy • inspiring • hopeful • joyous • light-hearted • optimistic • vivacious • welcoming • uneasy • alarming • idyllic • frightening • threatening • painful • warm

b) Analyse the development of the lesson and how it contributes to the creation of suspense. Take into account the end of the lesson too.

USEFUL PHRASES

Talking about the creation of suspense
to follow the plot closely • to attract • to maintain the reader's attention • to get a quick overview of • to get insight into the character's thoughts and feelings • to understand the character's thoughts • to feel uneasy about • to feel sympathy for • to identify with

Step 6 Your turn: Comment on the way the lesson is described

11 EVALUATION Explain Yaw's statement "History is Storytelling" and give reasons why you agree or disagree with him.

12 CREATIVE TASK Choose one of the following tasks:
1. In the evening of the same day, Yaw has dinner with a colleague from his school. He tells him about his new group and the way they reacted to his questions. Write down their conversation.
2. In the evening Peter writes a letter about his first history lesson with Mr. Agyekum to his family. Write his letter. → S24

TIP

Writing your texts, focus on the characters' behaviour, feelings and thoughts during the lesson and / or the conversation.

13 CREATIVE TASK Write a comment about the novel extract for your school magazine. Start with the information under Step 1 (fact file and Task 1). Include the expectations you have noted down under Task 1b) and explain whether your expectations have been fulfilled. Explain whether you enjoyed reading the extract and would like to read the whole novel.

Visions of the future
Warm-up

The following pages offer you material dealing with possible future developments – both from the past and the present. After engaging with the warm-up and the material in the sections A–D, it is time for a (group) project.

Step 1 Choose an aspect or theme – either from section A–D or make up your own.

Step 2 In groups, brainstorm, research and choose material to work on (e.g. literary texts, films, news articles or facts and figures).

Step 3 Analyse and evaluate your materials. Choose which ones to include.

Step 4 Plan your project (e.g. organise your group work by agreeing on roles and planning steps) and prepare a presentation. Use digital tools. → S6

Step 5 Present your results and be prepared to answer questions. → S30

> Destiny has two ways of crushing us – by refusing our wishes and by fulfilling them.
> Henri Frederic Amiel (1821–1881), philosopher

1

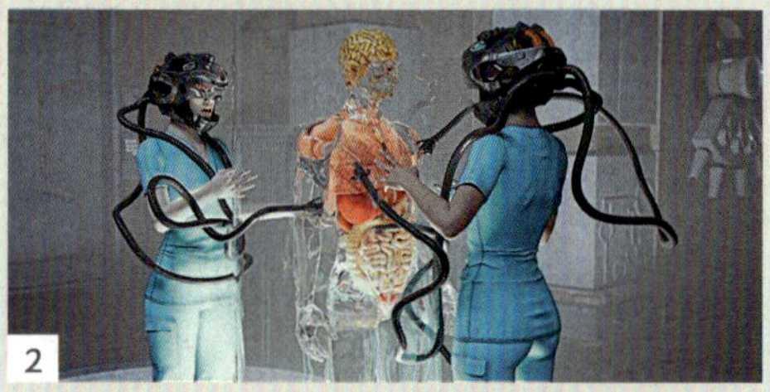
2

3

4

1 **BEFORE YOU START** Note down what hopes and fears come to your mind when you think about our planet's future. Think of possible ways to influence it. Discuss ideas in class.

2 **VISUALS** Talk about the photos and the quote. Explain what positive and negative aspects of the future they imply and how they are linked to the present.

3 **VOCABULARY** Work with a dictionary. Make a grid with useful vocabulary for talking about visions of the future. Start with the useful phrases and add more words for each heading. Write down translations, collocations, examples, related words, synonyms or antonyms to make sure you remember when and how to use them. → S1–2

USEFUL PHRASES

utopia / dystopia: humanity • progress • solarpunk art • an unsettling atmosphere • to face a moral dilemma • disturbing **society:** social beings • surveillance • to spy on sb • class **politics:** to manipulate • an oppressive regime **science / technology:** climate crisis • to exploit resources • vertical farming • genetic engineering • robotics • artificial intelligence

MK **4** **SPEAKING** Ideas of the future have always been the subject of books and films, one of the most popular genres being science fiction. If a concept of the future is positive, it is called utopia; if it is negative, it is called dystopia. What examples of literary works and films about future scenarios do you know? Share your knowledge about them in class. Collect the information, e.g. on a shared (digital) pinboard.

An extract from a classic novel

5 **BEFORE YOU READ** Some of you might know the phrase "Big brother is watching you". Discuss its meaning. Then read these passages from the beginning of the novel *Nineteen Eighty-Four*. It was first published in 1949 and is set in the fictional future of 1984.

It was a bright cold day in April, and the clocks were striking thirteen. Winston Smith, his chin nuzzled into his breast in an effort to escape the vile wind, slipped quickly through the glass doors of Victory Mansions, [...]. The hallway smelt of boiled cabbage and old rag mats. At one end of it a coloured poster, too large for indoor display, had been tacked to the wall. It depicted simply an enormous face, more than a metre wide: the face of a man of about forty-five, with a heavy black moustache and ruggedly handsome features. Winston made for the stairs. [...] On each landing, opposite the lift shaft, the poster with the enormous face gazed from the wall. It was one of those pictures which are so contrived that the eyes follow you about when you move. BIG BROTHER IS WATCHING YOU, the caption beneath it ran.

Inside the flat a fruity voice was reading out a list of figures which had something to do with the production of pig-iron. The voice came from an oblong metal plaque like a dulled mirror which formed part of the surface of the right-hand wall. Winston turned a switch and the voice sank somewhat, though the words were still distinguishable. The instrument (the telescreen, it was called) could be dimmed, but there was no way of shutting it off completely. [...] Behind Winston's back the voice from the telescreen was still babbling away about pig-iron and the overfulfilment of the Ninth Three-Year Plan. The telescreen received and transmitted simultaneously. Any sound that Winston made, above the level of a very low whisper, would be picked up by it; moreover, so long as he remained within the field of vision which the metal plaque commanded, he could be seen as well as heard. There was of course no way of knowing whether you were being watched at any given moment. How often, or on what system, the Thought Police plugged in on any individual wire was guesswork. It was even conceivable that they watched everybody all the time. But at any rate they could plug in your wire whenever they wanted to. You had to live – did live, from habit that became instinct – in the assumption that every sound you made was overheard, and, except in darkness, every movement scrutinised.

From: George Orwell, *Nineteen Eighty-Four*, 1949

2 **to nuzzle** to press your nose or face against sth gently
12 **pig-iron** *Roheisen*
12 **oblong** *rechteckig, länglich*
27 **to scrutinise** to examine very carefully

6 **COMPREHENSION | ANALYSIS**

a) Explain how surveillance works in the world described.

b) Describe the atmosphere and the narrative perspective of the extract. Guess what kind of literary genre it is and give reasons. → S10, 12, 14

MK c) Find a film adaptation of the novel. Watch the first 10 minutes of it and assess how well it brings Orwell's fictional world to life. Say why you think so. → S35

7 **EVALUATION** What effects does a surveillance society have on its people? Compare Orwell's vision of 1984 with an example of state surveillance today. Would you consider the book still worth reading today?

A Freedom and control

The Pedestrian

This short story was published in 1951, when TV was gaining popularity all over the US.

Author
Ray Bradbury
(1920–2012)

To enter out into that silence that was the city at eight o'clock of a misty evening in November, to put your feet upon that buckling concrete walk, to step over grassy seams and make your way, hands in pockets, through the silences, that was what Mr. Leonard Mead most dearly loved to do. [...] Sometimes he would walk for hours and miles and return only at midnight [...]. And on his way he would see the cottages and homes with their dark windows, and it was not unequal to walking through a graveyard where only the faintest glimmers of firefly light appeared in flickers behind the windows. Sudden gray phantoms seemed to manifest upon inner room walls where a curtain was still undrawn against the night, or there were whisperings and murmurs where a window in a tomblike building was still open. [...]

On this particular evening he began his journey in a westerly direction, toward the hidden sea. There was a good crystal frost in the air; it cut the nose and made the lungs blaze like a Christmas tree inside; you could feel the cold light going on and off, all the branches filled with invisible snow. He listened to the faint push of his soft shoes through autumn leaves with satisfaction, and whistled a cold quiet whistle between his teeth, occasionally picking up a leaf as he passed, examining its skeletal pattern in the infrequent lamplights as he went on, smelling its rusty smell.

"Hello, in there," he whispered to every house [...] as he moved. "What's up tonight on Channel 4, Channel 7, Channel 9? Where are the cowboys rushing, and do I see the United States Cavalry over the next hill to the rescue?"

[...] He turned back on a side street, circling around toward his home. He was within a block of his destination when the lone car turned a corner quite suddenly and flashed a fierce white cone of light upon him. He stood entranced, not unlike a night moth, stunned by the illumination, and then drawn toward it.

A metallic voice called to him: "Stand still. Stay where you are! Don't move!" He halted. "Put up your hands!"

"But –" he said.

"Your hands up! Or we'll shoot!"

The police, of course, but what a rare, incredible thing; in a city of three million, there was only one police car left, wasn't that correct? Ever since a year ago, 2052, the election year, the force had been cut down from three cars to one. Crime was ebbing; there was no need now for the police, save for this one lone car wandering and wandering the empty streets.

"Your name?" said the police car in a metallic whisper. He couldn't see the men in it for the bright light in his eyes.

"Leonard Mead," he said.

"Speak up!"

"Leonard Mead!"

"Business or profession?"

"I guess you'd call me a writer."

"No profession," said the police car, as if talking to itself. The light held him fixed, like a museum specimen, needle thrust through chest.

"You might say that," said Mr. Mead. He hadn't written in years. Magazines and books didn't sell any more. Everything went on in the tomblike houses at night now, he thought, continuing his fancy. The tombs, ill-lit by television light, where the people sat like the dead, the gray or multicolored lights touching their faces, but never really touching them.

"No profession," said the phonograph voice, hissing. "What are you doing out?"

"Walking," said Leonard Mead.

"Walking!"

"Just walking," he said simply, but his face felt cold. [...]

"Walking where? For what?"

"Walking for air. Walking to see."

"Your address!"

4 **to buckle** *nachgeben*
20 **tomblike** like a grave
40 **Where are the cowboys rushing** ... Westerns were the dominant genre on American TV in the 1950s and 1960s
75 **like a museum specimen** exhibits, e.g. insects, in a museum were often presented with a needle through their body
82 **ill-lit** badly lit

"Eleven South Saint James Street."

"And there is air in your house, you have an air conditioner, Mr. Mead?"

"Yes."

"And you have a viewing screen in your house to see with?"

"No."

"No?" There was a crackling quiet that in itself was an accusation.

"Are you married, Mr. Mead?"

"No."

"Not married," said the police voice behind the fiery beam. The moon was high and clear among the stars and the houses were gray and silent.

"Nobody wanted me," said Leonard Mead with a smile.

"Don't speak unless you're spoken to!"

Leonard Mead waited in the cold night.

"Just walking, Mr. Mead?"

"Yes."

"But you haven't explained for what purpose."

"I explained; for air, and to see, and just to walk."

"Have you done this often?"

"Every night for years."

The police car sat in the center of the street with its radio throat faintly humming.

"Well, Mr. Mead," it said.

"Is that all?" he asked politely.

"Yes," said the voice. "Here." There was a sigh, a pop. The back door of the police car sprang wide. "Get in."

"Wait a minute, I haven't done anything!"

"Get in."

"I protest!"

"Mr. Mead."

He walked like a man suddenly drunk. As he passed the front window of the car he looked in. As he had expected, there was no one in the front seat, no one in the car at all.

"Get in."

He put his hand to the door and peered into the back seat, which was a little cell, a little black jail with bars. It smelled of riveted steel. It smelled of harsh antiseptic; it smelled too clean and hard and metallic. There was nothing soft there.

"Now if you had a wife to give you an alibi," said the iron voice. "But –"

"Where are you taking me?"

The car hesitated, or rather gave a faint whirring click, as if information, somewhere, was dropping card by punch-slotted card under electric eyes. "To the Psychiatric Center for Research on Regressive Tendencies."

He got in. The door shut [...].

The police car rolled through the night avenues, flashing its dim lights ahead.

They passed one house on one street a moment later, one house in an entire city of houses that were dark, but this one particular house had all of its electric lights brightly lit, every window a loud yellow illumination, square and warm in the cool darkness.

"That's my house," said Leonard Mead. No one answered him.

The car moved down the empty river-bed streets and off away, leaving the empty streets with the empty sidewalks, and no sound and no motion all the rest of the chill November night.

Ray Bradbury, *The Pedestrian*, 1951

144 **bars** metal devices, e.g. in windows, to keep sb out or in
145 **riveted** fixed
154 **punch-slotted** early computers worked with punch cards for processing information
157 **regressive** ↔ progressive

1 COMPREHENSION | ANALYSIS

a) Summarise the plot and say what elements show you that it is a story about the future. In what way is it influenced by the time in which it was written?

b) Analyse how Mr Mead and the society he lives in are described. Think of content, style and the effect on the reader. → S11, 13, 14

c) Share ideas about how the story could go on.

2 EVALUATION "I don't try to describe the future. I try to prevent it." Interpret the quote by Bradbury, who mainly wrote fantasy and science-fiction.

FURTHER READING / VIEWING

Nineteen Eighty-Four • Fahrenheit 451 • Minority Report • Brazil • THX-1138 • Black Mirror: Nosedive • The Social Dilemma • The Handmaid's Tale • Equilibrium • The Circle • Daz 4 Zoe

B Science and technology

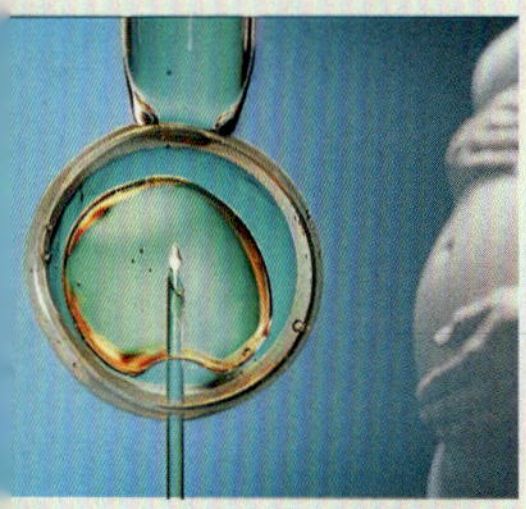

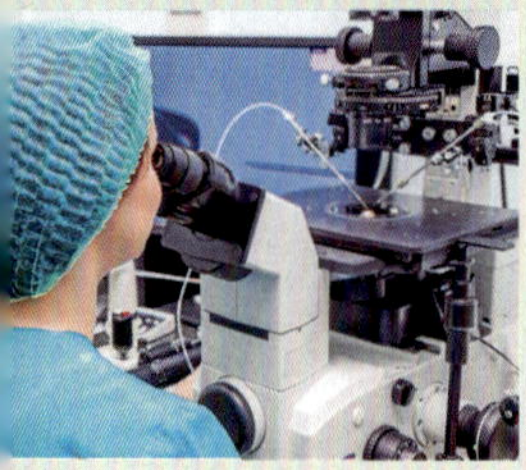

Forthcoming genetic therapies raise serious ethical questions

One of the greatest risks of gene editing tools "is that the people who would benefit most will not be able to access them".

The next generation of advanced genetic therapies raises profound medical and ethical issues that must be thrashed out to ensure the game-changing technology benefits patients and society, a group of world-leading experts has warned.

Medicines based on powerful gene editing tools will begin to transform the treatment of blood disorders, conditions affecting the heart, eyes and muscles, and potentially even neurodegenerative diseases before the end of the decade, but the cost will put them out of the reach of many patients.

Trials of gene editing in embryos will probably follow, researchers say, and while the procedure has limited clinical applications, some fear fertility clinics could embrace the technology and offer gene editing services that fuel "a new kind of techno-eugenics". [...]

Professor Françoise Baylis, a philosopher at Dalhousie University in Canada, said the cost of the new therapies will be prohibitively high for much of the global population, a situation that could "seriously threaten" the aspiration for all humans to be born equal.

The experts, who range from geneticists and public health researchers to bioethicists and philosophers, expect a wave of gene editing therapies to reach clinics in the next five years or so. [...]

The same technology paves the way for therapies to enhance healthy humans, to make them faster, smarter, stronger, or more resistant to disease, though enhancement is trickier than mending single faulty genes, according to Professor Ewan Birney, joint director of the European Bioinformatics Institute near Cambridge. [...]

Regardless, some see it as inevitable. Professor Mayana Zatz at the University of São Paulo, Brazil and founder of the Brazilian Association of Muscular Dystrophy, said she was "absolutely against editing genes for enhancement", but added: "There will always be people ready to pay for it in private clinics and it will be difficult to stop." [...]

At millions of dollars a shot, gene editing today is prohibitively expensive. But if costs fall substantially in coming decades, there is a risk that IVF clinics could start offering services, whether the benefits are proven or not. Prospective parents might feel obligated to use it to give their child "the best life", Baylis said [...]. Birney speculates that clinics could offer combined IVF, embryo screening and gene editing packages, but warned that this would be "misguided". "It is important countries work out how to regulate this before it becomes a more credible prospect," he said.

Despite the advances, Professor Alta Charo, a bioethicist at the University of Wisconsin-Madison, suspects most people will stick with having babies the old-fashioned way. "The biggest risk I see at the moment is that discussion around germline editing will continue to present such dystopian visions as realistic," she said. "IVF is uncomfortable, inconvenient and expensive. I don't see people abandoning conception through the more pleasurable means of sexual intercourse, unless there is a real need."

Ian Sample and Hannah Devlin, in: *The Guardian*, 2023

2 **to thrash out** to discuss
9 **fertility clinic** *Klinik für Reproduktionsmedizin*
9 **to embrace** to happily accept
11 **eugenics** practices aiming to improve the genetic quality of humans, a highly controversial term used by racists to legitimise systematic genocide
19 **to pave the way for sth** to make sth possible
19 **to enhance** to improve
21 **to mend** to cure, to repair
21 **faulty** damaged
23 **inevitable** unavoidable
28 **IVF** in vitro fertilisation
33 **prospect** possibility
35 **to stick with** to keep
37 **germline editing** gene therapy
39 **conception** *Empfängnis*

1 COMPREHENSION | ANALYSIS

a) Sum up what the article is about and what hopes and fears for the future are presented.

b) Analyse the way the topic and (different) opinions on the issue are presented.

2 **EVALUATION** Give your own opinion on the pros and cons of modern biotechnology.

3 **SPEAKING** Apart from genetic engineering targeting diseases, there are other innovations in science and technology which seem to advance us towards a 'brave new world'. Talk about advantages and disadvantages. These examples can give you ideas:

- Smart technology makes life easier, e.g. at home. Think of everyday life, entertainment, communication, shopping, administration, household chores etc.

- The internet allows people from all over the world to communicate and collaborate without meeting in person. This affects people's private and professional lives.

- New technology can help people with disabilities or health problems.

- Alternative forms of nutrition like insects, an extremely sustainable source of protein, can help to feed the world in a resource-efficient and healthy way.

4 **ANALYSIS** Interpret the following quote.

TIP

Always adapt your methods of analysis to the text type. Refer to the Skills section for stylistic devices in
- literary / factual texts, news reports, commentaries, letters, poems, songs → S9–11
- cartoons, diagrams → S37–38
- feature films, serials, documentaries → S35

> The factory of the future will have only two employees, a man and a dog. The man will be there to feed the dog. The dog will be there to keep the man from touching the equipment.
>
> Warren Bennis (1925–2014), organisational consultant and writer

5 **CREATIVE TASK**
1. Imagine a future product or invention. Advertise it with a slogan or a post. **OR:**
2. Advise against it with a news report or podcast. → S9, 25

FURTHER READING / VIEWING

Brave New World • The Island of Doctor Moreau • Gattaca • The Matrix • The Island • 2001: A Space Odyssey • Never Let Me Go • The Windup Girl • Black Mirror: Be Right Back

C Humans and machines

An artificial companion

Charlie, the narrator, who is fascinated by technology, is about to start a love relationship with his neighbour, Miranda. He has just spent a large amount of money to buy one of the first sophisticated androids that have been put on the market, a male called Adam (the female ones are called Eve).

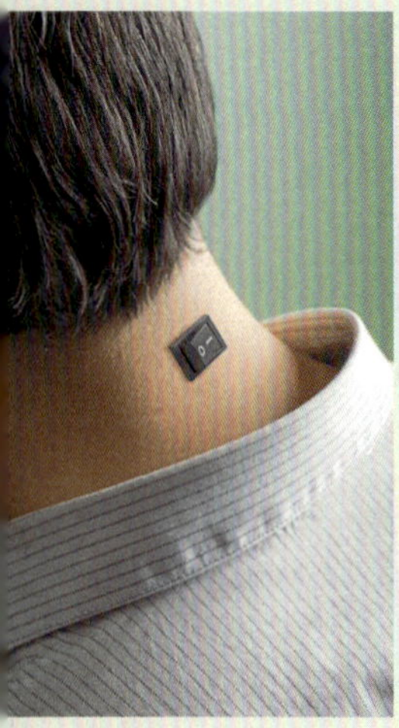

At last, with cardboard and polystyrene wrapping strewn around his ankles, he sat naked at my dining table, eyes closed, a black power line trailing from the entry point in his umbilicus to a thirteen-amp socket in the wall. It would take sixteen hours to fire him up. Then sessions of download updates and personal preferences. I wanted him now, and so did Miranda. Like eager young parents, we were avid for his first words. There was no loudspeaker cheaply buried in his chest. We knew from the excited publicity that he formed sounds with breath, tongue, teeth and palate. Already, his lifelike skin was warm to the touch and as smooth as a child's. Miranda claimed to see his eyelashes flicker. I was certain she was seeing vibrations from the Tube trains rolling a hundred feet below us, but I said nothing.

Adam was not a sex toy. However, he was capable of sex and possessed functional mucous membranes, in the maintenance of which he consumed half a litre of water each day. [...]

He was advertised as a companion, an intellectual sparring partner, friend and factotum who could wash dishes, make beds and 'think'. Every moment of his existence, everything he heard and saw, he recorded and could retrieve. [...] As for range, thanks to breakthroughs in electrical storage, he could run seventeen kilometres in two hours without a charge or, its energy equivalent, converse non-stop for twelve days. He had a working life of twenty years. He was compactly built, square-shouldered, dark-skinned, with thick black hair swept back; narrow in the face, with a hint of hooked nose suggestive of fierce intelligence, pensively hooded eyes, tight lips that, even as we watched, were draining of their deathly yellowish-white tint and acquiring rich human colour, perhaps even relaxing a little at the corners. Miranda said he resembled 'a docker from the Bosporus'.

Before us sat the ultimate plaything, the dream of ages, the triumph of humanism – or its angel of death. [...] It was a wintry late afternoon. I made toast and we drank more coffee. Miranda, a doctoral scholar of social history, said she wished the teenage Mary Shelley was here beside us, observing closely, not a monster like Frankenstein's, but this handsome dark-skinned young man coming to life. [...]

I couldn't think of myself as Adam's 'user'. I'd assumed there was nothing to learn about him that he could not teach me himself. But the manual in my hands had fallen open at Chapter Fourteen. Here, the English was plain: preferences; personality parameters. Then a set of headings – Agreeableness. Extraversion. Openness to experience. Conscientiousness. Emotional stability. The list was familiar to me. The Five Factor model. Educated as I was in the humanities, I was suspicious of such reductive categories, though I knew from a friend in psychology that each item had many subgroups. Glancing at the next page I saw that I was supposed to select various settings on a scale of one to ten.

I'd been expecting a friend. I was ready to treat Adam as a guest in my home, as an unknown I would come to know. I'd thought he would arrive optimally adjusted. Factory settings – a contemporary synonym for fate. My friends, family and acquaintance, all had appeared in my life with fixed settings, with unalterable histories of genes and environment. I wanted my expensive new friend to do the same. Why leave it to me? But of course, I knew the answer. Not many of us are optimally adjusted.

1 **polystyrene** a kind of packaging material
3 **umbilicus** navel
3 **to fire up** to get started
5 **avid** eager
7 **palate** the upper inside of your mouth
12 **mucous membrane** *Schleimhaut*
21 **pensively** *nachdenklich*
33 **extraversion** the qualities of being confident, lively, and enjoying social situations
34 **conscientiousness** the qualities of working hard and taking care to do things well

Gentle Jesus? Humble Darwin? One every 1,800 years. Even if it knew the best, the least harmful, parameters of personality, which it couldn't, a worldwide corporation with a precious reputation couldn't risk a mishap. *Caveat emptor.*

God had once delivered a fully formed companion for the benefit of the original Adam. I had to devise one for myself. Here was Extraversion and a graded set of childish statements. *He loves to be the life and soul of the party* and *He knows how to entertain people and lead them.* And at the bottom, *He feels uncomfortable around other people* and *He prefers his own company.* Here in the middle was, *He likes a good party but he's always happy to come home.* This was me. But should I be replicating myself? If I was to choose from the middle of each scale I might devise the soul of blandness. Extraversion appeared to include its antonym. There was a long adjectival list with boxes to tick: outgoing, shy, excitable, talkative, withdrawn, boastful, modest, bold, energetic, moody. I wanted none of them, not for him, not for myself. [...]

At the time, I was not to know that these graded options would have little effect on Adam. The real determinant was what was known as 'machine learning'. The users' handbook merely granted an illusion of influence and control, the kind of illusion parents have in relation to their children's personalities. [...]

Before lunch I'd sent Miranda an email inviting her to dinner that night. Now she'd accepted. She liked my cooking. During the meal I would make a proposal. I would fill in roughly half the choices for Adam's personality, then give her the link and the password and let her choose the rest. I wouldn't interfere, I wouldn't even want to know what decisions she had made. She might be influenced by a version of herself: delightful. She might conjure the man of her dreams: instructive. Adam would come into our lives like a real person, with the layered intricacies of his personality revealed only through time, through events, through his dealings with whomever he met. In a sense he would be like our child. What we were separately would be merged in him. Miranda would be drawn into the adventure. We would be partners, and Adam would be our joint concern, our creation. We would be a family. There was nothing underhand in my plan. I was sure to see more of her. We'd have fun.

From: Ian McEwan, *Machines like me*, 2019

47 ***caveat emptor*** (*Latin:* let the buyer beware) *Ausschluss der Gewährleistung*

68 **intricacies** *Feinheiten*

1 COMPREHENSION | ANALYSIS

a) Describe the situation and sum up the thoughts and expectations of the narrator. Analyse the choice of words and the stylistic devices used to describe Adam – either as a machine or as an individual. → S11, 28

b) Point out how it is shown that Charlie and Miranda are getting closer. → S13

TIP

Always give examples from the text to support your theses and give line numbers. → S4

2 EVALUATION Explain Charlie's difficulties with regards to Adam's personality settings and how they might impact their relationship. What would you do if you were him?

3 CREATIVE TASK Considering Charlie, Adam and Miranda, what potential conflicts can you see? Write a short summary of a possible storyline. → S25–26

MK **4 ACROSS CULTURES** More and more people are single. Some hope to find happiness in artificial or virtual companions with artificial intelligence that respond like humans. They may be holograms, androids or chatbots. With a critical eye, do research on the popularity of such companions in different countries and present your results.

FURTHER READING / VIEWING

Her • Do androids dream of electric sheep? / Blade Runner • West World • Ex-Machina • A. I. • Runaround / I, robot • Bicentennial Man • Klara and the Sun • Moon • Tron • Chappie

D Saving the planet

Last chance

Having left Earth because it has become uninhabitable, humans now live on a different planet. There, children are sent to Ikehara-Baasch Academy at the age of two. The academy is underground and teaches the students that the surface of the planet they live on has been destroyed by human activity. As part of their education, they are sometimes taken on above-ground visits to see how hostile the planet's environment is. Grace Swenson has been a teacher at the academy for twenty years, also training new teachers. She is going to give a speech at the graduation ceremony for the students who have finished school.

The transom light flashed. Grace scanned her palm and walked onto the stage. Thirty-four graduating seniors, all born during the same month sixteen years ago, watched her in expectant silence. None of them had any idea what would happen at the ceremony: the academy's graduates never returned to the dormitories.

"Congratulations," Grace intoned, "today you become full citizens in our society. But before you do, you need to understand the truth about our history."

"Millennia ago, humanity fled the smoking ruin of Earth. Your ancestors were among those select few lucky enough to find a place on those seventeen colonial ships."

Grace could feel the students' anticipation dissipating. They knew this by rote. She could see them only dimly through the harsh stage lights, but she knew they were leaning back, crossing their arms and legs, waiting for this remedial history lesson to end.

"Earth's survivors recognized the new planet they found for what it was and named it Salvation. And for a few generations, they treated the planet accordingly. But when the ruin of Earth had faded from living memory and was nothing more than a dry fact in a textbook, the colonists started to make exceptions, to take shortcuts for profit and comfort. And in the span of four hundred years, they destroyed the second Eden. *It can never happen again*, students. There are no more habitable planets within our reach. That's why our forefathers named this planet, your home, Last Chance."

Grace gestured and the floor-to-ceiling screen behind her glowed to life. It showed a red planet against the black backdrop of space. "This is the Last Chance you know." Grace flicked her wrist and the planet was replaced by an image of people in exposure suits struggling to assemble industrial machinery in a harsh red landscape. "This is what we've prepared you for: a brutal, painful life spent trying to scratch out something better for the next generation." Grace took a deep breath to steady her nerves. "But that was all a lie."

Grace let the silence draw out. When the students started to mutter, she gestured again. A new image filled the screen: a green and blue planet hanging in space. The camera plummeted toward the surface. Unblemished natural landscapes rolled by: craggy mountains, grassy yellow plains, sapphire blue lakes, and endless rows of towering trees.

1 **transom** part of the ceiling
4 **dormitory** a school or university building where students live together
9 **by rote** by heart

"This is the real Last Chance. The desert above us is only a tiny fraction of the planet. Our world is a paradise."

Grace gestured again, and the screen now showed a town square. Fit, smiling couples walked arm in arm down tree-shaded avenues. An elderly man rode a bicycle down the street, a loaf of bread and a bottle of wine in his basket. "And this is where you will be going to live: New Paris."

The screen went black. For a long moment, the room was dead silent – the students weren't even breathing. Grace waited. And then all the students began to shout at once. She let them howl for a full minute and then blew an earsplitting note on a whistle.

"You're outraged. I know. I felt the same way when I found out. But all we've done is justified – it's necessary. You'll never forget what a blessing this world is. You will live modestly, sustainably, and you'll never consider risking this planet – for anything."

"Your parents are waiting next door. You'll be leaving with them tonight, whenever you're ready. You'll have a month to reconnect with your family and explore New Paris. At that point, a counsellor will contact you to talk through your education and career options. I hope that some of you will have the courage to come back to the academy as apprentice teachers."

A boy scoffed loudly. Grace ignored him.

"For now, I'm here to answer any questions you might have."

She moved away from the podium and stood in the center of the stage. Within seconds, she was surrounded by students, some furious, some hurt, some plain lost. She didn't leave the auditorium for six hours.

From: Tyler Young, *Last chance*, 2017

1 COMPREHENSION

a) Explain the educational concept of the academy and sum up Grace's speech.
b) Sum up what we learn about Grace and her job from this extract.

2 EVALUATION → S19, 31

1. Comment on the way the school treats its students. Does the end justify the means?
   OR:
2. Imagine you were one of the graduates. What would you ask Grace? Write a short dialogue.

MK 3 SPEAKING

We know that we are overexploiting our planet's resources, our climate is changing and some places will become uninhabitable sooner or later. It will be difficult to provide food, water and energy to the world's growing population. Do research on innovative ideas and projects that could help and present them in class.

MK 4 VIEWING

a) Go online and watch the ad-free version of the commercial "Dear Alice". Describe and discuss what ideas for a livable future are shown.
b) Analyse the cinematic devices used and the effect on the viewer. → S35
c) Comment on the imagery and the original purpose of the film (advertising a yoghurt).

FURTHER READING / VIEWING

The Dispossessed • Ice on Fire • Interstellar • The Martian • Sunshine • Bewilderment • Rebuilding Paradise • David Attenborough: A Life on Our Planet • Aurora • WALL-E

3 Structural change
Introduction

1

2

1 VISUALS

a) Describe and compare the two pictures. Think of the time they are from, the aspect of life they show and how the people in the pictures might be feeling.

b) Find pictures to illustrate how people's lives have changed in other areas over the last 100–150 years (e.g. world of work, housing) and present them in a short talk.

2 SPEAKING

a) **Think:** Based on your own knowledge and the following quotes, make notes to define the term "revolution". Think of examples of revolutions you already know about, e.g. in politics, society or music.

b) **Pair:** Compare your notes with a partner. Agree on one definition and suitable examples.

c) **Share:** Present your results to the class.

> Revolutions are the locomotives of history.
>
> Karl Marx, German philosopher, economist and revolutionary
>
> A revolution can neither be made nor stopped.
>
> Napoleon Bonaparte, French emperor
>
> You never change things by fighting the existing reality. To change something, build a new model that makes the existing model obsolete.
>
> R. Buckminster Fuller, American writer and philosopher

3 SPEAKING

a) Discuss in which way the following inventions / ideas revolutionised the world:

printing press • steam train • vaccination • assembly line • personal computer

Consider the impact they have had on people's lives.

USEFUL PHRASES

a fundamental / significant transformation • a dramatic / major / profound change • changes in technology / everyday life • to bring about / to adapt to / to oppose change • to transform the workplace • to offer new possibilities • introduction of mass production • to have an impact on / to affect sb

b) In pairs, think of innovations that might revolutionise our lives in the future. Present one idea to the class. → S30

MK

4 VISUALS Describe the cartoon and explain its message. → S38

5 SPEAKING The changes in technology, industry and society in the 21st century are sometimes described as the "Fourth Industrial Revolution". Comment on the following statement.

> You cannot stop the Fourth Industrial Revolution, but you can influence its direction and impact in your life.
>
> Nicky Verd, South-African writer and keynote speaker

The Industrial Revolution(s)

The first Industrial Revolution

Britain was the first country to transform from a primarily agricultural to a primarily industrial society. This arose from many technological innovations, scientific discoveries and social changes that occurred from the mid-18th to the early / mid-19th centuries. In 1776, James Watt developed a much-improved steam engine which could be used to power industrial machinery. Prior to the Industrial Revolution, cloth was produced by hand in spinners' and weavers' homes. A series of inventions such as the power loom (1785) moved the production of cloth to steam-powered mills in rapidly expanding cities. Mechanisation hugely increased productivity, and textile production became Britain's leading industry.

Another important development was a new production process for iron in 1784, allowing it to be produced cheaply and in large quantities. In the mid-19th century, railways and steamships boosted industry and accelerated globalisation.

The Industrial Revolution had the biggest impact on the Midlands and parts of northern England. Reasons for this included:

- these areas had already been associated with textile production,
- nearness to ports (especially Liverpool) where cotton arrived from the United States,
- availability of coal from local mines to power machinery and to produce iron.

The profits from industrialisation made some people very rich and over time led to modest wealth for many more. However, the mechanisation of various industries and agriculture meant that many craftsmen and farmers lost their livelihoods.

In search of work in mills or factories, many migrated to Britain's new industrial cities, where living and working conditions were extremely bad. Slums, pollution, disease and child labour were the norm. Consequently, protest movements formed. The Luddites (named after their mythical leader Ned Ludd), for example, protested by smashing the machines that were taking their jobs. Conditions began to improve only slowly: The Cotton Mills and Factories Act (1819) set the minimum working age at 9 years and the maximum working hours for children at 12 hours per day, six days a week. But the new law was widely ignored. Trade unions were at first (sometimes violently) supressed by employers and the government, and it wasn't until 1871 that they were fully legalised.

Birmingham's population 1650–1950

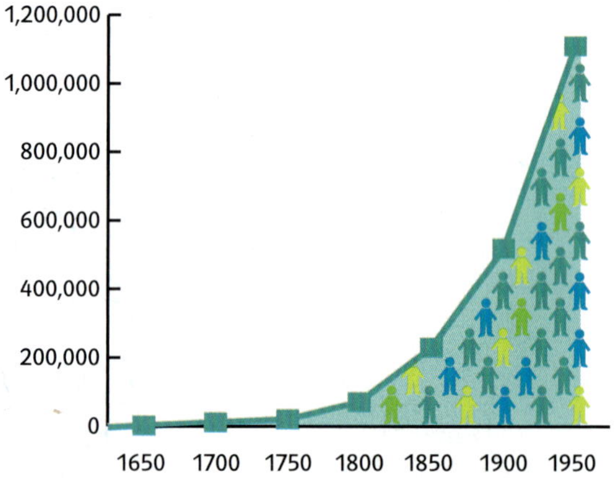

Wikipedia website, 2022

The second Industrial Revolution

In 1870 a technological advance enabled the production of high-quality steel, leading to a new phase of industrial development. Other major advances in this period included the emergence of mass-production manufacturing, chemical industries, electricity and telegraph / telephone networks. Britain consolidated its position as the world's leading industrial power. However, other countries such as France, Germany, the US and Japan had followed Britain's example of rapid industrialisation and had become strong competitors. In the UK, a series of Factory Acts gradually improved the conditions of industrial employment. So did labour movements in most industrialised nations, which led to improved pay and working conditions.

The third Industrial Revolution (or Digital Revolution)

After WWII, the economies of most nations from the first wave of industrialisation saw a decline in manufacturing and heavy industries such as mining and shipbuilding. In Britain, this had dramatic consequences for regions like the North or the Midlands that were economically dependent on these industries, and unemployment became a major issue. The miners' strike of 1984–85 unsuccessfully attempted to prevent the widespread closure of coal mines. The UK economy in general became more centred on service industries such as retail, financial services and tourism. However, many communities in former industrial areas remain economically disadvantaged even today.

The invention of the transistor (1947) led to computers and other digital devices. In 1969 the first electronic communications were sent via the ARPANET, the precursor of the internet. From the mid-20th century, the US became the world's dominant economic power. Key innovations in information and communications technology (e.g. modern smartphones in 2007) mostly originated there and led to the rise of high-tech corporations or 'tech giants'. Many of these are based in northern California's Silicon Valley, which has become the centre of the world's high-tech innovation. The internet and digital media transformed work and leisure in all industrialised economies, accelerating globalisation.

The fourth Industrial Revolution (or Industry 4.0)

In the 21st century, digitalisation and other technological advances such as artificial intelligence (AI) and 'the internet of things' are fundamentally transforming the global economy. China, where most high-tech devices are manufactured, is challenging the US's position as leader of the digital revolution. Working from home, the 'gig economy' (meaning businesses especially in IT or delivery that prefer short-term contracts and freelance work) and internet shopping have changed the ways that many people earn and spend their money. Challenges of 'new work' include lack of employment security, lack of separation between work and free time, and the prospect of AI taking jobs. Other concerns are data security, the economic effects of climate change and the impact of current economic trends on developing countries – the environmental damage caused by lithium mining for electric vehicle batteries being an example. Another key issue is sophisticated computer algorithms being used to target millions of social media users in order to influence or even manipulate people's opinions and behaviour.

1 **VOCABULARY** Collect useful words and phrases for describing economic development. → WB 17/1–2

2 **COMPREHENSION**

a) Explain how the chart about Birmingham's population illustrates points made in the text. → S37

MK b) Create a (digital) time line of the economic development mentioned in the texts.

c) Practise a two- to three-minute talk based on your time line. Explain how key historical events and processes transformed the economy (in the UK and other countries).

3 **EVALUATION** Choose 4–5 key developments / inventions from the texts and rank them according to their importance for our present-day economy / society. Give reasons for your choice.

V10 **4** **VIEWING**

a) Watch the video and take notes on these points: 1. the role the interconnection of inventions plays; 2. "Eurocentric" reasons for the Industrial Revolution happening in Europe; 3. the situation in China; 4. the two main advantages in Europe / the UK.

b) Explain what is said about the global aspects of the Industrial Revolution. Why do you think it is often seen as a (merely) European phenomenon?

MK c) Explain what type of video it is. Which elements did you find unusual? → S35–36

A Changing technologies, changing lives

The Age of Machinery

1 BEFORE YOU READ Describe the painting in detail and the effect it has on you. In what way does it symbolise the Industrial Revolution? → S38

USEFUL PHRASES

enormous / vast / powerful • factory floor • smoke • chimney • to toil • an atmosphere of cool / power • a sharp contrast • technological progress • a bright / promising future • dominance (over) / control (of) • a firm / strong / unquestioning belief

James Nasmyth, *A steam hammer at work*, 1871

1 **epithet** (by)name of an age / era
2 **devotional** religious
4 **exertion** act of doing sth
6 **shuttle** *Weberschiffchen*
7 **to ply** to use
7 **to furl** to roll up
7 **oar** long stick used for rowing
8 **vaporous** steaming
9 **harness** *Pferdegeschirr*
9 **fleet** *flink*
10 **fire-horse** *here:* train
10 **to invoke in his stead** *here:* to use instead of him
10 **nay** *ja … sogar*
11 **brood-hen** *Zuchthenne*
11 **to supersede** to replace (with sth better)
12 **furtherance** development
15 **spoils** *pl Beute*
16 **accession** addition, increase

Thomas Carlyle (1795–1881) was a Scottish essayist, historian and philosopher. His essay *Signs of the Times* was published in the Edinburgh Review in 1829.

Were we required to characterise this age of ours by any single epithet, we should be tempted to call it, not an Heroical, Devotional, Philosophical, or Moral Age, but, above all others, the Mechanical Age. It is the Age of Machinery, in every outward and inward sense of that word [...]. Our old modes of exertion are all discredited, and thrown aside. On every hand, the living artisan is driven from his workshop, to make room for a speedier, inanimate one. The shuttle drops from the fingers of the weaver, and falls into iron fingers that ply it faster. The sailor furls his sail, and lays down his oar; and bids a strong, unwearied servant, on vaporous wings, bear him through the waters. Men have crossed oceans by steam [...]. Even the horse is stripped of his harness, and finds a fleet fire-horse invoked in his stead. Nay, we have an artist that hatches chickens by steam; the very brood-hen is to be superseded! For all earthly, and for some unearthly purposes, we have machines and mechanic furtherances; for mincing our cabbages; for casting us into magnetic sleep. We remove mountains, and make seas our smooth highways; nothing can resist us. We war with rude Nature; and, by our resistless engines, come off always victorious, and loaded with spoils.

What wonderful accessions have thus been made, and are still making, to the physical power of mankind; how much better fed, clothed, lodged and, in all outward respects, accommodated men now are, or might be, by a given quantity of labour, is a grateful reflection which forces itself on every one. What changes, too, this addition of power is introducing into the Social System; how wealth has more and more increased, and at the same time gathered itself more and more into masses, strangely altering the old relations, and increasing the distance between the rich and the poor, will be a question for Political Economists, and a much more complex and important one than any they have yet engaged with.

From: Thomas Carlyle, *Signs of the Times*, 1829

2 COMPREHENSION Outline the main characteristics of the "Age of Machinery" and the changes this new age has brought about. → O 1

3 ANALYSIS Describe the prevailing spirit at the time and examine the author's attitude towards the "wonderful accessions" (l. 16) he depicts. → ○ 2

4 EVALUATION Throughout history, technological progress has often been – and still is – associated with increasing wealth and equality in society. Discuss if these hopes are justified in your opinion. → ○ 3 → S31

MK **5** CREATIVE TASK Find a catchy slogan to describe the age we live in and prepare a short presentation containing pictures or quotations to characterise it.

Coketown

VIP FILE

Charles Dickens (1812–1870) is one of the most famous authors of the Victorian era. In many of his novels and short stories he criticises the economic and social conditions of his time. His works enjoyed great popularity during the Victorian era and are still widely read today, just think of *Oliver Twist*, *Great Expectations*, *David Copperfield* or *A Christmas Carol*. In his novel *Hard Times* Dickens gives a description of a typical industrial city, the fictitious Coketown.

[Coketown] was a town of red brick, or of brick that would have been red if the smoke and ashes had allowed it [...]. It was a town of machinery and tall chimneys, out of which interminable serpents of smoke trailed themselves for ever and ever, and never got uncoiled.

It had a black canal in it, and a river that ran purple with ill-smelling dye, and vast piles of building full of windows where there was a rattling and a trembling all day long, and where the piston of the steam-engine worked monotonously up and down, like the head of an elephant in a state of melancholy madness. It contained several large streets all very like one another, and many small streets still more like one another, inhabited by people equally like one another, who all went in and out at the same hours, with the same sound upon the same pavements, to do the same work, and to whom every day was the same as yesterday and tomorrow, and every year the counterpart of the last and the next.

These attributes of Coketown were in the main inseparable from the work by which it was sustained; against them were to be set off, comforts of life which found their way all over the world [...]. You saw nothing in Coketown but what was severely workful. [...] [A]nd everything was fact between the lying-in hospital and the cemetery, and what you couldn't state in figures, or show to be purchasable in the cheapest market and salable in the dearest was not, and never should be, world without end, Amen.

From: Charles Dickens, *Hard Times*, 1854

3 **interminable** endless
4 **to uncoil** to make straight again
5 **ill** badly
7 **piston** *Kolben*
15 **comforts of life** luxury goods available thanks to the beginning global trade
16 **workful** *(old use)* focused on work
19 **world without end** biblical phrase, usually translated as "for ever and ever"

6 COMPREHENSION | ANALYSIS

a) Describe the impression the reader gets of Coketown and its inhabitants.
b) Examine the stylistic devices (e.g. repetitions, sentence structure, metaphors, similes) the author uses to create this impression.
c) The novel was first published in 1854. Compare and contrast the way of life portrayed in the novel with today's society. Think of the kind of work people do, the places they live in, the things that matter in their lives.

7 EVALUATION Based on the knowledge you have gained so far, write an argumentative essay on the positive and negative effects of the Industrial Revolution. → S17–18

Memorial recalls the hard history of British mining

8 **BEFORE YOU READ** Give possible reasons why the number of people working in coal mining in the UK declined from about 1.2 million in 1920 to about 11,000 in 2000. Talk about the effects this might have had on the life of coal miners.

Miners' strike, 1984

Miners' memorial

- 1 **cramped** uncomfortably small
- 6 **arduous** hard
- 6 **Boris Johnson** leader of the Conservative Party and UK Prime Minister (2019–2022)
- 7 **Margaret Thatcher** the UK's first female Prime Minister (1979–1990) whose policies of privatisation and deregulation polarised the nation
- 9 **Nicola Sturgeon** First Minister of Scotland (2014–2023)
- 31 **to stave off** to prevent from happening
- 39 **burly** *stramm*

They toiled far underground in dark, cramped and dangerous conditions, emerging at the end of their shifts caked in coal dust and often gasping for air.

Towns grew up around the collieries; boys followed their fathers and grandfathers down the pit. […] But by the end of the 20th century, miners had mostly been consigned to the post-industrial scrap heap as pit after pit shut down.

The arduous and risky labour of the nation's miners was not at the forefront of Boris Johnson's mind last week when, on a visit to Scotland, he thanked Margaret Thatcher's pit closure programme for giving the UK a "big, early start" on the transition away from fossil fuels. Nicola Sturgeon, Scotland's first minister, said his comment was "crass and deeply insensitive" to those whose lives and communities in Scotland had been devastated by the closures.

Now the nation's miners are to be commemorated in a monument at the National Memorial Arboretum in Alrewas, Staffordshire […]. The monument is the creation of Andy DeComyn, a public artist who specialises in commemorative sculpture. Five metres long, two metres high and a metre wide, it is made of Derbyshire stone with a bronze "seam of coal" running through it, and incorporates 25 plaques telling the 200-year story of the industry.

"It goes back to the 1800s, when women and children were working in appalling conditions, and right up to the 1990s when most of the pits closed," said DeComyn. "By then working conditions were a lot better, but statistically it was still the most dangerous job you could do."

Coalmining was "an important part of our industrial and social history", he added. "When I was at school, we learned about mining in geography lessons. Now kids learn about it in history. And today people tend to focus on the bad side – the environmental consequences of fossil fuels. But coalmining changed the world. It fuelled the Industrial Revolution and brought us to where we are today."

Many miners were killed or seriously injured in pit accidents, and thousands died of lung diseases brought on by working in enclosed spaces filled with coal dust. "But we felt we were doing a service to the country," Len, a former miner, told the BBC. "We kept the lights on. We powered industry. I was always proud of being a coalminer."

In 1984–85, miners fought to stave off pit closures under Thatcher's government in one of the UK's last great industrial disputes. The year-long strike caused terrible hardship in mining communities and bitter division between miners. It ended in defeat for the National Union of Mineworkers (NUM). […]

Plaque 18 is dedicated to the mines rescue service. Jack Brown volunteered with the service for more than 20 years and was present at the 1951 Easington Colliery disaster in County Durham, in which 83 men, including two rescuers, were killed. […] The plaque was a tribute to "marras", a miners' term for workmates you would trust with your life, [Phil Brown, Jack's son] said. "These were burly guys who looked after each other, relied on each other, and even washed each other's backs in the pit showers at the end of the day."

Jack, who served in the navy during the second world war, died in 1973 at the age of 52, four years after leaving the pits, when his son was just 18. "He'd been such a fit and proud man. But the dust made him really quite ill at the end," said Brown.

"Even now, I feel so bonded to my mining roots. Despite the pits going, it's still in my blood."

Harriet Sherwood, in: *The Guardian*, 2021

9 COMPREHENSION

a) Sum up what we learn about the history of coal mining in the UK and point out why a monument honouring miners was erected in 2021.

b) Describe the special attitude of miners as depicted in the text.

10 LISTENING Find the report about the British miners' strike (1984–85) from the BBC's series *Witness History* online. Listen and take notes on the following points:

1. reasons for the conflict between the government and the miners;
2. the effects the strike had on the Keating family and the whole community;
3. the relationship between pickets and strike-breakers;
4. the end of the strike. → ● 4

11 CREATIVE TASK Write a letter of complaint to Boris Johnson explaining to him why his statement mentioned in the article (ll. 7–9) might have been inappropriate and hurt the feelings of former coal miners and their families. → S21

West Midlands finds new role in electric vehicle industry

FACT FILE

The **Black Country** is an area located in the West Midlands. With its coal mines, mills and factories it is considered to be one of the birthplaces of the Industrial Revolution. It gained its name back in the 19th century when the area was covered with smoke and dirt from the factories. Another possible origin of the name is the thick black coal seam near the surface.

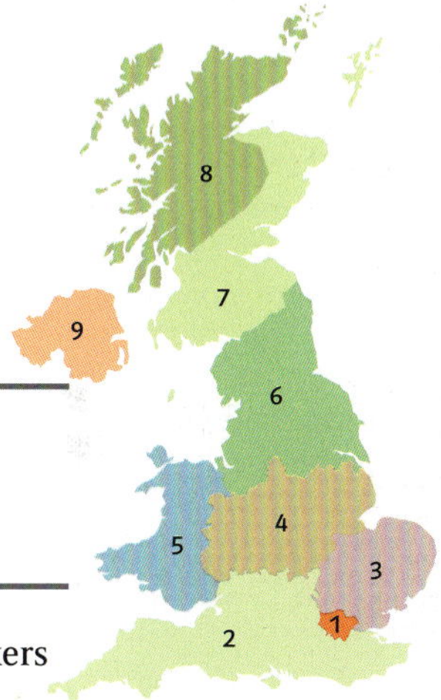

Regions in the UK

1 Greater London
2 South
3 East Anglia
4 Midlands
5 Wales
6 North
7 Lowland Scotland
8 Highland Scotland
9 Northern Ireland

Corners of the Alucast factory in the Black Country would be familiar to metalworkers several centuries ago. Workers pour molten aluminium at 720C into steel moulds. The cooling metal is then quickly pressed into shape before being sanded down into parts for gas-guzzling British sports cars.

Yet for all its traditional West Midlands manufacturing roots, Alucast is finding a role for itself in a fast-growing new industry: electric cars.

It needs to make the switch fast. The UK will ban the sale of all petrol and diesel cars by 2035, and other big car markets are following suit. The accelerated end of the internal combustion engine surprised and delighted environmental activists and has proven politically popular. Yet it has thrown into sharp relief the peril facing workers in the fossil fuel economy, who risk being left behind in the energy transition.

Nowhere is the challenge more acute than in the West Midlands, the traditional heart of British carmaking, home to companies from Jaguar Land Rover to Aston Martin, as well as an army of suppliers. The region hosts a third of all British car production and a 46,500-strong factory workforce – nearly a third of the UK total, according to the West Midlands Combined Authority.

New battery-powered technology will change the structure of the whole industry. Electric cars are mechanically simpler, with fewer moving parts, and carmakers are looking to bring more work in-house.

"There is the potential to maintain a viable [UK] automotive industry, but it probably won't employ as many people," said David Bailey, a professor of business economics at the University of Birmingham. [...]

For Alucast, that has meant bidding for work making parts such as battery casings. It has also invested millions of pounds in more precise computer-assisted machining [...].

Yet in any transition of the enormity and speed facing carmakers, there will be losers. The West Midlands already has its fair share of companies that failed to keep up. Longbridge, the former home of British Leyland and its successor MG Rover,

2 **molten** made liquid by heating
2 **mould** *Gussform*
3 **to sand down** *abschleifen*
4 **gas-guzzling** using a lot of fuel
10 **to throw into sharp relief** to make clearly visible
20 **viable** capable of success
23 **to bid for** *sich bewerben um*
23 **casing** protective covering

now houses a Marks & Spencer and flats named after its once-famous Austin cars. The Jaguar Land Rover factory at Castle Bromwich made Spitfires during the second world war, but its mass production days will end in 2025 – although Jaguar will still use the site for specialist operations. [...]

Batteries – by far the most expensive parts of electric vehicles – will be crucial to the fate of Britain's car industry. Britishvolt, a start-up, is hoping to raise money for a so-called gigafactory in Blyth, near Northumberland, while China's Envision will expand a plant in Sunderland beside Nissan's car factory. Yet the West Midlands is still waiting for a battery factory that would give its tens of thousands of workers hope for the future. Such is the concern that Coventry's politicians have pre-emptively applied for gigafactory planning permission despite lacking an investor. [...]

Brandauer, based in Birmingham's Newtown, is closing in on its 160th birthday. Yet bosses at the precision metal stamping company, which employs 60 people, realised about five years ago that they needed to start targeting the next generation of cars, or faced losing a large chunk of their business.

It has now branched out into metal lamination, producing plates that are being used in hydrogen fuel cells, a technology that could fuel zero-emission lorries. The new customers have helped it to its best year of new business on record.

"It's not too late," said Rowan Crozier, Brandauer's chief executive. "It's never too late, [but] it's certainly time to start thinking about how you're going to transition. The demand isn't here yet, but it's coming."

Jasper Jolly, in: *The Guardian*, 2021

29 **Marks & Spencer** retail company
30 **Spitfire** type of military aircraft
38 **pre-emptive** doing sth to prevent sb else from doing it
44 **to branch out into** to expand

12 COMPREHENSION Sum up the chances and challenges British carmakers are facing and explain which factors, according to text, are important in making a successful transition.

13 EVALUATION Research the advantages and disadvantages of electric cars. Then write an essay commenting on the planned sales ban on petrol and diesel cars. → ○ 5 → S17–19

Making the transition

14 VIEWING

a) Describe the photo. What problems do you think a place like this has?

b) Make sure you understand these terms: levelling up, pork barrel politics, devolution. → S1–2

V11 c) Watch the video. Contrast the situation in Scunthorpe in the 1960s and now.

d) Explain why, according to the video, the government's levelling-up plans haven't worked so far.

e) Outline the two main ideas for realising levelling up as presented in the video and comment on them. → ○ 6

Scunthorpe, Lincolnshire (East Midlands)

15 ACROSS CULTURES Collect information about a transformation project in a rural or economically underdeveloped area in Germany. Present the project and evaluate its outcome for the region and the people living there. → S3, 6, 30

MK

FACT FILE

There are various reasons why regions try **to make a transition**, e.g. to revive run-down neighbourhoods, reuse old factory buildings or avoid intensive farming. New ideas include creating cultural venues, providing shared living spaces, focusing on organic farming, …

Bottrop: Wenn eine Kohlestadt zum Klimavorreiter wird → WB 58–59/1–2

16 MEDIATION During a student exchange you have to write a report for a student newspaper about a successful example of structural change in Germany. Use the following article for your report. Outline Bottrop's past and how it managed to make the change. Also present the city's plans and hopes for the future. → ● 7 → S39

Jahrzehntelang war die Zeche Prosper-Haniel nicht nur der größte Arbeitgeber in Bottrop, sondern auch der einzige Großbetrieb in der Stadt. Keine großen Unternehmen zu haben, was im Vergleich zu anderen Städten lange als Nachteil galt, ist heute ein Vorteil: „Wir haben uns frühzeitig darauf konzentriert, viele kleine und mittelständische Firmen mit bis zu 600 Mitarbeitern anzusiedeln. Wir haben schon lange gesehen, was kommen wird, und konnten uns vorbereiten", sagt Stadtsprecher Andreas Pläsken. [...] Für Bottrop zahlte sich der Weg der kleinen Schritte mit kleinen Firmen aus. Mit rund sechs Prozent Arbeitslosen weist die Stadt eine der niedrigsten Quoten im Ruhrgebiet auf. In Gelsenkirchen gibt es beispielsweise doppelt so viele Arbeitslose. Im Gegensatz zu anderen Städten der Region verliert Bottrop auch keine Einwohner. Im Gegenteil – die Zahlen steigen sogar leicht an.

Um die positiven Entwicklungen in Bottrop besser begreifen zu können, muss man mehrere Jahre zurückgehen. 117 Kilometer schlängelt sich das unsichtbare Stollennetz unter der Erdoberfläche. Seit 1863 hat der Bergbau den Boden unter Bottrop und den angrenzenden Städten ausgehöhlt. Jahrzehntelang hat der Abbau der Kohle die Einwohner ernährt und Deutschland mit Wärme und Strom beliefert.

Dass irgendwann das Ende kommen wird, war klar. Daher waren die Planungen Anfang der 1990er Jahre mit der Internationalen Bauausstellung Emscherpark, IBA, von entscheidender Bedeutung für Bottrop. [...] Bottrop entwickelte für sich drei Säulen: Freizeit, Klima, Wissen. Als Freizeitstandort mit [einem Freizeitpark, einer Skihalle] und ähnlichen Angeboten werden jährlich rund zwei Millionen Besucher angelockt.

Die Entscheidung für Klimaschutz und Zukunftstechnologien verschaffte der Stadt auch international Geltung. „Innovation City" heißt das Zauberwort. Ziel der Innovationsinitiative ist es, die Ballungszentren klimagerecht umzubauen und dabei lokale Betriebe einzubeziehen. Dazu sollen auch die CO_2-Emissionen um 50 Prozent verringert und dadurch die Lebensqualität gesteigert werden. Das Projekt soll Vorbildcharakter für andere Kommunen an Ruhr und Emscher, aber auch international haben. [...]

Flankiert wird das Projekt vom Wissenstransfer mit der örtlichen Fachhochschule. Dort werden Ingenieure und Ökonomen ausgebildet. Sie sollen bei der Weiterentwicklung der Stadt helfen. Bottroper Firmen kooperieren mit der FH. Die Unis und Fachhochschulen hält auch Sozialwissenschaftler Jörg Bogumil für unabdingbar im Erneuerungsprozess: „Die Hochschulen werden zum Treiber der Stadtentwicklung im Ruhrgebiet." [...]

Für Bottrop kommt daher die Schließung des Bergwerks gerade recht. Das wird so natürlich nicht gesagt. Aber die nun frei werdenden Flächen des Bergbaus bescheren der Stadt im Ruhrgebiet eine dringend benötigte neue „Spielwiese". „Wir waren, was Gewerbeflächen angeht, an unsere Grenzen gekommen. Nun können wir im Projekt mit der Stadt Essen und [einer Immobilienfirma] zahlreiche Flächen neu gestalten", freut sich Pläsken.

Rund 1700 Hektar stehen dafür in beiden Städten zur Verfügung. Gewerbe mit Wohnbebauung soll entstehen. Dazu eine Umwelttrasse, die Bottrop mit Essen verbinden soll. Öko-ÖPNV, E-Bikes und selbstfahrende Autos sind die Zukunft für die Planer in Bottrop. Problemstadtteile sollen entwickelt werden und als Wohnquartier am Rhein-Herne-Kanal das Leben am Wasser ermöglichen. Noch ist das Zukunftsmusik. Doch die Chancen stehen nicht schlecht.

Carsten Grün, *Deutsche Welle* Website, 2018

Former mining tower at Prosper-Haniel coal mine

The walkable "Tetrahedron", a new landmark on the site of the former coal mine

B The digital age

Uncanny valley → WB 18/3, 20/6

1 CREATIVE TASK What do you associate with the term "start-up"? Write an acrostic.

2 SPEAKING Do some research to find out how Silicon Valley and its special start-up culture was formed. Based on your results, create a time line of the origins of Silicon Valley (1956–1971) and present it in a short talk.

The headquarters of a big IT company in Silicon Valley

3 BEFORE YOU READ **Think-pair-share:** Brainstorm what you know about the collection of data on the internet.

Anna Wiener is a young woman who worked as a freelance copy editor and literary agency assistant before she tried her luck in Silicon Valley. In her memoir *Uncanny Valley* she describes her work at different tech start-ups and criticises the work ethic there. In the following extract, Wiener describes her experiences at an analytics start-up. Noah is her 'onboarding buddy', a colleague assisting Wiener during her starting time.

It did not take long for me to understand the fetish for big data. Data sets were mesmerizing: digital streams of human behavior, answers to questions I didn't know I had. There was more every second. Our servers, and the company's bank account, absorbed this unstoppable wave.

Our bread and butter was engagement: actions that demonstrated the ways users were interacting with a product. This was a turn away from the long-running industry standard, which prioritized metrics like page views and time on site, metrics that the CEO called bullshit. Engagement, he said, was distinguished from the bullshit because it was actionable. Engagement generated a feedback loop between the user and the company. User behavior could dictate product managers' decisions. These insights would be fed back into an app or website, to dictate or predict subsequent user behavior.

The software was flexible, intended to function as easily for fitness trackers or payment processors as for photo-editing and ride-sharing apps. [...] Engineers and data scientists and product managers would inject snippets of our code into their own codebases, specify which behaviors they wanted to track, and begin collecting data immediately. Anything an app or website's users did – tap a button, take a photograph, send a payment, swipe right, enter text – could be recorded in real time, stored, aggregated, and analyzed in those beautiful dashboards. Whenever I explained it to friends, I sounded like a podcast ad.

Depending on the metadata, users' actions could be scrutinized down to the bone, at the most granular level imaginable. Data could be segmented by anything an app collected – age, gender, political affiliation, hair color, dietary restrictions, body weight, income bracket, favorite movies, education, kinks, proclivities – plus some IP-based defaults, like country, city, cell phone carrier, device type, and a unique device identification code. If women in Boise were using an exercise app primarily between the hours of nine and eleven in the morning – only once a month, mostly on Sunday, and for an average of twenty-nine minutes – the software could know. If people on a

2 **mesmerizing** hypnotic
21 **to scrutinize** to examine very carefully
23 **affiliation** connection (e.g. with a political party)
24 **bracket** group
24 **kink** *(infml)* a strange habit or taste
24 **proclivity** *(fml)* desire (usually for sth bad / wrong)
25 **carrier** provider

dating website were messaging everyone within walking distance who practiced yoga […], the software could know that, too. All customers had to do was run a report; all they had to do was ask.

We also offered a secondary product, a people-analytics tool, for which some customers paid extra. The people-analytics tool stored individual profiles of users on those customers' platforms. These contained streams of personalized, searchable activity, as well as any identifying metadata. The point of this tool was to facilitate outreach based on behavior, and incentivize re-engagement. An e-commerce store could search its own database to see which men, exactly, were filling online shopping carts with razor blades and beard oil but never checking out, and send those men an email, offering discounts or simply a passive-aggressive reminder that it might be time to shave. A food-delivery app, upon registering that a user had ordered a paleo TV tray six nights in a row, might trigger an in-app pop-up suggesting she try a carbohydrate. An exercise app could identify that a user had stopped a workout at the burpee section and automatically send a push notification asking him if he was still alive. […]

To do my job effectively, I had to be able to see customers' code, as well as their dashboards. This was true of anyone in a customer-facing role; it was almost impossible to solve users' problems if the problems weren't in front of us. The simplest way for the analytics start-up to achieve this was by granting those of us on the Solutions team access to all of our customers' data sets: to see the tool as if we were logged in to any given user's account, to experience our product through their eyes.

Some called this setting God Mode. It wasn't our customers' payment, contact, and organizational information – though we could see that, too, if we needed to – but the actual data sets that they collected on their own users. This was a privileged vantage point from which to observe the tech industry, and we tried not to talk about it. "We're not just selling jeans to miners," Noah said. "We're doing everyone's laundry."

[…] We all knew that internal permissions, limiting what we could see of customer data sets, would come eventually. We also knew, at least for the time being, that it wasn't a priority for our Engineering team. This level of employee access was normal for the industry – common for small, new start-ups whose engineers were overextended. Employees at ride-sharing start-ups, I'd heard, could search customers' ride histories, tracking the travel patterns of celebrities and politicians. Even the social network everyone hated had its own version of God Mode: early employees had been granted access to users' private activity and passwords. Permissioning was effectively a rite of passage. It was a concession to the demands of growth.

Besides, early employees were trusted like family. It was assumed we would only look at our customers' data sets out of necessity, and only when requested by customers themselves; that we would not, under any circumstances, look up individual profiles of our lovers and family members and coworkers in the data sets belonging to dating apps and shopping services and fitness trackers and travel sites. We would not, out of sociological curiosity, surf through data sets of neighborhood-watch platforms […]. We would not pry.

[…] It was assumed that if we had a publicly traded company using our software – and, if so moved, could chart the overall health of that public company based on its data set, or build out predictive models of when its overall value might grow or recede – we would resist buying or selling its stock.

Our tiny company of twentysomethings operated on good faith. If good faith failed, there was a thorough audit log of all employee behavior: the founders had implemented a product on our own back end, which tracked the customer data sets we looked at and the specific reports we ran. But nobody ever used the words "insider trading." Nobody had a press contact. There was no policy on leaks. Not that we needed one – we were all, as the CEO liked to remind us, Down for the Cause.

From: Anna Wiener, *Uncanny Valley*, 2020

36 **outreach** getting in touch
36 **to incentivize** to motivate, to encourage
40 **paleo** a special diet consisting of fruits, nuts and meat
40 **TV tray** a food platter to eat while watching TV
41 **carbohydrate** *here:* food containing carbohydrate
42 **burpee** exhausting full body exercise *(Liegestützsprung)*
59 **overextended** having too much work or work that is too difficult
63 **rite of passage** *Übergangsritus*
70 **to pry** to try to find out private facts about sb
76 **audit log** record of activities
80 **Down for the Cause** refers to the Bible ("Lay your life down for the cause of Messiah"); *here:* slavishly following all company rules

4 VOCABULARY

a) While reading, find words and phrases in the text belonging to the word field "collection of data". Then use a dictionary or online tools to add more words and phrases and compare your findings with a partner.

b) Collect other words you find useful from the text. Note them down together with "memory aids" (e.g. collocations, examples, related words, synonyms or antonyms) that will help you remember them.

5 COMPREHENSION

a) State your first reactions after reading. Which information was most surprising to you?

b) Briefly describe the tools the start-up offers. Explain what "engagement" means in this context and why it has been groundbreaking for the start-up.

c) Outline the different kinds of data collected by the start-up (2–3 examples) and explain why collecting data is so important for the start-up's customers.

6 ANALYSIS

a) Explain what "God mode" means and what is problematic about it.

b) Examine Wiener's attitude towards her job at the start-up. Consider the tone of the text, her choice of words and the use of stylistic devices. → S10–11

7 SPEAKING With a partner, discuss if you would like to work for this (or a similar) company. Can you relate to the enthusiasm of people working in Silicon Valley? → ● 8

A4 **8 LISTENING**

a) Listen to the interview with journalist Farhad Manjoo and do these tasks:

1. Sum up who the 'Frightful (or Big) Five' are and what makes them so frightful.
2. Explain in which ways / areas they are similar to governments.
3. Give examples of what kind of other companies (just name the area of business) the Big Five own and state your reaction to this information.

b) Considering your own everyday life, comment on Mr Manjoo's statement that the Big Five "blanket the entire society in their technology, and you can't really escape them".

9 VISUALS Describe and analyse the cartoon. Can you relate to its message? Why (not)? → WB 19/5

10 VIEWING

a) Find and watch the official trailer of the documentary "The Social Dilemma" online. Briefly sum up the main topics. Would you like to watch the whole film? Give reasons.

b) Analyse what makes the trailer convincing. Think of cuts, music, images / people shown etc. → S35

11 CREATIVE TASK Find out what you can do to limit how much data analytic tools can collect when you use the internet. Create an explainer video and present it to the class. → S36

MK

How to fight deforestation in the Amazon from your couch

If you've got as little as 30 seconds and a decent internet connection, you can help combat the deforestation of the Amazon.

"You don't have to be a climate scientist, you don't have to be a data scientist, you just have to be a citizen that is concerned about the issue of deforestation," said Elliot Inman, a researcher at [a US systems analysis company] which created an app that uses humans' sharp eyes to teach computers what deforestation looks like.

Some 15 % of the Amazon, the world's largest rainforest and a crucial carbon repository, has been cut or burned down. Around two-thirds of the Amazon lie within Brazil's borders, where almost 157 square miles of forest were cleared in April alone. In addition to storing billions of tons of carbon, the Amazon is home to tens of millions of people and some 10 % of the Earth's biodiversity.

Scientists are warning of an impending tipping point beyond which the Amazon will be irreparably transformed.

To stem the destruction, it is necessary to track where and when it's happening. To that end, [Inman's company] formed a nonprofit partnership with the International Institute for Applied Systems Analysis, or IIASA, a research institution based in Austria, to build an artificial intelligence model that can recognize signs of deforestation. [...]

To train its computer vision model to reliably recognize tree loss, [the systems analysis company] and IIASA turned to crowdsourcing. Visitors to the program website flip through pictures of the Amazon taken by European Space Agency satellites hundreds of miles above the Earth, looking for clues.

The interface is a lot like those reCAPTCHA boxes that ask you to prove you're "not a robot" by clicking on the parts of a picture that contain a truck or a stoplight. Here, the pictures show 31 square miles of forest divided into nine sections. Users simply select the squares in which they've spotted some indication of human impact: the tell-tale quilt of farm plots, a highway, a suspiciously straight edge of tree line. [...]

"We've been gathering data from human beings making these judgments and building an artificial intelligence model that will attempt to make judgments in the same way," [Inman] added.

It's not always easy; that's the point. For example, a brown patch in the trees could be the result of burning to clear land for agriculture (earning a check mark for human impact), or it could be the result of a natural forest fire (no check mark). Keen users might be able to spot subtle signs of intervention the computer would miss, like the thin yellow line of a dirt road running through the clearing.

The app serves up confounding images to more and more users until a clear answer emerges. [...] If users can't reach a consensus as to whether or not human impact is visible in a given image, [Inman's company] sends it to experts for analysis.

Since the app was launched on Earth Day in April, users have analyzed almost 41,000 images, covering an area of rainforest nearly the size of the state of Montana. Deforestation caused by human activity is evident in almost 2 in 5 photos.

The [...] team will add new images of the Amazon in Brazil, and expand west to Peru and south into Bolivia. The researchers hope to use historical images of these new geographies to create a predictive model that could identify areas most at risk of future deforestation. If they can show that their AI model is successful, it could be useful for NGOs, governments and forest monitoring bodies, enabling them to carefully track forest changes and respond by sending park rangers and conservation teams to threatened areas. In the meantime, it's a great educational tool for the citizen scientists who use the app.

Amanda Schupak, in: *Huffington Post*, 2020

8 **repository** a storage location
26 **tell-tale** *verräterisch*
27 **quilt** *here:* many small fields resembling a quilt *(Patchworkdecke)*
27 **plot** piece of land
36 **confounding** confusing

12 COMPREHENSION State the purpose of the app. Explain how it works and why the involvement of human beings is needed.

FACT FILE

Citizen scientists are nonprofessionals who conduct or take part in scientific research. Their participation helps accelerate scientific work and at the same time extends their knowledge. Examples: Measuring light pollution, bird count, dog behaviour research.

13 ANALYSIS Examine how the text tries to get the reader involved in the project.

14 EVALUATION

a) Discuss with a partner whether you would take part in a project like the one in the text or not.

b) Assess whether this kind of user engagement is an effective tool to deal with environmental issues. What other kind of measures should / ought to be taken? → S5

Artificial intelligence – boon or bane? → WB 18/4

Attitudes towards new technologies
Percentage of US adults who say the widespread use of each of the following applications has been / would be a …

	good idea for society	bad idea for society	not sure
Facial recognition technology that would be used by police to look for people who may have committed a crime or to monitor crowds	46 %	27 %	27 %
Computer programs, called **algorithms**, used by social media companies to find false information on their sites	38 %	31 %	30 %
Driverless passenger vehicles that are equipped with software allowing them to operate with computer assistance, and expected to be able to operate entirely on their own	26 %	44 %	29 %
Computer chip implants in the brain that would allow people to far more quickly and accurately process information	13 %	56 %	31 %

Pew Research Center / Survey conducted Nov. 1–7, 2021

15 VISUALS

a) Sum up the results of the survey.

MK b) Conduct the same survey in your class. Use digital tools to visualise and compare your results with the ones from a).

16 SPEAKING In groups, do some research on the benefits and risks of artificial intelligence (AI). Choose one area (e.g. medicine, protecting the environment, helping people with disabilities, transport vs privacy violations, loss of control, loss of jobs) and present your results. → ○ 9 → S30

17 EVALUATION Comment on the statement by famous physicist Stephen Hawking:

> The development of full artificial intelligence could spell the end of the human race [...]. It would take off on its own, and re-design itself at an ever increasing rate. Humans, who are limited by slow biological evolution, couldn't compete, and would be superseded.

Presenting facts and information

1 Inform a friend about what was said at a public meeting in Birmingham. Put the following sentences into indirect speech. Remember to use a suitable introductory verb in the simple past.

TIP

If you want to present facts and information properly / reliably, it is essential to report what different people said about a topic. To do so, use indirect speech.
Vary introductory verbs, e.g. *to mention, to explain, to promise, to demand, to warn, to want to know …*

1. Developer: "Birmingham has achieved a remarkable transformation in the city centre."
2. Mayor: "We mustn't give up even though there is still a lot of work to be done in some areas."
3. Inhabitant: "If we don't act now, some areas of Birmingham might be left behind soon!"
4. Former factory worker: "I've been unemployed for five years! Are there any measures the City Council is going to take to improve the situation? In my opinion, politicians must do a better job!"
5. Member of the City Council: "The City Council will meet here tomorrow and discuss what can be done to support disadvantaged neighbourhoods."

2 As a journalist you have interviewed different people about the transformation of Digbeth, an area of central Birmingham. Use the information from your notebook to write an article for the local newspaper. Use passive voice where appropriate and find a suitable headline.

TIP

The passive voice is often used to present facts and information in newspapers or in scientific work, especially if it isn't important or if you don't know who did something. It makes your text sound more formal.

- The government has invested a lot of money to regenerate disadvantaged neighbourhoods.
- Developers have submitted plans to transform Digbeth.
- Architects intend to convert old industrial buildings into new residential homes.
- They plan to bring the River Rea back into the city centre, running in a channel below street level.
- An important aim is that building companies should construct buildings with less carbon emissions.
- If the council grant planning permission, developers will build new riverside neighbourhoods including new homes, restaurants, shops, flexible workspace and parks.
- The council will hold several events to help answer the community's questions.
- Members of the public can view the plans and make comments.
- The people of Digbeth have never experienced a similar change to the district's face.

3 Write an article for the English version of your school's website about your school's technical equipment. Describe the changes that have been made and / or improvements that still need to be made. Do a survey in your class and include (real or fictitious) statements from students, teachers or parents.

C Chances and challenges for the future

Why the Midlands is the best place in Britain

Even in this great age of identity politics, coming from the Midlands is tantamount to coming from nowhere in particular. Professional northerners are legion, but professional Midlanders? Why, the very word "Midlands" is rarely employed outside the specialised news contexts of weather and travel. There are a lot of roads in the Midlands – it's a very popular place to travel through – and as for weather, there's as much of it in the Midlands as anywhere else. But beyond that, what are the term's associations? [...]

Aye, there's the rub (to quote that great literary Midlander William Shakespeare): no one is more sceptical about the existence of an overarching Midland identity than Midlanders themselves. Midlanders are spiky individualists who don't appreciate being lumped in together, thank you very much. [...]

The Midlands [...] has never really gone in for branding. We don't believe in blowing our own trumpet. Around Birmingham, tourist-board types like to talk about the region as "The Heart of England". But try saying "I'm a Heart of Englander" and it just sounds silly. The associations of the word "Midlands" itself are no better: fair to middling, stuck in the middle, middle age, middle management, midlife crisis.

But why does the Midlands deserve to be named and celebrated in national culture? Why should Midlanders start to identify themselves with their broader homeland as volubly and visibly as northerners do with theirs? Quite simply because almost everything of any value, ever, started life in England's belly: the Midlands has served as the womb and birthing pool for most of the ideas and innovations that have driven English, and indeed world, civilisation since the earliest times. We have just never been very good at telling people about it. We are too modestly capable, too contentedly accomplished. Just too Midland, in other words.

Robert Shore, in: *The Guardian*, 2014

1 **tantamount** being the same
2 **to be legion** to exist in large numbers
8 **there's the rub** *(idiom) da liegt der Hase im Pfeffer*
10 **spiky** *(infml)* easily annoyed
15 **fair to middling** *(idiom)* about average
19 **volubly** *(fml)* loudly
21 **womb** *Schoß*

Stilton cheese

A 'hobbit home'

1 EVALUATION

a) Point out features of Midland identity and the author's attitude towards his subject.
b) Explain what "ideas and innovations" (l. 21) the author hints at. Do you think an identity should be based on historical achievements? What else could matter? Discuss.

Focus on culture

We are a creative region, and this is reflected in our rich heritage, diverse cultures and our entrepreneurial spirit. The WMCA area has one of the largest cultural sectors when compared to other combined authority areas across the country. Coventry UK City of Culture 2021 and the Birmingham 2022 Commonwealth Games provide us with a great opportunity to showcase this nationally and internationally.

Arts, heritage and culture matter. They can help us to make sense of our lives, support our wellbeing, help us to understand others, as well as provide an opportunity to express our individual creativity. They are vital to skills development and can improve the attractiveness of our cities and towns, making residents feel better about the places they live and work in.

They also matter in economic terms. The economic footprint of our cultural sector (excluding film, television and wider creative industries) is £1.1 billion. It is estimated that the sector directly supports over 24,000 jobs, with further 22,700 jobs supported indirectly. A total of 28 million tourism visits to the WMCA area are attributable to culture – generating £2.8 billion of visitor expenditure.

West Midlands Combined Authority website, 2022

2 **WMCA** West Midlands Combined Authority (local government insitution)

2 EVALUATION Briefly sum up the text. Then comment on the idea of using culture as an "asset" to foster economic growth. → ● 10

3 ACROSS CULTURES As member of the local council, you've been asked to give a speech at an international conference about culture and economy. Think of economic or cultural aspects you could use to promote your region (2–3 examples) and write your speech. → S9, 11, 16

4 SPEAKING Find out more about Midland culture and give a presentation on one aspect. You can use aspects / events mentioned in the texts or one of these:

food (e.g. Stilton cheese, balti) • music (e.g. Black Sabbath, Robbie Williams, Jorja Smith) • film / TV (e.g. Peaky Blinders) • literature (e.g. Benjamin Zephaniah, the Midlands as inspiration for Tolkien's *Lord of the Rings*) • cave art at Cresswell Crags

Silicon Valley is falling short on climate change

5 BEFORE YOU READ
a) Describe and comment on the statistics. → S37
b) Think of ideas how to reduce your online carbon footprint.

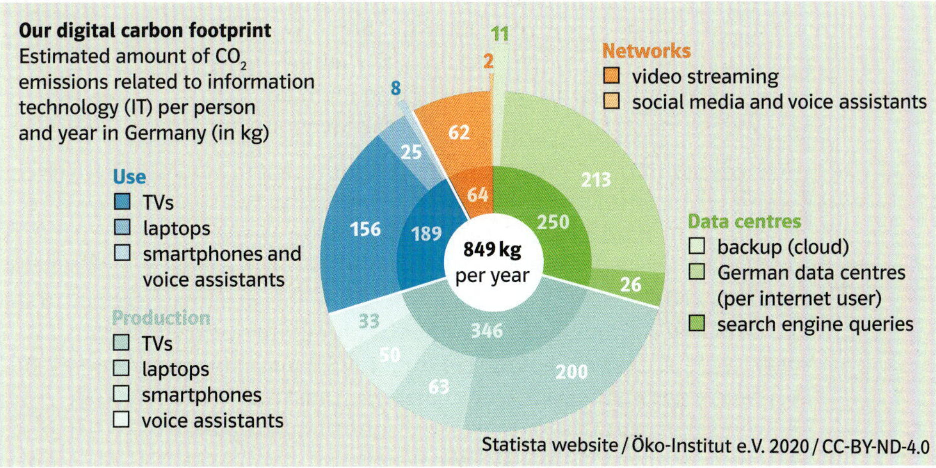

Statista website / Öko-Institut e.V. 2020 / CC-BY-ND-4.0

Living in San Francisco can insulate you from some of the world's problems. Climate change is not one of them. Over the past two years, residents have been advised to stay indoors on some days because of smoke from nearby wildfires. Another burning season is about to start in earnest. California's state government says climate change "has created a new wildfire reality".

In the long term, many Silicon Valley offices could be flooded if – or when – sea levels rise by two metres. Protecting the Bay Area against floods and storms would cost an estimated $450bn. Water shortages are also expected to worsen.

Yet few of Silicon Valley's amazing achievements have had a bearing on climate change. The world's most innovative place lacks answers to the world's existential problem. The contrast is striking, given that many tech employees worry about the issue.

The biggest companies act as if climate change is tangential. Although Google and Facebook power some or all of their data centres with renewable electricity they rarely engage more broadly with their role in increasing global energy use.

13 **tangential** of little relevance

Perhaps it's a clever ruse by Big Tech to demonstrate it isn't as powerful as politicians think: like a modern King Canute, it can't control the waves. More plausibly, it points to an underlying failure of the Valley.

Peter Thiel, a founder of PayPal, liked to say, "We wanted flying cars, instead we got 140 characters." Actually we wanted clean energy; we got cryptocurrencies that use as much electricity as Argentina. We wanted sustainable transport, instead we got millions of car-hire drivers.

Where are the tech products that help us slow global warming, and adapt to a warmer world? At this rate, parts of the world will gain access to multiple food-delivery apps just as they lose access to clean water. Alexa, tell me why it's 100 degrees outside.

One problem is that Silicon Valley's model of venture capital – which works so well on some problems – cannot easily address climate change. It excels in developing software for the US market and then spreads globally.

Clean technologies require much more capital and engineering, and often the low-hanging fruit – such as retrofitting dirty factories – lies outside of the US. The best green tech start-ups are not concentrated in California, undermining the network effect on which the Valley is built.

After Al Gore's 2006 film *An Inconvenient Truth*, one major venture capital fund, Kleiner Perkins, did bet heavily on clean tech – and fell from grace partly as a result. It didn't help that the US government failed to accelerate environmental regulation.

For years, this disengagement with climate change had one high-profile exception: Tesla's Elon Musk. Like Tom Cruise's character in *Top Gun*, the electric car pioneer was a mixed blessing. You could replace fossil fuels – but only if you were as unique and as rich as he was.

There are a couple more examples now: Impossible Foods and Los Angeles-based Beyond Meat have started selling meat alternatives with lower carbon footprints. But Kleiner's John Doerr says much of the investment in environmental technology still comes from family offices, rather than conventional venture firms. [...]

Of course the hard choices involved in stopping global warming don't fit well within the tech industry's usual optimistic, convenience-focused rhetoric. Facebook's Mark Zuckerberg and Google's Sundar Pichai hardly mention climate change in speeches. Apple has hired a former head of the Environmental Protection Agency, Lisa Jackson, to head its efforts, which include making suppliers use renewable energy. But the focus is still on mitigating the company's impact, rather than broader change.

Silicon Valley promises to tackle the world's biggest problems. When historians look back at our era, they may ask why the people with the most ambition, capital and appetite for risk failed to aim a little higher.

Henry Mance, in: *The Financial Times*, 2019

16 **ruse** trick
17 **King Canute** Legend says that in the 11th century, the Nordic king set his throne by the seashore and told the waves to stop before him, which they didn't do, thus illustrating that even kings can't rule over nature (or God).
20 **140 characters** refers to the limitation of 140 characters in a tweet
25 **Alexa** virtual voice assistant
29 **the low-hanging fruit** sth that is easy to get or achieve
30 **to retrofit** *nachrüsten*
33 **Al Gore** U.S. vice president 1993–2001
33 ***An Inconvenient Truth*** documentary about global warming
38 **mixed blessing** sth that has both advantages and disadvantages

6 COMPREHENSION Point out how California has been affected by climate change and why Silicon Valley doesn't seem to be able to tackle this problem.

7 ANALYSIS Analyse the line of argument and the stylistic devices the author uses to get his message across. → S10–11

8 EVALUATION "When historians look back at our era, they may ask why the people with the most ambition, capital and appetite for risk failed to aim a little higher" (ll. 50–52). Comment on this statement.

9 ACROSS CULTURES Find out about current innovative projects or tech products trying to combat climate change in different countries. Present your results and discuss if these ideas would work in your region too. Also consider possible reactions of the public.

Preserving the past and shaping the future

The way we live and work is constantly changing. Industries that used to be profitable in the past often lose their importance or die out completely. But what should we do with the remaining buildings and sites? In this task, you're going to develop a plan for a transformation project.

Step 1 Get started

Your task is to repurpose the site of a former porcelain manufacturer, which includes a few run-down factory buildings, and also to preserve its cultural heritage. Get together in groups and work on one of the projects 1–3:

1. Create a new living quarter with residential buildings, a school, …
2. Focus on tourism, e.g. by creating a hotel, restaurants, a park for (outdoor) leisure activities, …
3. Create a museum focusing on the region's / the porcelain industry's past

Step 2 Make a detailed plan

In your group, decide on the details of your project, e.g. what the new buildings will look like, what leisure activities you will offer, what exhibits there will be in the museum etc.
Also consider the following points:
- Sustainability: How could you save energy, avoid waste etc.?
- Social aspects: How could you bring together people from different ages or backgrounds?
- Funding: How could you generate money to realise your project (e.g. crowdfunding, sponsoring)?

TIP

Use digital tools for planning, communication and collaboration. Don't forget to assign one person the task of coordinating and managing your project.

Step 3 Choose a mode of presentation

Decide on a convincing way of presenting your project plan, e.g. use a combination of informative texts, visuals and slide shows, build a model (e.g. with plastic toy bricks) or use a digital home or garden planning tool.

Step 4 Make improvements

Plan 1–2 final group meetings to have a closer look at the material you have worked out. Improve texts or add new ideas where necessary.

TIP

Remember that you should try to convince your audience that your plan is a great idea for regenerating the place. Use rhetorical devices (→ S11) to support your message.

Step 5 Presentation and assessment

Present your project plan to the other groups. Then talk about the different presentations and assess if they meet your expectations:
- Do you think the project would work in real life?
- Will it benefit the people living in the region (e.g. by creating jobs, providing new sustainable ways of living etc.)?
- Do you have any suggestions for improvements?

Skills workshop 3
Dealing with mediation tasks

Step 1 Understanding the task

1 COMPREHENSION For each of the following tasks, make a grid to note down the addressee, the purpose (what information you're asked to give), the text type, a possible greeting and introductory sentence, and a possible last sentence / ending (think about appropriate style / register).

Task A Your exchange partner Josh from New York is preparing a class presentation on smart cities worldwide. He doesn't speak much German, so he asks you for help with the material he has found on Germany. Based on the following article **and** the information in the graph, write an e-mail to Josh explaining in more detail three ideas how smart cities can improve their citizens' lives. Also point out what possible concerns there are and how citizens can get involved in the process.

Task B You want to take part in an international youth competition showcasing ideas to make your hometown a 'smart city'. To apply, write an e-mail to the jury including an outline of your presentation. In your outline, use information from the article **and** the graph to explain in more detail three ideas you would use to improve citizens' lives. Also describe the main aims of smart cities and how citizens would be involved in the new developments.

Step 2 Finding relevant information

2 BEFORE YOU START Read the news article and reread Task B. Note down English keywords for the relevant parts and arrange your findings.

Smarte Städte sollen das Leben leichter machen

Auf welcher Strecke komme ich gerade am schnellsten durch die Stadt? Wo finde ich den nächsten freien Parkplatz? Wie ist der Füllstand beim Glascontainer um die Ecke? In smarten Städten sollen moderne Technologien eingesetzt werden, um sie klimaschonender, effizienter und lebenswerter zu machen. In Hessen gibt es mit Darmstadt [und] Kassel [... zwei] Kommunen, die mit Unterstützung vom Bund digitale Modell-Projekte erproben. Bundesweit werden 32 Städte und Gemeinden mit mehr als 300 Millionen Euro gefördert. Ihre Erkenntnisse sollen allen Kommunen zunutze gemacht werden.

„Mit der Digitalisierung der Stadt wollen wir den Alltag der Menschen erleichtern", erklärt José David da Torre Suárez, Geschäftsführer der Gesellschaft Digitalstadt Darmstadt. Die Stadt hat bereits 2017 den Wettbewerb „Digitale Stadt" des IT-Branchenverbandes Bitkom gewonnen. Seither ist sie im Umbau zu einer digitalen Vorzeigestadt. Anfang des Jahres etwa hat sie die bundesweit erste städtische Datenplattform mit Anwendungen zu Verkehr, Umwelt und Müll gestartet. Dort können in Echtzeit beispielsweise Daten zur Feinstaubbelastung, zum Ozongehalt und zu den Pendlerbewegungen abgerufen werden.

Möglich macht das ein Netz aus Sensoren, das die Stadt durchzieht. Es sammelt die Daten, die auf der Plattform eingehen und ein Abbild der Stadt liefern. Sorgen in Hinblick auf den Datenschutz kann da Torre zerstreuen: „Es werden keine personenbezogenen Informationen gespeichert."

Diverse weitere Projekte werden in Darmstadt bereits umgesetzt. Beispielsweise messen Sensoren im Zoo Vivarium rund um die Uhr die Temperatur und Luftfeuchtigkeit unter anderem im Terrarium der Riesenschildkröten. So kann da Torre zufolge unmittelbar auf Schwankungen reagiert werden. Ein anderes Beispiel sind intelligente Mülltonnen, die ihren Füllstand selbst mitteilen. Das System empfiehlt die Routen für die Leerungstour. Das spart Kosten, vermindert Emissionen und reduziert Lärm.

Die Liste der geplanten Projekte ist lang. In Arbeit ist laut da Torre etwa ein umweltsensibles Verkehrssystem, das abhängig von der Belastung den Verkehr lenkt und so die Schadstoffbelastung senkt. „Eine weitere Idee ist eine digitale Plattform, auf der jeder einfach und schnell sehen kann, welche Jungbäume im Stadtgebiet Wasser oder Schatten benötigen." Die Darmstädter könnten dann bestenfalls selbst aktiv werden. [...]

In Kassel ist das Smart City-Projekt gerade im Auftakt begriffen. Zu einer ersten Veranstaltung, bei der Ideen gesammelt werden sollten, hatten sich laut der Stadt 400 Bürgerinnen und Bürger angemeldet. „Wir wollen erfragen, wo es Probleme im Alltag gibt, bei denen digitale Werkzeuge helfen können", sagt Carina Wagener vom Projektbüro Smart Kassel. Wenn etwa die Bewohner eines Seniorenheims die Jalousien nicht mehr alleine betätigen könnten, könne vielleicht ein digitales Tool Abhilfe schaffen. „Unsere erste Aufgabe ist es, die Menschen dafür zu sensibilisieren, was Smart City bedeutet und dass sie diese Entwicklung selbst in der Hand haben."

Die Bürgerbeteiligung steht bei allen [...] Kommunen im Mittelpunkt, denn die Akzeptanz für Digitalisierungsprojekte ist bisweilen gering und den Begriff Smart City gilt es zunächst mit Leben zu füllen. In Workshops, Umfragen und Stadtlaboren werden die Bürgerinnen und Bürger als Experten für ihre Stadt befragt und mit Digitalisierungsthemen vertraut gemacht.

Die Bedeutung dieses Dialogs unterstreicht auch Korinna Thielen, Gastprofessorin für Stadtmanagement an der Uni Kassel und Smart Cities Koordinatorin in München. „Wichtig ist die Botschaft, dass die Projekte für und mit den Menschen entwickelt werden", sagt die Architektin. Sie sollten verständlich informiert und niedrigschwellig eingebunden werden, „damit sie sehen, dass es dabei um ihren Lebensraum geht und nicht nur um die Ansiedlung von Unternehmen", rät sie. Wichtig sei auch der Austausch der Städte untereinander. Denn klar sei: „Die Digitalisierung ist ein Megatrend, dem man nicht entgegensteuern kann."

dpa, 2021

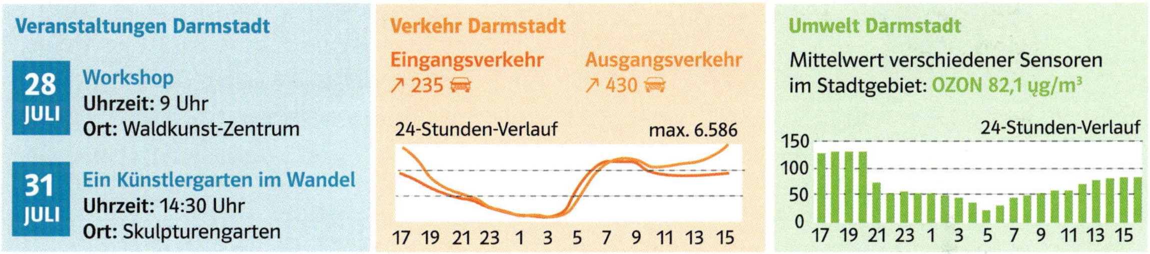

Datenplattform Darmstadt, 26.07.2022 (16 Uhr), adaptiert

3 VOCABULARY Find appropriate English expressions or paraphrases for the marked words in the text. Pay attention to the context.

TIP

Do not translate word for word! Remember:
- to use verbs instead of nouns, e.g. *Beim Ausbau (der Infrastruktur) … ⟶ When … is expanded …*
- to paraphrase words, e.g. by using relative clauses: *Seniorenheim ⟶ a place where …*
- to break down longer words into their parts, e.g. *Bürgerbeteiligung ⟶ …*
- to explain typical German phrases or concepts the addressee might not know.

Step 3 Producing a target text

4 MEDIATION

a) Write the e-mail and outline for Task B. Use your solutions from Tasks 1–3 and follow these steps:
1. Start with a fitting greeting for your addressee and a suitable introductory sentence.
2. Decide which examples from the text and the graph you really need – give only relevant information. Careful: Do not include ideas of your own.
3. Find an appropriate last sentence and ending.

b) Exchange texts with a partner. Focus on how Steps 1–3 are realised and give each other feedback. → S7

4 Postcolonial developments
Introduction

> India is a curious place that still preserves the past, religions, and its history. No matter how modern India becomes, it is still very much an old country.
>
> Anita Desai, Indian novelist

Lotus Temple, New Delhi

> Our children may learn about the heroes of the past. Our task is to make ourselves the architects of the future.
>
> Jomo Kenyatta, Kenya's first president

A veranda bar in Nairobi

> Our family of nations continues to be a point of connection, cooperation and friendship. It is a place to come together to pursue common goals and the common good, providing everyone with the opportunity to serve and benefit.
>
> Queen Elizabeth II, Commonwealth Day message 2022

Commonwealth Games, Birmingham, UK, 2022

> It's important for us to also understand that the phrase 'Black Lives Matter' simply refers to the notion that there's a specific vulnerability for African Americans that needs to be addressed. It's not meant to suggest that other lives don't matter. It's to suggest that other folks aren't experiencing this particular vulnerability.
>
> Barack Obama, former US president, ABC Town Hall meeting, 2016

Black Lives Matter protest, Manchester, UK, 2020

1 VISUALS

a) Choose the photo that you find most interesting and describe it. What does it show you about developments that have taken place since colonial times? Share what else you know about the country, organisation or movement in your photo with a partner. → ○ 1

b) Make a note of what you would be interested in finding out about it. Compare your notes with those of your partner. Then do research to find answers to your questions.

2 EVALUATION

a) Read the quotes and make a few notes on each one's meaning. Point out what they say about the past and the present and find links to the aspects in the photos.

b) Which quotes do you agree with, and why? Share your thoughts with a partner.

c) Collect useful words and phrases to talk about postcolonial developments in a mind map. → S1–2

3 CREATIVE TASK

MK

Get into groups and choose one of these tasks:

1. Find out more about the Commonwealth Games: how often they are held, the idea behind them and how they differ from the Olympic Games. Present your findings in a creative way using digital tools (e.g. as an explainer video or an audiovisual presentation). **OR:**
2. Choose another theme connected with postcolonial developments in the world, find visuals (photos or graphs) and a quote and give a short presentation. **OR:**
3. Go to the Commonwealth website and sum up what kind of information you can find there. Assess the way the information is presented, taking into account the structure and design of the website as well as the texts.

4 SPEAKING

Describe and interpret the cartoon about Thomas Jefferson, the 3rd president of the United States (1801–1809) and main author of the Declaration of Independence, which opens with the statement: "We hold these truths to be self-evident, that all men are created equal, that they are endowed by their Creator with certain unalienable Rights, that among these are Life, Liberty and the pursuit of Happiness." While Jefferson fought politically for the abolition of slavery, he owned a plantation himself and profited from hundreds of enslaved people working for him all his life.

TIP

- The prefixes "pre-" or "post-" **usually** have a **temporal** meaning, so in words referring to clearly distinguishable events, "pre-" simply means "before" and "post-" means "after", as in "pre-reading" or "postwar". Hyphens should be used to make words with prefixes easier to read (e.g. "rewrite" is OK without, but "re-enter" isn't).
- Colonialism, however, is a highly political issue, and its effects are undeniably still eminent. That is why some scholars argue that we cannot exactly tell when it started and whether it has ended yet. Therefore, the terms "postcolonial" and "post-colonial" may be used differently. Most people would agree that "post-colonial" with a hyphen refers to a period after colonialism. Especially in a context dealing with the lasting effects of colonialism which are still relevant and haven't been overcome in many different places, it is more suitable to use "postcolonial" because it does not suggest that there are periods that can be clearly defined as before, during and after colonialism.

Examples of postcolonial developments

The Commonwealth

The Commonwealth is a voluntary association of over 50 independent and equal countries that includes advanced economies as well as developing countries. It is home to nearly one-third of the world's population, over 60 % of whom are aged 29 or under. India is not only the Commonwealth's largest country by population but also its largest economy. The early Commonwealth had its roots in the British Empire and its members owed allegiance to the British monarch. Yet when India became independent in 1947, it wanted to remain a member of the Commonwealth even though it was a republic. Two years later at a meeting of Commonwealth prime ministers in London, it was agreed that republics and other countries could become members, resulting in the modern Commonwealth. The British monarch does not automatically assume the role – the member countries choose their leader.

Today, the member countries agree to work towards the goals of democracy, peace and prosperity. Their work is coordinated and facilitated by the Commonwealth Secretariat, an intergovernmental organisation founded in 1965. It is supported by 80 other organisations that focus on areas such as education, democracy and peace, and the environment.

The Commonwealth Games, often called the "Friendly Games", are held every four years. They aim to bring people together through sport and are open to amateur competitors from around the Commonwealth.

Kenya – a brief overview

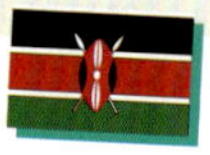

Official name: The Republic of Kenya, Jamhuri Ya Kenya in Swahili.
Largest cities: Nairobi (capital), Mombasa.
Religion: Christianity (85 % of the population), Islam (nearly 11 %).
Language: English and Swahili (official languages), but over 50 languages in total.
History: The first people to settle in Kenya were Africans from different parts of the continent. Coastal areas became a hub for traders and explorers from around the world. During Europe's 'Scramble for Africa' in the 1880s, the British acquired Kenya and set up the Imperial British East Africa Company to develop trade in the region. Shortly after, Britain declared Kenya a British protectorate and then a crown colony in 1920. Over the next 70 years, the British imposed damaging economic, social and political policies, including racial discrimination. From the early 1920s onwards, African protest movements began to grow, culminating in the so-called Mau Mau Uprising (1952–1960) against colonial rule led by the Kenyan Land and Freedom Army (KLFA). It was one of the Empire's bloodiest conflicts, resulting in the execution and torture of thousands of Kenyans. Kenya finally achieved independence from the UK in 1963.
Culture: Music and storytelling have been important parts of Kenyan culture for centuries.
Economy: Key sectors include agriculture (the majority of Kenyans work in this sector), manufacturing, and services. Tourism is also an important part of the economy.
Politics: Kenya is a presidential representative democratic republic, which also means that the president is both head of state and head of government.
Current issues: Government corruption, (youth) unemployment, poverty, crime, poor health care, lack of clean drinking water, poor infrastructure and inequality are the top issues according to a poll of Kenyans in 2016.

India – a brief overview

Official name: The Republic of India, Bharat in Hindi.
Largest cities: Delhi (capital), Mumbai (financial centre), Bengaluru, Kolkata.
Religion: The main religion is Hinduism, the world's oldest living religion. Muslims are the second largest religious group. Other religions include Christianity, Sikhism, Buddhism and Jainism.
Caste system: The caste system has existed in India for millennia. It divides Hindus into four hierarchical groups, subdivided into thousands of other groups, according to their karma (work) and dharma (duty). Below these come the Dalits, who do dirty work like cleaning latrines and sweeping streets. Discrimination based on caste was outlawed by the Constitution in 1950. K.R. Narayanan was India's first president from the Dalit community from 1997 to 2002.
Language: People in India speak hundreds of different languages. Many people use English as a lingua franca, although it is not an official language.
History: The subcontinent had experienced a vibrant history stretching back thousands of years before the British arrived in the1600s and established trading posts for the British East India Company. Over the next 150 years, their influence increased. Following a failed uprising in 1858, India became a British colony, and in 1877 the British made Queen Victoria the Empress of India. India finally gained independence after World War II and was partitioned into India and Pakistan.
Culture: India's culture is one of the world's oldest and richest. Many ideas and inventions originated there, e.g. in the fields of maths, astronomy, health (ayurveda, yoga, surgery) and everyday life (the button). Today, Bollywood, India's extremely popular film industry, is one of the largest producers of films in the world. They promote Indian culture, song, dance, values, and beliefs and generate a lot of revenue.
Economy: India is one of the world's fastest-growing economies. Its service sector – including IT, retail, entertainment, and finance – makes up 50 % of India's gross domestic product. Many people work in agriculture, but also in manufacturing and tourism.
Politics: India is a parliamentary democracy. The Indian parliament is made up of the President (the head of state) and the two Houses (the Lok Sabha and the Rajya Sabha). General elections are held every five years to elect the government.
Current issues: Corruption (amongst politicians and public officials), illiteracy, lack of basic sanitation, poverty, unemployment, women's safety, social divisions and pollution are some of the major issues in India today.

1 CREATIVE TASK Choose one of the aspects to do with India, Kenya or the Commonwealth and find out more about it. Give a two-minute presentation in class. Think about how you can present the information in a varied and interesting way, e.g. using visuals, statistics, facts, quotes or examples.
→ ● 2 → S30 → WB 21/1–2

Black Lives Matter

The Black Lives Matter movement was founded as an activists' hashtag campaign in response to the acquittal of George Zimmerman in the shooting death of the unarmed Black teenager Trayvon Martin in the US in 2012. Following many further incidents, it has become a global community, and some say the largest civil movement in US history. In early summer 2020, millions of people around the world took to the streets to protest the murder of George Floyd, who died when a police officer knelt on his neck for over nine minutes. Its members are dedicated to fighting racism, unfair treatment of and violence against Black people. That summer, Black Lives Matter protesters in the UK pulled down the statue of the slave trader Edward Colston in Bristol and a group of Black activists talked about racism and their struggle for equality.

2 SPEAKING Find out why the Black Lives Matter movement has been called the largest civil movement in US history. Which other civil movements have there been to do with Black people's rights and what do you remember about them?

A India – the world's largest democracy

A land of superlatives

1 ACROSS CULTURES Read the fact file, then find out about Germany's size and population and compare the two countries.

FACT FILE

India is the seventh-largest country in the world and the second-most populous country behind China; it is estimated that India will become the world's most populated country in 2030. In 2022, India had a population of 1.417 billion and it is one of the youngest populations globally. Its capital, New Delhi, was estimated to be home to almost 20 million inhabitants. It is one of the world's most ethnically and linguistically diverse countries.

2 VISUALS Choose one of the photos and describe it in detail. Explain what aspect of traditional or modern India it illustrates. → S38

1 Hindu pilgrims bathe in the River Ganges

2 Skyline of modern Mumbai with slums

3 The national pastime – cricket

4 A Bollywood actor on the set

Cricket is now an Indian game

Cricket probably remains, along with the English language, the railway system and the Indian army, the finest legacy of 200 years of British colonialism in India, one of the few areas in which imperialism gave more than it took. Like the other remnants of the colonial presence, cricket has been thoroughly Indianised without losing its essential British moorings. [...]

Cricket is now an Indian game; many who play it have no sense of owing it to England. Yet, just as Indian nationalists used British traditions and institutions to overturn British rule, so also Indians have taken up an English sport and delight in beating the English literally at their own game. [F]ew sporting triumphs are regarded with more satisfaction by Indians than a cricket victory over England.

Shashi Tharoor, *NDTV Sports* website, 2012

5 moorings *here:* roots

3 COMPREHENSION Explain the importance of cricket in India today. Give reasons.

4 VIEWING Find a video of Shashi Tharoor's 2015 Oxford Union speech on the internet and watch parts of it. Comment on his arguments and the quality of his speech. → S16

Social inequality in contemporary India

The narrator, Ramesh Kumar, is a young Indian from a deprived background, who by chance was able to get a good education at a school run by Europeans. In the first extract we learn about his business.

Rudi's parents had a nice little flat in Green Park – not the most desirable neighbourhood, but getting there. Aspirational location, the realtors would say, for those on the up. The cars were Hondas and Lexuses, no German ones yet. For my first meeting, I carried a bag that said *DeliveryFast* – no questions at gates, no hold-ups, just waved through. I was pretending to deliver pizza. Very Continental. Very chic. I was getting above my station, as the Britishers say in those old films where they beat coolies for making eyes at their virgin daughters.

Rudi's father was fat and wore a shirt advertising his golf club. He was rich. Of course he was. If you're fat and Indian, you're rich; if you're fat and poor, you're lying. It's only the West where the rich are thin and vegan and moral. His wife wore the usual tight pink workout clothes. Their home was filled with lots of stone, medieval tapestries vaguely Mughal, ostentatious prayer room by the front door, Mediterranean porcelain statues, marble goddesses […]. Three bedrooms, four crore on the market. […]

"So," Rudi's father said. His eyes were rotating round his pig skull, full of […] fantasies of how low a fee he could bargain me down to. […]

Thank God the foreplay was […] brief. I went immediately into my spiel.

Ramesh Kumar – Educational Consultant. That is what my business card says.

You want your little darling to get 99.4 per cent and become an IITian and lord it over the rest of us? You come to me. You want your little rasgulla to top the state boards, start his inevitable march to the corner office in Wall Street or London or, God forbid, if everything goes wrong, Bangalore? I'm your man. Any examination, any subject, four weeks. Or your money back. And they all try to, every single one.

"You got 0.1 per cent less than promised." "He only got into Vassar." "Rupa aunty's boy did better and he actually did his exams *himself*." I've heard it all.

I am one of the best exam-takers in Delhi, and so I must be one of the very best in the world. The Chinese are my only competition. There must be thousands of me over there, advancing the careers of the chubby children of communist officials, always fearing the bullet in the back of the head, or being packed off to one of those re-education camps they've put the Muslims in, or worse, being sent to make iPhones in the Shenzhen factories with the suicide nets. […]

The All Indias are the big one, the ones that everyone takes when they leave school. There are other entrance exams all year round for everything, one for law schools, one for the army, one for […] toilet inspectors, but the All Indias are the cream of the crop, my biggest earner for the year. They are the gateway to the best universities, the brightest futures, the whitest lives. […]

My form was thorough. Social security number, Aadhaar details, income, legal and illegal, school history, who they'd been referred by. I paid a contact at the income tax office to run checks. All my clients had the usual background of middle-class petty larceny. A few bribes paid here and there for construction permits, to private schools for exam-less admission, to the government to pass off their kids as low-caste for the quota admissions […].

Everyone knows what makes India great. China has the communists in charge, Xi Dada and his cronies, Europe has piazzas and art galleries, America has beef and tits

1 **Green Park** rich neighbourhood in South Delhi
2 **realtor** *(AE)* sb who deals in real estate
7 **coolie** unskilled worker, e.g. bearing loads
12 **Mughal** relating to the powerful Muslim empire before British colonisation
12 **ostentatious** showy
13 **crore** (number in Indian English) ten million (rupees)
19 **IITian** a graduate of one of the Indian Institutes of Technology
19 **to lord it over sb** to domineer over sb
20 **rasgulla** *here:* darling (name of an Indian dessert)
24 **Vassar** a top college in the US
37 **Aadhaar** the world's largest biometric ID system that citizens of India can apply for voluntarily
41 **to pass sb off as** to pretend sb is
46 **Dada** father (Hindi)
46 **crony** *(infml, pej)* close friend

and money. We have democracy. We argue, endlessly. We speak eight thousand different kinds of shit, we insult each other, we make things happen. This is the country of deals. This is the country of talk. Every brick might be halfbaked, every building might be missing the inside, held up more by belief than cement, but it gets done, at half the price, in half the time.

We signed the contract. I took a pile of the kid's textbooks. I was thrown out the back door. I went home, ready to spend a month filling my brain, eating junk food and grinding my way to a better life for myself and the generations of Kumars to come [...].

5 COMPREHENSION Explain what Ramesh's business is, and what we learn about his clients. What are the pros and cons of his business? → S8

Later, Ramesh describes how he grew up with his father after his mother had died. His father, who ran a tea stall, frequently beat and insulted him.

My father and I lived in a one-room concrete shell, down an alley, then down another, and another, from the place the tour guides said was the real India, the one with piles of spices, women in mango-coloured saris, men who smelled of hair oil and incense and dragged cows behind them, stately and fat; the ones where the whites got out of their AC jeeps and said how *overwhelmed* they were by the sights and the sounds. This India, my India, smells like shit. It smells like a country that has gone off, all the dreams having curdled and clumped like rancid paneer. It smells like the inhabitants have drugged themselves with cannabis and alcohol and incense, and exist only to turn wheat and corn and rice into babies and shit. You drink, you gamble, you watch cricket and bet money you don't have, you lynch Muslims, you beat your kids, and they grow up and do the same. [...]

We were right on the edge of Old Delhi, where the medieval gave way to the modern. On the road, impatient moustachioed men taking shortcuts zoomed past on Hero Hondas held together by tape and prayers. Women watched their purses and held their keys like knives to scratch any man who got too close. Children my age, five to a rickshaw, were carted to their schools, uniforms blue and grey and green, noses snotty, hair slicked back with oil, clutching plastic lunchboxes filled with chapatis and vegetarian curries made by their loving parents.

That was their world, an India that seemed a century away from ours. That was all I saw of it, just a brief glimpse, twice a day. I would never be part of it.

I was lower lower middle class. My father owned a business, it's true, one I was set to inherit. We weren't starving, we weren't Dalits or homeless, but we were not going anywhere either. The great social movements passed us by. Independence, socialism, capitalism, everything was the same. My life was grinding spices for tea. [...] I had a stone that I used to pulverise my spices, far too big for a kid, fat and heavy and dark grey with little veins of white running through it like cellulite on a politician's thighs. I spent my days hunched over behind the stall and beat those spices into dust, my back in painful little knots by the end of the day. [...]

"No shop-bought powders here, sir!" my father would shout. "All done fresh by my little runt of a boy down there. You, rat! Show [...] your muscles! Ha ha!" Sometimes a few insects, a little dirt, some spit found their way into the mixture, by accident, of course. My hate could have made India the world's leader in renewable energy.

From: Rahul Raina, *How to kidnap the rich*, 2021

3 **incense** material giving off an aromatic smell when you burn it
5 **AC** air-conditioned
6 **to go off** to go bad
7 **paneer** a kind of Indian cheese
16 **snotty** *(infml)* *rotzig*
26 **thigh** top part of the leg
30 **runt** a small and weak person

6 ANALYSIS Analyse how India is portrayed differently in both extracts. How does the author bring these images to life? Give examples. → O 3 → S10–14

7 EVALUATION Explain why the narrator criticises his home country so harshly.

What is at stake

This article was written while the rights of minorities were being limited by Indian Prime Minister Narendra Modi and his nationalist Hindu party.

Indian democracy is one of the 20th century's greatest achievements. Over 75 years, we built, against great odds, a nation that for the first time in its 5000-year history empowered women and the Dalits, people formerly known as untouchables. We largely abolished famine. We kept the army out of politics.

But I write this today to tell you: things in India are more dire than you realize. India is a country that is majority Hindu, but it is not officially a Hindu state. The people who are in power in India today want to change this. They want India to be a Hindu ethnocratic state, where all other religions live by Hindu sufferance. This has practical consequences: people of other religions are actively harassed, even lynched on the streets; their freedom to practice their religion in their own way is circumscribed. And when they protest, they are jailed and their houses bulldozed. Most worrying, much of the judiciary seems to be sympathetic to the Hindu nationalist agenda [...].

There is also sustained and systematic harassment of writers, journalists, artists, activists, religious figures – anyone who questions the official narrative. [...]

It is crucial that India remains a democracy for all its citizens. [...] A lot of India's standing in the world – the reason we're included in the respectable nations, the reason our people and our tech companies are welcome all over the world – is that we're seen, unlike, say, China, as being a multiethnic democracy that protects its minorities.

With over 200 million Indian Muslims, India is the third largest Muslim country in the world. There are 30 million Indian Christians. There are Sikhs, Buddhists, Jains, Zoroastrians, Atheists. They are as Indian as I am – a Hindu who's proud of being a Hindu, but not a Hindu as Narendra Modi and the BJP seek to define me. [...] The alienation of Indian Muslims would be catastrophic, for India and the world. They are being told: You are invaders, this is not your country, go back to where you came from. But Indian Muslims did not come from elsewhere; they were in the country all along, and chose which God to worship. After the Partition of India and Pakistan in 1947, they voted with their feet; they chose to stay, and build a nation.

The challenges facing India in the next 75 years are colossal, perhaps even greater than the first 75 years. This year, northern India saw the hottest temperatures in history, reaching 49 degrees Celsius (120F). Next year looks to be even hotter. By the middle of the century, New Delhi could become uninhabitable.

The country also has an enormous, restive, and largely unemployed youth population – half of its population is under 25. But only 36 % of the working-age population has a job. To meet these challenges, it is crucial that the country stay united, and not fracture along religious lines, spend its energies building a brighter future instead of darkly contemplating past invasions.

In this time when country after country is turning its back on democracy, India has to be an example to countries around the world, this beautiful dream of nationhood expressed in the Hindu scriptures as 'Vasudhaiva Kutumbakam' – the whole earth is a family. We should all be rooting for this incredible experiment in multiplicity to work. As goes India, so goes democracy.

Suketu Mehta, in: *India at 75*, published by PEN America, 2022

5 **dire** critical, terrible
8 **sufferance** toleration
10 **to circumscribe** to restrict
22 **BJP (Bharatiya Janata Party)** a political party in India
26 **Partition** the division of India into the separate states of India and Pakistan
27 **to vote with one's feet** *mit den Füßen abstimmen*
32 **restive** nervous, impatient
40 **to root for sth** to encourage

8 ANALYSIS

a) What major challenges are people in India facing according to the writer, and why?
b) Explain what he means by saying, "As goes India, so goes democracy".
c) Examine how Mehta gets his point across. Also think of how he uses structure and perspective to influence the reader. → ○ 4 → S14, 20

3 **vermilion** a bright red colour
6 **hamlet** a small village
7 **marble** a kind of precious white rock
8 **to denude** to cut down all the trees
8 **parched** dried up
8 **foliage** vegetation
11 **bout** period
16 **auspicious** favourable
19 **affidavit** a sworn statement
21 **to chip in** to contribute money
21 **fixed-deposit account** a bank account which cannot be closed until a certain date
27 **sari** a kind of women's dress

Piplantri: The Indian village where girls rule

In India, girls have historically been valued less than boys. But after a father tragically lost his daughter, he spearheaded a nationwide campaign to change gender perceptions.

Shyam Sunder Paliwal cracked open the pod and the blood-red seeds dribbled out. Holding it in his palm, he offered the fruit of the sindoor shrub up for inspection. The plant, which produces the vermilion powder that Indians often apply on their foreheads for cosmetic and religious purposes, doesn't normally grow in this region. But it is one of many types of trees that now grow in Piplantri, a collection of six connected hamlets in Rajasthan in north-west India.

In 2005 when Paliwal became the sarpanch, or village head, marble mining had denuded the hills; the surrounding land was parched and the foliage degraded. And like in most of India, daughters here were viewed as a financial burden and devalued compared to sons, who typically help support their parents economically.

Then in 2007, Paliwal's 17-year-old daughter Kiran died following a bout of dehydration. Heart-broken but eager to honour her memory, his family planted a tree near the entrance of the village in her name. As Piplantri's leader, Paliwal thought, why not turn this one-off event into a wider programme? Soon, other villagers began to follow his lead. Now, every time a girl is born in Piplantri, villagers plant 111 trees – an auspicious number for local Hindus – to both honour her and to regenerate the environment. [...]

In recent years, Paliwal's simple idea has expanded into a broader eco-feminist movement. Along with tree planting, new parents of daughters also sign an affidavit saying they won't marry them off before they turn 18 and will let them finish school. Villagers also chip in to open a fixed-deposit account for each girl with Rs 31,000 (£305) that she can access once she turns 18, either for her education or to help pay for her wedding. What's more, Piplantri's growing forest is now serving as an example of how Indian villages can literally go green while improving their water management. As Piplantri's trees have grown, its groundwater level has increased, and a marked cultural shift has improved the status of women.

Wearing a bright red sari and a broad smile, Nanubhai Paliwal [...] said she had two sons but as Piplantri started honouring its girls, she started wishing for granddaughters. Now she has two, and trees were planted when they were born.

"Earlier they were considered a burden. Now we don't think that way," she said. "We have no particular desire for sons." She then looked around, pointing at all the trees. "It was a small village. We worked hard, we made it special. And this way we get employment and income, too." [...]

"How can everyone be employed through industry?" Shyam Sunder asked. "Our approach is to create employment through natural resources."

Bhavya Dore, *BBC* website, 2021

9 EVALUATION Outline the project in Piplantri and comment on its effects.

V12 ▷ **10** VIEWING Watch the video material recorded in Kerala. Sum up what is said about the benefits of organic farming. Look up vocabulary you need to describe what you can see (e.g. work in the rice paddies) and write a voice-over for the video. → S2, 25–26

MK **11** ACROSS CULTURES Video channels featuring villagers in India or Bangladesh cooking lavish meals for large numbers of people have millions of subscribers. Find out about the origins of these channels and in what way the villagers benefit from their online presence. Watch one of the videos and try to explain what makes them so popular. Compare the videos to cooking videos on German TV. → S35

How India was colonised by Britain

Initially English traders were welcomed by the Mughal rulers. Both sides realised that there would be benefits for each of them if they traded with each other. In exchange for trading rights the English brought European products to India. Throughout the 1600s English trade in India expanded and English traders built many trading posts and factories across India. However, by the end of the century relations with the Mughal rulers had worsened.

When further English requests for trading privileges were turned down, the East India Company blockaded ports and fought battles against the Mughal army. This conflict became known as the Anglo-Mughal War, and it lasted from 1686 to 1690.

The English lost when the Mughal emperor, Aurangzeb, defeated the English merchants. He did not think the merchants were a serious threat and was satisfied with the English apologising and paying a fine. [...]

There was a big change after the death of Aurangzeb in 1707 as local princes fought to take the place of the emperor. The East India Company began to take advantage of the chaos and offer their support to the local princes in return for money and goods, which they used to build a private army that could challenge the local princes. [...]

In the 1700s much of India was divided into individual principalities and different empires. Following the British victory at the Battle of Plassey, some Indian princes were removed from their positions of power by the East India Company's private army. This army was largely made up of Indian soldiers called sepoys.

However, other Indian princes kept their positions if they promised to support the East India Company and favour British interests.

Some ordinary Indians turned British control to their financial advantage, such as shipbuilder Jamsetjee Bomanjee Wadia. He became wealthy by building ships for the British East India Company.

However, for many Indians, life under the control of the East India Company meant poverty and violence from British merchants. Indian workers were forced to sell their goods to the British at very low prices and were then made to buy British products at much higher prices. High levels of poverty and high taxes left Indians particularly vulnerable when famines hit the region, as they struggled to afford food. [...]

From 1757, the East India Company began to control the government, economy and education system of India.

By 1857, the sepoys in the East India Company's army began a rebellion [...]. [T]he British defeated the rebellion after 18 months of fighting. In August 1858, the Government of India Act was passed and direct British rule of India began.

It is estimated that several thousand British were killed during the rebellion, while the estimates for the Indian death toll are in the hundreds of thousands. Many British and Indian civilians were also killed in the violence, and many lives were also lost to a famine that occurred at the same time as the rebellion. [...]

The huge amount of money made from colonising India, as well as the fact that some of the current crown jewels were taken from India, is one of the reasons some historians say the colony became known as the 'jewel in the crown'. [...]

The East India Company's control of India significantly impacted the British economy. Britain was able to export vast quantities of goods such as tea and pepper and sell them for a great profit. This profit helped to fund the Industrial Revolution in Britain. For example, it was used to build textile factories, which employed many people. Imports such as silk and cotton were brought from India and turned into expensive clothes and fabrics before being sold at a higher price back in India. The profits made by the East India Company were invested in Britain. Factory owners in particular earned a lot of money from trade with India.

BBC Bitesize website, 2023

Gwalior Fort, a typical example of Mughal architecture

1 **Mughal** relating to the powerful Muslim empire before British colonisation

18 **Battle of Plassey** battle between the East India Company and Indian ruler Siraj-ud-Daulah in 1757

MK **12** **VOCABULARY** Look at these words from the text. Use a dictionary or digital tools to do the following tasks. → S2

request (l. 7) • turn down (l. 7) • merchant (l. 11) • fine (l. 12) • take advantage of (l. 14) • in return for (l. 15) • make up (l. 20) • vulnerable (l. 30) • famine (l. 30) • rule (l. 35) • death toll (l. 37) • occur (l. 39) • silk (l. 47) • fabric (l. 48)

1. Which words can have different word classes (e.g. verb and noun, adjective and noun etc.)? Which is the correct word class in the given context?
2. For nouns: Which ones can be used in the singular only (uncountable nouns)? Which of the uncountable nouns can be used in the plural too, in what kind of context?
3. Write example sentences showing the meanings of the words. When you are unsure where to place the object of a phrasal verb in a sentence, go online and cross-check with similar sentences from reliable sources.

13 **COMPREHENSION**

a) Read the text and put these events in the historically correct order.

A. The East India Company (EIC) was in control of most parts of public life in India.
B. A flourishing trade between Indians and the British developed during the Mughal era.
C. A new law marked the beginning of direct British rule in India.
D. A rebellion led by Indian soldiers broke out but finally failed.
E. Conflicts between Indian rulers caused confusion and disorder.
F. More and more conflicts between Indians and the British broke out towards the end of the 17th century.
G. The EIC created a private army.

b) Decide if these statements are true or false. Refer to the text to give reasons.

1. Due to conflicts between local rulers in the 18th century, the EIC was able to strengthen its position and even establish its own army.
2. The EIC's army consisted mostly of British merchants.
3. The EIC's control of India led to poverty for ordinary Indians because they couldn't sell their products to the British.
4. The EIC had been controlling India for decades, but in 1858 the British government took over control.

c) Take notes to answer these questions.

1. What do you learn about the rebellion that started in 1857?
2. Why was India called the "jewel in the crown"?
3. What effects did colonising India have on the development of the Industrial Revolution and the British economy?

14 **VISUALS** Describe and analyse the scene in the picture and how the different kinds of people are portrayed. → S38

Shah Alam, Mughal of Hindustan, with troops of the British East India Company in a woodcut of 1781

15 MK **CREATIVE TASK** Imagine a successful Indian shipbuilder and a poor Indian textile worker from the 18th century meet in the market place of their village. They start a discussion about the changes the trade with the British has brought about. Make prompt cards for each character. Then act out the conversation or use digital tools to record and present it. → S31

Independence and Partition

16 CREATIVE TASK Find out about these people as well as the organisations they belonged to and write a short fact file about them and their role in India's becoming independent from Britain: Mohandas (Mahatma) Gandhi, Lord Louis Mountbatten, Jawaharlal Nehru, Muhamad Ali Jinnah. → ● 5 → S3

Jawaharlal Nehru

Muhamad Ali Jinnah

FACT FILE

In 1947 Britain granted British India independence and it was partitioned into two countries: India (mainly Hindu) and Pakistan (mainly Muslim). As tensions between Hindus and Muslims were high (and had been exploited by the British), millions of people rushed to move to the other country as they were frightened that they would be discriminated against because of their religion. Around 15 million people were displaced and around one million died.

V13 **17** VIEWING Watch the video with historian Yasmin Khan. Make notes and sum up:

1. what she says about the time of Partition and the people involved in the decision,
2. what the results were,
3. how her family was affected,
4. why there was so much violence. → ○ 6

This novel extract is set in New Delhi in June 1947, shortly before the Partition of India.

The afternoon air hung heavy and thick. In the classroom, it remained in the aisles between desks like phantoms. Sweat dripped down Deepa's forehead and settled in the nests of her eyebrows, the hair of her sideburns. She fanned herself with her [...] notebook but it did not help. Her fellow classmates scribbled the final lines of an essay on their favorite poem from *Gitanjali*. How unfair that she should have to choose only one to write about! Rabindranath Tagore's words swirled in her mind, flowed into her dreams. She could reach out and touch them, drink them like water. [...]

Oh, to write like Tagore, Kalidasa, or Shakespeare. If only she could take in some of their gifts when she read them, borrow just a tiny little bit of their styles, their voices, imbed them in her own writing. Bells rang throughout the building, each one louder than the next. She pushed out her chair, dropped her notebook into her bag, slung it over her shoulder. "Faseelah," she called to her friend three desks in front of her. "Can you come over later tonight to study?" Faseelah pushed her glasses higher on her nose, adjusted the front of her hijab. "I wish I could, Deepa." Her gaze shifted to the floor. "Yesterday, some boys started harassing my mother and me. They said that we'd soon have to move to our prison in Pakistan and followed us all the way home. I'm not allowed to leave home anymore, except to go to school."

"Oh, Faseelah," Deepa said. "How terrible." She walked over to her friend, hugged her tightly. Tensions had been steadily rising over the last several months, more so since Lord Mountbatten formally announced the Partition the previous week. Delhi was no longer safe for her Muslim friends and Deepa's heart felt heavy under the weight of it all, like it might throw her into some kind of an abyss, the way a wave drags sand into the ocean. Was this grief? She had been lucky in life. She had never experienced it before.

"Please be careful, Faseelah," she said.

Deepa had once considered herself good at offering comfort to her friends when they needed it, of always knowing the right thing to say. But these words were all she could muster, and in the midst of this crisis, they seemed shallow. Muslims were being forced to flee north. Deepa wondered how many more times she'd be able to hug her friend and how long it would be before she learned that Faseelah and her family, too, had escaped to what would become the new Pakistan.

"You be careful too," Faseelah said, squeezing Deepa's hand.

3 **sideburns** strips of hair in front of your ears
6 **Tagore** (1861–1941) a famous Bengali poet and philosopher
6 **to swirl** *herumwirbeln*
8 **Kalidasa** a famous poet in ancient India
14 **to adjust** *zurechtrücken*
14 **hijab** a kind of headscarf
22 **abyss** a deep pit you can fall into
23 **grief** extreme sadness
28 **to muster** *aufbringen*

A sea of white salwar suits, hijabs, and bobbing black braids crowded the central corridor of St. Magdalene School for Girls. Here, and in the school's courtyard, Muslim, Hindu, Sikh, Christian, Buddhist, Parsi, and Jain students gathered together as they always did to study together or exchange gossip. It could be easy to forget that India was on fire when Deepa saw the love and laughter shared between her classmates regardless of their faith. [...]

Another set of bells rang, another set of doors flung open, this time belonging to St. Francis, the boys' school next door. Students ran through the [...] iron gates, play-punched shoulders, knocked books out of one another's hands.

Father Michael in his long black cassock jabbed his finger at an older student who had wrestled a child half his size to the ground. He taught Science at both schools and was a favorite instructor among the students. He didn't give too many exams, told jokes at the end of class. Lately though, he admonished, quite harshly, those who earned poor marks and instead sent rowdy children straight to Sister Louisa, keeper of the switches. Sister Ann, the music teacher, no longer sang cheery gospels in the mornings before classes started. All of the teachers at the two schools seemed on edge lately.

A page from a yellowed newspaper was lifted up by the wind, caught onto the back of Deepa's sandal. She picked it up, flattened the paper on her hand. The date was October 27, 1946. Death toll high from latest riots in Bihar; citizens fearful of more bloodshed with upcoming Partition, it read. [...]

She shuddered, crumpled the paper, put it in her bag. She and her father had listened to the radio during the sectarian violence that broke out in Calcutta, Noakhali, and finally in Bihar late last October. He smoked one beedi after another as he adjusted the dial to quiet the static.

"How can we march together with Gandhi during the day and destroy one another at night?" he had cried between puffs on his cigarette. "How can brother kill brother? For thousands of years, Indian identity was never so closely tied to religion. The blood of Partition is on British not Indian hands."

From: Anjali Enjeti, *The parted earth*, 2021 (adapted)

[33] **salwar** a kind of traditional trousers
[33] **braid** *Zopf*
[36] **gossip** *Klatsch und Tratsch*
[42] **cassock** a priest's dress
[42] **to jab** *stechen, piksen*
[45] **to admonish** *tadeln, ermahnen*
[47] **switch** a kind of whip used to punish children
[48] **on edge** very nervous
[52] **death toll** number of people killed
[55] **sectarian** sb who wants to break away from a group
[56] **beedi** Indian cigarette
[56] **to adjust the dial to quiet the static** to tune in to a radio station to hear the sound clearly

18 COMPREHENSION

a) Briefly describe the individual characters as well as the relationships between them.
b) Name the groups of people mentioned in the text and sum up what is said about them.
c) Explain why Deepa is so sad and why the teachers at the two schools have started to behave differently.
d) Summarise how Deepa's father comments on the outbreaks of violence he hears about on the radio.

19 ANALYSIS

a) Write a characterisation of Deepa, also showing what we learn about her experience of Partition. Make sure you refer to the relevant lines in the text. → S4, 13
b) Examine the first two sentences. Say what kind of atmosphere is created and how the author achieves this. Find other examples of how the author creates atmosphere in the text.

20 CREATIVE TASK Do you think Deepa and Faseelah can keep up their friendship after Partition? Will Faseelah's family have to move? Write 2–3 paragraphs to continue the story. → S26

21 ACROSS CULTURES Germany has also experienced a partition. Discuss similarities and differences to the Partition of India. → ○ 7

B Kenya – a country on the rise

City and country life

1 VISUALS

a) Describe and compare the two photos of Kenya. Then read the fact file. Discuss to what extent the information matches what you expected. → ● 8

b) Find out the population density in Kenya and compare it with that of Germany. Research if more people live in rural or in urban areas and explain why.

FACT FILE

Agriculture in Kenya Agriculture is key for Kenya's economy. The agricultural sector employs over 40% of the population (and 70% of those living in rural areas). The main crops for domestic consumption are maize (corn), wheat and sugarcane. Cattle, goats and other livestock are also raised. The main exports are tea, coffee, cut flowers, fruit and vegetables. Kenya is the leading exporter of roses to the European Union. However, productivity has stalled over the past years. A lack of water, infrastructure and land that is suitable for farming are holding back further expansion. Kenya typically has two rainy seasons, but due to climate change, there have been more droughts, affecting agricultural production.

Different ways of life → WB 60–61/1–3

Wandia and Aoro, who live with their children in Nairobi, have gone to visit Aoro's brother, who lives to the west of the Rift Valley.

The farm in Njoro was now solely under the able management of Odongo Sigu, Aoro's youngest brother, a burly and powerful looking man. He was assisted by his wife Jael, a friendly and gregarious person – who nevertheless managed her husband and five children with impressive efficiency. Opiyo, Odongo's twin brother, had sold his share of the farm to his brother, preferring to live in Nakuru Town with his wife – a well dressed and highly made-up woman who had been truly horrified at the idea that anyone at all, least of all her husband, should expect her to touch soil except as a ceremonial gesture during funerals.

Jael was normally up at five, woke her husband and children by five-thirty and all were ready for breakfast by six. By six-thirty her husband made his way to the dairy to supervise the milking while the older children started on their way to school, about a kilometre and a half away. At seven-thirty she walked the fourth child, four-year-old Aoro, to his nursery school about a kilometre away at the church hall. On the way she told stories and sang songs to whichever child was lucky enough to be in nursery school at any particular time. This was the way they would remember their mother all their lives, not the not-so-rare times she had used her slippers to swat recalcitrant bottoms.

Jael was a remarkable woman. This year alone they had twenty acres under wheat, ten under maize, five under potatoes and two acres under an assortment of

2 **burly** ↔ thin
3 **gregarious** sociable
16 **to swat** to beat
16 **recalcitrant** stubborn, disobedient
17 **bottom** behind (part of the body)
18 **acre** unit of area measure, ca. 4,047 m²

horticultural crops supposedly for home use, but each year she seemed to have an impressive surplus for the market at Nakuru. She spent quite a bit of time behind the wheel of her little pick-up delivering farm produce.

Aoro had been touched when his brother had named his second and youngest son after him. "Oh, but he will be a doctor one day, just like his uncle," Jael had said happily. Everyone had smiled indulgently for had not her husband Odongo been the dunce of the Sigu family and had she herself not dropped out of high school – due to lack of fees, yes, but a drop-out was a drop-out. But a few years later the smiles had changed to whistles of amazement and chagrin when her oldest child, Elizabeth, had passed her primary exam at the top of the entire district, was the third best in the province and probably among the top twenty in the entire country. With that the young lady had also won a scholarship to the top national school for girls.

"Hala! But her father never could negotiate his way beyond 10 + 10!" someone remarked.

"That has not prevented him from being a highly successful farmer and I believe richer than all of us put together. Don't be deceived by the simplicity of his personal lifestyle."

"She is a throwback!" some other family member remarked, his pride wounded. He meant a throwback to some illustrious ancestor on the father's side.

"Nonsense. Her mother, behind all those smiles, is one smart woman! Besides she has a way with her husband and children."

Jael busied herself with her guests, wanting them to have the best that she could offer.

"But you don't have to wake up early at all. I know just how hard doctors work and how tired you must be," she said solicitously. What a nice person, Wandia thought, relaxing immediately in her sister-in-law's presence. She will succeed where others fail because she does not dwell on what can't be done, but rather on what can be done and does it.

From: Margaret Ogola, *I swear by Apollo*, 2002

25 **dunce** a stupid person
28 **chagrin** irritation
37 **throwback** a person showing unexpected features of a remote ancestor
40 **to have a way with sb / sth** to be good at dealing with sb / sth
44 **solicitous** caring
46 **to dwell on sth** to keep focusing on sth unpleasant

2 ANALYSIS

a) Outline what the reader learns about life in rural Kenya.

b) How is Jael presented by the narrator? Give a characterisation of her and compare her attitudes to those of the people around her. → ○ 9 → S10, 13

3 EVALUATION Discuss what makes Jael a traditional or a modern woman.

V14 **4 VIEWING** Watch the video about Wangari Maathai and take notes. Be prepared to give a short presentation of her background, education, goals and achievements. Explain why she was a modern woman and why she is considered a global icon.

V15 **5 VIEWING**

a) Watch the video, outline what the women's business is and explain why it is of great importance for the villagers.

b) Comment on the project and the problem at the root of it. Do you know of any other projects which involve recycling plastic? Share your ideas in class.

A5 **6 MEDIATION** You are on an English-speaking tour of Nairobi with a small group of German tourists, not all of whom are very good at English. Two of them ask you for some help – one of them is a former history teacher, and the other is particularly interested in the issues Kenya is currently facing. Listen carefully and interpret. Ask suitable questions and sum up the relevant parts of the guides' answers for the addressees. → S39 → WB 23–24/4–7

A young country

7 ACROSS CULTURES Compare the two population pyramids. What kinds of challenges might each country face due to the age of their population? → S37

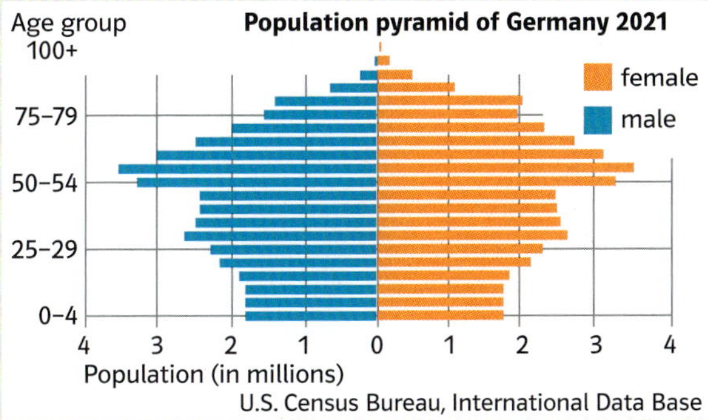

U.S. Census Bureau, International Data Base

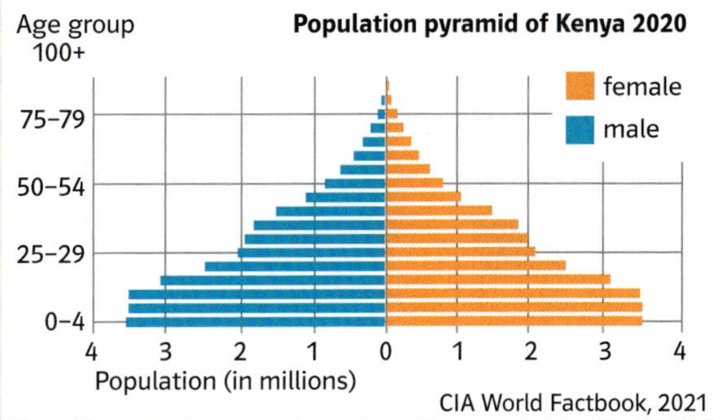

CIA World Factbook, 2021

Who are the Kenyan youth?

A study focusing on young people in Kenya was conducted in 2018, when already more than one in every five Kenyans was between 15 and 24 years old.

Young people have a strong sense of pride in Kenya – 91 per cent of those who responded to our household survey love their country, and 86 per cent agree that the heritage and identity of the country are important to them. The majority feel the country has made progress in recent decades – 62 per cent of respondents believe their generation's lives are better than those of their parents' generation. [...]

As well as loving their own country, Kenyan youth have a growing interest in the outside world, with 71 per cent willing to move from where they live if they had the opportunity. Some of these want to move within Kenya, mostly to towns and cities. [...] But more would like to move abroad. Overall, 38 per cent of young Kenyans would be willing to relocate overseas given the opportunity. [...]

This desire to emigrate is partly spurred by the youth's increasing connectivity with the outside world. Traditional media such as television and radio remain the most important sources of local and global news for young people, but Facebook and other social media applications are becoming an ever more important part of their lives. Forty per cent of 15- to 24-year-olds have access to the internet, mostly through their mobile phones, and the majority of these use social media. Young people believe social media is helping them to integrate with the global community; 88 per cent say it makes them more tolerant of other people's points of view, and 84 per cent that it has made them feel more of a global citizen. Those with internet access are much more likely to want to move overseas than those without. This increased openness is also reflected in a high level of tolerance for foreigners – three-quarters say foreigners from other countries in Africa and elsewhere who live in Kenya are not a problem.

There are push factors, too, behind the desire to relocate, for many young Kenyans are deeply worried about the future of their country. Corruption, violence, crime and unemployment are their key concerns, and as well as causing them anxiety now, they believe these problems will become more serious in future.

From: *Next Generation Kenya, British Council* website, 2018

10 **to relocate** to move elsewhere
11 **to spur** to motivate
23 **push factor** ↔ pull factor

8 ACROSS CULTURES Agree on a list of questions that may have been asked in the study. Use them to gather information on how young people in Germany feel. Evaluate similarities and differences to the answers from the Kenyan survey. → S9

MK

Politics and the young

This article was written a few days before the 2022 elections in Kenya.

NAIROBI – The election jams play at nightclubs and on YouTube, at gas stations and on the minibuses speeding through traffic.

Ahead of Kenya's presidential election [...], the catchy songs are an ever-present soundtrack. With the contest projected to be a neck-and-neck competition, former prime minister Raila Odinga and Deputy President William Ruto have both turned to Kenya's young musicians for a boost.

"Politicians need ground game," said Malaak Ayuen, 25, a member of Mbogi Genje, a popular hip-hop group supporting Odinga, "and musicians, we are on the ground."

[T]he contenders are especially eager to reach Kenya's massive youth population. Those under the age of 35 make up more than three-quarters of the population, and people ages 18 to 35 make up a whopping 40 percent of the registered electorate.

As Ayuen walked through Eastlands wearing sunglasses and an Mbogi Genje hoodie, fist-bumping kids who recognized him in the poor Nairobi neighborhood where the group's three members grew up, he listed the problems he hears from peers. Joblessness. Public corruption. Police violence. Lack of opportunities. When it comes to choosing Kenya's next leader, many young people, he said, "have given up".

To capture their votes, politicians are turning more than ever to music – including groups like Mbogi Genje, who are part of a genre of Kenyan hip-hop called gengetone – said Patrick Monte, a musicology lecturer at Kabarak University in Nakuru who studies the intersection of politics and music. Whether the strategy will succeed, given the extent of youth disillusionment, is an open question, he added.

But what is clear, Monte and artists said, is that this campaign season represents a financial opportunity for artists, many of whom are struggling. While musicians sometimes genuinely support the politicians they promote, other times they say it's about the money. Often it's a combination of the two. [...]

Sitting outside his mansion in Kisumu in Western Kenya, Odinga, 77, smiled when asked about his campaign's use of young musicians. [...]

Young people, whose unemployment rate jumped in recent years to 14 percent, are experiencing a crisis, Odinga said. He said he has a plan to boost employment, including more effective job training, but communicating his plans to younger voters has been hard. Music proved among the best ways. "That's why we went in that direction," he said.

Rachel Chason and Rael Ombuor, in: *The Washington Post*, 2022

1 **election jams** music events organised to support candidates in an election
7 **ground game** (football) work close to the basis (*here:* the people)
9 **contender** a candidate
11 **whopping** very large

FACT FILE

President William Ruto Now one of Kenya's wealthiest men, President Ruto often talks about his humble beginnings in the Rift Valley: going to primary school barefoot, getting his first pair of shoes at the age of 15, and selling chickens from a roadside stall to help his family. During the election he portrayed himself as a champion of the poor. He promised a "bottom-up" economic model to improve the lives of poorer Kenyans.

9 EVALUATION Outline how politicians in Kenya were trying to reach out to younger voters, and why musicians decided to work with them. What do you think of this kind of campaign?

MK **10** CREATIVE TASK In 2008, a development programme "Kenya Vision 2030" was launched. Go to the programme's website to find out about its three key pillars. Choose an aspect you find interesting and give a short presentation on it.

Running with the Kenyans

Kenyans have been extraordinarily successful in long-distance running. The author, a journalist and a runner himself, in 2011 visited Iten, a village in the Great Rift Valley, where almost all internationally successful Kenyan runners have trained. He wanted to find the secret of their success. His book *Running with the Kenyans* gives an insight into the life of the runners and the methods of their managers and has received a lot of praise.

In 2002, when Chris was thirty-three [...], he came second in both the Boston and the New York City marathons. He was flying, one of the top athletes at the illustrious training stable of the Italian agent Dr Rosa. Almost immediately, though, he became distracted. He used his money to build a school, named after his home village, Salaba. Like all Kenyan runners, when he was young Chris had to run to school, 4 km, back and forth twice a day every day.

"Unknowingly, we were already training," he says. "But it was hard." He says he built Salaba Academy so that his own children didn't have to suffer as he did.

"It's also an investment. It's his retirement," says Godfrey.

A fee-paying boarding school just outside Iten, Salaba Academy takes up a lot of Chris's time. He seems to do everything, from buying the flour for the ugali to attending meetings with education officials in Nairobi. One day we arrange to leave for an early morning run at 5 a.m. and he asks if we can pick him up at the school.

"Why will you be at school at that time?" I ask.

"I'm always at school early," he says.

"But is anyone even awake?"

"They are in class already," he says, affronted, as though I'm suggesting his children are lazy.

"At 5 a.m.?"

"They have exams coming up. They must work hard." Once his school was up and running, Chris never reached the same level of performance in his running again. [...]

"So, what did you want to know?" he [Renato Canova] says. I ask him why the Kenyans often have short careers. Unlike the great Ethiopian runners [...], most Kenyans run well for a few years and then disappear. He looks at me over the top of his fingers, held in a prayer position on the table. "The runners all come from poor backgrounds, with less education," he says. "When they win, the whole village celebrates their victory, and everyone asks for support. The successful athlete becomes like the chief of the village, so then everyone goes to him with their personal problems." He says he once had an athlete at the World Championships who was being phoned up every two hours by people back in Kenya asking where they should put the windows in a building they were constructing.

"The athletes need to concentrate on their training," he says. "They need to educate their villagers about their life." This is why the training camps were started, to remove the athletes from the distraction of their families and relations, and the rest of the outside world. But once they become successful, often the athletes decide they don't want to live in the camps any more, where daily life is stripped down to the bare essentials of run, sleep and eat, so they move out. "They start dealing with building projects, borrowing money," says Canova. "This is normal behaviour for a Kenyan." It is normal behaviour in most other countries, too, even for athletes. It is the ones who live in the camps who are unusual. But the difference it makes is huge. Without the same intense levels of dedication and focus, and the time to rest, when an athlete leaves a camp it often signals the beginning of the end.

9 **Godfrey** A Kenyan runner who shows the author around and introduces him to runners and managers in Iten
11 **ugali** the staple food of Kenya, a kind of porridge made of maize flour
22 **Renato Canova** a famous Italian coach

11 COMPREHENSION Explain what distractions there are for Kenyan runners and why they often finish their athletes' careers early. Give examples from the text. → S4

The following extract is about a training camp called Run Fast.

Once an aspiring runner arrives in Iten and finds a group to train with, his next aim is to run fast enough to attract the attention of a manager, who will sign him up and send him abroad to race. In return for his services, the manager takes a percentage of the prize winnings. Virtually all the managers are foreigners who have set up training camps in Iten and the surrounding area. Once an athlete gets signed up, he usually lives in the manager's training camp, where he receives food and lodging and gets to train with the other athletes in the camp. Most camps also have a masseur on hand to revitalise tired limbs and treat any niggling injuries. It's amazing how some heavy-duty thumb pressing can usually fix an injured athlete, as though he's simply made of plasticine. […]

The Run Fast manager is an Englishman called Peter McHugh. He has told the group that by the end of the week he will pick six of them to travel to Europe to run a series of races. Once they get there, all they have to do is run like Kenyans and watch the money start rolling in. Last year, the camp's star runner won enough prize money to buy himself a plot of land in Iten when he got back.

There's a lot of tension in the group right now as the runners wait to find out if they will be among the chosen six. Most of them have never raced abroad before. They stand on the threshold of the door to the promised land. This is what they've been training for, dreaming about. But if their name is not on the list, they'll be left standing outside in the cold, watching as their friends head off without them. One of the athletes, Eliud, has been running for twelve years and has made a total of 1,000 Kenyan Shillings – or about £8 – in his entire career. Even a small race abroad could net him £1,000. But only if he gets picked.

The problem is, Peter tells me, that finding races for Kenyans is getting harder and harder. […]

Peter only set up his Run Fast camp recently, but the other managers I speak to don't think he has much chance of making it a success. It's not that he doesn't know what he's doing, but that the landscape is dominated by a handful of über-managers.

"The governing body passed a new rule recently," explains one US manager, who is pulling out of Kenya after twenty years working with athletes here. "Contracts need to be renewed every year. It's good for the athletes, because it means they can move on if they're not getting a fair deal. But it makes it easy for athletes to get poached by other managers." He says that once a smaller manager like Peter discovers a promising talent, the bigger names will simply move in, offering short-term incentives to the athlete to switch. "There's no loyalty any more," he tells me. "The Kenyan runners don't understand the longer-term view. So if you offer them $500 up front, they'll jump at it, even if the terms of the contract mean they'll lose out in the long term."

From: Adharanand Finn, *Running with the Kenyans*, 2012

8 **limbs** arms and legs
8 **niggling** irritating
10 **plasticine** a soft modelling material for children
18 **threshold** doorstep
18 **promised land** the land where your dreams come true
32 **to poach sb** to make sb give up their job with sb else to work for you
34 **incentive** *here:* a sum of money
36 **up front** in advance, before they start
37 **in the long term** considering a longer period of time

12 EVALUATION Explain and comment on the system behind the Kenyan runners' international careers. What pros and cons are there for the athletes? → ● 10

V16 **13** VIEWING Watch the video and compare it with what you read. Find out if "the conveyor belt of talent" is still running in Iten and what has changed since the author's visit.

A6 **14** LISTENING Listen to the podcast and sum up:
1. who Philip Boit and Bjørn Dæhlie are,
2. what was special about the 10-kilometre Classic race in 1998,
3. what happened when Boit reached the finishing line,
4. what effects Boit's participation had on Africa,
5. how the events have personally affected Boit and Dæhlie. → S34

C Postcolonial developments worldwide

"Sey yuh sorry!"

There's a wind of change blowing through the Commonwealth Caribbean and it's beginning to pick up. When Queen Elizabeth reached Jamaica during her tour of the Commonwealth in 1953, the British Pathé newsreel described 35,000 schoolchildren waiting to welcome her in Spanish Town. "Their eyes shine with excitement – their Queen has come from a far-off land to see them." The grainy footage shows the Queen and Prince Philip driving past ranks of children in a Land Rover on a day "warm not only with the bright sunshine but with the affection of the Queen's people ... the great wealth of loyal affection that awaits them at every stage of their Commonwealth tour." The Land Rover was one of the few things that the 'New Elizabethan' visit had in common with the tour of the region Prince William and Kate, Duchess of Cambridge, embarked on last month. The young couple may have used the same open-top car, but for most Jamaicans the Windrush scandal, the Black Lives Matter protests and George Floyd probably resonated more than the post-coronation visit.

After Barbados, the 'Little England' of the Caribbean, became a republic last year, William's trip was meant to strengthen the British monarchy's links with Caribbean Commonwealth states as well as mark the Queen's Platinum Jubilee. Instead, the tour may have "accelerated moves to ditch the Queen as the head of state". There were protests, placards telling the prince to apologise and to go home, and demands for reparations for slavery. Jamaica's prime minister, Andrew Holness, baldly told William: "It is inevitable that we will move towards becoming a republic."

The tour got off to a bad start, with the couple flying into a row in Belize because of a dispute between indigenous Q'eqchi Maya people and Flora & Fauna International, a conservation charity that counts William as a patron and has land nearby, over the alleged appropriation of 5,000 hectares of communal land. Belize's Channel 7 TV reported villagers demonstrating against the 'colonial' visit and use of their football pitch for the couple's helicopter without them being consulted. The visit was hastily scrapped. Days later, the Belize government said the People's Constitutional Commission would be consulting on becoming a republic. [...]

While an estimated 250,000 Jamaicans – a sixth of the population – turned out to see the Queen in 1953, William arrived to a cooler reception. [...] An open letter from 100 prominent Jamaicans, organised by the human rights alliance Advocates Network Jamaica, gave 60 reasons for apologies and reparations from Britain and its royal family, going back to pre-colonial history. "We will not participate in your Platinum Jubilee celebration," it stated. "We will, however, celebrate 60 years of freedom from British colonial domination. We are saddened that more progress has not been made given the burden of our colonial inheritance ... just sey yuh sorry!" [...]

A speech in which William expressed his "profound sorrow" over the "appalling atrocity of slavery" was roundly criticised for falling short of an apology. An estimated 600,000 Africans were shipped to Jamaica as slaves, according to the National Library of Jamaica, but Britain has never formally apologised for the trade it helped instigate for fear of vast reparation claims.

Oren Gruenbaum, *The Round Table* website, 2022

2 **to pick up** to gain speed and power
5 **grainy footage** low-resolution film material
11 **to embark on** to start
12 **Windrush scandal** a political scandal in the UK (2018) concerning the children of Commonwealth citizens who were wrongly detained and threatened with deportation
12 **George Floyd** Black person killed by police brutality (2020)
16 **Platinum Jubilee** a celebration marking 70 years on the throne
17 **to ditch the Queen ...** *(infml)* to abolish monarchy
19 **baldly** frankly
24 **alleged** supposed
27 **to scrap** to cancel
37 **profound** deep
38 **to fall short of** to fail to achieve
40 **to instigate** to introduce

1 COMPREHENSION | ANALYSIS Summarise what the article is about and state how stylistic devices, arguments and examples are used in the article to illustrate criticism of Britain's royal family. → ○ 11

2 EVALUATION Do you agree with the people who criticised the royal visit to the Caribbean in 2022? Explain why / why not and comment on their two demands. → S19

The global impact of George Floyd

Even after the end of colonialism, Black people are still facing systemic racism.

George Floyd's murder in Minneapolis in May 2020 sparked the largest racial justice protests in the United States since the Civil Rights Movement. But the movement went far beyond this nation's borders – it inspired a global reckoning with racism.

This time last year, countries across the globe had some of the largest Black Lives Matter protests in their history, all inspired by the video of Floyd's brutal death in police custody on May 25, 2020. Crossing continents and cultures, Black activists saw Floyd's death as a symbol of the intolerance and injustice they face at home.

Some of these countries had their own George Floyd – a Black person whose death by police brutality or racial violence created national outrage. Everywhere, activists knew there was no going back to the way things were before they witnessed Floyd's final moments. President Biden said that when he met with Floyd's young daughter Gianna, she told him, "Daddy changed the world." These worldwide protests show how right she was. [...]

The United Kingdom had the largest Black Lives Matter protests in the world last summer outside of the United States.

"England is not an overtly racist country, in my humble opinion," Imarn Ayton, an organizer of the London protests, told CBS News at the time. "It is a covertly racist country. So we are much more subtle and polite with our racism."

But the time to be polite was over.

Protesters and police clashed at some of the demonstrations. Some protesters tore down and vandalized statues of slave traders and political leaders – even some who were considered national heroes. A statue of Winston Churchill in London's Parliament Square was spray-painted with a message calling him a "racist".

Within days, London's protests exploded from about 20 people outside the U.S. embassy to more than 20,000 people flooding the streets. Celebrities joined, including Madonna and John Boyega, who gave an impassioned address to protesters. [...]

As the summer of protests blazed through the U.S., Washington, D.C. became a national center for the Black Lives Matter movement. The city created Black Lives Matter Plaza, near the White House, less than two weeks after Floyd's death, and it is now a regular gathering space for protest and activism. [...]

On August 28, thousands gathered for the 2020 March on Washington at the Lincoln Memorial, with George Floyd's brother Philonise addressing the crowd.

Meanwhile, the local Black Lives Matter chapter started mutual aid initiatives in all eight wards of the city to work to bring about some of the changes that they've yet to see from institutions. "We have built a stronger community and reimagined a world where we keep us safe and we can build a world without police," Neenee Taylor, the former mass engagement and rapid response coordinator for Black Lives Matter D.C., told CBS News. "And so that's what has changed for our community since George Floyd in D.C. But as far as the government – hasn't nothing changed."

Jason Silverstein, *CBS News* website, 2021

1 **to spark** to start
3 **reckoning with racism** openly addressing the problem of racism
6 **custody** detention
9 **outrage** shock and anger
16 **overtly** openly
17 **covertly** secretly, subtly
20 **to tear down** to pull down
27 **to blaze** to move like flames
33 **chapter** part of an organisation
34 **ward** quarter, district

3 COMPREHENSION Point out the similarities and differences between the Black Lives Matter protests in the UK and the US.

4 ANALYSIS Show how the writer uses language and quotes to influence the reader and reflect the power of the Black Lives Matter movement. → S11, 14

MK **5** ACROSS CULTURES Find articles online about the protests in Germany at the time and discuss what is said about them. → WB 22/3

Improving your writing style

Hindu gods

The most important Hindu gods are Brahma, Vishnu and Shiva, each having a specific role. Brahma, usually depicted with four faces and four arms, is the creator of all things and beings. There are many legends about him: One says he was born in a lotus flower growing out of Vishnu's navel. Another says when creating the cosmic waters, Brahma planted a seed in them which turned into a golden egg. Having emerged from it, the egg expanded and became the universe.

Vishnu preserves and protects life and the universe. Responsible for returning to earth to restore the balance between good and evil whenever necessary, he has been reincarnated nine different times. It is believed that he will return a tenth and final time, thus indicating the end of the world. Like Brahma, he has four arms, each holding a different symbol of power: a discus, a lotus flower, a shell trumpet and a club.

Shiva is the destroyer. Although sometimes viewed negatively, destruction is seen as an essential part of creation, enabling positive change. He is often shown carrying a trident and wearing a cobra around his neck. A third eye is located in the middle of his forehead. According to legend, Shiva was once meditating when his wife Parvati covered his eyes, without thinking of the consequences. Not having the light from Shiva's eyes, the universe was plunged into darkness. To be able to give light back to the universe, Shiva created a third eye.

1 Identify the non-finite constructions (which contain participles, gerunds or infinitives or no verb at all) in the text. Say what purpose they fulfil and, if possible, rewrite them using clauses with finite verbs.

Examples: *The participle constructions ("each having …", "usually depicted …") in lines 2 and 3 are used to give additional information. They are shorter and considered stylistically better than additional main clauses ("and each of them has …") or relative clauses ("each of whom has …").*

2 Rewrite these sentences about the Hindu god Ganesh using non-finite constructions.

1. The elephant-headed god Ganesh **is said to remove obstacles and bring happiness** and is a very popular Indian god.
2. People often ask for Ganesh's blessing **before they begin a new project, move into a new house or go on a journey.**
3. According to a legend, Parvati made a boy out of some paste **because she did not want anyone to disturb her bath.**
4. **After she had breathed life into it**, she told the boy to guard the door to the bathroom.
5. **As he had been told not to let anyone pass**, the boy did not even let Shiva go inside.
6. Shiva became very angry and cut off the boy's head **and killed him immediately.**
7. **As Parvati was extremely sad**, Shiva promised to cut the head off the next living creature he saw **so the boy's head could be replaced**.
8. Shiva saw an elephant and **after he had put its head on the boy's body**, Shiva said that the boy would be the leader of his ganas (assistants) and called him Ganesh.

3 Improve this text about Diwali using non-finite constructions.

Diwali is a special festival for Hindus and is called the Festival of Light. The word comes from the Sanskrit *dipwali* and means "row of lights". It takes place every autumn and marks the start of the Hindu New Year. People all around the world celebrate the holiday which represents the triumph of light over darkness and good over evil. They often decorate their homes with oil lamps which are called *diyas*. They light them so that the goddess Lakshmi can find her way into their homes. She is the goddess of wealth and fortune, and people say she brings prosperity for the coming year. It is a time when people exchange gifts, wear new clothes, eat together, and enjoy fireworks. The festival, which is not just celebrated by Hindus but also by Sikhs, Jains and Buddhists, goes back to ancient times.

D Breaking bad habits

Activists toppled a statue of 17th-century slave trader Edward Colston at a Black Lives Matter protest in Bristol on 7 June 2020. Vanessa Kisuule, Bristol's city poet from 2018–2020, wrote a poem in response to this event.

hollow empty inside
2 **wrench** *here:* push
3 **grand plié** bending your knees in ballet dancing
4 **to corkscrew** to turn like a tool for opening wine bottles
6 **loose change** coins
12 **to carve** to shape
15 **virtuous** righteous
15 **plaque** a piece of metal with writing on it
16 **odourless** without a smell
17 **sneaky** doing things in a secret and unfair way
19 **saliva** liquid produced in your mouth
24 **tadpole** early developmental stage of a frog
29 **succinct** short and precise
34 **bougie** *(AE infml disapproving)* middle class
34 **to flaunt** to show off
38 **to throb** steadily beat
43 **plinth** a pillar for a statue
44 **marble** precious white rock

Hollow

You came down easy in the end.
The righteous wrench of two ropes in a grand plié.
Briefly, you flew, corkscrewed, then met the ground
With the clang of toy guns, loose change, chains, a rain of cheers.
Standing ovation on the platform of your neck.
Punk Ballet. Act 1.
There is more to come.
And who carved you?
They took such care with that stately pose and propped chin.
Wise and virtuous, the plaque assured us.
Victors wish history odourless and static.
But history is a sneaky mistress.
Moves like smoke, Colston,
Like saliva in a hungry mouth.
This is your rightful home,
Here, in the pit of chaos with the rest of us.
Take your twisted glory and feed it to the tadpoles.
Kids will write raps to that syncopated splash.
I think of you lying in the harbour
With the horrors you hosted.
There is no poem more succinct than that.
But still you are permanent.
You who perfected the ratio.
Blood to sugar to money to bricks.
Each bougie building we flaunt haunted by bones.
Children learn and titans sing
Under the stubborn rust of your name.
But the air is gently throbbing with newness.
Can you feel it?
Colston, I can't get the sound of you from my head.
Countless times I passed that plinth,
Its heavy threat of metal and marble.
But as you landed, a piece of you fell off, broke away,
And inside, nothing but air.
This whole time, you were hollow.

Vanessa Kisuule, 2020

1 VIEWING
a) Find the video of Vanessa Kisuule reading the poem online and watch it. Listen to the rhythm and the emphasis she places on certain words. Pay attention to the way she divides the poem into sections and outline what each one is about. → S15
b) What effect is created by the use of 'you' and 'us'?

2 EVALUATION Explain what Kisuule thinks of Colston and his legacy. Find examples to support your answer in the poem.

3 SPEAKING Discuss the pros and cons of pulling down statues of people like Colston or renaming streets named after people who were honoured for acting in the name of imperialism. → S31, 33

Postcolonial approaches to education

How can democratic societies educate their members in order not to repeat the mistakes of the past? First you are going to look at educational goals. Then you are going to discuss how they can be achieved. Work in groups. Make notes of your results for each step.

Step 1 Examine the actual situation

a) Compare the following two extracts from exemplary curricula in English-speaking countries. Summarise what kind of society the institutions promote and explain what historical events may have led them to do so.
b) Point out the skills a person is supposed to develop during the educational process.
c) Give your own opinion on the ideas expressed in the statements.

Teaching should equip pupils to ask perceptive questions, think critically, weigh evidence, sift arguments, and develop perspective and judgement. History helps pupils to understand the complexity of people's lives, the process of change, the diversity of societies and relationships between different groups, as well as their own identity and the challenges of their time.

From: *National curriculum for History*, UK government website, 2013

The social studies, history, geography, and Canadian and world studies programs will enable students to become responsible, active citizens within the diverse communities to which they belong. As well as becoming critically thoughtful and informed citizens who value an inclusive society, students will have the skills they need to solve problems and communicate ideas and decisions about significant developments, events, and issues.

From: *Ontario curriculum for Canadian and World Studies*, Canadian government website, 2018

Step 2 Develop suggestions for postcolonial curricula

You as representatives of the target group are asked to make suggestions on how to achieve the goals described in Step 1. Get into groups and choose a concrete topic, e.g. the British colonisation of India, Canada or Australia or the international slave trade. Collect ideas on what to study (themes, events, people, dates), what sources to use (authors, text types) and how to practise the skills needed. Discuss what potential dangers there are (focus, perspective, what to leave out) and make a checklist of what to avoid.

USEFUL PHRASES

bias • to keep sth back • to shift focus • compare opposing views • to rely on traditional texts • to not accept opinions as facts • to read exclusively European / Indigenous authors • to question traditional perspectives • to introduce new perspectives • to present information • to do research • legitimate / serious scholars • a balanced presentation • minorities

Step 3 Organise a debate

Conduct a class debate on the motion:
To teach people about colonial history, you must confront them with authentic texts written by the colonisers, even if their perspective and language may be racist. → S32

Skills workshop 4
Writing an argumentative text

Being able to argue convincingly will help you not only to succeed in your exams but also to represent your interests and to make better decisions. The structure of an argumentative text depends on your aim (or the task you're given), e.g.
- getting your opinion across, convincing or persuading readers (tasks with ***Comment on***);
- giving a balanced view on a topic that includes your own opinion (tasks with ***Discuss / Evaluate / Assess***).

Step 1 Collecting and structuring ideas

1 SPEAKING With a partner, talk about how important sports are to you. Could you imagine doing professional sports? Why (not)?

In 2019 Kenyan athlete Brigid Kosgei broke the women's marathon world record (2:14:04h).

2 BEFORE YOU START

a) You're going to deal with the task:
Discuss the following statement: "Training to be a champion – blessing or curse?"
With a partner, collect arguments for and against doing professional sports. You can use grids like these:

Pro (main arguments)	**Support** (examples / statistics / quotes)
…	…

Con (main arguments)	**Support** (examples / statistics / quotes)
…	…

TIP

Make sure your arguments are not too similar. Pick arguments from **different areas**, e.g. career / money, work-life balance, health, media, satisfaction, or ethical principles. Leave out any arguments that aren't really convincing.

b) Research examples, statistics or quotes to support your arguments and add them to the grids.

c) Note down ideas you could use for the introduction and conclusion. Brainstorm with a partner or do more research if necessary.

d) Define your own position on the topic.
Then arrange your arguments in a logical and convincing way, e.g. first cons (strong to weak), then pros (weak to strong). → S18

Step 2 Main body

3 VOCABULARY Revise how to use linking words. Complete the sentences with two of the given phrases. Cross-check with online resources.

above all • as a result • consequently • contrary to • first of all • for example • for instance • however • in addition • in contrast to • most importantly • moreover • nevertheless • to start with

1. **Starting:** 1 , it is important to mention that training to become a professional …
2. **Giving examples:** 2 , ballerinas will not stop dancing even if …
3. **Contrasting:** 3 ordinary teenagers, professional athletes …
4. **Emphasising:** 4 , training to be a champion means to …
5. **Adding:** 5 , it also takes willpower to …
6. **Making concessions:** 6 , it might not be a good idea to …
7. **Concluding:** 7 , athletes often suffer from …

4 EVALUATION

a) The following example paragraph could be part of the main body of your essay. Have a closer look at each sentence and identify the main elements of a paragraph given in the tip box.

> Moreover, being an athlete is a hard and time-consuming occupation. Professional runners, for example, have to follow a meticulously organised routine day in and day out. To improve their performance, they have to accomplish different training sessions from light jogging to long distance running every day. Following this tight schedule obviously requires strict discipline and leaves little space for other activities like hobbies or friendships.

TIP

A convincing paragraph is similar to a "mini-essay" and consists of these elements:
- **Topic sentence**: Presents the main idea.
- **Support**: Sentences explaining your point and giving evidence (examples, statistics, quotes). Careful: Do not just list this evidence, but use it to illustrate your argument.
- **Concluding sentence**: Rounding off and / or restating the topic sentence. → S17

b) Choose your strongest argument and write a paragraph following the clues in the tip box. Then exchange paragraphs with a partner and give each other feedback. → S7

Step 3 Introduction and conclusion

5 EVALUATION Explain what is good / not so good about the introductions below (→ S18) and improve them. Then choose one you'd like to use for your essay.

1. In this essay I want to discuss the question "Training to be a champion – blessing or curse?".
2. Since I first watched the Olympic Games as a child with my father, I have been fascinated by the endurance runners prove when they finally dart through the finish line with light-footedness after having run the distance of a marathon. Since that day, I have dreamed of becoming an athlete myself. So I would like to discuss whether …
3. Many young teenagers living under poor conditions dream of a better life and cheer on athletic heroes from their country who have made it to the top. And now I am going to discuss the task.

6 VOCABULARY The following sentence beginnings can help you to conclude your essay in a convincing way, e.g. by summarising your arguments or giving an outlook on the future. First put in the missing words, then complete the sentences with your own ideas.

in other words • no doubt • to matter • to remain • very (un)likely

1. There is [1] that the advantages of doing sports …
2. [2], training to be a champion …
3. It is [3] that a career in professional sports will …
4. In the end, what actually [4] is that …
5. It [5] to be seen what …

Step 4 Writing an argumentative text

7 EVALUATION Use your ideas from the previous tasks to complete the body paragraphs and the conclusion of your essay.

8 EVALUATION

a) Choose one of these tasks:
1. Discuss how Bollywood influences the way Indian culture is perceived internationally.
2. Comment on the following statement: In today's world, monarchy is an outdated concept. → S19

b) Exchange texts with a partner. Give each other feedback. → S7

5 Global matters
Introduction

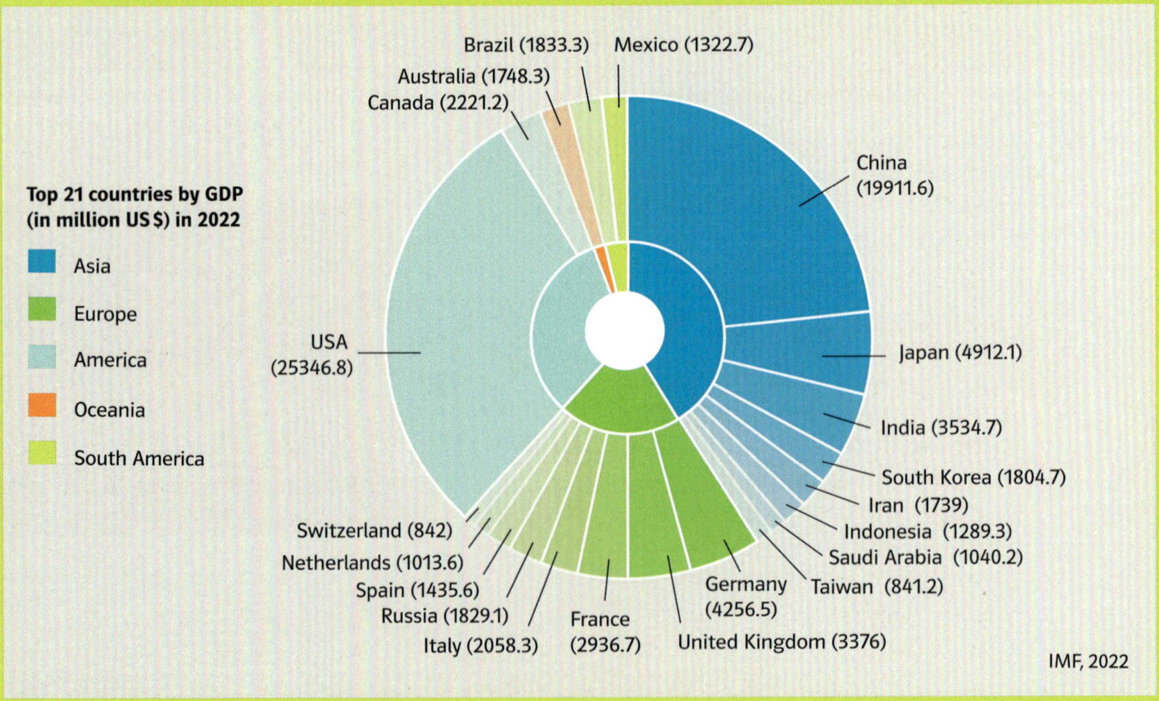

1 SPEAKING
Match the photos, statistics and quotes to these five aspects of globalisation: economy, politics, culture, environment, communication. Discuss other ways these aspects have been affected by globalisation. Give examples from your knowledge and personal experience. → ○ 1

> "Globalisation, with inexorable speed, has changed the world we live in. For all of us. Jobs have changed, the way we trade has changed, who we employ has changed and the feel of where we live has changed. Katty Kay, British-Swiss journalist
>
> Our biggest challenge in this new century is to take an idea that seems abstract – sustainable development – and turn it into a reality for all the world's people. Kofi Annan, Ghanaian diplomat
>
> We are aware that globalization doesn't mean global friendship but global competition and, therefore, conflict. That doesn't mean we will all destroy each other, but it is no happy global village, either.
> Rene Girard, French anthropologist
>
> Mobile technologies have become an opportunity to boost economic, health, educational and technological development. [...] Mobile technology can become a powerful weapon against poverty. UNICEF, children's fund
>
> I think globalization actually maintains and fosters various elements of national and cultural identities. I don't think everything is being homogenized. If anything, your food, your culture, and your ethnicity might become part of the globalized world, and thus absorbed by other countries. Nouriel Roubini, US economist"

2 EVALUATION

a) Evaluate each quote about globalisation: Where do you think it belongs on a spectrum between 'very positive' and 'very negative'? Comment on the quotes' combined effect.

MK b) Do research on one of the people / organisations quoted on this page, their reputation and the context of the quote. Discuss whether the new information changes how you interpret the quote.

c) Take another look at the pie chart. Assess which countries play a big role globally. Think of reasons for their importance now and guess which countries may become more relevant over the next years. Say why.

3 EVALUATION What could the public's reactions to each of the statements have been? Write at least one pro and one counter argument for each statement.

4 VISUALS Describe and analyse the cartoon explaining the irony in it. Point out the clichés in the drawings of the people. Interpret why the cartoonist chose to use these clichés. → S38

5 EVALUATION How does globalisation affect you personally? Collect positive and negative examples.

Global chances and challenges

Why globalisation?

Looking back, the path to globalisation seems inevitable. Evidence of trade between people from faraway places stretches back into prehistory. As long ago as the second century BC, merchants on the Silk Road were travelling between China and the Mediterranean.

The Age of Discovery from the 15th to the 18th centuries enabled contact among continents, which brought about colonisation and exploitation led by the three Cs: Christianity, civilization and commerce.

The first phase of globalisation in the modern sense (or 'Globalisation 1.0') was from the mid-19th century up to the start of WWI in 1914. Beginning in Britain, the Industrial Revolution hugely accelerated worldwide trade. Improved manufacturing technology and transport of goods by steamship and trains made it possible for Britain and other rapidly industrialising nations to produce goods like iron and textiles that were in high demand around the world. Investments also became global with, for example, European companies creating the Suez Canal, building thousands of kilometres of railway in India and establishing mining operations in Africa.

In 1929, the Wall Street Crash led not only to the Great Depression in the USA, but also to economic decline in many other parts of the world, showing how interconnected economies had become.

After WWII, a new phase of globalisation (Globalisation 2.0) began, as the USA became the world's dominant nation, both culturally and economically. Rapid developments in technology, communications and financial systems led to the nations of the world becoming ever more connected. The collapse of the Iron Curtain in 1989 suddenly brought Russia and several countries in Eastern Europe into the global economy. In 1995, 123 nations established the World Trade Organization (WTO) with the goal of promoting free trade worldwide. Today there are more than 160 members, including of course China, which some economists predict will become the world's largest economy in the 2030s.

Globalisation in today's world

Globalisation 3.0 started around 2000, when the internet began to transform many aspects of work and leisure. While the poorest people stayed poor, the middle classes (especially in countries like China and India) experienced fast income growth. The big winners were the richest 1 % of the world, who received 60 % of the world's income.

Globalisation and the shrinking world have also emphasised the world's vulnerabilities: supply chains that can be interrupted, the worldwide financial crisis of 2008, international terrorism and the fact that trade agreements are no guarantee for peace. Meanwhile, digitalisation, while bringing many benefits, has also resulted in cross-border cyber-attacks and political manipulation by foreign powers via social media. Some commentators have suggested that, due to increasing awareness of the drawbacks of globalisation, the world is entering a phase of deglobalisation. Others predict Globalisation 4.0, a new phase of rapid technological, social and economic change which shrinks the world even further.

1 CREATIVE TASK Make an infographic to show the four phases of globalisation. For each phase, create one very simple image or icon to represent that phase, give (approximate) dates and write a short list of key features that sums it up. → O 2

2 VOCABULARY Create a word bank and / or mind maps with words and phrases that are useful for talking about economics and globalisation. Add to it as you work through this topic. → WB 25/1

3 SPEAKING Discuss what you know about winners and losers of globalisation. How could globalisation become fairer? → S31

Why English?

One in four people in the world speak English. 750 million of them do not come from an English-speaking country. In more than a hundred countries, English is the main foreign language taught in schools in many parts of the world because English is believed to be the key to success.

Some may wonder how English developed from the language spoken by a few people on an island in northwestern Europe into a global language in less than 400 years, dominating in business, technology, politics, education, science and entertainment.

Largely, English owes its global dominance to Britain's colonial expansion. Settling in or colonising countries around the globe in the 17th to 19th centuries, the British imposed their language on the inhabitants. Many of the 55 sovereign states and 27 non-sovereign entities in which English is a main or official language (see the map at the end of this book) are former British colonies, including Canada, Australia, South Africa, India and the US.

Throughout the 20th century, the United States evolved as the world's political and business superpower. This strengthened the use of English as the language of global trade. America's influence, combined with Hollywood films and popular music from both the US and the UK, made English the language of entertainment as well.

English has long been used as a worldwide lingua franca for commerce and communication by non-native speakers who each speak different languages and could not otherwise understand each other.

English in today's world

English is still seen in many countries as an essential requirement for studying at university, reading and producing international literature, research or technology, and achieving a maximum international audience. It is, however, facing growing competition from other languages, such as Chinese and Spanish.

There are countless different varieties of English today. Vocabulary, pronunciation and style depend on the situation and status of the people in the conversation (register) or the country, region and culture. It can hinder understanding when the participants in a conversation are not familiar with the local dialect or vocabulary.

English words have been integrated into many other languages (e.g. *le weekend* in French), while words from other languages were and are still being added to the English language (e.g. *juggernaut* from India, or *karaoke* from Japan), which is always changing to reflect new inventions or trends.

In lingua franca and similar contexts, communication should be reduced to a basic, polite and clear standard vocabulary of non-idiomatic words and phrases to avoid confusion. 'Globish' is one example of this attempt to simplify communication. Yet new translation technology is developing which could make lingua francas unnecessary.

4 COMPREHENSION

a) Outline how English became such an important global language.

b) State how and where English is used today, and how that use is changing.

5 SPEAKING Discuss the role of English in your life now and how essential it will be in your future life and career. → O 3

MK **6 CREATIVE TASK** → S3

a) Indian linguist Braj Kachru defines the spread of English around the world with a 'three circle model of World Englishes'. Research this model and explain it in key words.

b) Research the role of English as a main or official language in a country of your choice (not the UK or the US) and present this aspect of your chosen country in class.

A Economic and political impact

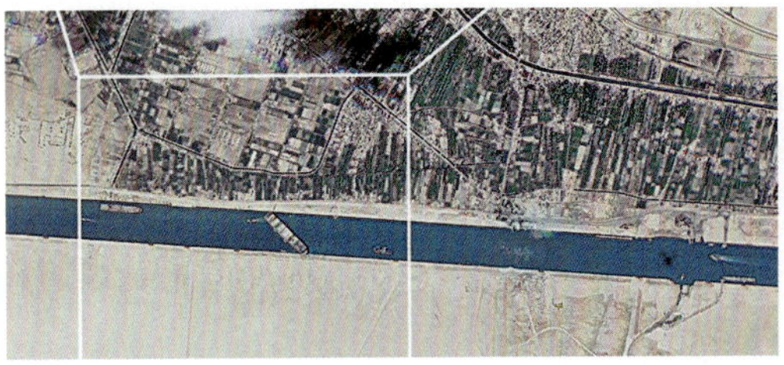

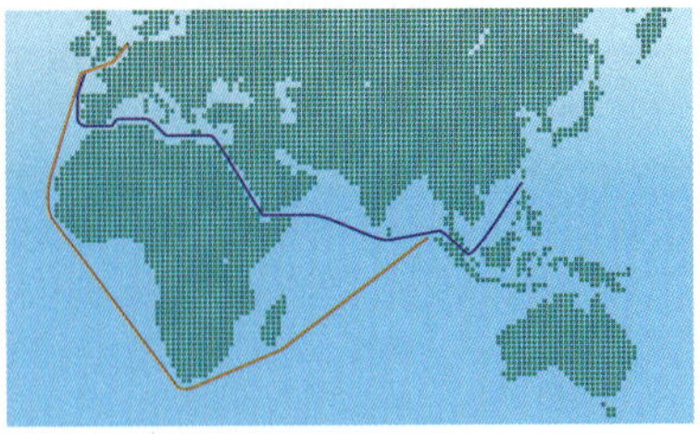

Standardized shipping is on the move → WB 25/2

Today's global economy runs on standardized shipping containers, as the Ever Given fiasco illustrates.

Take a look around you. Perhaps you're snacking on a banana, sipping some coffee or sitting in front of your computer and taking a break from work to read this article. Most likely, those goods – as well as your smartphone, refrigerator and virtually every other object in your home – were once loaded onto a large container in another country and traveled thousands of miles via ships crossing the ocean before ultimately arriving at your doorstep.

Today, an estimated 90 % of the world's goods are transported by sea, with 60 % of that – including virtually all your imported fruits, gadgets and appliances – packed in large steel containers. The rest is mainly commodities like oil or grains that are poured directly into the hull. [...]

In short, without the standardized container – like the thousands that helped to keep the Ever Given stuck in the mud along the Suez Canal, snarling traffic for almost a week – the global supply chain that society depends upon would not exist. [...]

Trade before the container [...] Even as trade grew more advanced, the process of loading and unloading as goods were transferred from one method of transportation to another remained very labor-intensive, time-consuming and costly, in part because containers came in all shapes and sizes. Containers from a ship being transferred onto a smaller rail car, for example, often had to be opened up and repacked into a boxcar. [...]

A trade revolution [...] it was not until the 1950s that American entrepreneur Malcolm McLean realized that by standardizing the size of the containers being used in global trade, loading and unloading of ships and trains could be at least partially mechanized, thereby making the transfer from one mode of transportation to another seamless.

This way products could remain in their containers from the point of manufacture to delivery, resulting in reduced costs in terms of labor and potential damage. In 1956, McLean created the standard cargo container, which we basically still use today. [...]

One of the key advantages is that whatever size a ship uses, they all, like lego blocks, fit neatly together with virtually no empty spaces. This innovation made the modern globalized world possible. The quantity of goods carried by containers soared from 102 million metric tons in 1980 to about 1.83 billion metric tons as of 2017. Most of the containerized traffic flows across the Pacific Ocean or between Europe and Asia – usually through the Suez Canal.

Ships get huge The standardization of container sizes has also led to a surge in ship size. [...] In fact, the average size of a container ship has doubled in the past 20 years alone. The largest ships sailing today are capable of hauling 24,000 containers [...].

8 **appliances** devices
9 **commodities** goods
10 **hull** body of a ship
12 **to snarl** *ins (Verkehrs-) Chaos stürzen*
18 **boxcar** *Güterwagen*
24 **seamless** smooth
30 **to soar** *here:* to dramatically increase
34 **surge** increase

Cost of success But the growing size of ships has a cost, as the Ever Given's predicament showed. Maritime shipping has grown increasingly important to global supply chains and trade, yet it was rather invisible until the recent logjam and blockage of the Suez Canal. As the Ever Given was traversing the narrow 120-mile canal, fierce wind gusts blew it to the bank, and its 200,000 tons of weight got it stuck in the muck.

About 12 % of the world's global shipping traffic passes through this canal. The blockage had, at one point, at least 369 ships stuck waiting to pass through the canal from either side, costing an estimated $9.6 billion a day. That translates to $400 million an hour, or $6.7 million a minute.

Ship-building companies continue to work on building ever-larger container vessels, and there's little evidence this trend will stop anytime soon. Some forecast that ships capable of carrying loads 50 % larger than the Ever Given's will be plying the open seas by 2030.

In other words, the standardized shipping container remains more popular – and in demand – than ever.

Anna Nagurney, in: *The Conversation*, 2021

[38] **predicament** dilemma
[39] **logjam** block
[40] **to traverse** to cross
[47] **vessels** ships
[48] **to ply** to go back and forth

1 COMPREHENSION Outline the importance of the shipping industry to the global economy as well as the advantages of shipping containers. → S5, 8

2 EVALUATION
a) Assess the risks that come from shipping industry's central role in global economics.
b) Give examples of problems caused by the shipping industry which ordinary people (could) notice in their everyday lives.
c) Find the Suez Canal on a map. Assess why the Suez Canal has been one of the most politically sensitive places in the world for many decades.

V17 **3 VIEWING**
a) Sum up the problem and the solution that the video presents.
b) Explain the significance of these numbers, symbols and dates.

9 billion • 3% • $H_2 + H_2 + O_2 \rightarrow 2H_2O$ • 2017 • CH_4 • 6th

c) Outline the pros and cons of hydrogen fuel cells for powering ships.
d) Think of political reasons why continuing to use fossil fuels in the shipping industry may continue for a long time before greener alternatives become the norm.

4 ACROSS CULTURES Container ships typically have international crews, but poor command of English, stereotyping crew members, and different attitudes towards work or safety can make working together complicated. What could be done to improve the team spirit at sea and lower the risk of misunderstanding each other? Agree on three strategies and present your findings.

A7-8 **5 LISTENING** → ● 4 → S34
a) Listen to the first part of the podcast "Forward thinking: Globalisation". Take notes on the positive and negative aspects of globalisation mentioned by Kathleen Whitehead.
b) Now listen to the second part of the podcast. Add further aspects to your notes.
c) Listen again to both parts of the podcast and answer the following questions.
1. Why do many global players have a bad image?
2. What have some of the achievements of the UN been so far?
3. Which arguments are given by those who deny a collective spirit of globalisation?
4. How could globalisation become fair according to Kathleen Whitehead?

Is globalisation really doomed?

With the end of the Cold War, there was a widely shared sentiment in the West that the world had reached the End of History: "That is, the end-point of mankind's ideological evolution and the universalization of Western liberal democracy as the final form of human government," according to Francis Fukuyama. This was one of the reasons why WTO members decided to admit China in 2001. The prevailing view in Brussels and Washington, at the time, was that China's WTO membership was bound to transform the country into a Western liberal market economy and democracy. When it became clear [...] that neither would happen soon, there was huge disappointment in many capitals. In Washington there has also been fear that, having already become the world's largest exporter of goods and perhaps soon the economy with the largest GDP, China is fast becoming a major geopolitical rival.

Against this background, the dependency of the United States on imports from China, and of China on exports to the United States, led the two rivals to adopt measures to curtail their bilateral trade after the Great Recession [...]. The COVID-19 pandemic was a further reason for many economies, including the European Union, to adopt measures to gain 'strategic autonomy' and to reshore production, mainly from China. The final nail in the coffin of hyperglobalisation was Russia's invasion of Ukraine, which has reinforced the voices of those claiming that trade dependency on economies with illiberal political regimes had gone too far and that near- or friend-shoring is essential.

Similar calls for self-reliance abound in China, where President Xi believes that his country has become too reliant on liberal democracies as markets for its exports and suppliers for crucial inputs. All this may or may not qualify as deglobalisation, but it certainly sounds like partial decoupling. [...]

A healthy domestic social contract is essential in general, and to sustain globalisation in particular. But fears are increasing that in countries where the domestic social contract is lacking, policy will deliver protectionism rather than improved social policies. If this happens, deglobalisation will not reverse the trend towards greater income and wealth inequality seen in many advanced countries, though more in the United States than in Europe, during the relatively short period of hyperglobalisation. Instead, by decreasing international competition, deglobalisation risks worsening the plight of workers through lower labour productivity and higher prices for some of the goods they consume.

Those who genuinely seek better social protection for workers – to better withstand not only globalisation but also the digital and climate transitions – would do well to remember that this will require better social policies rather than restrictive trade policies.

André Sapir, *Bruegel* website, 2022

1 **the Cold War** period of hostility and tension between the Soviet bloc and the Western countries (ca. 1947–1991)
4 **Francis Fukuyama** American political scientist and writer
14 **to curtail** to reduce
14 **Great Recession** period of worldwide economic decline 2007–2009
21 **to abound** to exist in large numbers
32 **plight** a bad or difficult situation
34 **to withstand** to cope with

MK **6** VOCABULARY Find definitions for the marked words and phrases in the text. Use digital tools for help, e.g. a (specialised) dictionary or thesaurus. When using a search engine, always cross-check your results with other sources. → S2

7 COMPREHENSION Take notes on the following points as mentioned in the text:
1. the hopes of the Western countries in the WTO after the Cold War (ll. 1–11)
2. the reasons for the trend towards "deglobalisation" and "decoupling" (ll. 12–24)
3. the risks of deglobalisation if social policies are neglected (ll. 25–37)

MK **8** EVALUATION Do research on possible social policy measures and comment on the author's view that "a healthy social contract" rather than protectionism will help to ameliorate the negative effects of globalisation on workers. → S3, 19

Vom Manufacturing Belt zum Rust Belt

9 MEDIATION For his English class, your younger brother has to write a reference article about the Rust Belt. He found the following article and asks you for help. Make an outline in English for him, explaining which regions play a major role for the US economy, how their importance has changed and how the Rust Belt got its name. → S39 → WB 63/1–3

Schon seit dem Zweiten Weltkrieg durchlaufen die USA einen Wandel von der Industrie- zur Dienstleistungsgesellschaft. Doch in Kombination mit der intensivierten Globalisierung und Digitalisierung führt diese Entwicklung seit den 1980er-Jahren verstärkt zu ökonomischen Ungleichheiten – mit großen regionalen Unterschieden.

[...] Im Zuge der industriellen Revolution nahm in den USA seit Ende des 19. Jahrhunderts zunächst die Bedeutung der Landwirtschaft stetig zu Gunsten der verarbeitenden Industrie ab. Bis in die 1970er-Jahre dominierte dieser Sekundärsektor die Wirtschaftsstruktur, und seitdem gewannen zunehmend Dienstleistungen, der sogenannte tertiäre Sektor, an Bedeutung. Diese Verschiebungen hatten weitreichende Auswirkungen auf die räumliche Verteilung wirtschaftlicher Aktivität innerhalb der USA. Während der *Manufacturing Belt* (deutsch etwa: Produktionsgürtel) im Nordosten zum *Rust Belt* (Rostgürtel) wurde, erstarkten der *Sun Belt*, ein Großraum vom Südwesten bis zum Südosten des Landes, und die Metropolregionen. [...]

Knapp 100 Jahre konzentrierte sich die wirtschaftliche Aktivität in den USA vor allem im Nordwesten und Mittleren Westen des Landes, dem sogenannten *Manufacturing Belt*. Um 1900 wurden vier Fünftel des gesamten industriellen Bruttoinlandsprodukts (BIP) der USA in dieser Region produziert, auch wenn der *Manufacturing Belt* nur ein Sechstel der gesamten Landfläche der USA ausmachte und nur etwas über die Hälfte der gesamten Bevölkerung dort lebten. Ursächlich für die Ansiedelung der Industrie in diesem Gebiet war das Vorkommen natürlicher Ressourcen, wie Kohle und Eisenerz. [...]

Im Laufe der 1970er-Jahre wurden Investitionen allerdings größtenteils außerhalb des *Manufacturing Belts* getätigt. Die Stahlkrise, die Binnenmarktsättigung und eine zunehmende Konkurrenz aus dem Ausland ließen den traditionellen ökonomischen Kernraum immer mehr an Bedeutung verlieren. Dem Stilllegen großer Anlagen der Schwerindustrie folgte zunehmend die Schließung weiterer Unternehmen und der *Manufacturing Belt* wurde schließlich zum *Rust Belt* (Rostgürtel), benannt nach dem Rost, der sich an den verlassenen Fabriken ansammelte. Verstärkt wurde diese abnehmende wirtschaftliche Bedeutung der Region durch die zweite Welle der Globalisierung seit den 1980er-Jahren. Das weltweite Exportvolumen hat sich von 1980 bis 2021 nahezu verzehnfacht (UNCTAD 2021). Die lange den Welthandel dominierenden Mitgliedsstaaten der Organisation für wirtschaftliche Zusammenarbeit und Entwicklung (OECD) begannen verstärkt mit großen Schwellenländern wie China, Indien, Brasilien und Russland zu handeln, welche ein besonders niedriges Lohnniveau aufwiesen. [...]

Regionale Ungleichheiten innerhalb der Länder steigen seit den 1990er-Jahren wieder an. Der Handel mit China hat Schätzungen zufolge zu einem Verlust von nahezu 2,7 Millionen Jobs in den USA geführt. 2,1 Millionen dieser Jobs gingen zu Lasten von US-Beschäftigten in der Industrie. Auch wenn die Zahlen für die USA insgesamt relativ klein sind, so sind sie durch ihre räumliche Konzentration sehr gewichtig. [...]

Die daraus resultierenden regionalen Ungleichheiten führten auch zu einem Erstarken des Populismus. Dies spiegelte sich im Brexit-Votum in Großbritannien 2016, bei der Wahl von Donald Trump zum US-Präsidenten 2016, den Französischen Präsidentschaftswahlen 2017 oder der Deutschen Bundestagswahl 2017 wider.

Prof. Dr. Julia Püschel, Website *Bundeszentrale für politische Bildung*, 2021

26 **UNCTAD** United Nations Conference on Trade and Development

'Take back control'? With this Pacific trade deal, Brexit Britain has just signed it away

Goodbye, food standards. Hello, corporate lobbyists. Why are we doing this, for no real economic benefit?

Last night [30 March 2023], the government announced that Britain has joined a trade deal [...]. While hardcore Brexiters would like to pretend this is the ultimate payoff of our decision to leave the EU and write our own rules, the reality is somewhat different. In signing the Comprehensive and Progressive Agreement for Trans-Pacific Partnership (CPTPP), Britain has ditched environmental standards, signed up to terms that will undermine British farmers, and left us open to being sued by multinational corporations in secretive courts. And all for no real economic benefit. [...]

The most pressing issue reported from the talks is that Britain has been forced to lower environmental standards as a condition for entry to the deal. Palm oil plantations in Malaysia are a driver of deforestation, threatening biodiversity including the survival of orangutan populations. European tariffs on palm oil aim to stop deforestation, but the UK is understood to have agreed to scrap the tariffs as a condition for entry into the Pacific deal, in effect reneging on deforestation pledges made at the UN climate conference in Glasgow.

But it gets worse, because the Pacific trade deal isn't a one-time set of rules, but rather gives corporate lobbyists permanent power to force governments to lower standards over time. The whole point of the CPTPP is to get countries to recognise standards as equivalent to each other – and to accept imports even where there are real differences in standards.

Britain still endorses the precautionary principle, which places the burden of proof on the producer of a product to demonstrate that it is safe. Most signatories to the Pacific trade deal do not, and there will be inevitable pressure to accept food containing pesticides that have been outlawed here, antibiotics in livestock farming or hormone-treated beef. [...]

And all of this in the absence of evidence that the deal will boost jobs or growth. By the government's own estimates, the deal will add a mere 0.08% of GDP after running for about 10 years – a number so small as to be meaningless in the uncertain world of economic predictions. [...]

In order to prove we've taken back control, we are, in reality, relinquishing it as quickly as possible. [...]

Nick Dearden, in: *The Guardian*, 2023

10 VOCABULARY Find expressions in the text with the same meanings (some have more than one match). Use online resources to cross-check your solutions.

to abandon • to abolish • to break • certain to happen • condition • to give up • only • a promise • a representative of a big company • reward • to support • to take legal action against sb • a tax on imports • to weaken • without

11 COMPREHENSION | ANALYSIS

a) Choose the main topics in the text from the following list. → S8

A Britain signing the CPTPP • **B** the history of the CPTPP • **C** climate change • **D** the concessions Britain has to make to join the CPTPP • **E** sustainable farming methods • **F** Brexit effects • **G** economic growth in Britain

b) Examine the title, the introduction and the conclusion of the article to sum up the author's main point. State what arguments he uses to make his point. → S10

B A greener world?

The toxic effects of electronic waste in Accra, Ghana

Sorting through used electronics is a livelihood for many in the Agbogbloshie area, but toxic e-waste poses serious health risks.

Heavy, acidic gusts of smoke billow across the Agbogbloshie dump, a wasteland dotted with burning mounds of trash in Ghana's capital, Accra. Up to 10,000 workers wade through tons of discarded goods as part of an enormous, informal recycling process, in what has become one of the world's largest destinations for used electronic goods.

Burns, back problems, and infected wounds are common ailments among these workers, as well as respiratory problems, chronic nausea, and debilitating headaches – brought on by the hazardous working environment and toxic air pollution.

"When I was a small boy, I used to be a footballer – but not anymore," said Abdullah Boubacar, a 28-year-old who moved to Accra from the northern Ghana town of Tamale in 2008. "I have stomach ulcers and I run out of energy very easily." Boubacar spends his days smashing up old computers and televisions in search of valuable parts and burning insulated cables to recover copper.

The Agbogbloshie dump is a result of the world's increasing demand for electronic equipment as consumers continually upgrade their devices and throw out the older ones. A significant proportion of this electronic waste is sent, often illegally, from the West to developing countries across Africa and Asia.

Around 50 million tons of electronic waste, or e-waste, is being thrown away each year, according to a report published this year by the United Nations. That figure is projected to double by 2050. At the same time, only 20 percent of e-waste is thought to be recycled appropriately. The rest "ends up in landfill, or is disposed of by informal workers in poor conditions," the UN found. [...]

In total, about 80,000 men, women, and children subsist from the Agbogbloshie dump, living either on-site or in the adjacent slum. [...]

Abdrahaman Daouda, 34, came to Agbogbloshie from Niger two years ago. "Unemployment was so bad, my father was embarrassed for me," he said. "So I left my country."

Some days, Daouda earns up to 40 Ghanaian cedis ($7.50) collecting used water sachets or scrap metal, but on others he earns nothing at all. [...] He hopes to save enough money to buy his own taxi one day. [...]

There are signs that some countries are beginning to acknowledge this responsibility. The German development agency GIZ is in the midst of delivering a €5 million ($5.5 million) project to build a sustainable, efficient recycling system at Agbogbloshie, as well as a health clinic and football pitch for workers.

Peter Yeung, in: *Bloomberg*, 2019

1 **acidic** *säurehaltig*
2 **mound** hill
3 **to discard** to throw away
5 **wound** injury
5 **ailment** illness
6 **respiratory** breathing
6 **nausea** vomiting
6 **debilitating** weakening
10 **stomach ulcer** *Magengeschwür*
12 **to insulate** to cover
12 **copper** *Kupfer*
20 **to dispose of** to throw away
22 **to subsist** to survive
23 **adjacent** next to sth
28 **sachet** small bag

1 COMPREHENSION

a) Sum up daily life for workers at the Agbogbloshie dump.
b) Outline the reasons why places like the Agbogbloshie dump exist. → S8

2 ANALYSIS Comment on how stylistic devices influence the article's effect. → ○ 5

3 EVALUATION

a) Explain what is being done to solve this issue according to the article. Do you think the measures are helpful? If so, why?
b) Collect ideas about what people in developed countries can do to help with the global e-waste issue.

4 CREATIVE TASK Write a letter to the editor to voice your opinion on e-waste dumps. Appeal for change by suggesting a solution. → S21

5 MK SPEAKING Different solutions counteract the huge amount of e-waste. Research and evaluate one of them and present your findings to the class. → WB 26/3

> extracting valuable metals from e-waste • refurbishing and reselling used electronic items • campaigning for the 'right to repair' • lobbying for companies to use more recycled materials • offering a recycling service • publishing tips about how to make electronic items last longer • making sculptures from e-waste • …

Five reasons to invest in African green energy in 2022

Abundantly blessed with a variety of natural resources, the African continent is eager to tap into its significant renewable energy potential in a bid to expand energy access, meet rising global demand, and drive economic growth, while at the same time addressing the fundamental challenges of climate change. Accordingly, Africa has risen to the forefront of the global investment agenda, with several overarching reasons motivating green investment across the continent.

Multi-sector opportunities: Africa is considered the most opportune market for renewable energy, with current estimates placing solar at 10TW; hydro at 350GW; and wind at 110GW. [...] Much of Africa's resources remain largely untapped, offering lucrative opportunities for investors. [...]

Demonstrated political will: Recognizing the role that renewable energy will play in mitigating climate change while boosting socioeconomic growth, many African countries have put in place clear green energy development targets. [...]

High demand for energy: Africa's energy crisis continues to serve as a direct inhibitor to economic growth. Currently, over 600 million people lack access to electricity while over 900 million people lack access to clean cooking fuels. Electrification, particularly in rural areas, has in turn become a priority for many African governments whereby significant levels of investment are required. [...]

Scalability and deliverability: [...] The potential for micro- and off-grid renewable systems in Africa is immense. [...] Low-cost energy derived from hydro, solar and wind is considered the best method to power isolated communities, enabling governments and private sector players to deliver affordable, viable, and sustainable energy.

Significant economic potential: [...] Africa's young, vibrant population, and significant economic potential has made it an attractive prospect for foreign investors. Political and economic reforms, new intra-African trade agreements, and the creation of enabling environments continue to attract major players from across the world and within multiple industries.

Charné Hollands, *Energy Capital & Power* website, 2022

2 **to tap into** to use
2 **bid** offer
5 **overarching** *übergreifend*
7 **opportune** with opportunities
8 **TW** terawatt
8 **GW** gigawatt
12 **to mitigate** to make less bad
15 **inhibitor** block, disadvantage
19 **scalability** ability to change in size
19 **off-grid** *abgekoppelt vom Versorgungsnetz*
22 **viable** practical, profitable
25 **intra-** within

6 ANALYSIS → ○ 6

a) Why is Africa "at the forefront of the global investment agenda" (l. 5)?

b) Assess what type of reader the text is aimed at. Give examples of the language and stylistic devices that tell you this. → S11

c) Comment on the way that the information is organised and presented. How effective is the form? → S10

7 EVALUATION → ● 7

a) Explain benefits for the whole world of developing green energy in Africa.

b) Guess reasons why Africa may not have been so attractive to international investors in the past.

Globalisierung gerecht gestalten

8 MEDIATION

a) You are representing Germany in an international "Model UN" workshop, where a debate is on the agenda: "Globalisation has made the world more equal". To prepare, take notes on the central ideas of this speech by the former German federal minister for economic cooperation and development, Dr Gerd Müller, and write prompt cards. → S39

b) Prepare more arguments for each side of the motion. Hold the debate. → S32

Dr. Gerd Müller thematisiert Vor- und Nachteile der Globalisierung und gibt seine Antwort auf die Frage, wie Globalisierung zukunftsfähig und gerecht gestaltet werden kann.

Erstens, die Grundlage: Globaler Markt braucht globale Regeln. Freihandel darf keine Einladung sein, die Zukunft kommender Generationen oder der Menschen anderswo aufs Spiel zu setzen! Die Politik muss den Rahmen für Fairness und Nachhaltigkeit setzen. [...] Wir brauchen eine öko-soziale Marktwirtschaft weltweit. Standards für Menschenrechte, Umwelt und Arbeit müssen weltweit umgesetzt werden! Wir müssen Nachhaltigkeit leben – sozial, ökologisch, wirtschaftlich und kulturell. Dafür braucht es starke internationale Organisationen. [...]

Zweitens: Globalisierung muss Ressourcen schonen. Der Konsum hat sich in den letzten 50 Jahren verzehnfacht. Unser Lebensstil in den westlichen Ländern verbraucht Ressourcen von 1,7 Planeten. Das geht nur, weil die Menschen in Afrika und Indien weniger verbrauchen. Wir leben auf Kosten der Menschen in anderen Teilen der Welt! Und auf Kosten kommender Generationen.

Es muss Schluss sein mit der Externalisierung! Wir brauchen Wahrheit bei den Preisen! Wir brauchen ein Wachstumsdenken, das Umwelt- und Ressourcenverbrauch einrechnet, eine wirksame CO_2-Steuer. Die Folgen von Abgasen, giftigen Chemikalien und Treibhausgasen in der Produktion tauchen auf keinem Preisschild auf. Aber Naturverbrauch darf es nicht gratis geben! Globale öffentliche Güter wie Luft, Wasser und Klima müssen geschützt werden.

Wir brauchen drittens ein neues Wachstumsmodell. Ein Wachstumsmodell, das sich am Welt-Gemeinwohl orientiert, statt an einem neo-liberalen Wirtschaftssystem! Wir werden jedes Jahr 80 Millionen Menschen mehr. Was ist unsere Empfehlung an Afrika oder Indien? Sollen wir sagen: Macht es wie wir?

Wir brauchen Steuersysteme, die global greifen, die Fairness und Nachhaltigkeit fördern – wie eine Finanztransaktionssteuer oder eine Digitalsteuer. Und wir brauchen mehr Teilhabe: Vor allem Frauen müssen mehr profitieren.

Werte müssen zum Fundament unseres Lebens und Tuns werden: Wir müssen Verantwortung gegenüber kommenden Generationen und für den Erhalt der Schöpfung übernehmen.

Was kann Entwicklungspolitik dafür tun? Wir müssen Entwicklung ermöglichen und gleichzeitig die Schöpfung erhalten. Wir fördern saubere Energie von Anfang an. 70 Länder haben nach deutschem Vorbild eine Einspeisevergütung eingeführt – das ist die Welt-Energiewende! Wir setzen uns ein für faire globale Lieferketten. Das Textilbündnis ist ein Schritt in die richtige Richtung. Notfalls brauchen wir gesetzliche Regelungen! [...]

Aber auch Konsumenten tragen Verantwortung! Greifen Sie nicht immer nach dem Billigsten, sondern achten Sie auf Langlebigkeit und Recyclingfähigkeit. [...] Politik muss Regeln für gerechte und nachhaltige Globalisierung setzen. Aber die Öffentlichkeit muss auch bereit sein, sie mitzutragen. Globalisierung ist eine Chance, wenn sie einen Interessenausgleich schafft: zwischen Starken und Schwachen, zwischen Markt und Menschen, zwischen Profit und Gemeinwohl.

Bundesministerium für wirtschaftliche Zusammenarbeit und Entwicklung, 27.11.2018

C Say it in English

Decolonising the mind

VIP FILE

Ngũgĩ wa Thiong'o (born 1938), the first East African author to publish a novel in English (1964) and write the first novel in Gikuyu, fled Kenya in 1978 and became a professor of literature, teaching at several US universities. *Decolonising the mind*, his 1986 essay, has become a classic. Since 1978, all of his creative literary works have been written in Gikuyu.

I was born into a large peasant family: father, four wives and about twenty-eight children. I also belonged, as we all did in those days, to a wider extended family and to the community as a whole. We spoke Gi kuyH as we worked in the fields. We spoke Gi kttyu in and outside the home. I can vividly recall those evenings of storytelling around the fireside. It was mostly the grown-ups telling the children but everybody was interested and involved. We children would re-tell the stories the following day to other children who worked in the fields picking the pyrethrum flowers, tea-leaves or coffee beans of our European and African landlords.

The stories, with mostly animals as the main characters, were all told in Gi kuy U. Hare, being small, weak but full of innovative wit and cunning, was our hero. We identified with him as he struggled against the brutes of prey like lion, leopard, hyena. His victories were our victories and we learnt that the apparently weak can outwit the strong. We followed the animals in their struggle against hostile nature – drought, rain, sun, wind – a confrontation often forcing them to search for forms of co-operation. But we were also interested in their struggles amongst themselves, and particularly between the beasts and the victims of prey. These twin struggles, against nature and other animals, reflected real-life struggles in the human world. [...]

The language, through images and symbols, gave us a view of the world, but it had a beauty of its own. The home and the field were then our pre-primary school but what is important, for this discussion, is that the language of our evening teach-ins, and the language of our immediate and wider community, and the language of our work in the fields were one. [...]

FACT FILE

The colonisation of Kenya Colonialism in Kenya began in 1895, when Britain established the East Africa Protectorate, known as the Kenyan Colony from 1920. English became one of the two official languages and also the language of instruction in schools. When the 'Mau Mau rebellion' against the British regime started in 1952, a state of emergency was declared. The fighting went on for years. Kenya finally became independent in 1963.

It was after the declaration of a state of emergency over Kenya in 1952 that all the schools run by patriotic nationalists were taken over by the colonial regime and were placed under District Education Boards chaired by Englishmen. English became the language of my formal education. In Kenya, English became more than a language: it was Slanguage, and all the others had to bow before it in deference.

Thus one of the most humiliating experiences was to be caught speaking GikuyU in the vicinity of the school. The culprit was given corporal punishment – three to five strokes of the cane on bare buttocks – or was made to carry a metal plate around the neck with inscriptions such as I AM STUPID or I AM A DONKEY. Sometimes the culprits were fined money they could hardly afford. [...]

2 **extended family** aunts, uncles, cousins, grandparents etc.
3 **Gi kuyH, Gi kttyu *and* Gi kuy U** Gikuyu language variants in Kenya
7 **pyrethrum** flowers used to make insecticide
10 **hare** a large, fast-running wild rabbit
10 **wit** skill with words and jokes
10 **cunning** cleverness in planning tricks
11 **brutes of prey** animals hunting and killing other animals for food
13 **hostile** unfriendly
20 **teach-in** a meeting to share information on important issues
27 **to bow in deference before sth** *sich vor etw. in Ehrerbietung verneigen*
28 **humiliating** embarrassing, shameful
29 **in the vicinity of** near to
29 **culprit** *der / die Schuldige*
30 **cane** stick
30 **buttocks** *Hintern*

The attitude to English was the exact opposite: any achievement in spoken or written English was highly rewarded; prizes, prestige, applause; the ticket to higher realms. English became the measure of intelligence and ability in the arts, the sciences and all the other branches of learning. English became the main determinant of a child's progress up the ladder of formal education. [...]

Selections from primary into secondary were through an examination, in my time called Kenya African Preliminary Examination, in which one had to pass six subjects ranging from Maths to Nature Study and Kiswahili. All the papers were written in English. Nobody could pass the exam who failed the English language paper no matter how brilliantly he had done in the other subjects. I remember one boy in my class of 1954 who had distinctions in all subjects except English, which he had failed. He was made to fail the entire exam. He went on to become a turn boy in a bus company. I who had only passes but a credit in English got a place at the Alliance High School, one of the most elitist institutions for Africans in colonial Kenya. The requirements for a place at the University, Makerere University College, were broadly the same: nobody could go on to wear the undergraduate red gown, no matter how brilliantly they had performed in all the other subjects unless they had a credit – not even a simple pass – in English. Thus the most coveted place in the pyramid and in the system was only available to the holder of an English language credit card. [...]

Literary education was now determined by the dominant language while also reinforcing that dominance. Orature (oral literature) in Kenyan languages stopped. [...] Thus language and literature were taking us further and further from ourselves to other selves, from our world to other worlds. [...]

For colonialism this involved two aspects of the same process: the destruction or the deliberate undervaluing of a people's culture, their art, dances, religions, history, geography, education, orature and literature, and the conscious elevation of the language of the coloniser. [...] But since the new, imposed languages could never completely break the native languages as spoken, their most effective area of domination was the third aspect of language as communication, the written. The language of an African child's formal education was foreign. The language of the books he read was foreign. The language of his conceptualisation was foreign. Thought, in him, took the visible form of a foreign language. [...]

There was often not the slightest relationship between the child's written world, which was also the language of his schooling, and the world of his immediate environment in the family and the community. [...] This resulted in the disassociation of the sensibility of that child from his natural and social environment, what we might call colonial alienation. The alienation became reinforced in the teaching of history, geography, music, where bourgeois Europe was always the centre of the universe.

This disassociation, divorce, or alienation from the immediate environment becomes clearer when you look at colonial language as a carrier of culture. Since culture is a product of the history of a people which it in turn reflects, the child was now being exposed exclusively to a culture that was a product of a world external to himself. [...] The images of his world and his place in it implanted in a child take years to eradicate, if they ever can be.

From: Ngũgĩ wa Thiong'o, *Decolonising the Mind*, 1986

35 **realm** area of power, activity or influence
36 **determinant** sth that controls or affects what happens
43 **distinction** an excellent grade
44 **turn boy** an assistant to the driver of public transport
45 **pass** the lowest successful grade
48 **gown** university students' long, formal clothing
50 **to covet** to want to have sth very much
57 **deliberate** intentional
57 **to undervalue** to consider sth as less important than it actually is
63 **conceptualisation** forming an idea or principle in your mind
68 **sensibility** the ability to feel and react to sth
69 **alienation** *Entfremdung*
69 **to reinforce** make sth stronger
70 **bourgeois** middle-class
74 **to expose sb to sth** *jmdm. etwas aussetzen*
76 **to eradicate sth** to get rid of sth, eliminate sth

1 COMPREHENSION | ANALYSIS

a) Outline the writer's view on English as the language of education in Kenya.

b) Contrast the roles of the different languages in the author's life.

c) Analyse the stylistic devices used for persuasion. Explain their effect. → ○ 8, ● 9

A9 **2 LISTENING** Listen to David Crystal talking about World Englishes. Explain why he uses the plural and how and why "the Englishes differ". → S34

Can English remain the 'world's favourite' language? → WB 27–28/4–8

In the Hispanic neighborhood of Santa Ana, California

About 1.5 billion people around the world speak it – but fewer than 400 million have it as their first language. [...] English is the world's favourite lingua franca – the language people are most likely to turn to when they don't share a first language. [...]

Five years ago, perhaps. But not any more. Thanks to advances in computer translation and voice-recognition technology, they can each speak their own language, and hear what their interlocutor is saying, machine-translated in real time. [...]

In California, Wonkyum Lee, a South Korean computer scientist for Gridspace, is helping to develop translation and voice-recognition technology that will be so good that when you call a customer service helpline, you won't know whether you're talking to a human or a computer. [...]

But this is not the only challenge English is facing. Because so many people speak it as their second or third language, hybrid forms are spreading, combining elements of "standard" English with vernacular languages. In India alone, you can find Hinglish (Hindi-English), Benglish (Bengali-English) and Tanglish (Tamil-English). In the US, many Hispanic Americans, with their roots in Central and South America, speak Spanglish, combining elements from English and the language of their parents and grandparents. [...]

English owes its global dominance to being the language of what until recently were two of the world's most powerful nations: the US and the UK. But now, especially with the rise of China as an economic superpower, the language is being challenged. If you are an ambitious young jobseeker in sub-Saharan Africa, you might be better off learning Mandarin Chinese and looking for work in China than relying on your school-level English and hoping for a job in the US or UK. [...]

In Uganda, however, all secondary schools must conduct classes entirely in English, and some parents teach their young children English as their first language. In many parts of the world, English is still regarded as a passport to success.

So is the future of English at risk? I don't think so, although its global dominance may well diminish over the coming decades. [...] But I continue to count myself immensely fortunate to have been born in a country where I can cherish and call my own the language of Chaucer, Shakespeare, Milton and Dickens, even though the language I call English is very different from theirs.

Robin Lustig, *BBC* website, 2018

6 **interlocutor** partner in conversation
13 **vernacular** dialectal
18 **to owe sth to sb** to have success only because of what sb has done
29 **to cherish** to adore, to love

3 COMPREHENSION | ANALYSIS → ○ 10

a) Outline the reasons why English may no longer be the "'world's favourite' language".
b) Analyse the language and style used in the text and the author's opinion on English as a global language. → S9–11

4 EVALUATION Discuss the pros and cons of translation software in today's world. → S18

A 10 **5** LISTENING

a) Listen to "The language called Globish" and take notes on its features. → ○ 11
b) Guess which of these words are included in Globish and explain why.

informed • agree • antsy • brother • converse • hell • opposite • please • quid • sincerely • shrinkable • thirsty • unusual • zebra

c) Discuss whether it is possible to have a "language without culture". → ○ 12

A 11 **6** LISTENING Listen to the extract from Robin Lustig's podcasts "From Language to Algorithm" and "Too Much English?". Take notes to prepare a short report on the impact of new technology on the future of English and its status as a lingua franca.

D Mixing languages and cultures

1 BEFORE YOU START Talk about your experience with different cultures or languages. What have you noticed? Do you have a funny anecdote where there has been a misunderstanding due to different cultures / languages?

Native speaker → WB 62/1–3

VIP FILE

Chang-Rae Lee (born 1965) is a Korean-American novelist and professor. Growing up in the US with Korean parents has led him to write about issues concerning his Asian-American experience such as the challenges of racism, the encounter of diverse cultures, or what it means to be American.

Henry Park, the main character, grew up in America with Korean parents. The following three excerpts highlight his struggle to fit into either culture as well as the role language has played in his everyday life as a child and as an adult. In the first part, Henry discusses his supposed accent with his wife, Lelia, who is an English teacher for students with other native languages.

A We sat on a bench among the sleepers. It was a clear night, the moon, a few high clouds. I'd given her my suit jacket. Some others were awake, talking and drinking like us. I heard them speaking Spanish, and I heard English, and then something else that Lelia said was called *mixup*. Its music was sonorous, rambling, some of the turns unexpected and lovely. Everywhere you heard versions.

"People like me are always thinking about still having an accent," I said, trying to remember the operation of the salt, the liquor, the lime.

"I can tell," she said.

I asked her how.

"You speak perfectly, of course. I mean if we were talking on the phone I wouldn't think twice."

"You mean it's my face."

"No, it's not that," she answered. She reached over as if to touch my cheek but rested her arm instead on the bench back, grazing my neck. "Your face is part of the equation, but not in the way you're thinking. You look like someone listening to himself. You pay attention to what you're doing. If I had to guess, you're not a native speaker. Say something."

"What should I say?"

"Say my name."

"Lelia," I said. "Lelia."

"See? You said *Leel-ya* so deliberately. You tried not to but you were taking in the sound of the syllables. You're very careful."

"So are you."

She took a sip from the cup. "It's my job, Mr. Henry Park. Unfortunately, I'm the standard-bearer."

Henry's father owned a small chain of grocery stores around the city and always worked. Unfortunately, his mother died when Henry was 10 years old, so things had to change.

B He started speaking, but in English. Sometimes, when he wanted to hide or not outright lie, he chose to speak in English. He used to break into it when he argued with my mother, and it drove her crazy when he did and she would just plead, "No, no!" as though he had suddenly introduced a switchblade into a clean fistfight. Once, when he

[4] **sonorous** vibrant
[4] **rambling** on-going
[14] **to graze** to lightly touch
[14] **equation** calculation
[25] **standard-bearer** overseer, leader
[27] **outright** straight
[29] **switchblade** pocketknife
[29] **fistfight** *Faustkampf*

[30] **to berate** to reprimand *(beschimpfen)*
[32] **cowardice** ↔ courage
[37] **to hurl** to throw
[38] **to whack** to hit
[40] **to dress down** *(infml)* to reprimand *(anschnauzen)*

was having some money problems with a store, he started berating her with some awful stream of nonsensical street talk [...]. I broke into their argument and started yelling at him, making sure I was speaking in complete sentences about his cowardice and unfairness, shooting back at him his own medicine, until he slammed both palms on the table and demanded, "You shut up! You shut up!"

I kept at him anyway, using the biggest words I knew, whether they made sense or not, school words like "socioeconomic" and "intangible," anything I could lift from my dizzy burning thoughts and hurl against him, until my mother, who'd been perfectly quiet the whole time, whacked me hard across the back of the head and shouted in Korean, *Who do you think you are?*

Fair fight or not, she wasn't going to let me dress down my father, not with language, not with anything.

"Hen-*ry*," he now said, accenting as always the second syllable, "you know, it's difficult now. Your mommy dead and nobody at home. You too young for that. This nice lady, she come for you. Take care home, food. Nice dinner. Clean house. Better that way."

I didn't answer him.

"I better tell you before, I know, but I know you don't like. So what I do? I go to store in morning and come home late, nine o'clock, ten. No good, no good. Nice lady, she fix that. And soon we move to nice neighborhood, over near Fern Pond, big house and yard. Very nice place."

"Fern Pond? I don't want to move! And I don't want to move there, all the rich kids live there."

"Ha!" he laughed. "You rich kid now, your daddy rich rich man. Big house, big tree, now even we got houselady. Nice big yard for you. I pay all cash."

"What? You bought a house already?"

"Price very low for big house. Fix-her-upper. You thank me someday ..."

"I won't. I won't move. No way."

Byong-ho, he said firmly. His voice was already changing. He was shifting into Korean, getting his throat ready. Then he spoke as he rose to leave. *Let's not hear one more thing about it. The woman will come with us to the new house and take care of you. This is what I have decided.*

Learning English proved to be a challenge for Henry growing up.

[62] **Peanut Butter Shelley** reference to Percy Bysshe Shelley, English Romantic poet
[64] **realm** domain
[67] **booby trap** *(Stolper-)Falle*
[68] **scabrous** shocking
[71] **to torture** *foltern*
[75] **to fumble** to screw up, *patzen*
[78] **to conflate** to mix up
[79] **to conflagrate** to set on fire
[79] **friction** *Reibung*
[80] **affliction** defect

C Peanut Butter Shelley, I'd murmur beneath my breath, unable to remember all the poet's womanly names. It was my first year of school, my first days away from the private realm of our house and tongue. I thought English would be simply a version of our Korean. Like another kind of coat you could wear. I didn't know what a difference in language meant then. Or how my tongue would tie in the initial attempts, stiffen so, struggle like an animal booby-trapped and dying inside my head. Native speakers may not fully know this, but English is a scabrous mouthful. In Korean, there are no separate sounds for L and R, the sound is singular and without a baroque Spanish trill or roll. There is no B and V for us, no P and F. I always thought someone must have invented certain words to torture us. *Frivolous. Barbarian.* I remember my father saying, Your eyes all *led*, staring at me after I'd smoked pot the first time, and I went to my room and laughed until I wept.

I will always make bad errors of speech. I remind myself of my mother and father, fumbling in front of strangers. Lelia says there are certain mental pathways of speaking that can never be unlearned. Sometimes I'll still say *riddle* for *little*, or *bent* for *vent*, though without any accent and so whoever's present just thinks I've momentarily lost my train of thought. But I always hear myself displacing the two languages, conflating them – maybe conflagrating them – for there's so much rubbing and friction, a fire always threatens to blow up between the tongues. Friction, affliction. In kindergarten, kids would call me "Marble Mouth" because I spoke in a garbled voice, my bound tongue wrenching itself to move in the right ways.

"Yo, China boy," the older black kids would yell at me across the blacktop, "what you doin' there, practicin'?"

Of course I was. I would rewhisper all the words and sounds I had messed up earlier that morning, trying to invoke how the one girl who always wore a baby-blue cardigan would speak.

"Thus flies foul our fearless night owl," she might say, the words forming so punctiliously on her lips, her head raised and neck straight and her eyes fixed on our teacher. Alice Eckles. I adored and despised her height and beauty and the oniony sheen of her skin. I knew she looked just like her parents – lanky, washed-out, lipless – and that when she spoke to them they answered her in the same even, lowing rhythm of ennui and supremacy she lorded over us.

Alice used to sneer at me when I left our class for my special daily period upstairs. The class was Remedial Speech, and I accepted my own presence there if only because of the very trouble I had pronouncing it. The other students were misfits, they all seemed to have dirty hair and oversized mouths and shrunken foreheads and in my estimation were as dumb as the dead. By association, though, so was I. We were the school retards, the mentals, the losers who stuttered or could explode in rage or wet their pants or who just couldn't say the words.

From: Chang-Rae Lee, *Native Speaker*, 1996

81 **marble** *Murmel*
81 **garbled** mixed up, confused
81 **to bind** to tie
82 **to wrench** *sich zerreißen*
83 **blacktop** asphalt
86 **to invoke** *here:* to remember
89 **punctiliously** formally
93 **ennui** boredom
93 **to lord over** to dominate
95 **remedial** corrective
99 **retard** *(pej)* someone who is considered stupid
99 **mental** *(pej)* someone with a mental illness

2 COMPREHENSION

a) For part A, outline how Henry feels about languages spoken around him and his own English skills. Summarise Lelia's opinion of Henry's English in your own words.

b) Sum up the role English plays in part B for each character as well as in the relationships between (a) Henry's parents, (b) Henry and his mother and (c) Henry and his father.

c) Outline what Henry says in part C about his relationship with English in kindergarten and in his first year at school. Point out which sounds were new to him. Explain why he adores and despises his teacher Alice Eckles at the same time.

3 ANALYSIS

Get together in small groups and choose one part of the text that you want to work with. For your part, do these tasks:

a) Analyse Henry's relationship with English with regard to the challenges he faces and the words used to describe his feelings towards it.

b) Analyse the other characters' relationships with English in comparison to Henry's. Explain how the way they use English and describe the characters' roles in the story. Give quotes from the text. → S4, 13

c) Examine the narrator's perspective and techniques. Focus on communicative strategies, stylistic devices and style used to highlight Henry's difficulties with (part A) fitting in as a native speaker, (part B) using English at home, or (part C) learning English at school.

4 EVALUATION

Interpret how the probably autobiographical text excerpts relate to Chang-Rae Lee's own Asian-American experience regarding language and culture (e.g. feeling non-native, differences in sounds, learning environment, parents' expectations). Find illustrating examples in the text.

5 ACROSS CULTURES

Give your thoughts about the excerpts. Explain how the context in which Henry learns English is different to your experience of learning English. Discuss your own experience of learning a foreign language. → S31

Improving written texts

Globalisation 4.0 or deglobalisation?

Globalisation 4.0 is a new idea. This idea says that we are at the start of a new era of globalisation. Some old ideas about economics will end. New ideas about economics will replace them. There will be big improvements in technology. The world will become more globalised. It will be better for everyone. It will also be better for the environment.

There is a problem with this idea. There have been problems with supply chains in the whole world. These problems have led to the prices of things going up. These problems have led to not enough food. These problems have led to energy prices going up a lot. Reasons for these problems include the COVID-19 pandemic and the war in Ukraine. Some people are saying that there will be less globalisation because of these problems. These people include important business and political leaders. These people think that businesses and governments are going to do things about these problems. These things will 'deglobalise' the world economy.

Many businesses have 'just-in-time' supply chains. This means that they move things they need between countries just before they need them. This could change to a 'just-in-case' system. This means keeping a lot of things that you need. This is in case there are problems with supply chains. Some businesses use factories in faraway countries because it is cheaper. This could change to using factories that are more expensive but much nearer. This could be less risky for economic reasons. It could be less risky for political reasons. It would mean a less globalised economy.

1 Outline problems with the writing style of the text. → S29

2 Write a version that is improved stylistically and makes logical connections regarding these aspects:
- Avoid repeating words and add a good variety of adjectives.
- Make complex sentences and connect ideas by using linking words.
- Make longer sentences by using relative clauses and participle constructions.
- Continue improving it until you have a text which sounds good when you read it aloud.

3

a) Explain the meanings of the loanwords in **bold**. Use a dictionary. Find out which languages they come from. Find alternative ways of saying them.

1. Whenever I read about the latest global economic crisis, I sense a **déjà vu**.
2. The 2008 global financial crisis was mainly caused by a **gung-ho** attitude to lending in the USA followed by a **tsunami** of bad debts.
3. The internet has become, amongst other things, a global **bazaar**.
4. Being able to speak English still brings **kudos** in many parts of the world.
5. Some celebrities avoid the **paparazzi**, but others feel that appearing in newspapers around the world can only help their careers.
6. The government has appointed a new climate **czar**.
7. Look, this is my latest gaming **avatar**.
8. There have been some **glitches** in our supply chain recently.

b) Think about how the words from a) have come to be used in English. What may be reasons to borrow words from other languages in general? Comment on the effect of using loanwords.

c) Find examples of loanwords from English used in your native language(s). Comment on any difference in the meaning and usage in English if you can.

MK **4**

a) Note down and research indicators that we are or are not moving into a period of deglobalisation rather than into the next level of globalisation. Then discuss which point of view you find more convincing. Give reasons.

b) Use your discussion insights to individually write an argumentative essay. Exchange texts and give each other feedback. → S7, 18

E Rethinking economics

The 'Doughnut Economics' model

If a doughnut isn't the first thing that pops into your head when you think about saving the planet and fixing the economy, I wouldn't blame you. But, as it turns out, a doughnut might be just what we need right now.

As the world continues to crumble around us, communities and cities have been turning to an economic model known as 'Doughnut Economics.' The 'doughnut' is an idea that was first presented by renegade economist Kate Raworth in her bestselling 2017 book, *Doughnut Economics: Seven Ways to Think Like a 21st-Century Economist.*

The idea is based on an image that contains two rings. The inner ring represents our social foundation and the outer ring represents our ecological ceiling. The goal of the 'doughnut' model is to get humanity into the doughy center – the space where we are meeting our economic needs while remaining within planetary boundaries. [...]

The most prominent image that is associated with economics is probably the supply and demand curve. And while useful in certain contexts, Raworth wants to replace this image with that of a doughnut. Her vision is one which rejects our current attachment to endless economic growth while making sure that humanity is thriving.

"What is the goal of the economy?" Raworth says. "The old diagram that told us what the goal of the economy was that of GDP growth, which is just an ever-rising line going up and up – this deeply rooted notion that forward and up is good. But we know that GDP growth and growth itself is not bringing all the wellbeing that we want in the world. The process we have now is leading to extraordinary environmental degradation and extraordinary inequalities as well."

By creating policies and frameworks which reject blind, endless growth – policies that lie within the doughnut's sweet spot, Raworth believes that we can structure our societies in a way that provides communities with the economic securities they need while maintaining a habitable planet.

"The doughnut is trying to represent a vision of the world in which we can meet the needs of all within the means of our planet," Raworth says. "That is the vision of human wellbeing that it's depicting. So that every person has the resources and abilities to meet their needs and their rights to food, water, health, education, housing, community, connection, energy, and political voice. [...]"

And Raworth is not alone in her vision. Many communities and even entire cities have begun exploring the 'doughnut' model as a goal for community and environmental wellbeing as well as for public policy. And although the goal is a global doughnut, all of them will not look the same. The model is flexible and can be applied in a grassroots way by a diversity of communities, cities, states, and even countries.

In fact, earlier this year the city of Amsterdam embraced the model as a starting point for public policy decisions. [...]

"We need to turn those linear lines into circular lines," Raworth told Shareable. "We need to create economies in which resources aren't used up, where instead they're used again and again and again, far more carefully, more collectively, more creatively, and more slowly." [...]

After realizing how much interest there was in the doughnut model, Raworth and co-founder Carlota Sanz launched the Doughnut Economics Action Lab, or DEAL to create a global network of communities that want to embrace doughnut economics.

"Ever since Kate Raworth came up with the ideas, people have been spontaneously applying them in different contexts – so neighborhoods, cities, and businesses have been picking up the idea," Rob Shorter of DEAL told Shareable. "The ideas have been put into action for many years now.

4 **to crumble** to fall apart
6 **renegade** rebel
10 **doughy** *teigig*
15 **attachment** connection
15 **to thrive** to boom, to grow
21 **degradation** ruin
25 **habitable** a place in which you can live
33 **public policy** *öffentliche Ordnung*
36 **to embrace** to hug, *here:* to incorporate

What DEAL is about is creating space for this emerging community of change makers who are applying these ideas spontaneously and helping people connect around the ideas."

DEAL's approach to economic transformation includes reframing economic narratives, influencing strategic policy, and innovating with the DEAL community itself by providing the tools for communities to co-create methodologies that turn the ideas of Doughnut Economics into action.

Robert Raymond, *Shareable* website, 2021

52 **to reframe** *umgestalten*
54 **methodology** approach, method

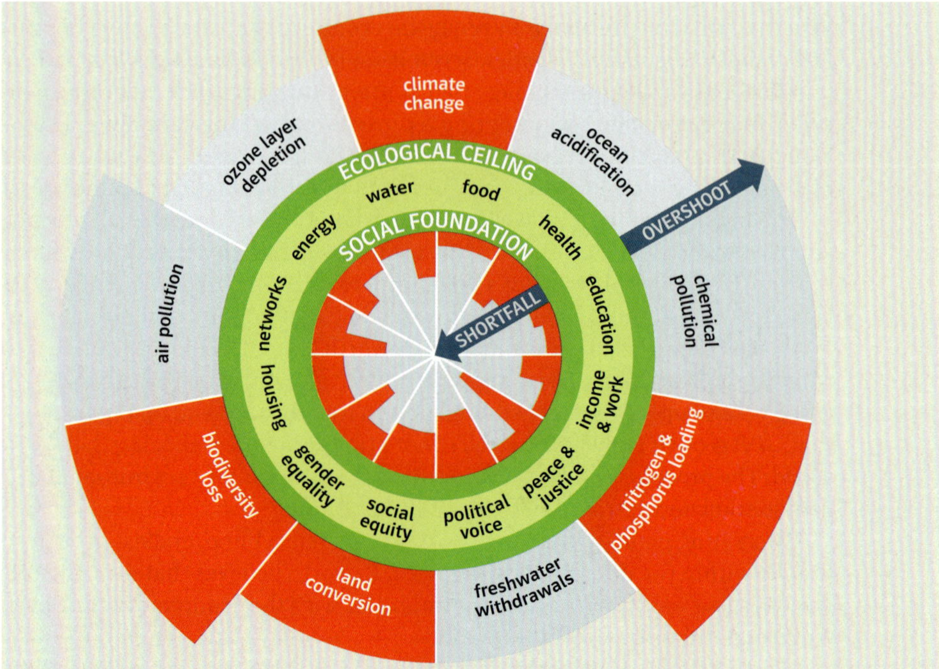

Raworth, K. (2017), Doughnut Economics: seven ways to think like a 21st century economist. London: Penguin Random House

depletion complete emptying
shortfall deficit
overshoot ↔ shortfall
social equity *soziale Gerechtigkeit*
land conversion *Landnutzungsänderung*
freshwater withdrawal *Wasserentnahme*

1 COMPREHENSION Outline Doughnut Economics for somebody who doesn't have much knowledge of economics and economics vocabulary. What is your opinion on the model? Give reasons.

2 VOCABULARY In this text the word 'doughnut' is used figuratively: It does not refer to an actual doughnut. Find more words in the text that are used figuratively. Explain their literal and their figurative meanings. How could it be said without figurative language? Describe the effect of figurative language in the text. → ○ 13 → S1–2, 4

3 ANALYSIS Analyse the way that the text uses descriptions of shapes, lines and movement to represent economic processes. Assess how well this strategy works as a communicative strategy. → S5, 11

4 VISUALS Outline the information that the graphic adds to the text. Explain why this information is very suitable for being presented in a graphic rather than as more text.

5 SPEAKING Look at the issues in the outer ring of the graphic. Discuss their relative importance based on your existing knowledge. Rank them in order 1–9 of how much risk you think they currently present to the human race. Be prepared to explain the reason for your order.

Judging global news sources

In this task, you will compare news items from different sources, discuss your findings in class and produce a wiki for future reference.

Step 1 Choose your topic and find your sources

a) As a class, choose a topic that has been covered in the news recently and which has had a global impact, or which has been reported on world-wide.

b) Get together in small groups. Go online to find five to seven English-language news reports on your chosen topic. Make sure that your sources are from different countries (which should differ in political leadership or economic zone) and in different formats, e.g. quality newspapers, tabloids, TV news channels, news on social media, podcasts etc.

Step 2 Analyse and compare your sources

a) Go through your sources one by one. Analyse each news item's
- text type (e.g. interview, comment)
- addressee, intention, register
- structure (e.g. length, amount of details / context, headline, structure of arguments, visual information)
- arguments (e.g. based on facts / opinions)
- sources (e.g. experts, statistics)
- language (vocabulary, style)

b) Now compare your news items with each other. Is there a bias? Make notes about:

facts / details presented • highlighted / omitted aspects • language supports one-sided view (e.g. 'government-run' vs. 'public') • sources • owner of source (conflict of interest)

USEFUL PHRASES

Talking about bias (un)reliable • impartial • (un)trustworthy • well-researched • useful • accurate / correct • serious enquiry • in-depth reporting • superficial • (un)biased • political bias • left / right wing • left / right of centre • liberal • conservative • one-sided • progressive • selective presentation of facts • manipulative • (un)supported statistics • propaganda • intolerant views • disinformation • fake news • clickbait • satirical news • fact-checking

Step 3 Evaluate your sources

a) Place your sources on a scale from 'untrustworthy / strongly biased' to 'very trustworthy / unbiased'. Give reasons for your evaluation. Discuss reasons why news sources in different countries / regions might have different perspectives. Discuss the risks of using a news source without understanding its perspective and political bias.

b) Which source would you prefer to use for which purpose? Give reasons.

to stay informed • to do research for school • to understand different points of view • to get detailed information • to strengthen your vocabulary and language skills • to confirm a hypothesis

c) Try to find an objective / independent rating of your news sources. Search for the name plus 'media bias'. Compare your evaluation with your search results and other groups' findings. Here's an example:

Africanews (Africa)

A pan-African news channel and website. The main focus is Africa, but with world news too. It claims to 'empower African people by giving access to independent, trustworthy and relevant national, regional and international news'. The reporting seems well-researched, with many articles in both video and text format. It appears to be mildly left-of-centre, with prominent coverage of development and environmental issues. It has been accused of viewing African issues from a European perspective: its parent company is Euronews.

Step 4 Write and revise

Turn your notes into an overview of the news sources as exemplified in Step 3. After writing your first drafts, compare your texts and give each other feedback on content (e.g. structure, analysis of the perspective / trustworthiness of the sources) and language (e.g. grammar, repetition). Then improve your texts.

Step 5 Create a wiki

Create a class wiki with your entries. Improve it and add to it in the future. → S7

Skills workshop 5
Analysing non-fictional texts

Step 1 Dealing with different text types

1 BEFORE YOU START

a) Discuss how governments can encourage their citizens to lead a (more) sustainable way of life.

b) Reactivate your knowledge of text types. With a partner, name the main purpose(s) of these non-fictional texts. (Don't forget that authors may have various intentions, from neutrally informing to manipulating readers!)

advertisement • blog entry • comment / editorial • encyclopedia entry • instructions • news article / report • review • speech

c) Skim the following text (title, structure, source) and state the text type. → S8–9

How do we make the move to electric cars happen? Ask Norway

I've just been standing for 10 minutes at a moderately quiet junction near where I work in Cambridge. During that time I've seen six electric vehicles (EVs) – three VW ID.3s, a Nissan Leaf, a Nissan white van and a Renault Zoe. Three years ago, if I'd been standing at the same spot, I'd have seen precisely zero such vehicles. And what that brought to mind was Ernest Hemingway's celebrated reply to the question: how does one go bankrupt? "Two ways," he said. "Gradually, then suddenly."

Something similar is going on in relation to adoption of EVs in Britain. The hockey-stick graph is common in consumer technologies. We saw it in the early years of mobile phones, when text messaging was ignored by adults as an inferior form of email. But when pay-as-you-go tariffs arrived and teenagers could have phones, SMS use suddenly shot skywards. The arrival of kids represented a tipping point – a point in time when a group rapidly changes its behaviour by widely adopting a previously rare practice.

Britain hasn't reached a tipping point with EVs yet, and so the first question is: when is it likely to occur? It needs to be earlier than most people think, because the government has decreed that sales of new petrol and diesel cars must cease by 2030. The second question, then, is: what will persuade – or force – people to change their cars?

The best place to look for answers is Norway, the one country that has been through the tipping point. Ten years ago, diesel cars accounted for 75 % of new sales there. Today they make up just 2.3 %. Two-thirds of all new cars sold there in 2021 were EVs and the predictions are that proportion will reach 80 % this year. Ye olde internal combustion engine seems destined for extinction in that particular part of the frozen north.

How did Norway do it? Partly through luck: it's a small country (population 5.5 million) which has abundant supplies of hydroelectric energy and – ironically – massive fossil-fuel reserves, the income from which is placed in a sovereign wealth fund and can be invested in all kinds of better ideas than burning them. The second factor was public opinion: people have been campaigning for EVs in Norway since the 1990s when a celebrated pop star and an environmentalist put an electric motor into a Fiat Panda and continually drove it through motorway tolls without paying until the resulting publicity made electrification a public issue.

But the third – and most significant – factor was government action. Norway, like all the Scandinavian democracies, is a high-tax society, and the taxes on imported cars were high – 25 % VAT and a hefty registration fee. Both were waived for EVs. Motorway toll charges were removed for electric vehicles in 1997, city parking was made free for EVs in 1999 and access to bus lanes granted in 2005. The country installed 16,000 public charging stations (including 3,300 fast chargers). In the end, if you were a Norwegian contemplating buying a new car, going electric became a no-brainer. And Norway is well on its way to being an EV-only society by 2025.

So that's how to do it. You just need lashings of money, a political system that responds to public opinion and a government that knows what it's doing. Which is why it would be unwise to bet on the UK meeting its deadline of being an EV-only society by 2030 – a failure that would have pleased Douglas Adams (of blessed memory). "I love deadlines," he once said, "I love the whooshing noise they make as they go by." And the great thing about EVs is that they don't growl, they merely whoosh.

John Naughton, in: *The Guardian*, 2022

13 **hockey-stick graph** a graph showing an even line, then steeply rising 36 **ye olde** the old *(pseudo-old English; often used ironically)* 56 **hefty** huge 56 **to waive** *(fml) erlassen (Gebühren)* 66 **lashings of** lots of

Step 2 Writing a step-by-step analysis

2 COMPREHENSION

a) Read the text and sum up each paragraph.
b) State the main purpose of the text.
c) Point out in which kind of newspaper the article was published (broadsheet or tabloid).

TIP

Characteristics of **broadsheet newspapers**: distinction between articles with neutral information and opinion pieces; clear / objective style; arguments and facts supported by dates, examples or quotes.
Characteristics of **tabloids**: sensationalised headlines; often mix facts and opinion; vivid descriptions and exaggerations.

3 ANALYSIS To prepare your analysis, have a closer look at the strategies the author uses to make his text convincing. Do the following tasks and take notes.

1. Find adjectives (including superlatives) expressing an attitude as well as casual / informal phrases in the text. Explain the effect this choice of words has on the reader.
2. Find examples of enumeration, (rhetorical) questions, imagery, humour / irony and onomatopoeia in the text and collect them in a grid like this one:

stylistic device	example in line ...	function / effect on the reader
...	...	...

3. Examine how the author develops his line of argument and the effect this creates: link between introduction and conclusion, structure and function of the paragraphs, use of facts and figures.

USEFUL PHRASES

to start off with ... • to follow the same / a different structure • to return to / to take up (an issue) again • to round sth off • the use of ... emphasises ... • getting the reader's attention • raising awareness (of) • stressing the need to act • showing solutions

4 ANALYSIS Use your results from Task 3 to analyse how the author tries to convince the reader of his opinion. → S10–11

Step 3 A step further

5 CREATIVE TASK Choose one of these tasks.

1. Rewrite a paragraph of the article into a piece for a tabloid newspaper. → S9, 26
2. Write a letter to the editor giving your opinion on the article. → S21

6 SPEAKING Discuss which ideas from Norway could help to promote electric cars (or other green technologies) in Germany.

Practice pool

Topic 1 New York – aspects of a world city

Bird's eye view of an anthill

1 VISUALS ○ → *Help with Introduction/7*

Guided analysis for Cartoon 1: In the analysis, the central element to be explained is why Gahan Wilson has chosen ants to represent human beings. A close look at the photo of an anthill might help you. Now write the interpretation: Point out what Wilson intends to express about people in big cities and explain how he conveys this.

Guided analysis for Cartoon 2:

1. **Description:** Name the three major elements of the cartoon and then describe in which situation they are depicted exactly. Do not forget to describe the body language and the facial expressions.
2. **Interpretation:** Compare the role and the status of the three elements in this scene and in 'normal life'. What might Gustavo Rodriguez want to criticise about human behaviour by depicting the three elements in this 'absurd' situation?

2 VISUALS ○ → *Help with Spot on facts/3a)*

You can use these words and phrases to describe the chart.

a pie chart • career choices • a large majority / a small minority of workers in … are … • the percentage of workers • Black people make up … percent of … • white people only rarely / frequently work as … • the number of … workers is a lot higher / lower than … • only few … workers seem to prefer job opportunities in the … sector

3 LANGUAGE ○ → *After Spot on facts/4*

Correct the grammar and spelling mistakes in this text about crime in New York.

In the 90s New York City has had a bad reputation for being one of the dangeroust cities in the world. The crime rate was higher than it has ever been before and people felt unsafe because the number of shootings was extreme high. A major reason of the high crime rate was the crack epidemic: Many people were dependent on a drug called crack and in order to get it, they did crimes. In the beginning of the 21st century though, the situation improved. One of the reasons were that politicians succeeded to control the drug trade. Another was that more police officers patrolled the streets.

Today, the New York crime rate is relativly low, but in the last years there has been an new increase. People feel particularly unsafe when they using public transports. On the 12th of April 2022 there was for example an attack at the subway, when a psychopath shoot at people, injuring 29 passengers. Some New Yorkers wish there were more police in the streets to give peoples the feeling of security. Others say that police patrols in the streets have a adverse effect because Black young men tend to react negative on the presence of mostly white police officers. Black youngsters feel harassed by police officers which control them more often than other people. They see this as a sign for discrimination and unjustice.

A1 **4 LISTENING** ○ → *Help with Texts A/4*

Listen to Cook Monsta da Illest, take notes and work on the following tasks.

1. Note down the things the rapper names to show how productive New York is.
2. Explain what, according to him, makes New York different from other cities.
3. What does he say about noise in New York City?
4. What is special about the language he uses?
5. Outline how he feels about NY and characterise his view of the city.

5 LANGUAGE ○ → *Help with Texts A/5*

Read what a student says about New York and put in the missing words / phrases.

You want to know what life in New York is [1]? Well, I can tell you, 'cause I [2] born here in Manhattan 20 years [3]. New York is a fantastic place to grow [4]. The city [5] you just about everything, you get the entire [6] in one place. As a teenager, I [7] a high school with young people from all corners of the earth, I learned four languages and could [8] them with my friends. How amazing is that? I don't need to talk of all the cultural [9] on offer here, the delicious [10], the crazy street artists. You can't imagine life in New York if you [11] it yourself. The Big Apple really is the city [12] never sleeps.

Mind you, there are also disadvantages. Downtown Manhattan is loud, noisy, dirty. [13] violence sometimes. But [14] are practical people, they are good [15] problems. And all the problems mean nothing in comparison to the freedom [16] enjoy here. At present I [17] law here at the City University of New York. It is a very international place but [18] interesting is that those of my fellow students [19] come from the countryside are rather unsure of [20] and incredibly naive. [21] in a world city has made me strong and self-confident. I feel I [22] more lives [23] many of my fellow students.

6 VIEWING ● → *After Texts B/3*

a) Find a virtual tour with the topic 'walking across the Brooklyn Bridge'. Take notes on when and why it was built, what was special about it and who managed the work.

b) Explain why walking across the Brooklyn Bridge is such a memorable experience.

7 ANALYSIS ○ → *Help with Texts C/3*

Choose adjectives that fit Raheem and explain your choice.

hard-working	arrogant	ignorant	boastful *(angeberisch)*	angry
reserved	frustrated	light-hearted	envious *(neidisch)*	proud
emotional	intelligent	aggressive	carefree	lazy
naïve	disciplined	self-confident	inferior *(unterlegen)*	calm

8 VISUALS ○ → *Before Texts C/12*

a) Describe the statistics on the common means of transportation in NYC and state what information the bar chart provides.

b) Comment on the results and point out which numbers you find surprising.

c) After Task 12, compare the New York numbers to those of other world cities.

9 ANALYSIS ○ → *Help with Texts D/6*

Explain the following argumentative strategies and the effect on the reader:
- the mention of people holding a different view on the subject (ll. 14–25) and of negative aspects of diversity (ll. 38–43)
- the reference to London's history and the British Empire (ll. 26–29)
- the opinion poll (ll. 31–33) and the London School of Economics (ll. 34–38)

Explain the following linguistic devices and the effect on the reader:
- metaphors (e.g. in the headline, l. 19, l. 28, l. 48, l. 51)
- enumerations (e.g. in l. 27 and ll. 32–33)

10 VOCABULARY ● → *After Texts D/11*

a) Collect phrases and techniques which the author uses to make (cautious) predictions about the future (ll. 22–52).

b) Use your expressions from a) to make six to eight predictions about what life in big cities will be like in 100 years.

Topic 2 Colonial legacies

Shops in a South African township

1 VOCABULARY ○ → *Help with Introduction/1a)*

Match the words with their definitions. You will need them to talk about the pictures on the Introduction page as well as colonial legacies in general.

1. lingua franca	a) buildings from the colonial era, often in a style typical of the colonising country
2. signage	b) a formal visit by a head of state, monarch or monarch's representative
3. state visit	c) a language used for communication between native speakers of various languages
4. left-hand traffic	d) public signs of various types
5. colonial architecture	e) vehicles drive on the left side of the road

2 COMPREHENSION ○ → *Help with Introduction/2*

Read the wiki text and explain in your own words what it means to be a Commonwealth country.

The official Commonwealth logo

The Commonwealth of Nations is a voluntary association of more than 50 countries, almost all of which are former British colonies. It only accepts members who commit themselves to a common set of values: democracy and democratic processes, including free and fair elections and representative legislatures; the rule of law and independence of the judiciary; good governance, including a well-trained public service and transparent public accounts, and protection of human rights, freedom of expression and equality of opportunity.

3 EVALUATION ● → *After Introduction/2*

Discuss whether a country can experience any benefits from having been a British colony, and (if so) what they may be. Do research first, so you can support your views with examples from former British colonies. Write a short argumentative text.

4 LANGUAGE ○ → *After Texts A/5*

A German student has started to write a wiki text about apartheid. Help to improve the text by editing out any language mistakes. Write down the corrected sentences.

The Apartheid has been a system of racial segregation. It introduced in South Africa in 1948. South Africa was colonised by the British and the Dutch, and the word is coming from Afrikaans, the language of the Dutch settlers. When it translates as 'separateness', in reality it was meaning suppression and control of the non-white majority by the white minority. Even in front of apartheid, non-white South Africans had been already severe discriminated against. Under apartheid, all South Africans were divided into four categories: black, 'coloured', Indian, and white. Black South Africans were forced living in certain areas, often at overcrowded and unhealthy conditions. Mixed-race marriage was illegal, and numerous other laws controlled almost every aspect of black South Africans lifes. If they would not follow these laws, they could be arrested or worse. Despite of international condemnation of apartheid, it's laws were not until 1991 repealed. In 1994, multiracial elections were held, resulting in Nelson Mandela to become South Africa's first black president.

5 SPEAKING ● → *After Texts A/6*

Find another example of a 'police state' (today or in the past). Explain how the system works or worked and point out similarities and differences in comparison with apartheid-era South Africa. Present your research as a short talk.

6 **ANALYSIS** ○ → *Help with Texts A/14*

Find examples of the following criteria for a good speech in the text:

good explanation of the cause • concise list of demands • clear, persuasive examples • acknowledging other points of view • counter-arguments • emotions • personalisation • statements of future intent • quotable phrases • powerful ending

7 **VOCABULARY** ○ → *Help with Texts A/20*

Fill the gaps in the following sentences with the correct forms of the words below.

frustration • household • deep inequalities • to struggle to cope • running water • candle • to flare up • to sprawl • lack of basic services • paraffin • cramped conditions • to be testament to

1. Violence [1] when people protested in the streets, expressing their [2].
2. Currently, settlements outside big cities [3] for various reasons.
3. Poor people in townships are often [4].
4. They still experience a [5].
5. For example, there is no [6].
6. Without electricity, people light [7] or fuel their lamps with [8].
7. A lot of family members often live in one [9], which means they live in [10].
8. Although the emergence of a new middle class [11] slight improvements, there are still [12] in South African society.

8 **ANALYSIS** ○ → *Help with Texts B/7*

a) Find examples of anaphora, exaggeration, metaphors or rhetorical questions in T'seleie's speech.
b) Point out how light, colours and perspective emphasise what is said in the text.

9 **SPEAKING** ● → *After Texts B/17*

Find out about the role of missionaries, the Roman Catholic Church and the Canadian government in the residential schools tragedy and what the organisations involved have done in response to these issues becoming public. Present your results in class.

10 **COMPREHENSION** ○ → *Help with Texts C/3*

Sum up the two views of colonialism that were held during its existence and the reasons behind those views. Point out the relationship between the two perspectives.

The primary goal of European colonialism was to extract as much wealth as possible from colonised territories. Another major motivation was to gain geopolitical advantage over other European nations by controlling as much of the globe as possible. Britain was even more successful in both these objectives than its closest rivals France, Spain and Portugal. However, these aims were hard to present as noble causes even then, and so the colonialist project needed some kind of moral justification. This came in two forms. One was bringing 'civilisation' to 'savages', despite the fact that the 'savages' had ancient, complex cultures and societies that in some cases predated their colonisers' by many millennia. Another justification was the supposed benefit of imposing Christianity on faraway places that were already well supplied with their own religions. While in its heyday the British Empire was widely regarded as a positive thing by those who benefitted from it, there were also dissenting voices which saw through the so-called justifications, criticised the morality of colonialism and questioned whether it was compatible with the teachings of Christianity.

Topic 3 Structural change

1 VOCABULARY ○ → Help with Texts A/2

Match these definitions with words from the text.

1. to damage the good reputation of sb / sth • 2. sb doing skilled work by hand • 3. a place where things are made or repaired • 4. not living, lifeless • 5. to be born or to cause to be born from an egg • 6. to cut up into tiny pieces (esp. food) • 7. a round vegetable with green or purple leaves • 8. to throw • 9. to change sth • 10. to deal with

2 ANALYSIS ○ → Help with Texts A/3

To complete the analysis task, take notes on these points:

1. Explain the images the author uses to contrast "old" and "new" ways of life and the message these contrasts convey.
2. Find examples of exaggeration and irony (e.g. "we remove mountains", l. 13). Explain what they tell the reader about how technological progress and the relationship between humankind and nature were seen a) at the time and b) by Carlyle.

3 VOCABULARY ○ → Help with Texts A/4

Sort these arguments into pros and cons of technological progress. Add more if you wish to.

environmental damage • improved communications • labour-saving devices in the home • less sense of local community • quicker, easier and cheaper travel • people become less connected with nature • raised living standards • improved medical treatments, higher life expectancy • some (business)people become extremely rich / powerful • unfulfilling jobs • access to (cheap) goods from around the world

4 COMPREHENSION ● → After Texts A/10

a) Outline features of a miner's job and the attitude to that job conveyed in the song.

A miner's life is like a sailor's
Aboard a ship to cross the waves
Every day his life's in danger
Still he ventures being brave
Watch the rocks, they're falling daily
Careless miners often fail
Keep your hands upon your wages
And your eye upon the scale

Chorus:
Union miners, stand together
Do not heed the Coal Board's tales
Keep your hands upon your wages
And your eye upon the scale

You've been docked and docked again, boys
You've been loading three to one
What've you to show for working
When your mining days are done?
Worn out shoes and worn out miners
Blackened lungs and faces pale
Oh, keep your hands upon your wages
And your eye upon the scale

Chorus

In conclusion, bear in memory
Keep this watchword in your mind
Worker's strength cannot be broken
When in union we combine
Stand up tall and stand together
Victory for you prevails
Oh, keep your hands upon your wages
And your eye upon the scale

Chorus

Traditional miner's trade union song

4 **to venture** to do sth risky
8 **scale** *Waage* (miners were paid by the ton)
11 **to heed** to listen to
11 **(the National) Coal Board** the UK's state-owned coal mining corporation
14 **to dock** to reduce sb's wages
16 **to load three to one** to do work of three
25 **watchword** slogan
28 **to stand (up) tall** to feel proud / confident
29 **to prevail** *here:* (victory) will come

b) Find a recording of the song performed by Billy Bragg online. Give your reaction on voice, music and instrumentation. Would you like to listen to more songs by this artist?

c) Discuss how important the job role (tasks and responsibilities) and the industry or type of business will be for you when deciding on a job / career.

5 VOCABULARY ○ → *Help with Texts A/13*

You can use the following phrases to talk about the pros and cons of electric vehicles.

shorter range than conventional vehicles • zero on-the-road emissions, but only if charged with electricity that isn't generated from fossil fuels • more expensive to buy • much cheaper to run • more energy efficient than internal combustion vehicles • less noise pollution • in comparison, producing electric cars leads to more emissions • raw materials needed for the batteries are often mined under problematic circumstances

6 LANGUAGE ○ → *After Texts A/14*

Complete the blog post with the missing words / phrases.

The great scientist and son of Lincolnshire Sir Isaac Newton [1] proud if he had seen what I [2] *(just see)*. [3] the county's capital Lincoln today, I hardly recognised the city of my 1970s childhood. Back then many of the grand, elegant houses and once busy industrial [4] were run-down and it seemed that Lincoln's [5] days were behind it. Jobs [6] rare since manufacturing [7] [8] *(dramatic)* in the 1960s, and to many young people it [9] that [10] was the only option. That's [11] I did anyway – I fled to London a few weeks after my 18th birthday. Nowadays, Lincoln is a vibrant regional hub [12] not only investment and workers, [13] students and visitors. There is a fast-growing IT economy and many former industrial buildings [14] *(repurpose)* for multi-occupancy residential, leisure and small business uses. Apart [15], Lincoln has a very rich past [16] back to Roman times, with tourism [17] to both its industrial and pre-industrial heritage now [18] a major role in the local economy.

7 SPEAKING ● → *After Texts A/16*

Find out which of the plans for Bottrop have been realised so far and comment on your findings. Do you think Bottrop could be a model for other places?

8 EVALUATION ● → *After Texts B/7*

Imagine you'd like to work for that company. Write a letter of application explaining why.

9 VOCABULARY ○ → *Help with Texts B/16*

Match the phrases with the categories 1–7. Some can go with more than one category.

1. medicine • 2. protecting the environment • 3. helping people with disabilities • 4. transport • 5. privacy violations • 6. loss of control • 7. loss of jobs

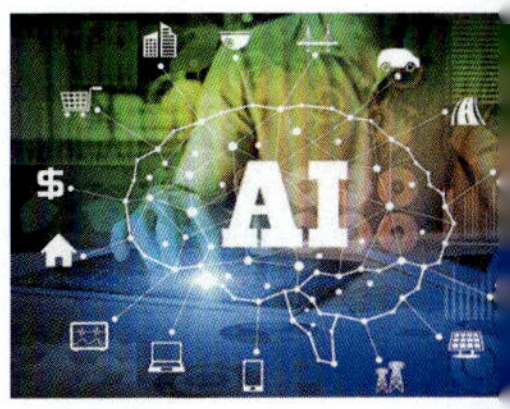

cybernetic implants • data mining • driverless vehicles • apps for audio transcripts • more accurate diagnoses • eliminating human error • systems to detect / predict wildfires • political manipulation • user profiling • reducing waiting times, e.g. for operations • traffic control • workers made redundant • voice / facial recognition • digital maps showing wheelchair accessibility • systems to monitor endangered species

10 SPEAKING ● → *After Texts C/2*

Imagine local politicians have suggested hosting the next Olympic Games in your region. Hold a panel debate on the pros and cons with representatives from different areas (e.g. politicians, business people, residents, environmentalists). → S32

Topic 4 Postcolonial developments

1 COMPREHENSION ○ → *Help with Introduction/1a)*

Read the statements from an essay about developing countries and pick out the words and phrases which you find useful to talk about developments in society, economy and politics.

1. Independent countries have the chance to profit from their resources themselves. They can act for the good of their own people. With the wealth generated by selling raw materials, agricultural products or manufactured goods, or by providing services countries can invest into infrastructure, modern buildings and education.
2. Economic growth and better employment opportunities have often led to the emergence of a relatively wealthy middle class that can afford to spend money on entertainment and free-time activities as well as consumer goods.
3. Better education helps people to find qualified jobs in the cities in the service sector when there is not enough work for everyone to live on agriculture.
4. When a country's sovereignty is recognised, it can join international organisations and collaborate with other countries.
5. If people get a vote in a democratic system, they can influence political decisions in their own country, such as the protection of minorities, religious and cultural tolerance, as well as international relations. People who live in diverse democratic societies and are granted the same civil rights can learn from each other and start to participate in political processes to achieve equality and solve social issues.

2 CREATIVE TASK ● → *After Spot on facts/1*

Find out more about a big city in India or Kenya, focusing on its importance for its country today. Create a wiki text with visuals to showcase the city.

Hyderabad, India

3 ANALYSIS ○ → *Help with Texts A/6*

a) Scan the text for the narrator's views on India and the different descriptions he gives of life in India. What different perspectives on India can you find (past / present, Indian / foreign, rich / poor / personal)? Make notes to go with those different perspectives.

b) Look for important adjectives, metaphors or similes the author uses.

TIP

These questions may help you
Where and how do people live?
What have they got? What are they good at? What chances do they have?
What do these chances depend on?
What are the hopes and worries of each group?

4 ANALYSIS ○ → *Help with Texts A/8*

Follow these steps:

1. Divide the text into sections and find suitable headings to describe them.
2. Sum up the content of each paragraph and identify the most important key words.
3. Find out how the author supports his arguments (e.g. use of emphasis, superlatives, strong adjectives, comparison and contrast, personification, examples, dates and figures).

5 CREATIVE TASK ● → *After Texts A/16*

Mahatma Gandhi was the primary leader of India's Independence Movement.
Create a class time line of Gandhi's life. Find out key dates in and facts about his life and write short texts. Find fitting visuals to illustrate some of them.

6 VOCABULARY ○ → *Help with Texts A/17*

Match the words with their definitions and write down the pairs before you watch the video.

intercommunal • settlement • reluctantly • slippery • culpability • to unravel • cord • uprooting • toddler • wireless • job prospects • to be buried • to flee • to hound out • ethnic cleansing • to exterminate • militia • deliberately • demobilised • vigilantes • to consolidate

agreement • to be laid into the ground • between different communities • to chase • to completely destroy • employment opportunities • to escape, to run away • to fall apart • guiltiness • killing a particular ethnic group as a whole • little child • on purpose • problematic • radio • recently released from the army • separating people from their roots • slowly, hesitatingly • tie • to unite • unofficial fighters (two words)

7 LANGUAGE ○ → *Help with Texts A/21*

Fill the gaps in this wiki text about German partition with suitable words or phrases.

After the Second World War, Germany experienced 1. Its territories east 2 the Oder-Neisse line 3 to Poland and the Soviet Union, and the rest 4 into four parts and temporarily occupied and 5 the USA, the UK and France on the one 6 and the Soviet Union on the other. 7 deteriorating relations between the Soviet Union and the other three powers during the period 8 as the Cold War, Germany 9 into the Federal Republic of Germany and the German Democratic Republic. The division 10 1949. Consequently, the border 11 *(gradually)*, and in 1961 a wall 12 to separate East and West Berlin. 13 1952, people in the GDR were prevented 14 to Western countries, 15 the FRG, and many of 16 who tried to 17 were 18 or shot. The division of Germany 19 about forty years. When the GDR experienced substantial economic problems and protests 20 more and more powerful, the Berlin Wall 21 and Germany was reunified at last. Since 3rd October 1990, Germany 22 *(officially)* one country again, freedom 23 an important right 24 to its 25 by the constitution.

8 CREATIVE TASK ● → *After Texts B/1*

Find out more about Kenya's flower industry and its economic importance. Prepare a short presentation.

9 ANALYSIS ○ → *Help with Texts B/2b)*

1. Brainstorm female roles and the qualities associated with them. Look up the vocabulary you need.
2. Compare your results with what you find in the text. How are the women described (adjectives, the way they act and communicate)? What information is there on why and in what context these qualities are important?
3. Give your opinion on the female characters in the text.

10 CREATIVE TASK ● → *After Texts B/12*

The Kenya Lake System in the Great Rift Valley is on the World Heritage List. Find out what makes this area so special and create a (digital) poster to showcase it.

11 COMPREHENSION ○ → *Help with Texts C/1*

1. How does the author use comparison as a means to structure the text? Collect the events of 1953 and 2022 in a grid.
2. Make notes of what is said about the situation in Barbados, Belize and Jamaica and the reasons why people in Belize and Jamaica are annoyed with the British royals.

Topic 5 Global matters

1 VOCABULARY ○ → *Help with Introduction/1*

Find more words and phrases to talk about globalisation:

connectedness: to bring (closer) together • to share • to interact • …
influence: to have a (political) voice • to regulate • to be informed • …
distance: to move (away / to) • to switch jobs • to be a global citizen • …
issues: …

2 COMPREHENSION ○ → *Help with Spot on facts/1*

Read the tip box to create your infographic. These words and phrases may help you:

pre-industrial • industrialisation • industrialised nations • transformation (of) • to increase • to decline • to lead to • to result in • to cause • to bring about

TIP

To create your infographic, make sure you work on each feature:
Text preparation: scan the text • note down any important dates and turning points • write the text • find headings • refine the text
Visual presentation: on paper or digital? • make sketches of images / icons • organise the page • finalise order and icons
Then put the text and visuals together. Infographics about history often use the **historic present**, which uses the present tense to describe past events. This makes the text more dramatic.

3 SPEAKING ○ → *Help with Spot on facts/5*

a) Imagine a possible future life for yourself. Consider these factors: your future location, your future job, your future leisure interests and how the world may be different then.

MK b) Search online for job ads you might find interesting and create a list. Which jobs require proficiency in English and why?

MK **4 SPEAKING** ● → *After Texts A/5*

Do research on another international organisation besides the UN. Find out what goals they have and which problems of globalisation they solve / address. Prepare a short presentation of your findings. Here are some examples of international organisations:

INTERPOL • NATO • WHO • WTO • COE • ICC

5 ANALYSIS ○ → *Help with Texts B/2*

Point out examples of these narrative techniques and stylistic devices in the text. → S11, 14

setting the scene • dramatic language to describe a scene • emotive language • enumeration • personal accounts • explanation of a process • presenting statistics / facts and figures • switching between information about the topic and personal experiences • focus on future plans / possibilities

6 VOCABULARY ○ → *Help with Texts B/6*

Match these definitions with words from the text.

1. to make bigger
2. act of increasing
3. the very front
4. guesses based on numbers
5. high paying
6. goals to shoot at
7. liquid used to power sth
8. making possible
9. outlook, opportunity

MK **7** **CREATIVE TASK** ● → *After Texts B/7*

Research and present a green energy project being developed in Germany or another country. Outline the project and explain the benefits that it will deliver.

8 **ANALYSIS** ○ → *Help with Texts C/1c)*

Find these stylistic devices and narrative techniques in the text and comment on their effect on you:

> different points of view • emotionally-charged words • metaphors • parallelisms • enumeration • repetition • superlatives • passive voice • anecdotes

9 **EVALUATION** ● → *After Texts C/1*

What is the importance of language for a nation's identity? Write an essay. Think about:

> popular culture • literature • traditional stories • customs and traditions • festivals • food • music • religion • vocabulary for local plants, animals or weather

10 **LANGUAGE** ○ → *After Texts C/3*

Complete this blog entry about translation technology with the missing words and phrases.

Have you [1] how online translation seems to be getting better and better? In its early days, the results [2] frequently disappointing and sometimes bizarre. [3] languages can be ambiguous as [4] phrases can have two meanings. [5], if asked to translate the phrase 'I saw my doctor', the translation software [6] between the meanings 'I had a medical consultation with my doctor' and 'my eyes identified my doctor'. In the past, the wrong choice [7] in strange mistranslations. [8] able to obtain information from increasingly large databases, translation software is becoming [9] intelligent as it analyses contexts instead of [10] word for word. If our example was processed today, a correct translation [11] very likely. So [12] there still are [13] mistakes in them, the translations [14] much more accurate. This means that online translation [15] now reliable enough to use without [16] misunderstandings.

A 10 **11** **LISTENING** ○ → *Help with Texts C/5a)*

How are grammar, vocabulary, idioms and jokes used in Globish and why?

12 **SPEAKING** ○ → *Help with Texts C/5c)*

Talk about where language is used. Write short dialogues for the situations below. Evaluate if some sentences / gestures would be different in another culture. What would the dialogues be like if you left out cultural conventions?

> having an interview • talking on the phone to make an appointment • meeting someone you know in town • checking out at the supermarket

13 **VOCABULARY** ○ → *Help with Texts E/2*

Find the words in the text that are used figuratively with the meanings below. The first letter is given as a clue. Write sentences using each word in its literal meaning.

> 1. upper limit – c • 2. aim, ambition – g • 3. restriction around an area – b • 4. lacking the ability to see – b • 5. mental image of the future – v • 6. not fixed, can be changed – f • 7. involving ordinary people – g • 8. accepted enthusiastically – e

Skills

A Study skills

S1 Guessing new words

Here is a list of guessing techniques that can be applied to texts containing new words. There will always be some words you don't know, but this should not prevent you from understanding the most important points in the texts.

Guessable words

- words that are used in a German context: *boycott, clown, laptop, track, …*
- words that are similar to German words – but watch out for false friends (*actual* ≠ aktuell)! *campaign, globalisation, lyrical, province, …*
- words that are similar to words you know from another foreign language (French, Latin, Spanish, Italian, Greek) – but watch out for false friends! *capital, community, destruction, dignified, minor, mural, phase, to renounce, to suspend, …*
- compounds of words you already know: *knowledge-based, passer-by, postcolonial, …*
- words from a word family you already know: *applicant, beneficial, entrepreneurial, …*
- words you already know, but with a different meaning (which is guessable from the context) *a large retail **company** – a new theatre **company***
- words whose meaning you can guess from the context: *The riots, then, he says, were partly about turning the tables on **despised** representatives of authority. "It was to give them a taste of their own medicine".* In this example you guess that *despised* must be a negative adjective (*despised* = *hated*).

S2 Working with a dictionary

An **English–German, German–English dictionary** is best suited for the purpose of **translation**, whereas an **English–English dictionary** helps you get to know the **usage** of words. Practise using them before exams!

- pronunciation
- word category / part of speech
- style / usage
- different meanings with definitions and examples showing typical usage
- idioms

> **decline** /dɪˈklaɪn/ **verb; noun**
> ▶ verb GO DOWN ▶ **1** B2 [I] to gradually become less, worse, or lower: *His interest in the project declined after his wife died.* ○ *The party's popularity has declined in the opinion polls.* ○ formal *The land declines sharply away from the house.* REFUSE ▶ **2** B2 [I or T] formal to refuse: *I invited him to the meeting but he declined.* ○ *He declined my offer.* ○ [+ to infinitive] *They declined to tell me how they had got my address.* GRAMMAR ▶ **2** [I or T] specialized If a noun, PRONOUN, or adjective declines, it has different forms to show if it is the subject or object, etc. of a verb or if it is singular or plural, etc. If you decline such a word, you list its various forms: *In Latin we learned how to decline nouns.* IDIOM **sb's declining years** the last years of someone's life: *He became very forgetful in his declining years.*
> ⍰ noun [S or U] B2 when something becomes less in amount, importance, quality or strength: *industrial decline* ○ *Home cooking seems to be on the/in decline (= not so many people are doing it).* ○ *a decline in the number of unemployed* ○ *She seemed to be recovering*

- grammatical details ([I] = intransitive verb)
- frequency (relative importance of the word according to the Common European Framework of Reference for Languages)
- collocations

An example from the Cambridge Advanced Learner's Dictionary

Good online dictionaries, best for everyday use,
- are easily and quickly accessible online
- include authentic pronunciation soundbites
- provide some common example sentences.

Translating tools have access to huge data pools, but often include incorrect English sentences. Check for user comments!

Online corpus searches show many examples and detailed information using a 'corpus', a collection of authentic speech recordings and texts.

Portable electronic dictionaries have a smaller but also trustworthy data pool for their example sentences and definitions.

S3 Doing research

You will often have to research a topic before you can talk or write about it. Always use multiple sources of information and be very careful to check the quality of the author(s) and content.

Step 1 Choosing sources

- Look in **books, newspapers** and **magazines.**
- **Research online** (see tip box).
- Go to your school, local or state **library.**
- **Write to an organisation** or an agency that might be able to send you brochures, posters or information sheets, e.g. tourist offices, museums, government agencies, NGOs (non-government organisations), or political parties.
- **Talk to someone** who knows a lot about the subject, e.g. English / American friends or exchange students at your school.
- Carry out an **interview** with an expert or do a **survey** and document the results. → S9
- **Always note down your information sources and quote them correctly!** → S4

Step 2 Checking author and source quality

- **Don't believe everything you read!** Anyone can publish anything on the internet, even in online encyclopaedias. Printed articles and books have normally been more carefully chosen and edited, but these can also be biased or too generalised and simple.
- Check up on the author or writing team. Avoid any texts without a named author or team of authors.
- Is the source background serious, reliable and trustworthy? Was it written by a respectable journalist, professor, expert, institution or government agency? Are the survey results really representative? Or is the text trivial? Avoid sources generally known to be sensationalist and superficial, e.g. something written by a hobby historian, or something from the popular press.
- Is the source up to date or too old to be useful?

TIP

How to find the best information
- Plan plenty of time to research, read through and check up on what you have found.
- If you find that the quality of your sources is not good enough, look for new sources or ask for help!
- Your local or state library will offer research tips, recommend specialist journals on the topic and explain how to use academic search engines.

Step 3 Checking the quality of the contents

- Is the text **neutral** and **objective** or is the writer / speaker expressing a personal, biased opinion?
- Is what has been said or written just **hearsay** or **fake information**, without expert **proof** or **personal experience?**
- Does the source include reliable information on **both sides of a controversial topic** or is all of the information one-sided?
- Check the **sources of information** the author has used. Are they listed? Are they good quality sources?
- Follow links to quoted sources to check their validity. You may find some good information there too. If not, don't trust the original text!

TIP

Researching online

Safer and more effective search engine use
- There is a variety of search engines, many of which include options on privacy settings or a non-tracking mode.
- If you're looking for a set phrase, use inverted commas, e.g. "Martin Luther King's speeches".
- You can use **+** (= require), or **-** (= exclude).

Finding information quickly on a website
- Many websites offer a search function. If not, use the search function in the edit (Bearbeiten) menu or **Ctrl** (Strg on German keyboards)**+F** to find certain words on the page.

Fact and picture checking
- Always use multiple sources! Check information from your sources with other reliable sources to find any discrepancies (different contents or quality).
- Put (part of) a sentence from the text you want to check into a search engine to see if (and where) it has been used before.
- Use a reverse search engine to find out where a picture or photo has been used before.

S4 Using quotes and sources

1 Quoting

Always make a clear difference between the text you write yourself and texts or facts written by others. You can cite a text **directly**, with quotation marks: **"..."**, or **indirectly**, paraphrasing in your own words. Use **[...]** to add to or leave words out of a direct quote, **l.** for line, **ll.** for lines, **p.** for page, **pp.** for pages and **ff.** for following pages / lines. Use **'...'** for direct speech in a quote, and cite from a poem or play with / between the lines:

> In her poem "Life", Emily Dickinson uses the metaphor of a bird: "Hope is the thing with feathers / That perches in the soul" (ll. 1–2). It "sings the tune [...] and never stops at all"; and in contrast to poetry itself, hope works "without the words" (ll. 3–4), which presents it as a universal emotion not connected to language.

TIP

Paraphrasing techniques

- Make sure you understand the original.
- Think about how you can say the same thing in your own words.
- Use synonyms.
- Change the sentence structure, e.g. use a gerund or participle instead of a relative clause.
- Introduce your paraphrase (see Useful phrases).

USEFUL PHRASES

Direct quotes (whole sentence):
In his / her book / article ..., X states, "..." (p. 7 ff.).

Direct quotes (built into your sentence):
The advantage is that "the ... are ...", claims X (l. 6). •
X presents ... as "...", which ... (p. 12). •

Indirect quotes (paraphrasing)
X claims / reports / writes in *(title)* that ... •
According to X, ... is / has / was / could ... (ll. 7–9). •
In X's article there is a good description of ..., which is based on / gives reasons for / explains why ... (l. 4). •
While X argues against ..., Y gives reasons for ...

2 Documenting sources

You must document all **sources** used for longer texts or written work, e.g. a term paper. It's best to start your list early, in the research and writing phase. Ways of listing details vary, but they all follow the same principle: List the **author** / original **source** and **title** first; then the **publisher** and **date**.

2.1 Making footnotes and citing sources

- The **first footnote** for a source should list the full details. Use your software's automatic function.

> Bill Smith analyses British migration problems.[1]
> [1]Smith, Bill, *Real Life in the UK*, London: Brown, 2020, p. 3.

- If you quote the **same source again**, it can be written in a short form like the Harvard system: **author, year and page number** in a footnote or in brackets in the text: *Smith 2020*: 37, or: *ibid., p. 3*.

> Smith writes that real life is about integration.[2]
> [2]Smith 2020: 23.

- For more than one book by the same author, add a short form of the title.

> For these problems (Smith, *Real Life*, 2020: 37 ff.) Smith suggested some solutions in his next book (Smith, *What Next?* 2021: 3).

2.2 Creating a list of references (Bibliography)

- Write your list in alphabetical order of authors' surnames. References can be in sections, e.g.: Books • Articles • Internet sources • Other sources (e.g. your photographs, interviews).
- Include the following details: author's surname • first name • "article title" *or book title* • place of publication • publisher • publication year • page number(s) if relevant
- If you read just one chapter, add Chapter X.

> Adiga, A., *The White Tiger*. London: Atlantic, 2008.
> Eggers, Dave, *The Circle*. New York: Knopf, 2013.

- For a newspaper / internet article or a text from a compilation or journal, write author, "title", then in: newspaper, date and page number or in: website 'online' with date or in: first editor's name, (ed.), book title, and publishing details.

> Jones, Owen, "Brexit, one year on", in: *The Independent*, 31 January 2021, p. 5.
> Stone, Daniel, "This Land Is Your Land", in: *National Geographic* online, 23 April 2014.
> McAteer, M., "Ireland, Modernism and Imperialism", in: Nash (ed.), *Review of English Studies 298*. Oxford: OUP, 2020.

S5 Dealing with exam tasks *(Operatoren)*

When you are preparing for exams, you need to know all of the relevant information and check which strategies are important for each task type. There are three task sets *(Anforderungsbereiche)* you should recognise when you read the task and see key instruction words *(Operatoren)*. Note that listening skills are often tested with standardised tasks such as *tick, match* or *complete / fill in*.

1 Orientation, comprehension (understanding) and reproduction

Key word	What you have to do	Example task
describe	Say what sth / sb is like by giving details.	Describe the setting in the story.
outline, point out, state	Present certain aspects briefly and clearly.	Point out the differences between … State the reasons for the family crisis.
present	(Re-)Structure something and write it down.	Present the situation of the characters.
summarise, sum up	Give a concise account of the main points or events.	Summarise the information given in the text about the consequences of water pollution.

2 Analysis and restructuring

Key word	What you have to do	Example task
analyse, examine	Describe and explain in detail certain aspects and / or features of the text.	Analyse the opposing views on class held by the two protagonists.
characterise, give / write a characterisation of	Analyse thoroughly how sb is presented.	Characterise the two brothers in the story.
compare	Point out similarities and differences.	Compare the two pictures.
explain	Describe something and give reasons.	Explain the cartoon's message.
illustrate	Explain / make sth clear with examples.	Illustrate the author's use of imagery.

3 Evaluation, discussion and / or text production

Key word	What you have to do	Example task
agree on	Decide together on one opinion / compromise.	Agree on the best three tips for …
argue	Build a case with evidence for / against sth.	Argue against the view that racism is obsolete.
assess, evaluate	Form an opinion after presenting advantages and disadvantages.	Evaluate the success of the campaign as presented in the text.
comment (on)	Express your opinion on the topic, giving evidence to support your view.	Comment on the author's view.
discuss	Consider the sides of an issue by reasoning for and against, with examples.	Discuss how the internet influences our communicating behaviour.
interpret	Analyse the form and content of something and explain its meaning in a wider context.	Interpret the message of the poem.

S6 Group projects

When working collaboratively, it can help to use apps and digital tools because many steps can be done online. An advantage is that every group member has access to all the information at any time and can edit or add to it. Different types of tools or apps may be used at different stages of your project. Of course, you can still do steps non-digitally. Combine analogue and digital tools for the best outcome.

TIP

Agree on rules to collaborate successfully. How should team members behave? How do you want to work together? Additionally, you can assign special responsibilities:
- **Timekeeper:** keeps track of time during meetings and the whole project's time line.
- **Secretary:** takes notes of ideas and results.
- **Moderator:** regulates the group's communication.
- **Presenters:** visualise results, structure the presentation, prepare discussion, answer questions.

Step	Digital tools	Analogue tools
1. Organising meetings and distributing tasks	conference tools / chat apps / checklist tools	plan meetings in person / write a list of tasks
2. Collecting ideas	writing programmes / collaboration platforms / mind-mapping tools	pen and paper
3. Gathering information	search engines	books / magazines
4. Writing process	collaborative writing programmes / storytelling tools for creative ideas	distribute topics and work on them individually, pass them around for feedback and corrections
5. Presentation	presentation programme / video clips / audio tracks / interactive board / projector	flip chart / pens / poster / slides / (white) board

S7 Giving feedback

Evaluating your classmates and getting feedback yourself has several advantages.
- You get a quick response and immediate tips.
- Your classmates understand problems you have because they are at a similar learning level.
- You get the chance to speak more in English.
- Positive criticism is better than not knowing what you could do to improve your techniques.

You can give your feedback orally and / or write notes on different aspects, e.g. preparation • content (topic made interesting, easy to understand) • structure (paragraphs, line of argument) • language (spelling, grammar) • presentation (fluency, voice clear and loud, time management, media competence)

It's important to follow these rules:
- Talk / Write about several different aspects and don't forget to mention what was good; not all aspects of a talk or text will be bad.
- Criticise parts of the work, but not the person!
- Formulate criticism positively, e.g. as a tip.

USEFUL PHRASES

Positive feedback
I was impressed by … • I really liked the way you … • You're really good at …

Positive criticism
… was really good, and I think your presentation / text would be even better if you … • Why don't you try this: … • I noticed that you often say … • I think you often make this mistake: … Correcting it is easy; concentrate on … • Look out for … when you're writing … • It might help if you always check for … • When I …, people often tell me … Maybe it's the same for you. • I'm sure the reader would be impressed if you … • I'm afraid I didn't understand this paragraph. Could you explain what you meant? • It might be better to break that long sentence up into shorter / simpler sentences.

B Text skills

S8 Reading methods

Skimming
When you skim a text, you read it quickly to get the general idea. This is also called 'reading for gist'. Read the title, the headings, the first sentences of paragraphs and the last paragraph because it often summarises the text. Look at pictures. Don't read every word, concentrate on looking for key words.

Scanning
When you scan a text, you look for specific information. This is also called 'reading for detail'. Look out for relevant key words. Stop when you find one and read that part of the text carefully. Mark the text or take notes on the relevant information.

Taking notes
Step 1 Deciding what you need
Depending on what you want to do with your notes later, decide what you want to note down, i.e. just the gist (e.g. for a summary or to prepare a talk) or particular details (e.g. for a comparison of particular aspects in different texts).

Step 2 First reading
Read the text and mark important phrases, if possible. You can use symbols or abbreviations for quick notetaking, as shown in the table.

Step 3 Taking notes
Skim the text to find the most important questions or key words. Write them down and add your own comments, if necessary. You can use mind maps, grids, flow charts or other ways of collecting and visualising information.

Step 4 Adding more points
If you need more detailed information for some aspects, you can add these points to your list after scanning the text.

TIP

- Use simple language for your notes.
- Avoid copying words you don't properly understand.
- Structure your notes by writing them in a sensible order with headings. Use numbers, bullets (•) or dashes (–) to list subordinate points.

Using abbreviations	
and / yes	+
not / no	–
the same as, equals, means	=
not the same as, does not equal	≠
becomes, will be, develops into	→

S9 Dealing with frequent text types

While the standard for texts is that you read them from a printed page, don't forget that other media outlets such as video, audio and the internet make texts available for analysis too. If you need to search for a text, think about where you could find it and which form will suit your use best. For example:

Text type	Printed	Online	Audio	Video	Live
Speech	✔	✔	✔	✔	✔
Play	✔		✔	✔	✔
Interview	✔	✔			✔
Blog		✔	✔	(✔)	
...					

1 Fictional texts

Drama A play is intended to be performed on stage by actors and actresses. The plot develops directly through spoken language and how actors portray characters. To interpret plays, analyse facial expressions, gestures and the actors' way of speaking or read the stage directions to gain insight in characters' traits, feelings and thoughts. The scenery, costumes, sound, lighting and props contribute to action and atmosphere.
A play is usually divided into acts and scenes. Differentiate between comedies, tragedies and tragicomedies.

Novel A long fictional text that often includes a large number of characters, different settings (i.e. the time and place) and a complex plot (storyline) (→ S12). For **graphic novels**, pay attention to the panels (images): As is the case with films, the images can be close-ups, medium shots or long shots (→ S35).

Poetry A poem is usually a short piece of writing divided into lines which may or may not be grouped into verses / stanzas. (→ S15)

Short story A short fictional text that usually focuses on a single event in one setting, often with only one or two main characters. A short story often starts in an unexpected way (in the middle of the action), and there is often a turning point and a surprise ending. (→ S12)

Song A song is usually divided into verses and chorus, so its lyrics can be analysed like a poem. Pay attention to how music style, melody, voice and instruments support the content.

2 Non-fictional texts

Non-fictional texts provide information, facts, and often opinions. They are usually well-structured and written in clear, direct prose. It is important to know the purpose of the text. The most common types are:

- informative texts (e.g. newspaper article, report)
- descriptive texts (e.g. feature, biography)
- argumentative / commenting texts (e.g. argumentative essay, comment)
- persuasive texts (e.g. flyer, brochure, speech)
- instructive texts (e.g. recipe, handbook, instruction manual)

Take into account the typical characteristics of each text type. When working with informative texts, it is particularly important to evaluate if the writer wants to inform neutrally (as usually done by public news sources like the BBC) or if they have an agenda aiming to manipulate the reader's opinion. The text may not be trustworthy if you find these features: sensational headlines, shocking pictures, one-sided depiction of the topic, emotional style, figures given out of context or without sources. Spreading false information on purpose, called fake news, has also become more frequent.

Ad / Commercial Ads aim at persuading their addressees of their product, organisation or company. Using elements such as pictures / text / sounds to attract attention (eye- / ear-catcher), a slogan, visuals (colours, logo), sounds (music, voice) and contact details support this.

Argumentative essay In an argumentative essay, your goal can be to persuade your reader of one side of a topic (persuasive essay) or to give insights into pro and contra arguments equally (neutral essay). (→ S18)

Comment Give your opinion on a controversial topic by presenting arguments or suggesting a solution. (→ S19)

Diary entry Past and upcoming events are narrated and commented on from a personal perspective, usually under the assumption that nobody else will read the diary. Use strong adjectives and adverbs to describe thoughts and feelings accurately.

Formal and personal letters / e-mails Pay attention to the correct greeting and be polite. In formal e-mails or letters, it is common to use the long forms, e.g. *I am* instead of *I'm*. For letters, remember to state the addresses of recipient and sender as well as the date. (→ S21, 24)

Interview The interviewer asks the interviewee questions that were prepared beforehand. The questions should be simple and precise; avoid wh-questions which only give you one-word or yes / no-answers. As interviewee, be polite and answer in complete sentences or even give some additional information where possible.

Newspaper article Newspaper articles inform the public about interesting events in an unbiased way with all the relevant points. The three basic types are news reports (news) (→ S20), features (news and background) and editorials (the writer's opinion on a news topic; the structure can be different from a comment). Differentiate between broadsheet newspapers and tabloids: tabloids are associated with shorter stories and more illustrations, often reporting in a sensational or biased way and using easier language. While tabloids are likely to write about crimes or gossip, broadsheet newspapers tend to topicalise serious news, weighing arguments for and against from various sources. The vocabulary is usually more sophisticated, giving reports a sober writing tone.

Reference article An article in a reference book (where you can look up definitions and explanations) contains the most important information regarding a topic or term. Think about what somebody who doesn't know anything about a specific topic should know. Leave out detailed information, which is only important for experts. The article begins with a key word. Typical online examples are Wikipedia articles.

Review A review provides a basis for decisions, e.g. whether a theatre visit is worth the money or whether to read a book. First, the most important details are given, then you give your opinion on certain aspects and support it with arguments.

Speech A central feature of speeches is that they are given publicly to a predefined audience, so the addressees, the location and the topic are very important. (→ S16)

Survey In a survey, data is collected to answer specific questions. Decide on your target group (age, gender, interests) and note your hypothesis: What will you prove with the survey? For simple results use yes / no questions, multiple choice for alternatives, or rating questions to collect opinions or trends. The results are often presented as graphs or statistics. Pay attention when analysing statistics (→ S37): the headline tells you the main topic, the legend helps you interpret them correctly.

3 Mixed text types

TIP

Some text types have come into existence with the internet, e.g. wiki texts, blogs, vlogs, or social media posts. While the characteristics are still largely the same, many online text types are more flexible than printed ones: They include direct links to other articles and offer comment opportunities or opinion meters to interact with readers. Online texts can be shared and commented on in real-time by people world-wide – keep this in mind to understand their purpose, characteristics and advantages. Also pay special attention to the text type: podcasts, e.g., can be presented in the form of interviews, discussions, comments, advertisements or a combination of these.

Blog / Vlog A blog (weblog) or vlog (video-blog) entertains readers / viewers with regularly published posts. Blogs can have a theme, e.g. a music or a travel blog. They are usually written from the viewpoint of the blogger and address the blog readers.

Post A social media post can have different purposes (informative, persuasive, etc.) and include a variety of media, e.g. a text, picture or video.

Wiki text Wikis are websites with collections of articles (wiki texts). Wiki texts mostly are reference articles, which are commonly written and edited by multiple authors.

S10 Analysing texts

When asked to analyse a given text, first identify the type of text. Then decide which of the following points are relevant for this text type and make notes. Use examples from the text with line numbers (→ S4) to support your arguments.

For all texts

1. **Basic information**
   - text type, author
   - when / where published, (historical) context
2. **Content and purpose**
   - main topic/idea
   - main intentions (to inform, to entertain, …)
3. **Form (How is it written?) and effect**
   - structure / line of argument
   - language, style, tone (choice of words, use of stylistic devices) (→ S11)
   - effect on the reader
4. **Conclusion**
   - short summary of your results
   - your personal impression (if asked for it)

TIP

Style, tone and register
The three are difficult to separate and mainly considered together to note the way a character speaks or how a text is written. **Style** is the typical way of writing / speaking used by a person; their choice of tone, grammar and narrative techniques. **Tone** is the general mood, feeling or attitude being expressed; it is the emotional content of a text rather than the devices used. **Register** is the choice of words, style and grammar to match the status of and relationship between people in different social contexts.
Don't forget: Form follows function. Comment on the way these instruments are used to convey an impression.

Additionally for literary / fictional texts:

- literary genre (e.g. novel, short story, fable)
- setting (Where and when does the action happen?)
- plot (What happens in the story?) and structure (e.g. exposition, climax, turning point, rising / falling action)
- characters (e.g. personal data and appearance, actions, mood, relationships with others, function in the story) (→ S13)
- narrative techniques and perspective (e.g. first-/ third-person narrator) (→ S14)

USEFUL PHRASES

Non-fictional texts
Giving information on the text
The article / text was published in / written by … • The text is a typical example of … • The text deals with … • The author / writer describes … • The aim / purpose of the text is to …

Talking about the structure, language and style
The author / writer uses … in order to show … • He / She tries / intends to / aims at … • The way the topic / problem is presented suggests … • The repetition / description of … evokes / makes the reader feel … • The use of words such as … emphasises … • everyday / colloquial / vulgar / formal / complex language / slang / literary expressions and rich / basic vocabulary • clear / academic / impersonal / familiar / eloquent style • foreign words • incomplete / ungrammatical sentences • dialect • On the one hand … on the other hand … • That's why … / For this reason …

Conclusion
All in all, the author gives an unbiased account of the situation / the events. • The author convincingly proves / shows … • Personally, I feel that … / In my opinion …

Fictional texts
The novel / short story / … was written by … in … • It tells the story of … • It is written from the point of view of … • It is set in … / The action takes place in … • The main characters are … / The narrator is … • The poem / play / novel is divided into … stanzas / acts / chapters • At the beginning … / Later on … / At the end … • The climax / turning point is …

Narrative devices
The writer creates a relaxed / tense atmosphere by using … • Suspense is created by … • Providing the backstory of *(character)* gives insights into … • The author uses foreshadowing / flash-forwards / flashbacks to highlight …

S11 Stylistic devices

Here are some of the most important stylistic devices, used to make a text more interesting and effective.

alliteration [əˌlɪtə'reɪʃn]	Alliteration is a figure of speech in which consonants, especially at the beginning of words, are repeated. E.g. "**B**etty **B**otter **b**ought some **b**utter."
allusion [ə'lu:ʒn]	A reference in a literary work to a character or theme found in another literary work. E.g. "Carrying the weight of the world on your shoulders" alludes to Atlas in Greek mythology.
analogy [ə'nælədʒi]	A comparison in which one thing is compared to another that is quite different from it. E.g. "What you're doing is **as useful as** rearranging deck chairs on the Titanic."
anaphora [ə'næfrə]	Repetition of words or phrases at the beginnings of neighbouring sentences or clauses for emphasis. E.g. "**I didn't** like his hairstyle. **I didn't** want to tell him. **I didn't** care."
antithesis [æn'tɪθəsɪs]	Two opposite ideas are put together in a sentence to achieve a contrasting effect. E.g. "It was the **best of times**, it was the **worst of times**" (from Charles Dickens' *A Tale of Two Cities*).
contrast ['kɒntrɑ:st]	A way of creating a strong effect on the reader which puts two extremes in opposition, e.g. the features of two characters or the way they talk, or the atmosphere of two places.
direct address [daɪ'rekt ə'dres]	A way of communicating directly to the audience / reader by using the pronouns you and we in order to be more relatable therefore persuading them more easily. E.g. "What do you do to reduce CO_2 emissions?"
enumeration [ɪˌnju:mə'reɪʃn]	A number of points set out in a list. E.g. "old, grey, suave, majestic."
euphemism ['ju:fəmɪzm]	More gentle expression used instead of the more direct one to express unpleasant, frightening or embarrassing facts, e.g. "The old dog was **put to sleep** (i.e. killed)."
exaggeration [ɪgˌzædʒə'reɪʃn]	Making something seem better or worse than it really is. E.g. "Today was **the worst**."
hyperbole [haɪ'pɜ:bəli]	A figure of speech that involves exaggeration in order to produce a more noticeable effect. E.g. "He couldn't live without her." The difference to exaggeration is that it is usually used intentionally in a literary context and is often unrealistic.
imagery ['ɪmɪdʒri]	Use of language which represents objects, actions, feelings, thoughts, and ideas through the use of simile and metaphor. E.g. "Her smile embraced me like a warm hug."
irony ['aɪərəni]	Using the contrast between what is said and what is meant in order to create humour. E.g. "Well, that was **clever**! Now it's broken."
metaphor ['metəfə]	One thing is represented by a word which normally describes something different, e.g. "She **is** a little monkey." Unlike a simile it contains no words of comparison ('like', 'as').
onomatopoeia [ˌɒnəˌmætə'pi:ə]	Words that contain sounds similar to the sounds they refer to, e.g. "meow" or "buzz".
oxymoron [ˌɒksɪ'mɔ:rɒn]	Combining contradictory things with opposite meanings, e.g. "organised chaos".
paradox ['pærədɒks]	A statement which, on closer inspection, reveals a kind of truth which at first seems contradictory, e.g. "**Deep down** he's really **very shallow**."
parallel structures/ parallelism ['pærəlelˌɪzəm]	Using parts of a sentence that are grammatically the same or similar in their construction, sound, meaning or metre. Parallelism examples are found in literary works as well as in ordinary conversations. E.g. "It's great **for** me, **for** you, **for** all of us."
personification [pəˌsɒnɪfɪ'keɪʃn]	Attribution of personality to an impersonal thing, e.g. "The **wind cries** softly outside the window."
repetition [ˌrepɪ'tɪʃn]	Single words or phrases that appear several times in one text, a way of creating emphasis. E.g. "'**March** for your rights!' he cried, and we **marched** and **marched**."
rhetorical question [rɪˌtɒrɪkl 'kwestʃn]	A question that need not be answered because the answer is either obvious or else it cannot be answered at all. It is mainly there for effect. E.g. "Wouldn't we all like a holiday?"
simile ['sɪmɪli]	A comparison between objects or ideas, using 'like', 'as' or 'as if', e.g. "He fought **like** a tiger."
synecdoche [sɪ'nekdəki]	Synecdoche is a literary device in which a part of something represents the whole or it may use a whole to represent a part. E.g. "I need a new **set of wheels** (i.e. a car)."

S12 Novels and short stories

Characteristics of a novel

Novels tell a fictional story, which transports the reader into a fictional world (close to real life or fantastical).

Focus	• any number of **characters / protagonists** • different **narrative perspectives** are possible (→ S14) • may cover several **events** or **locations** over a long period of **time**
Structure	• long **introduction** or direct start 'in the middle of things' *(in medias res)* • **plot / structure:** chronological and / or using various narrative techniques, e.g. flashbacks or cliffhangers • usually separated into **chapters** • **ending** can be closed, open, predictable or unexpected
Language and style	• in **prose**, many **styles** possible, may be artful • contains descriptive sections, indirect speech and direct speech

Characteristics of a short story

Short stories give a short glimpse of a life-changing event or revelation and capture an important moment or feeling.

Focus	• only one or two main characters • single event, single setting, short time span
Structure	• direct beginning, little or no introduction • central turning point or surprising 'twist in the tale' near the end • ending usually unexpected
Language and style	• often **elliptical** (details or sentence parts left out) • one distinctive language or style

TIP

The novel is a flexible literary genre with many subgenres for different reader interests. Authors can parody or mix sub-genres. Common sub-genres are: coming-of-age • crime • dystopia • family saga • fantasy • fictional diary • Gothic • horror • historical • psychological • romance • science fiction

S13 Characterisation

When dealing with a novel, film or play, you will often be asked to analyse or examine a certain character and their behaviour.

Types of characterisation

- **direct characterisation:** The narrator or a character tells the reader explicitly what a character is like.
- **indirect characterisation:** The reader interprets a character by what the character thinks, says, feels or does, and how he / she interacts with others.

Types of characters

- **protagonist / hero / heroine** (main character)
- **antagonist** (important character who is in conflict with the protagonist)
- **flat character** (does not change; has no depth)
- **round character** (changes; is presented in detail)

- Collect any relevant information given in the text about the character (personal data and appearance, what he / she does / thinks and what others say about him / her, his / her relationship with others, any changes in the character during the course of the story). In your characterisation, analyse what your findings reveal about the character and use evidence from the text (quotes and lines, → S4).
- Don't forget to edit and check your text. (→ S29)

USEFUL PHRASES

Personal data
The protagonist is a young / middle-aged / elderly / a 38-year-old single / married person / child of … origin.

Outward appearance
He / She is described as being tall / small • good-looking / handsome / ugly • obese / slim • healthy / sickly. He / She has a bony / wrinkled / square / round face • bright / dull eyes • a long / flat / pointed nose • straight / curly hair • … is bald. He / She has tattooed / smooth / scarred skin • a loud / soft voice.

Positive character traits
He / She is / seems to be cheerful • open-minded • modest • decent • good-natured • honest • trustworthy • generous • optimistic • self-confident • sympathetic • sensitive • reasonable • ambitious • determined • courageous.

Negative character traits
He / She is / seems bad-tempered • cheeky • rude • violent • narrow-minded • spiteful • deceitful • stingy • inconsiderate • ruthless • dishonest • unreliable • anxious • pessimistic • shy • lazy • insecure because he / she …

Drawing conclusions about a character
The body language / This action reveals that … • X's statement "…" (l. x) shows / proves that he / she … • X appears to be / is portrayed as …

Talking about relationships
to build up / continue / break off a relationship • Their relationship is characterised by deep affection / hostility / suspicion / feelings of … • The difficult / poor / close / casual relationship changes over the course of the story / remains unchanged until the end.

S14 Narrative techniques and narrative perspectives

The way a fictional text is told – using **narrative techniques** – influences the way the reader sees it.

Structure
- The **plot** (what happens) can be told directly to the reader, or by one character to another.
- The **exposition** (or introduction) gives basic information about setting, characters and plot.
- The main part often shows a development (**rising action – climax / turning point – falling action**).
- The ending may be surprising, abrupt or open.
- A **frame story** presents a story within a story.

Chronology
- A **back story** gives the history of characters, objects, places or other elements.
- A **flashback** or **flash-forward** switches to another time in the storyline.
- **Foreshadowing** means there are clues in the story that hint at a future development.

Narrative situation
- **Suspense** is created by not giving away too much information; typical of crime or adventure stories.
- More **distance** is created by using **irony** (→ S11) or indirect speech.
- To convey what a character is thinking, an **interior monologue** or, from a third-person viewpoint, **free indirect speech** *(erlebte Rede)* are often used. Unstructured thoughts are called **stream of consciousness**.

The effect of a story is influenced by the **narrative perspective**, which may change within the story.

Third-person omniscient narrator
- narrator: not visible, tells the story from the outside, but knows everything (is omniscient) about the characters and background. Sometimes comments on the characters' behaviour, the events coming later in the story, or even on the writing itself.
- style: mainly neutral and more distanced than first-person narrator.

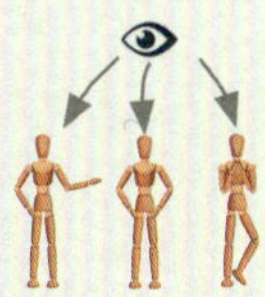

Third-person limited narrator
- narrator: tells the story from the outside, but only describes feelings and thoughts of one character
- We sympathise more easily with the character we are told most about.

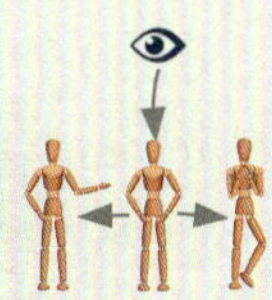

First-person narrator
- narrator: tells the story from his / her own perspective. ("I …") We only know what this character thinks, knows, sees or hears. He / She is often (not always) the main protagonist.
- We sympathise most easily with this narrator.

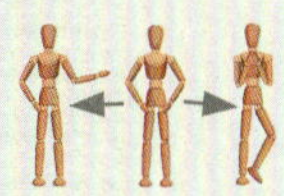

S15 Analysing poetry

- **Formal poetry types:** ballad, elegy, epic poem, haiku, ode, sonnet, …
- **Free verse:** No rhyme or fixed rhythm pattern, sounds like natural speech. Often used in the 20th / 21st century to express strong feelings or concentrate on unusual words / thoughts / associations.
- **Enjambement** (run-on line): connects lines and content, increases flow or tension.

From **Poem in October**
Pale rain over the dwindling harbour
And over the sea wet church the size of a snail
With its horns through mist and the castle
Brown as owls [...]

Dylan Thomas, 1945

Making cocoa for Kingsley Amis
_ / _/ _/ _ /
It was a dream I had last week a
And some kind of record seemed vital. b
I knew it wouldn't be much of a poem c
But I love the title. b

Wendy Cope, 1986
(Kingsley Amis: English novelist and poet)

- **Style:** A poem can be lyrical, song-like, descriptive, narrative, comparative, humorous, reflective, …
- **Title:** Don't forget: The title is part of the poem!
- **Metre (rhythm):** pattern of accented or stressed (/) and unaccented (–) syllables
- **Rhyme:** Words are labelled with letters to show the rhyme scheme.

Step 1 Introduction

- State in your own words: the poem's main theme • its message or the story it tells • who the speaker is (if there is one) • who he / she is addressing.

Step 2 Examining the formal elements

- Look closely at **structure** and **form** (stanzas, rhyme scheme, rhythm / metre, any changes) and **language** (simple / complex, repetitions, comparisons / contrasts, images / symbols).
- Describe how these formal elements are used to create a certain atmosphere / feelings; explain how they support the message of the poem.

Step 3 Additional points and conclusion

- Say (if asked) whether you find the poem convincing, or describe your own feelings.
- When **interpreting songs**, answer the following question: Do the musical genre, melody, vocals or accompanying instruments support the lyrics?
- Conclude with the main effect / impression.

TIP

In a poem, **every single word** is important. Reading the poem several times (aloud) will help you to understand it.

USEFUL PHRASES

Introduction / Main theme
The poem / sonnet "…" by … deals with / is about … • The speaker describes / reflects on … in order to … • The title makes the reader think of / that …

Talking about structure and form
The poem is divided into … stanzas / sections / lines. • The poem follows / does not follow a clear rhyme scheme. • Lines x and y rhyme / do not rhyme at all. • The rhyme scheme is (aabb). • The poem is an example of free verse. • The poem is based on a regular metre. • It has a flowing / monotonous / staccato rhythm.

Talking about language
The poet uses complex imagery / emotive language / ambiguity / contrasts / unusual associations in order to … • The words (mainly) belong to the word field / area of …

Form and function
The poem conveys / creates a feeling / atmosphere of … • The repetition of the word "…" stresses / emphasises … • The change of (rhythm) in line x indicates … • The run-on line (ll. x–y) intensifies the feeling of …

Conclusion
The poem is convincing / moving / special because … • … the reader can identify with the speaker / situation. • The reader is left with the impression that …

S16 Analysing a speech

Three elements are often mixed in a speech, but depending on the purpose, one of them is dominant:

- **informative:** telling people what you know about a topic
- **explanatory:** showing people how something works or why it is effective
- **persuasive:** trying to win people over and persuade them to take action

Step 1 Preparing an analysis

Gather all the necessary information:

1. **Context:**
   - speaker, audience, occasion, purpose

TIP

Speeches are usually prepared for one special occasion, e.g. political speeches given at summit meetings, campaigning events, press conferences or inaugurations. Knowing this helps you find out its purpose.

2. **Content:**
   - introduction (hook, catch the audience's attention etc.)
   - main thesis / main arguments
   - conclusion (rounding off, restate aspects from the introduction, call for action, outlook on the future etc.)
3. **Form and effect:**
   - line of argument / structure
   - style and register (→ S10)
   - language (choice of words) and stylistic devices (e.g. direct address, rhetorical questions → S11)
   - effect on the reader
4. **Presentation** (when watching/hearing a speech)
   - presentation style (intonation, stress, gestures, facial expressions etc.)
   - visual aids (e.g. slides)
5. **Conclusion**
   - short summary of your results
   - your impression (if asked for it)

TIP

Take a close look at how arguments are supported to evaluate the speaker's trustworthiness. Emotive language is often used to build a relationship with the audience, but can be manipulative or support prejudice. Even arguments based on feelings should, when possible, also be supported by facts and figures.

Step 2 Writing

Having all information ready, you can start writing your analysis. In your introduction, present the context the speech was given in. Include a brief summary and state the speaker's intention.
Your body paragraphs highlight the findings of your analysis. The concluding paragraph is used to summarise the main results of your analysis. Give your personal opinion if asked for it.

Step 3 Editing and checking → S29

USEFUL PHRASES

Introduction
The speech titled "…" was given on (date) by (name) on the occasion of … • The purpose of the speech was to … • … introduces the topic of his / her speech by … • … aims to get the audience's attention with …

Form and analysis
The speaker / orator claims / argues / states / acknowledges that … • He / she provides examples of … which support … • … uses humour / direct address to engage with the audience. • Frequent use of hyperbole / imagery, such as (example), gives the impression that … • … emphasises the importance of … by using repetition. • … draws historical parallels to … • By developing the line of argument step by step, the audience can easily follow. • Many arguments are based on feelings / prejudices / facts, which reduces / increases the speaker's trustworthiness. • The formal register suggests that … • The use of emotional adjectives highlights …

Presentation style
The orator's facial expression when speaking about … conveys shock / support / confidence. • His / Her body language suggests … • The speaker's gestures support … • Moving around the room for different arguments conveys … • The combination of his / her gestures and facial expressions underline the speech's goal to …

Conclusion
The speaker concludes the speech by … • All in all, he / she clearly states the aim: … • By ending with an appeal, the message of the speech is highlighted. • With his / her gestures / slides / congruent arguments, the speaker successfully persuaded / convinced / questioned …

C Writing skills

S17 Writing paragraphs

Writing compact paragraphs helps the reader to recognise the structure and understand your text better. An introductory paragraph catches the reader's interest with a question you can answer in steps and come back to in your conclusion. Most paragraphs state, support and comment on one aspect, argument or idea:

Ideal paragraph structure

- The topic sentence (the first sentence of the paragraph) is a 'mini-thesis' which states one main idea, clearly and without detail.
- Supporting sentences have a connecting word or phrase to the topic sentence and give facts, details or examples which support the main idea.
- Paragraph conclusions comment on the information and round off the paragraph.

TIP

Writing good sentences

- Vary **sentence structures.** Highlight important aspects by putting them at the beginning of a sentence.
  Use linking words:
  also • although • as … as • as well • even if • for example • however • in order to • in spite of • not until • since • so • therefore • unless • whereas • while
- **Link paragraphs** with structuring devices:
  first of all • secondly • on the one / other hand, … • furthermore • consequently • it is true that … • but • finally • last but not least
- Use **adverbs of degree (least to most):**
  (not) at all • hardly • rarely • at least • rather • quite • really • particularly • almost • most of all • absolutely • completely • extremely • drastically • utterly
- Add **adverbs of comment:**
  (judging extent) possibly • apparently • probably • in fact • actually • basically
  (adding opinion) naturally • of course • obviously • frankly • understandably
  (influencing emotion)
  sadly • unfortunately • fortunately • luckily • thankfully • amazingly

This is an example of a short essay on the task "Assess which of the problems caused by rainforest deforestation are most urgent."

Introduction

Rainforests are disappearing rapidly. **Naturally**, problems arise when these unique tropical forests are cut down. But which of them are the **most urgent**?

Main part, in paragraphs, from the weakest to the strongest point

Sadly, one result of deforestation is that more than half of the world's animals are endangered. The tree kangaroo and the jaguar are **almost** extinct. Animals play an important role in the forests, **for example** the spider monkey for seed dispersal. **So** if these animals die, not only the food chain, but also plant survival will be affected.

Furthermore, food from plants like avocados, guavas, bananas or pineapples can no longer be harvested in these forests if they are cut down. Medicines and other products are made using plants from the forests **as well**. We lose valuable resources if we clear forest areas.

The **most** worrying effect **of all, however**, is that when logging companies cut down these trees, they are also cutting the great ability of these trees to absorb carbon dioxide. According to the WWF, 15 % of all greenhouse gas emissions are a result of deforestation. We simply can't afford to lose more trees.

Conclusion, referring to the introduction

Although it may seem **most urgent** to save the climate, the whole interconnected ecosystem is vital for a healthy planet. **Consequently**, we need to save animals, plants *and* the air that we breathe.

S18 Argumentative essay

An argumentative essay (or composition) presents a controversial topic from opposing points of view in a clear and logical way. Typical tasks will ask you to **discuss**, **assess** or **evaluate** a topic or statement.

Step 1 Preparation

Collect ideas and information about the topic; note arguments for and against it. Use mind maps or lists.
Make an outline of what you are going to write and in which order. For the body of your essay choose a logical structure which fits the topic / task best:

- **Dialectical approach:**
  - Present all of the negative points first, then the positive or alternate between arguments and counter-arguments for each aspect.
  - Arrange points, e.g. from weakest to strongest.
- **Other approaches:**
  - chronological order
  - comparative: similarities, then differences
  - enumerative ('list' form): neutral sequence of paragraphs

Decide if you want to persuade the reader to agree with you or if you want to remain neutral.

Step 2 Writing

Introduction
Present the issue and attract the reader's attention, for example by using background facts about the problem and its relevance today or mention a suitable quote or short anecdote or question(s) that you will give answers to in the essay.

Body
Based on your outline, present each point in a separate paragraph. → S17
Support your points with evidence (examples, statistics, personal experience etc.).

Conclusion
Give a short summary of what you have written, but do not introduce any new ideas here. You may: give an outlook on further consequences / future developments / possible solutions; state your own opinion / give a recommendation or appeal to the readers to reach their own conclusion.

Step 3 Editing and checking → S29

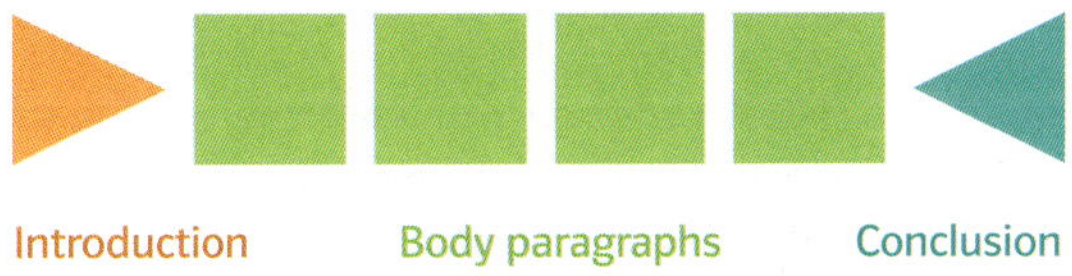

USEFUL PHRASES

Introduction
In the past, this issue was … • … consists of (two) aspects. • … should also be considered / mentioned. • The question that needs to be answered is …

Presenting aspects and examples
First of all / Secondly / Thirdly … • … consists of (two) aspects. • It is a … rather than a … problem / issue. • … should also be considered / mentioned. • … is relevant / completely irrelevant to … • My main argument is … • For example, … • in contrast to • There are various reasons why … • This also raises questions about … • Studies show … • On the one hand …, on the other hand … • Proponents / Opponents say / point out …

Using linking words → S17
Initially, it appears that … • It could be argued that … • However, / Conversely, / In direct contrast, it could also be argued that … • There is much evidence to suggest that … • Ultimately, / On balance, it is clear that …

Talking about developments and results
… can / will / should lead to / cause / result in … • The main / short-term / long-term consequences are … • … could have serious / far-reaching consequences for …

Countering arguments
Certainly, the author makes a good point. Nevertheless, … • This certainly sounds good. However, … • I would like to mention that … • I strongly question / support …

Summing up / Conclusion
Therefore, / Consequently, / As a result, people should / might / must … • In conclusion, … • Having examined the pros and cons, I would suggest / recommend … • In other words, … • And here's what really (matters / happens / is at stake): … • At the end of the day everybody has to decide (for themselves) …

S19 Comment

A comment is a type of essay in which you give your opinion on a topic. It usually deals with a controversial issue or statement, which can be based on a text. The task is "**comment on**".

Step 1 Preparation

- Form your opinion on the topic.
- Collect all the material you can (arguments and examples) to support your opinion.
- Think of possible counter-arguments. Refuting them can be a good way to convince the reader.
- Make an outline to structure your material. It is a good idea to start with the weakest argument and end with the strongest.
- To make your text convincing, plan stylistic devices, e.g. rhetorical questions or hyperbole. → S11

Step 2 Writing

Introduction
Present the issue and attract the reader's attention. When commenting on a given text, briefly summarise the point the author makes.

Second part
If you disagree: Build up your arguments from agreeing with part of what the author says (and / or giving counterarguments) to giving the strongest argument for your opinion.
If you agree: Go through the author's points and give more examples / proof, ending with the strongest argument.
Present your arguments in paragraphs. → S17

Conclusion
Summarise your opinion and give an outlook on further developments or possible solutions. Do not introduce any new ideas here.

Step 3 Editing and checking → S29

Example of a comment

Peace and wealth

The author claims that competition is the key to global peace and wealth. There are a few aspects which would support this view, but can it really be true that this behaviour, essentially a battle between opponents, can produce peace and riches?

It is true that healthy competition between businesses prevents corruption, monopolies and over-inflated prices. Large-scale corruption and poverty makes people dissatisfied with leaders or managers. This could lead to riots.

Maybe the author also assumes that competition increases productivity, which does indeed raise short-term profits for employers and employees.

I find it hard to believe, however, that competition is the most important factor. Concentrating on a supportive social atmosphere instead of on competition makes people less stressed, more secure and more productive. Companies who care for their workers earn more money in the long run.

World peace is obviously much more affected by violence, crime and terrorism. I disagree with the author; good government, diplomacy and education are certainly the key to global peace, and hard work in a cooperative environment is the real key to wealth.

USEFUL PHRASES

Expressing opinions / Convincing people
Those who advocate … often argue that … • It might be argued that … • We have to bear in mind, however, that … • With this in mind you can better understand why … • So what is it that (makes people do sth… / leads to…)? • So why …? • I believe / suppose … I am sure / convinced / certain that … • As far as I can see, … • Looking at … from this / their point of view, you have to admit that … • It is quite obvious that … / There is no doubt that …

Countering arguments
I agree / do not agree at all with … • However, I agree with … only to a certain extent. • Certainly, the author has a point. Yet / Nevertheless … • This certainly sounds good. However, … • I would like to mention the fact that … • I strongly question / support / object to … • I find it hard to believe that … • Instead of adopting this (simplistic) stance, we should … • There is something fundamentally wrong with this idea / point of view.

Summing up / Conclusion → S18

S20 News article / Report

Whether online or in print, there are three basic types of newspaper articles: **reports** (news), **features** (news and background) and **comments** or **leaders / editorials** (including the writer's opinion). News reports inform the public about interesting and important events in an unbiased way. As total objectivity is not possible, they should at least be fair, with all the relevant points included, even if the writer does not agree with them.

Step 1 Preparation

- Research the topic and make sure you can answer the wh-questions: Who? What? When? Where? Why? – and sometimes How? or So what?
- Remember the ABC of news writing: Accuracy (be exact – all the facts have to be correct), Brevity (keep it short and to the point), Clarity (make sure everyone understands).

Step 2 Writing

- Attract the reader's attention with the headline and the lead (usually the first sentence or paragraph) which contains the most important or exciting point and makes the reader want to go on reading. → S17
- The structure of a news article is an inverted pyramid with the most important aspect at the top. More facts and additional details follow, with the least important ones at the end, so readers can stop reading when they feel they have enough information. If the story is written well, however, he / she will read on.

Step 3 Editing and checking → S29

TIP

Using the right style

- Good news style is objective. Stick to the facts and do not give your opinion.
- Be informative, use mainly active voice and write to the point, with nothing repeated and no unnecessary information.
- Keep everything logical and easy to understand.
- Quotes, examples and anecdotes are often used in news writing. Make sure quotes match the speaker's intention. Without the right context, they may be misunderstood. Only use quotes to make a point clearer.
- In a tabloid report, however, use emotive language and include vivid descriptions.

Here is an example of the same story as reported in a serious news article and a tabloid news article.

Australia fires: tens of thousands stranded while attempting to flee

Tens of thousands of people remained stranded on Thursday evening while attempting to flee bushfire-ravaged areas of the south-east Australian coast – having earlier been urged to leave before the return of extreme and dangerous weather conditions. [...]

The prime minister, Scott Morrison, urged people to be patient, as he again deflected criticism about his government's policies to address the causes of climate change. [...]

On Thursday afternoon an angry protester told Morrison he should be "ashamed of himself" and that he had "left the country to burn" during a tour of the burnt out town of Cobargo.

Ben Smee and Luke Henriques-Gomes, *The Guardian online*, 2 January 2020

Australia fires – Tens of thousands in path of killer flames told to 'flee or die' as death toll hits 18

Huge areas between Bateman's Bridge and the border with Victoria state have been ruled "unsafe", sparking monster traffic jams as thousands flee for their lives through choking smoke. [...]

Meanwhile today Aussie PM Scott Morrison was forced to retreat into his limo after residents of a devastated town hurled abuse at him. He went to visit Cobargo in New South Wales – where a father and son died on New Year's Eve – but one woman refused to shake his hand and said: "You're an idiot".

Felix Allen, *The Sun online*, 2 January 2020

S21 Writing a formal letter / email or letter to the editor

This is the letter type you would write to an employer, a company, a government office or any other respected person to
- make a request for information / service
- introduce your job / university application or submit a petition
- express a concern, wish or complaint
- write to a news editor to express your opinion about an article

The style **must** be formal, factual and polite.

Writing your formal letter or email
- In a letter, type your address and then the recipient's address on the left, followed by the date on the right.
- In an email, type your name and full contact details at the end of the email.
- In the reference line, clarify the topic.
- If you do not know the name of the person, write "Dear Sir or Madam," If you do know their name, write "Dear Mr / Ms / Dr Jones,"
- The first line begins with a capital letter. Begin by stating the topic / explaining why you are writing.
- Write each point in a clear, compact paragraph.
- In the last paragraph of your letter / email, summarise the most important point and offer the recipient the option of contacting you.
- Finish a "Sir" letter with "Yours faithfully" and a "Dear Ms (Name)" letter with "Sincerely, / Yours sincerely," (or less formally, "Best / Kind regards"). Then sign it **and** type your full name.
- If you have enclosed a document, write after your typed name Enclosures / Encl.: with its title or a clear description.

Daniel Borchert
Alleenstrasse 42
35396 Giessen
Germany

Creative Concepts Ltd.
62 Denmark Street
London WC5 10B
England

24th March 20…

Your invitation to an interview

Dear Mr Jones,

Thank you very much for your letter. I am writing to accept your invitation to the interview for the position of Director's Assistant.

Please find enclosed a new reference from my last employer, which I received yesterday.

Thank you for giving me this opportunity. I am looking forward to discussing this matter with you on the 10th of April.

Should you have any further questions, please do not hesitate to contact me.

Yours sincerely,
Daniel Borchert

Encl.: Reference from Deutsche Bank

Exceptions for a letter to the editor
- In the reference line, say exactly which article you are referring to (title, date).
- Write "To the editor:" or "Sir," or "Madam,", not "Dear".
- Make the letter short, to the point and polite, even when criticising the article.
- Make your opinion convincing. → S18
- End with your name and the town you live in. Do not use "Yours faithfully / sincerely".

USEFUL PHRASES

Starting the letter
I am writing regarding / to ask about / to thank you for … • In last week's / In reference to your letter dated …

Middle of the letter
I appreciate / apologise for / would be grateful if … • Please send me / Would you please be so kind as to …

Ending the letter
Please feel free to contact me if you have any questions. • Thank you very much in advance for your help / advice. • I am looking forward to meeting / hearing from you soon. • For your convenience I have enclosed …

In a letter to the editor
With reference / I am referring to your article of … • In his / her article dated / from …, the author stated that … • After carefully studying the article, I am sorry to say that / would like to express doubts about / to add that … • I definitely support / agree with the author's opinion on … • I am very glad that this topic has finally been … • I was hoping for a more impartial treatment of / would appreciate more objectivity when … • In my experience … • An option the author did not consider would be to … • Undoubtedly, it would be more acceptable if …

S22 Writing an application

In a letter of application, which is usually accompanied by a CV (BE)/resume (AE), write your address and the company's (US: your address on the right) and add the date. In an email, leave out the company address and date. Put your contact details at the end of the email and the reference line becomes the subject line (Re:).

Laura Borchert
Altmuehlweg 20
35396 Giessen
Germany

Ms L. Johnson
Creative Concepts Ltd.
62 Denmark Street
London WC5 10B
England

19th February 2021

Application for a work placement

Dear Ms Johnson,

I am a pupil at a grammar school in the town of Giessen in Germany. This summer I would like to gain work experience at Creative Concepts, contribute my knowledge of German market trends and enhance my proficiency in English, IT and marketing skills in an international business environment.

As you will see from the enclosed CV, I have visited the USA, South Africa and the UK and I can speak and write English fluently. I will complete my studies in a year's time when I take the Abitur exams, which are similar to British A-levels. My aim is to study business and marketing in the UK after that. You will also see that I have already had some work experience in my father's web applications company here in Giessen.

I am particularly interested in working with you as Creative Concepts is one of the most innovative app development companies in London. It was recommended to me by my brother, Daniel Borchert, who did three weeks' work experience at Creative Concepts in 2018, enjoyed it immensely and gained valuable experience, especially in the app design department.

I am keen to gain practical experience and learn how Creative Concepts attracts and retains customers. I have good computer skills and I am able to carry out many office duties. I would be most interested in working in the customer development department.

I am sure I could make a valuable contribution to your company. A placement would be possible for me at any time between 25th July and 5th September 2021. I would be very grateful for a positive reply and look forward to hearing from you.

Yours sincerely,

Laura Borchert

Laura Borchert

Encl.: CV

You can – but you don't have to – put your name above the address.

For German words, write ß as ss and ä, ö and ü as ae, oe and ue.

BE: work placement
AE: internship

Include a **reference** (in bold print) to show what the letter is about.

Important: Find out exactly who you should write to!

Introduce yourself in the first paragraph. Say why you are writing the letter.

In the second paragraph, mention important points from your CV (AE: resume).

Say why you want the job, what you know about it and what you think you can bring to it.

End with a friendly sentence which looks forward to a reply.

In a letter, sign AND print your name and list what you are enclosing. In an email, type your name and list any attachments (in PDF format) with clear file names, e.g.
Attached:
L_Borchert_CV.pdf

S23 Curriculum vitae – CV

Here is an example of a CV (BE). For a resume (AE), present the information in a short text. You may be given a word limit, e.g. 1500 words. Concentrate on what is really relevant. Keep your CV short and clear.

Curriculum vitae
Laura Borchert (b. 20th January 2004)
Altmuehlweg 20, 35396 Giessen, Germany
laura.borchert@....de / +49 (0)641 34838

I am creative, skilled at computers and speaking English, hard-working and a supportive team player. I would like to add international experience to my marketing knowledge.

Work experience
2020 Borchert App Solutions, Giessen
Three-week summer placement in marketing
– assisted in marketing planning
– dealt with telephone inquiries
2018 Maximus Engineering AG, Gießen
Work experience week
– learnt about international customer relations

Education
Since 2014: **Herderschule, Giessen**
(Grammar school) *Abitur* exams
(equivalent of British A-levels) to be taken in 2022.

Language skills
German: native speaker (C2)
English: fluent speaker and writer (B2/C1)
French: good working knowledge (B1)

Interests
Computers – passionate about programming and travel blogging
Sports – responsible for publicity in my handball team (national champions in 2019)
Travel – developed linguistc and intercultural skills in South Africa (2013), the US (2015) and the UK (2018, 2019)

Voluntary work
Weekly learning support for two refugee students since 2018

- Always match your CV to the job / course requirements.
- Leave out irrelevant experience or keep it short to avoid gaps in your time line.
- Give a short personal statement describing what makes you the right person for the job / place.
- Don't include a photo, your marital status, religion, nationality or information about your family. Your date of birth may not be necessary either.
- Start with the most recent / relevant events and work backwards.
- Explain but don't translate names of schools, companies or qualifications.
- Describe what you did in each job: Show the skills relevant to what you are applying for.
- Describe AND give language levels according to the Common European Framework of Reference for Languages (CEFR).
- Use your interests to show skills and personality.
- Alternatively arrange CV information under skills and achievements titles. Check online for examples.

Don't forget to check your CV for mistakes before you send it.

S24 Personal letter or email

You can use **informal language** for private contact with friends and relations, e.g.

short forms: I'm • we're • there's • didn't;
question tags: don't you? • aren't we? • OK?
and colloquial / emotional terms with friends of your age: Hi • fed up with ... • guys

Letters: Your address and the date (top right).
Emails: Email address, subject line.
Start like this: Dear Grandad, • Hi Jen, ...
First line: Start with a capital letter!
Use paragraphs for each different point.

Understand your role: Be considerate, e.g. use a similar style, ask how they are, say why you're writing, respond to previous interaction and / or give a reason for finishing.

Finish like this: Best (wishes / regards), • Love, • All the best, • See you soon, • Miss you, • Take care, • Hope to see you / hear from you soon, Tim / Lea (first name only).

Check (emails: use the spell check function) for any mistakes or sentences that could be misunderstood before you send your text.

S25 Free writing

Step 1 Preparation
- Brainstorm ideas for your creative text and organise them, e.g. in a mind map.
- Decide who you are writing the text for, the purpose of the text, the genre and text type. → S9
- For fictional texts: Consider how you can express your ideas best and which techniques are the most suitable for your story. Look at → S14 for point of view and narrative techniques, and → S13 for characterisation.

Step 2 Writing
- If you decide to tell a story, cover these points: Who? When? Where? What? How? Why? The first four can be used in an exposition to introduce the main characters, setting and theme.
- The main part deals with the main action. End with an interesting conclusion.

Step 3 Editing and checking → S29

TIP

Your free writing text
- Both fictional and non-fictional texts need to develop logically, so use structuring devices and connectives. → S10
- Your style should be consistent. → S11
- If you are writing a poem, remember that the form is very important. Choose formal elements which suit what you want to convey. → S15
- If you are writing a dialogue, consider stage directions to support the spoken text.

S26 Material-based writing

Your creative writing can be based on a printed text or on an audiotext, video / film or cartoon / visual.
- Printed texts: Your task may be to tell a part of the story that is not in the text, write about a different subject using the same text type, to change the point of view, or to tell the same story using a different text type.
- Audiovisual material: You may be asked to relate what happened before / after the situation shown, or do a similar task to printed texts.

Step 1
First make sure you have understood the original text properly. Make notes on typical characteristics and style.

Step 2
Use what you know about text types and features to create a new text that matches the original. → S9–15

Here is an example of how the plot of the play ***Othello*** by Shakespeare was turned into a news report:

Army general kills wife in night of bloodbath
Racial violence or jealousy?

CYPRUS. Last night a terrible crime was committed in the castle lodgings of Venetian general Othello (42), a dark-skinned gentleman famous for fairness and courage until today. His wife Desdemona (18) was found dead in her bed after screams had woken the neighbours.

Lieutenant Cassio (25), quickly on the scene, expressed his shock at the terrible act. Othello had smothered his own wife, Cassio claimed, then stabbed himself to death.

Our reporter W. Shakespeare asked how this could have happened. Was racial tension involved?

But Cassio attributed this murder to a more scandalous cause. Othello had apparently been fooled by his ensign Iago (28), making the general so jealous that he killed his wife in a blind rage. A handkerchief seems to have convinced Othello of his wife's infidelity. "I mourn for my good friend Othello that he was forced into this madness by such a villain," Cassio said.

The dead lady's father, Senator Brabantio (49), said to reliable sources, "I knew that violent Moor was not to be trusted!" Rumour has it that these were not the only deaths last night. More news to come in our evening edition.

S27 Term paper

A term (or research) paper records your research on a particular subject. Follow these steps:

Step 1 Choosing a subject
- You may be given a list of subjects, or you may be able to make suggestions yourself. Choose the subject you like most.
- Don't choose a subject that is too general. Answer concrete, relevant questions in logical steps, using facts to prove or support what you say.

Step 2 Finding sources → S3
- Don't use sources more than twenty years old unless you are working on historical aspects.
- Use books, newspapers, magazines and the internet. Using several different sources is best.

Step 3 Organising your search
- Make a list of key words and phrases you might need in your search for material.
- Start a file card for each source: subject, author, title, publishing information, relevant pages.

Step 4 Taking notes
- Skim through sources to find what is useful for answering your question(s), then read carefully.
- Write down notes and quotes and make a note of page numbers / key headings you need to use for footnotes or to find the information again.
- Do not misrepresent the author's meaning.
- Collect material which supports and opposes your thesis to write a well-balanced text.
- Collect facts, not just opinions. Comment on authors' statements and why they are important.

Step 5 Planning
- Check that your task can be answered in your own words using the material you have found.
- Sort your notes into groups under headings you can use in the steps / sections of your paper.

Step 6 Writing
- **Introduction:** Present the topic of the paper and the question(s) which will be answered.
- **Body:** Write points or answers in logical sections and paragraphs supported by quotes and reasons.
- **Summary and conclusion:** Summarise / Comment on important research results or conclusions.

Step 7 Editing and checking → S29
- Read the whole paper as if you were reading it for the first time. Reading aloud will help you.
- Check spelling, phrasing and sentences.
- Check there is a footnote for each quote and that every source was cited correctly. → S4

Step 8 Formatting and documenting sources
- Format your text with consistent font style / sizes, spacing, margins, footnotes and page numbers.
- Create a contents page, checking sections for correct headings and page numbers, and a front page with the following information: name, class, subject, teacher, task, date.
- List your different sources in alphabetical order in a list of references at the end. → S4
- Include a signed statement of authorship, e.g.: *This term paper is my own work and no sources have been quoted without due reference.*

S28 Summary

When you write a summary, you have to briefly restate the author's main ideas (non-fictional texts) or retell a story in your own words (fictional texts). Your summary should be much shorter than the original, usually about a quarter to a third of the length of the original text.

Step 1 Preparation (NON-FICTIONAL TEXT)
- Read the text carefully to find out the main idea (thesis). Underline it.
- Read the text again and highlight ideas, facts or arguments (words and phrases rather than whole sentences) that support the thesis.

OR

Step 1 Preparation (FICTIONAL TEXT)
- Read the text carefully and underline the main characters and setting.
- Divide the text into sections. When there is a new aspect or development, underline key words, main points and the turning point in the plot.

Step 2 Writing, for both types of text
- In the first sentence mention the source (author, title), text type and the main idea / theme.
- Write short paragraphs summing up the major arguments (non-fiction) or what happens, who contributes to the action, and how the events are connected (fiction). Follow these rules:
  - Use your own words as often as possible.
  - Use the present tense.
  - Leave out non-essential information (e.g. examples, descriptive details, direct quotes).
  - Do not include your own ideas and opinions.

Step 3 Editing and checking
- Check and, if necessary, revise your summary. You can do this best if you imagine you are a reader who knows nothing about the topic. → S14, 29

USEFUL PHRASES

Non-fictional texts
According to the author, … • The author says / writes / claims / states that … • In addition / conclusion, the author argues that …

Fictional texts
X makes an important discovery / decision here. • The relationship between X and Y takes a turn for the worse / better. • There is a change in …, which causes … to …

S29 Editing and checking

Plan in enough time to read through your draft several times. Take a break before you start checking, if possible. While checking, concentrate on just one aspect (see questions below). Then read again for the next.

Content
- Have you included all important aspects / points?
- Have you used a logical structure (introduction, main body, conclusion)? Have you started a new paragraph for each new idea? (→ S17)
- Are your ideas logically connected (linking words, structuring devices)? (→ S17)
- Is the sentence structure clear?
- Do style and register (→ S10) fit the text type / situation / character / reader?

Spelling
- Have you spelled everything correctly? You may use a spell-checker / dictionary for help.

Grammar and vocabulary
- Have you used the correct tenses?
- Is the word order in your sentences correct?
- Have you checked any grammar points you are unsure about?
- Add variety by using synonyms for overused words (nice, say etc.).

Punctuation
- Have you used apostrophes, commas, quotation marks and periods in the correct places?

TIP

Keep improving
- Keep a list of your most **frequent mistakes** and check for these first.
- **Peer editing:** You can also give your text to a partner and see if they have any suggestions for improvement. → S7

D Speaking skills

S30 Presentation

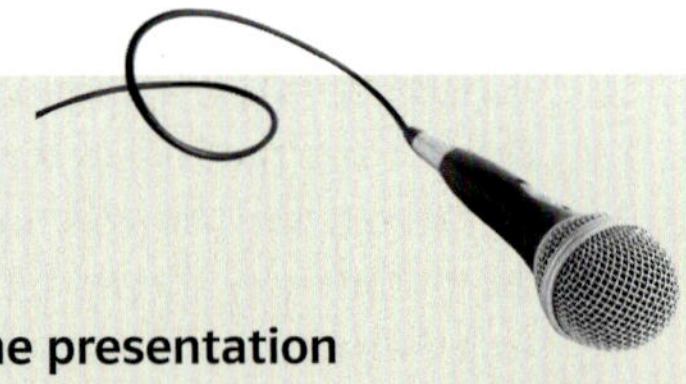

Step 1 Research and sources

- Collect information and material from different sources, including books. Check their quality.
- Document all sources and graphics. → S4
- You can also use statistics / interviews / surveys.
- Use at least two sources for every aspect of the presentation. It makes your statements reliable.

Step 2 Preparation

Making notes

- Plan and visualise the structure on a mind map.
- Write key words and notes for each section on prompt cards. Don't write complete sentences!
- Note facts or details you find interesting, funny or surprising. Use them throughout the talk.
- Quote from experts of your topic.

Visuals (maps, photos, video clips, diagrams, digital presentation slides, flip chart, objects)

- Visuals should be big enough to be seen easily from the back of the room. Comment on the visuals.
- Use one main visual element for each section to help the audience to remember each aspect.
- Use little or no text; your talk is the text!

TIP

Public speaking

- Introduce yourself.
- Announce what you're going to talk about. Then say it. Then sum up what you have said.
- Speak in a slow, clear, natural way, using promt cards.
- Make sure you don't talk for too long. Most people start to lose concentration after ten minutes.
- Rehearse your speech / presentation. Ask someone to listen and give you feedback.

Language

- Choose the right register for your audience.
- Use short and simple sentences with examples.
- Use the phrases below, and adverbs of degree and comment → S17 to make the talk lively.
- Repeat important points. Use rhetorical devices. Explain important / difficult words. → S11, S16

Handout

- Write only the most important points from your presentation, on just one page. Include sources.
- Include name, class, subject, teacher, task, date.

Step 3 Giving the presentation

- Test any equipment as early as possible. Check all you need and give handouts to the audience.
- Smile, interact with the audience and be friendly, polite and self-confident. You are the expert!
- Speak loudly, clearly and slowly.
- Use the tips for public speaking (see tip).

Step 4 Defending your arguments

- Think of questions people may ask at the end and prepare answers and further information.
- Be ready to give more reasons for your arguments.

USEFUL PHRASES

Introduction
Good morning / afternoon / evening, my name is … and my topic today is / I'm going to talk to you about … • I will begin by explaining / describing … and continue with a list of the most important … Finally, I will …

Interactive and rhetorical questions
Have you ever thought … / been in a situation where … • If you think about …, what comes to mind first? • Did you know that …? / I'm sure you will have … • Is there anybody here who has heard of … who / which …

Linking / summarising / repeating points → S17
Therefore, the advantages / disadvantages of … are … • Similarly / In contrast to …, recent developments in … have been surprisingly …

Quotes
X once said that / X, an expert in …, stated that … • According to X … / Although X said …, Y …

Integrating and commenting on visuals
This is an example of a …, which is / was used in … • X, who you can see in the picture, is / was a … who …

Conversational elements and troubleshooting
Can everybody hear me? If not, please let me know. • I'm afraid I lost my train of thought. Let me go back to …

Conclusion
So what we have learned today / the most important … is. / To summarise, then, the most important point … • I've now reached the end of my presentation. Thank you for listening. Does anyone have any questions?

S31 Taking part in discussions and dialogues

One part of your oral exam is often a **dialogue**. You discuss a topic with a partner and / or your examiner. **Discussions** often arise when controversial topics are spoken about. Prepare for both by revising your topic knowledge and reviewing useful phrases. During the dialogue or discussion, make clear, logical arguments and give reasons for your opinion while accepting other people's perspectives. Pick up on what others say or ask friendly questions to show that you are listening carefully.

Remember that non-verbal communication can be as important as what you say!

USEFUL PHRASES

Getting along in dialogue and discussion

Stating your case
Let me begin with … • In my opinion / view, … • I am convinced that … • There are three points I would like to make: First of all, … Secondly, … Thirdly, … • Finally, … • Take …, for example. • To illustrate this point, … • There is strong evidence that … • I'd like to draw your attention to the fact that … • It is also important to know … • What we haven't discussed yet is the question whether / if … • I'd like to emphasise …

Defending your case
My point is that … • I see your point, but I still feel … • That's not quite what I mean. • If I were you, I would … • On the one hand …, (but) on the other hand … • Although …, we mustn't forget that … • I'm glad you asked me that. • That's possibly true, but … • I'm afraid there has been some misunderstanding. What I actually said was … • Don't get me wrong. I meant … • The logical consequence is … • That's why …

Interacting with others
May I interrupt you for a second? • As we have just heard from … • I strongly criticise / disagree … • I'm sorry, but I don't agree with you on that. • What is your position / view on …? • So, if I understand correctly, … • What exactly do you mean by …?

Polite phrases instead of just saying yes or no
No, I'm afraid I don't think so. • Yes, that's partly true. • I agree, but nevertheless, / to be honest … • That's interesting, but what do you think about … ? • Yes, but may I suggest …? • Well, actually …

Feedback phrases to keep a friendly atmosphere
Please • Oh, well • of course • I see • you know • I mean • really? • Are you sure? • I understand that … • I hadn't seen it from that angle before. • You're absolutely right. • That's a good idea. • That sounds very convincing. • I can go along with that.

S32 Debate

All around the world there are debating societies and contests. A debate is a formalised discussion following clear rules. It is a contest between teams of speakers for (proposition) and against (opposition) a statement or 'motion' (e.g. "This house believes that …") which ends in a vote. Taking part in debates can help you to express opinions and arguments clearly and improve your English. Join or start a school debating club! Here is an example structure for a debate.

Step 1 The chairperson ('chair') introduces the issue and presents the motion to be voted for.

Step 2 In the first round, four speakers speak alternately for and against the motion without being interrupted. The audience (called 'the floor') listens.

Step 3 An open debating phase follows, in which the floor takes part, raising hands and, if allowed by the chair, making comments or asking questions.

Step 4 In the second round, speakers summarise positions or make prepared 'rebuttal' speeches against the other party's arguments.

Step 5 The chair calls for a vote by raising hands for / against the motion and concludes the debate.

S33 Chairing a discussion or talk show

Your role as a chairperson
- Be neutral. Do not express your own opinion.
- Do not judge opinions expressed by others.
- Avoid dominance. Let the participants talk.
- Give all speakers an equal chance to talk.
- Ask open or provocative questions.

Step 1 Preparation
- Note the topic's main aspects and vocabulary.
- Write prompt cards with key words on important aspects. Note the order of the speakers.
- Make notes during the discussion to help you to refer to speakers' statements and sum up.

Step 2 Introduction
- Greet the audience and participants and state the topic and its importance.
- State the question / controversy being discussed.
- Introduce the speakers.
- Ask all participants to sum up their opinions in an introductory statement.

Step 3 Conducting and concluding
- Ask open, precise questions encouraging speakers to give a detailed answer (not just yes / no). See the useful phrases box below.
- Ask for closing statements, sum up, conduct a vote (in a debate) and thank speakers.

USEFUL PHRASES

Structuring the discussion

Introduction
Good morning and welcome to our discussion of / debate on the topic of … • The question now / The motion to be discussed today is … • To my right, I'd like to introduce … and …, who are … • I'd like to start with … and I would like you to make an introductory statement about where you stand on this issue / your opinion about …

Introducing a new aspect
Most of you argue that … This raises the question whether / if … • We haven't yet talked about the statistics, which show … • Does that mean / Would you all agree that …?

Conclusion
Time is almost up now. Could each of you briefly summarise your main point again, please? • What has become clear in our discussion is that … • Thank you for your attention.

Keeping order and involving all speakers

Avoiding digressions and repetitions
Can we please stay with … for the moment? • I would like to return to / Going back to … • Would you please come to the point? • Could you please answer …'s question?

Including everybody, dividing time fairly
Mr …, we haven't heard your opinion on … yet. • Ms …, what is your opinion on … / how do you feel about …? • I have a number of people on my list who would like to say something about … • Ms …, would you like to reply to this?

Keeping order
Would you please let … finish his / her statement? • Would you please listen to …? • I have your name on the list; you'll have your turn in a minute. • If I could just stop you there – … would like to comment on your statement.

E Listening skills

S34 Listening comprehension

In everyday life, one-way listening situations can be radio programmes, speeches, presentations, songs and announcements. Purely listening tasks in lessons and exams are the same. You don't have to reply; you just have to understand them. First, you will understand the gist, then the details.

Combined listening and viewing situations can also be one-way, such as TV programmes or films in the cinema, or experiencing presentations using visual media. Here you can observe the speaker's body language, visual clues, and tone to help you understand what is being said.

Step 1 Preparation for note-taking while listening

- Note the task title, situation and information you already know; for example, say who is speaking.
- For a particular task, write suitable headings to give you a frame for collecting important information. Make these as simple as possible.

World without media London 2021
– Mr Smith's opinion: no real loss
less loneliness, more personal contact
– Reason 1: more time to talk
– Reason 2: fewer distractions

Step 2 Listening for the first time: gist

Make notes while you listen:

- First write down **key words and phrases** which sound important. Listen for stresses on words or the repetition of words to help you find them.
- Leave space between your first notes for more notes when you listen again.
- Write down **names, dates, numbers, times and places** when you hear them, with one or two words to explain them. They may be useful later.

Step 3 Using the break between listening times

- Read through the words you wrote and look at the task again.
- Check what you easily understood to see if it still seems logical.
- Write an answer to the first task(s) if necessary.
- Check what you still need to listen for.

Step 4 Listening again for more detail

- Concentrate on what you still need to know.
- Listen for grammatical signs to help you understand the meaning. Present, future or past tense? Singular or plural?
- Listen for connecting words *(and, but, because, on the other hand, …)* which help you to understand how the information is being used.

TIP

Strategies for understanding quickly

- **Don't panic** if you don't hear or understand every word! You will probably still understand the most important information.
- **Intonation patterns** will help you to recognise a speaker's attitude or intention. Does what the speaker says sound like a question, criticism, suggestion, statement, agreement, ironic statement, or a joke?
- Use **anticipation** to help you. What do you think they are going to say?
- Remember **words you know** for the topic.

USEFUL PHRASES

Coping in two-way listening situations (telephone call, conversation, debate)

I'm sorry, I didn't quite catch what you said. • Could you say that again, please? • Could you please repeat that? • Sorry, I don't understand the word '…'. What does it mean? • Can you spell that for me, please? • Did I understand you right when you said … • I've never heard that word before. Could you please explain what you mean by '…'? Does it mean …? • I think you said … Am I right? • Could you possibly speak just a little bit more slowly, please?

F Visual skills

S35 Dealing with films

To understand the contents of a film, that is the **setting, location, plot** and **characters**, use the skills you know from reading and listening tasks (→ S8, S34). In addition, pay attention to the **film type** and what **cinematic devices** are used to complete your analysis.

Film types

Entertainment

- Anyone can post **video clips** online.
- Professional **music videos** give visual atmosphere and / or a context to songs.
- **Film series**, made for home viewing, encourage viewers to continue to watch by using cliffhangers.
- **Feature films** are full-length films made for presentation in the cinema or for home viewing. They may correspond to, parody or mix typical genres e.g. action, adventure, animation, comedy, police procedural, docudrama, historical, horror, musical, romance, sci-fi, thriller or western.

Information, education and advertising

- **Newscasts** provide information on current events.
- **Documentaries** show, explain and guide the viewer through topics such as history, politics, environmental issues, science or wildlife.
- **Explainer films** teach you about a topic. → S36
- **Commercial clips** for advertising.

Cinematic devices

Camera techniques

The **field size** is how much you can see on the screen. A wide-angle or full shot gives an overall impression and is often used to set the scene. Medium and close-up shots focus on action and interaction; extreme close-ups show facial expressions and emotions.

The **camera angle** influences how the viewer sees the characters. A high angle, bird's eye view makes people look small and insignificant. A low, worm's eye view makes them look big and powerful. An over-the-shoulder shot shows interaction between two people and how close they are. A reverse-angle shot shows the reaction of the person talked to, not the person talking.

Camera movement ranges from a static shot (no movement, a calm, slow scene) to a tracking shot, following a moving person as if walking or running with them, emphasising movement and the emotions connected with the speed.

Editing techniques

Cuts are film stops / changes between one camera angle / scene and the next. The more cuts, the quicker and more hectic the pace. Fade-out and fade-in are calmer than cuts. A flashback or flash-forward switches to another time in the storyline.

The **playing speed** changes to slow motion to intensify moments, to time lapse for slow change or fast motion to exaggerate speed.

Motifs, music and atmosphere

Repeating elements (motifs) like symbolic objects, lighting, sounds, music, words or colours influence the mood and emphasise the theme of the film. E.g. red suggests heat or violence; gold and light for luxury or riches; black and shadows for fear and death. Music both reveals and influences emotions.

USEFUL PHRASES

Cinematic devices
In the establishing shot the audience can see … • This brings … close. / This creates distance between … • The viewer sees … from above / below / behind / from a … perspective, which makes … look … • The tracking shot follows (the movement of) … • The shots follow each other quickly / slowly, creating a sense of … • Suspense is created by … • The camera pans from left to right / tilts from top to bottom, shifting the focus from … to … • … is shown in slow motion, intensifying … • … moves the action forward / surprises the viewer. • The relationship between … is shown to be … by … • The characteristic / repeated use of … emphasises …

Action and language
There is more action than speech / more speech than action in the scene, which emphasises … • X's body language / reactions show(s) that …

S36 Creating explainer films

Explainer films take larger concepts and break them down into parts, making complicated ideas easy to understand. They are typically quite short, entertaining, and **informative**. Providing audio, visual and visible text simultaneously can have different advantages for the learner.

Planning and making an explainer film

- You are the expert: Know your topic.
- Decide on the learning target (the one thing the viewer should know at the end) and length (2–4 min.). Make a sequence of short clips rather than just a long film. Use cliffhangers to connect them.
- Collect ideas; choose a suitable film type (e.g. stop motion film, animation, real film sequences).
- Assign roles to team members (→ S6) to create your clip. Follow these golden rules:

1. **Show, don't just tell:** Think of a realistic, interesting situation / picture that can explain a lot simply by showing it. Start with a hook that draws attention.
2. **Visual input + text:** Use the voice-over to give additional information in simple language. Use visual elements to add humour or to show how / why. Keep on-screen text to an absolute minimum.
3. **Viewers who enjoy learn better:** Activate viewers by asking questions or using a storyline, plot twist, real-life scenario or surprise.
4. **Make a storyboard:** Plan each step with a sketched scene, text, moves, sound, actors, camera settings etc. Don't forget the title screen and credits.
5. **Use creative commons resources** (pictures, sounds and music) and quote them correctly.
6. **Concentrate on language and clarity:** Allow enough time per slide or sequence for the viewer to understand the information. Test your film on someone who doesn't know the topic.

S37 Analysing statistics

Diagrams visualise statistics and make them much easier to understand and analyse. Check for relevant details, clarity, up-to-date content, and reliable sources to assess the quality. **Infographics** show what statistics, facts or quotes mean by visualising numbers as this makes it much easier to understand, remember and interpret them.

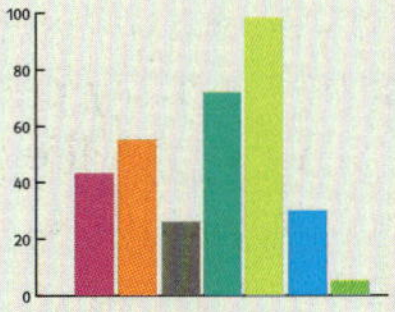

bar chart
for comparing figures directly

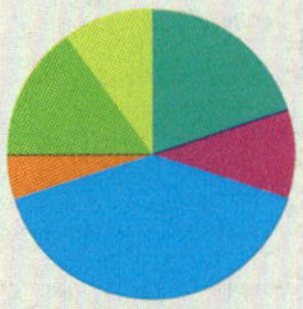

pie chart
for percentages or proportions

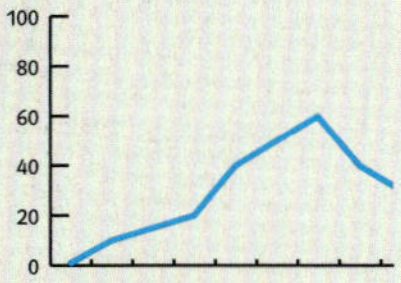

line graph
for trends / developments

USEFUL PHRASES

Introduction
The bar chart / pie chart / line graph from *(source)* in *(year)* shows how many … are … in relation to … • … represents the results / amounts of … in percent in / for *(year / country / …)* • … displays the development of … from *(start)* to *(end)*. • The horizontal / vertical axis … •

Description
The majority / minority of … have … • The chart shows the amount / proportion / number of … from *(year)* to *(year)*. • The longest / shortest bar shows … • The segments highlight that the amount / share of … is larger / smaller than … • Surprisingly, nearly half / all / a third of … • … reached its highest / lowest point in …, which was probably because … • The number of … increased / rose / remained constant / decreased / fell (gradually / rapidly / significantly) until … • Since then there has been a marked / slight … • Comparing the charts for … • On average, there are twice / three times as many … • A total of …

Analysis / Conclusion
This illustrates / could be a result of / proves that / makes it clear that … • The change was possibly caused by … • The numbers / figures suggest that … • This chart indicates that … • We can draw the conclusion that …

S38 Analysing visuals

Visual material, for example a **picture** or **cartoon**, often sends a message or draws our attention to a certain aspect or issue. It can be described and analysed systematically by following these steps.

STEP 1 Introduction

Note what the picture / cartoon shows in one sentence. Add any information you know (creator's name, picture type, when / where / why it was created) and emotions the visual evokes and, if asked, your first reaction to it.

STEP 2 Description

Imagine you're describing the visual to a blind person. Start with the most important elements and the background. What other information is needed to explain it and its message? Check for speech bubbles, captions, people's body language or facial expressions, and their relationship with each other. Use the present progressive for describing people, and the simple present for objects and the setting.

STEP 3 Analysis

Describe the message the picture conveys. Is it aimed at a target group? What effect does it have on the viewer? How are language, light, colours, focus and perspective used to support the message?

TIP

Pictures can contribute to fake news, e.g. when they are taken out of context or evoke strong emotions. Editing pictures or creating memes may manipulate the original context or meaning.

STEP 4 Evaluation / Interpretation

State whether the visual is effective and which elements are responsible for its success / failure. If asked, give your personal opinion. Do symbols, stereotypes, or feelings come to your mind?

Some kinds of visuals require you to analyse additional features. **Paintings** often have a historical component. Compare the original intent / effect with the one it has now. **Cartoons** usually pick up on current news events and criticise people, institutions, or developments in society and politics. They may often just be entertaining, e.g. making fun of public figures, but can also make a serious / important point clear using visual means.

TIP

Cartoonists often use the following techniques:
- highlighting prominent features / actions / events by caricature (exaggerating characteristic elements)
- exposing inconsistencies (e.g. contrasting a statement with a picture showing the opposite)
- irony (depicting the opposite of what is really meant)
- making use of puns, word play or symbolic elements

USEFUL PHRASES

Introduction / First impression
The cartoon / photograph was drawn / taken by … • It was published / appeared in *(source)* on *(date)*. • It was created in response to / during the time of … • It shows / deals with / refers to / comments on … • The cartoonist / photographer / artist makes fun of … / criticises … • It gives a detailed / realistic / shocking / dramatic view of …

Description
The picture / cartoon consists of / is divided into … • There is a (short / an ironic) caption / speech bubble / thought bubble / description in / on / next to … • The caption says / states that … • In the foreground / background / middle / centre there is … • In the top / bottom left- / right-hand corner … • The perspective is from above / below / eye level / the side. • It's a close-up / medium shot / long shot field of view.

Analysis / message
The eye is drawn to … • There is a contrast between … • … is clearly visible, whereas … does not stand out as much. • The light / colours / position of / elements of … create an … atmosphere / give an impression of … • The cartoon stands for / represents / is a caricature of … • It plays on the stereotypical view of … • … is exaggerated / symbolic of … • The humour / irony lies in the discrepancy / contrast / parallels / misunderstanding between …

Interpretation and evaluation
The overall effect of the drawing / cartoon is … • The cartoon (only partly) achieves its aim of (doing sth). • It reminds me of … • In my opinion, the artist / cartoonist is (not) successful in presenting / criticising … because … • The picture is a (non-)stereotypical view of … because … • In my opinion, it is convincing / simplistic / confusing / (un-)fair. • It skilfully / effectively shows …

G Mediation skills

S39 Mediating written and spoken texts

What is mediation?

- You are the **mediating link**, passing on information from a source in one language – text(s), statistics, visuals, infographics or spoken information – to a recipient / addressee who (normally) only speaks another language and needs some of this information for a particular purpose.
- Your job is to pass on the relevant parts of this information in a new text type and language for a new purpose.
- Name the source(s) to clarify whose ideas / facts you are stating. Don't mix this information with what you know or think.
- **Never just translate every sentence or summarise all of the text.** Some parts are irrelevant for your task!
- You will need to go through the whole text to find all the information you need, then restructure and / or paraphrase it to make your own communication clear.
- Add suitable context for your recipient, e.g. if you are writing an email, greet the reader, say why you are giving him / her this information and end the email – formally or informally, according to the situation.

Step 1 Looking carefully at the task

- Note what points the addressee needs to know. Keep that in focus as you read / listen.

Step 2 Reading the original source(s)

- After reading / listening once for gist, note the source type, title, author's / speaker's name and the intention / tone for passing on information about the source. → S8
- Read again. Mark / Note the task-relevant key words or paragraphs. Don't stop after finding one point. Check for more!

Step 3 Preparing your mediation

- Check the task again for:
  - **text type and length**
  - **addressee**
  - **relationship** between you (for register and style).
- **Rearrange** all points into a useful order.

Step 4 Writing your mediation text

- Use appropriate language and style for the situation.
- Introduce the source(s) and explain why you are passing this information on.
- Write each section in your own words in a suitable structure for the addressee.
- Paraphrase if you can't translate. Explain cultural or idiomatic terms, e.g. 'ARD', a German public TV channel, or 'Fernweh', a longing to travel far away.

Step 5 Editing and checking → S29

Check for 'false friends' and correct wrong spelling, word order, tenses, prepositions and style.
Read again: Your text should sound natural.

Grammar

In this short grammar section, you can look up selected difficult grammar points again. The rules and examples will help you to remember why each construction is used and to improve your writing / speaking.

G1 Tenses referring to the past

Basic rules

- As a rule, you use the **past tense** for actions / events that were completed in the past.
- Use the **present perfect** for actions / events that happened in the past and whose results are still relevant to the present.
- Also use it for actions / events completed in the past if you want to stress that they have taken place one or more times (without actually saying when).
- Also use it for actions / events that started in the past but are not over yet.

- To express chronological relations between two actions / events of the past in one sentence, follow the sequence of tenses.
- Use the **past tense** for two actions / events happening at the same time or shortly after one another.
- Use the **past perfect** and the past tense to clarify that one thing happened before or after the other.
- Referring to the past, use **substitute forms** for modal auxiliaries.
- If you want to shift the focus from somebody doing something to something being done, use the **passive**.
- If you introduce a statement in **indirect speech** with a past tense verb, **backshift** the tenses.

Reflection

Look at the examples, examine the differences in meaning and explain why each of the tenses is used.

1. The British **focused** on Africa, Asia and the Pacific because their North American colonies **had become** independent.
2. The British **didn't focus** on Africa, Asia and the Pacific until their North American colonies **became** independent.
3. Imperialists **claimed** that the British **had to shift** their focus to Africa, Asia and the Pacific in order to be able to compete with other colonial powers.
4. When production methods **were industrialised** and large factories **were built**, people **came** to live and work in the towns and cities of the Midlands.
5. **Have** you ever **been** to the US? – Yes, **I've visited** New York three times.
6. My brother **has lost** his ticket. Now he's in trouble.
7. We**'ve been living** in Leicester for four years.

TIP

Know your **irregular verb forms.** Know the substitute forms of modal auxiliaries. Use suitable linking words.

Immigrants on Ellis Island in New York City, 1905/1907

G2 Aspect

Basic rules

- Referring to a state or a regular activity / event rather than to a dynamic action / event, use the **simple form**.
- If you want to focus on the duration of an action / event in progress, use the **progressive form**.

Reflection *Look at the examples and explain why each of the tenses is used.*

1. In some deserts, it never **rains**.
2. It **was raining** all the time while we **were walking** home.
3. I **was waiting** for the meeting to begin when my phone **rang**.
4. Listen! They**'re talking** about their plans for the new cultural centre.
5. They **meet** and **talk** about new suggestions every Tuesday.
6. The athletes **had been training** all morning when the press **arrived** to interview them.
7. I **joined** the training camp because I **had heard** of the new coach.
8. Sea levels **have been rising** constantly due to global warming.
9. I **had known** all along that it **was** a big mistake.

TIP

- Remember: Most English verbs are **dynamic** (e.g. *run, change, write*) and can be used in the simple form or in the progressive form. **Stative verbs** describe 'states' (e.g. *belong, know, cost*). Therefore, they are normally only used in the simple form.
- Use the progressive form when you want to focus on the duration or progress of an action or event.

G3 Conditional sentences

Basic rules

- If you want to refer to a condition and its consequence, choose the correct tenses in the *if* clause and the main clause according to the degree of probability of the condition being fulfilled and depending on whether you refer to the past, the present or the future.
- The order of the tenses given in brackets applies to conditional sentences in which the *if* clause comes before the main clause.

- Use **type 1** conditional sentences (**present tense / will future**) to refer to a possible future.
- Use **type 2** conditional sentences (**past tense / conditional**) to refer to a theoretically possible future.
- Use **mixed** conditional sentences (**past tense / conditional perfect**) to refer to consequences in the past of conditions that haven't been fulfilled in the present.
- Use **type 3** conditional sentences (**past perfect / conditional perfect**) to refer to possible consequences in the past of conditions that were not fulfilled in the past.
- Use **mixed** conditional sentences (**past perfect / conditional**) to refer to possible consequences in the present of conditions that were not fulfilled in the past.

Reflection *Look at the examples and explain what type of conditional sentence each of them is.*

1. If the British **had taken** more time to prepare independence in India, there **may not have been** so many deaths.
2. If global trade **stopped**, our lives **would change** considerably.
3. Our lives **would be** completely different if there **hadn't been** a digital revolution.
4. If you **were interested** Bollywood movies, you **would have heard** about Shah Rukh Khan.
5. There **would be** no need for Black Lives Matter protests if racism **were wiped out**.
6. If we **don't learn** from the mistakes of the past, life **will be** harder for future generations.
7. If I **spoke** Mandarin, I **could have applied** for work experience in China.

TIP

- Never use a conditional form in the *if* clause! ~~*If you would study hard, you would pass the exam*~~.
- Use commas in conditional sentences only when they start with the *if* clause.

G4 Non-finite constructions with participles or gerunds

Basic rules

These **non-finite constructions** can be used **instead of adverbial clauses, relative clauses or main clauses**. They can express a sequence of events. They can have an active or a passive meaning. Sometimes they have a **subject of their own**.

Reflection *Look at the examples and show you understand their meanings by replacing them with finite constructions instead.*

1. **Wanting** to get to know the city, we flew to New York.
2. Always **having wanted** to get to know the city, we flew to New York.
3. **After checking in**, we had a coffee in the airport lounge. / **Having checked in**, we had a coffee in the airport lounge.
4. He answered the police officer's questions, still (**being**) in shock.
5. **His things being** in total disorder, it took him some time to find out what had been stolen.
6. My mother, **having returned** from work, was surprised to find me at home.
7. The boss appreciated the job **done** by her team.
8. **Confused** by the way the questions were asked, I wasn't able to answer them immediately.
9. He tried to walk away quickly, his dog **following** him and **barking** loudly.

TIP

- Decide if a linking word (e.g. *after, while, thus*) is needed to make the logical connection between the participle construction and the main clause explicit.
- Using participle constructions, make sure your participle always refers to the right word or phrase in the sentence, unlike in these examples:
  ~~*Arriving at the station, the train had already left.*~~
  Grammatically, the participle refers to the subject of the main clause (= *the train*). This doesn't make sense. The information on who arrived at the station needs to be added.
  *Arriving at the station, **my parents** learned that the train had already left.*
  ~~*Covered in dirt, he gave the dog a bath.*~~ In this sentence, it isn't quite clear who is covered in dirt: *he, the dog* or both?
  ~~*Having repaired the damaged windscreen, the car looked good again.*~~ Again, there is no reasonable subject for the participle to refer to. If you don't know who repaired the car, you can change the participle from active to passive and make the object the subject of the participle construction:
  ***The damaged windscreen (having been) repaired**, the car looked good again.*

G5 Non-finite constructions with gerunds or infinitives

Basic rules

There are non-finite constructions with **infinitives** or **gerunds** which do not correspond to clauses with finite verbs.

Reflection *Look at the examples, explain the function of each non-finite construction and / or translate it into German.*

1. Malcolm McLean revolutionised global transport **by standardising** shipping containers.
2. **To be able** to assess market developments, internet companies collect, store and evaluate large amounts of customer data.
3. In the near future, Californians **expect water shortages to become** more frequent.
4. **Instead of saving** energy, we are looking for new energy sources.
5. I think **it's worth trying** to find out how we can live more sustainably.

G6 Relative clauses

Basic rules

- Use **defining relative clauses** to give information about people or things that are not clearly defined without that information. Don't use commas to separate main clause and relative clause.
- Use **non-defining relative clauses** to give additional information about people or things that are clearly defined without that information. Always use commas to separate main clause and relative clause.
- Use **commenting relative clauses**, which are a special type of **non-defining relative clauses**, to refer to entire statements or sentences.
- Use suitable **relative pronouns** (**who** for people and **which** for things or neutral pronouns like **that** and **whose**). Relative clauses can be used without relative pronouns when the subject of the main clause is not identical with the subject of the relative clause. This kind of relative clause is called **contact clause**.

Reflection *Look at the examples and explain what kind of relative clause is used.*

1. The children **who were taken away** from their families suffered from the separation.
2. The children in residential schools, **who had been taken away** from their families, suffered from the separation.
3. The children **(whom) the government had taken away** from their families suffered from the separation.
4. The residential school system was a system **which was established** by the Canadian government to assimilate Indigenous children into the dominant Canadian culture.
5. About 150,000 children in residential schools were forced to give up their traditional culture, language and religion, **which amounts to cultural genocide.**
6. The residential school tragedy is a historical truth **(that) Canada is not proud of.**

TIP

- Never use *what* as a relative pronoun! Use ***which*** for commenting relative clauses.
- Prepositions are usually moved to the end of a relative clause because introducing a relative clause with a preposition and a relative pronoun as its object sounds very formal *(... a historical truth **of which** Canada is not proud.).*

G7 Emphasis

Basic rules

- Use **emphatic pronouns** to stress that a particular person has done something in person or without help from others. Also use them to stress that somebody or something is meant as such.
- Use **emphatic *do*** to stress an action/event expressed by a verb phrase.
- Use **cleft sentences** to put emphasis on any part of a sentence you want to stress.

Reflection *Look at the examples and explain why each kind of emphasis is used.*

1. Even monarchs cannot decide everything **by themselves.**
2. She has designed the poster **herself.**
3. The king **himself** spoke to us at the meeting.
4. The house **itself** is nothing special, but the garden around it is like a beautiful park.
5. Most white people do not mean to be racist, but they **do** tend to ask people with darker skin where they come from.
6. **It was** the Industrial Revolution **that** started in Britain in the 18th century.
7. **It was** in Britain **that** the Industrial Revolution started in the 18th century.
8. **It was** in the 18th century **that** the Industrial Revolution in Britain started.
9. **What** people associate with the Midlands **is** the Industrial Revolution.

TIP

Always make cleft sentences with *It is/was ...* or *What ... is/was ...*, even if a noun in the plural follows: ***It is*** ***the people*** *who make all the difference.*

Thematic vocabulary

This part of the book contains a selection of useful vocabulary for each of the five *Topics* and *Visions of the future*. It is organised thematically. Each section is divided into three to five themes. The vocabulary is listed in alphabetical order under each theme heading.

You may find that some of the words are not new. You should know them from working with *Green Line 1–6*. They were added to the lists because they are useful in the given contexts. You may also find some words that are not in the texts but that have been added because they are helpful to talk about the themes.

At the end of each part, there are exercises to revise and expand your vocabulary. You can find the solutions on p. 226ff.

Unlike in *Green Line 1–6*, there is no printed chronological vocabulary to go with the *Topic* texts in the book itself, but you can find vocabulary sheets for each of the texts online (in: *Medien zum Schulbuch*).

AE	American English	*infml*	informal	↔	is the opposite of
BE	British English	*pl*	plural	→	is related to
CE	Canadian English	*sg*	singular	!	usage note
fml	formal	*	irregular verb		

Topic 1 New York – aspects of a world city

Visiting a world city

architecture ['ɑːkɪtektʃə]	Architektur	New York is world-famous for its spectacular *architecture*. *architecture* → architect
attraction [ə'trækʃn]	Attraktion; Sehenswürdigkeit	The Empire State Building is a popular tourist *attraction*. *attraction* → to attract → attractive
awe-inspiring ['ɔːɪnspaɪrɪŋ]	beeindruckend; Ehrfurcht einflößend	When he first saw the skyline of New York, it was an *awe-inspiring* moment. ! an *awe-inspiring* sight/landscape/moment
breathtaking ['breθˌteɪkɪŋ]	atemberaubend	The landscape was so beautiful it was *breathtaking*. *breathtaking* → to breathe
contemporary [kən'temprəri]	zeitgenössisch; zeitgemäß	In the city you can find a mix of historic and *contemporary* buildings. *contemporary* ≈ current *contemporary* ↔ old-fashioned, traditional
historic [hɪ'stɒrɪk]	historisch	They didn't know at the time that they were witnessing a *historic* moment. ! Careful: 1. *historic*: The president's speech was a *historic* moment. (= important in history). 2. historical: Do you love historical films? (= related to history). *historic* → history
hub [hʌb]	Zentrum; Mittelpunkt	Lots of people want to work in Silicon Valley, the technological *hub* of the US.

landmark ['lænmɑ:k]	Wahrzeichen	The Statue of Liberty is an important *landmark*.
marvellous ['mɑ:vləs]	fabelhaft; herrlich	We had a *marvellous* time at the Broadway show. ! *marvellous (BE)* = marvelous *(AE)*
megacity ['megə,sɪti]	Millionenstadt	Do you know how many people live in this *megacity*?
memorial [mə'mɔ:riəl]	Denkmal; Gedenkstätte; Denkschrift	There are thousands of Civil War *memorials* in the United States. *memorial* → memory
metropolis [me'trɒpəlɪs]	Metropole; Weltstadt	You can find everything in this city. It's a *metropolis*!
monument ['mɒnjəmənt]	Monument; Denkmal	This *monument* shows an important person in history.
reputation [,repjə'teɪʃn]	Ruf	This food truck has an excellent *reputation*. You can get the best tacos there.
sight [saɪt]	Sehenswürdigkeit; Anblick	You can't visit all of New Yok's *sights* in just one weekend. A *sight* is an interesting thing to see in a city. *sight* → sightseeing

Population

to **adapt to sth** [ə'dæpt ,tə]	sich etw. anpassen	It's not always easy to *adapt to* a new situation.
to **assimilate** [ə'sɪmɪleɪt]	integrieren; eingliedern	Some immigrants find it difficult to *assimilate* into a new culture. *to assimilate* → assimilation
to **cooperate** [kəʊ'ɒpreɪt]	kooperieren; zusammenarbeiten	We all need to *cooperate* to find a solution. *cooperate* = to work together *to cooperate* → cooperation
cosmopolitan [,kɒzmə'pɒlɪtn]	weltoffen; international; kosmopolitisch	London is a *cosmopolitan* city. Lots of different cultures live there together.
crowd [kraʊd]	Menschenmenge	A huge *crowd* has come to see the show. *crowd* → crowded → crowdedness
custom ['kʌstəm]	Gewohnheit; Brauch; Sitte	Trick-or-treating is a Halloween *custom*.
diversity [daɪ'vɜ:səti]	Vielfalt; Verschiedenheit	Cultural *diversity* describes people with different ethnic, national, or language backgrounds living in one community. *diversity* → diverse
ethnic ['eθnɪk]	ethnisch; Volks-	What's your *ethnic* background? *ethnic* → ethnicity
habit ['hæbɪt]	Gewohnheit	It isn't always easy to give up bad *habits*. A *habit* is something one usually does. *habit* → habitual
heterogeneous [,hetrə'dʒi:niəs]	heterogen; verschiedenartig	We live in a *heterogeneous* society with people from different cultural and social backgrounds. *heterogeneous* ↔ homogeneous
immigrant ['ɪmɪgrənt]	Immigrant/-in; Einwanderer/Einwanderin	Her parents came to the UK as *immigrants*. ! Nigerian/Jamaican/first-generation/second-generation/illegal *immigrant* *immigrant* → immigration → to immigrate

influx ['ɪnflʌks]	Zustrom	This country has experienced a large *influx* of immigrants over the past years.
inhabitant [ɪn'hæbɪtnt]	Einwohner/-in; Bewohner/-in	All the *inhabitants* of the building were informed that gas would be disconnected for two hours. All the people who live in a place are its *inhabitants*.
migrant ['maɪgrnt]	Migrant/-in	Big cities attract *migrants* because of the opportunities they offer. ! climate/economic/undocumented *migrant* *migrant* → migration → to migrate
minority [maɪ'nɒrəti]	Minderheit	This organisation is fighting for the rights of *minorities*. *minority* = less than half of the people or things in a group *minority* ↔ majority
multicultural [ˌmʌlti'kʌltʃrl]	multikulturell	Canada is a *multicultural* society. *multicultural* → multiculturalism
population [ˌpɒpjə'leɪʃn]	Bevölkerung; Population	This country has a large Spanish-speaking *population*. *population* → populated → populous
social status [ˌsəʊʃl 'steɪtəs]	gesellschaftliches Ansehen	Does one's *social status* entirely depend on money?
variety (of) [və'raɪəti‿əv]	Vielzahl (an); Vielfalt (von)	They say that *variety* is the spice of life. *variety* → various → to vary

Living and working in a world city

anonymity [ˌænə'nɪməti]	Anonymität	The artist wants to preserve his *anonymity*. *anonymity* → anonymous
borough *(AE)* ['bʌrə]	Bezirk; Stadtteil	New York consists of five *boroughs*. Manhattan is one of them.
*to **come true** [ˌkʌm 'tru:]	wahr werden; in Erfüllung gehen	Wouldn't it be wonderful if our dreams *came true*? ! to make a dream *come true*
commercial [kə'mɜ:ʃl]	kommerziell; profitorientiert	The movie was a *commercial* success, but the critics hated it. ! *commercial* activity/advertising/centre *commercial* → commerce
community [kə'mju:nəti]	Gemeinde; Gemeinschaft	Are you active in your *community*? ! a close-knit/religious/Asian/English-speaking/sense of *community*
to **commute** [kə'mju:t]	pendeln	Every day she takes the train to *commute* to work. *to commute* → commuter
concrete ['kɒŋkri:t]	Beton	New York is often called a *concrete* jungle.
to **consist of** [kən'sɪst‿əv]	bestehen aus	The US *consists of* 50 states.
downtown *(AE)* [ˌdaʊn'taʊn]	Stadtzentrum; im Stadtzentrum	I think malls are boring. Shopping *downtown* is cooler! Our hotel is close to *downtown*. *downtown (AE)* = in the city centre *(BE)*
green space [ˌgri:n 'speɪs]	Grünfläche	This city doesn't just consist of concrete. There are lots of *green spaces*.
job opportunity [ˌdʒɒb‿ɒpə'tʃu:nəti]	Stellenangebot; Arbeitsgelegenheit	I'm moving to Now York because I've been offered a great *job opportunity* there.

*to **make it** ['meɪk‿ɪt]	es schaffen	If I can *make it* here, I can *make it* anywhere. *to make it* = to be successful
neighbourhood ['neɪbəhʊd]	Stadtviertel	We love our *neighbourhood* because there are lots of small shops, nice restaurants and green spaces. *neighbourhood* → neighbour
office space ['ɒfɪs ˌspeɪs]	Bürofläche	This new building offers a lot of *office space*.
residential [ˌrezɪ'dentʃl]	Wohn-	We live in a *residential area* close to downtown. ! *residential* area/building/street *residential* → resident
suburb ['sʌbɜːb]	Vorort	We moved from a small apartment downtown to a large house in the *suburbs*. *suburb* → suburban
transit system *(AE)* ['trænsɪt ˌsɪstəm]	Transportsystem	The subway is part of New York's *transit system*.
urban ['ɜːbn]	städtisch; Stadt-	We live in an *urban* area. *urban* ↔ rural
to **work from home** [ˌwɜːk frəm 'həʊm]	im Homeoffice arbeiten	In the past, I had to commute over an hour to and from work, but now I can *work from home*.

Urban development

*to **be located** [ˌbi ləʊ'keɪtɪd]	gelegen sein; liegen	Where *is* the museum *located*? = Where exactly is the museum? *to be located* = to be situated *to be located* → location
to **benefit (from)** ['benɪfɪt]	von etw. profitieren	The whole area *benefits from* tourism. *to benefit (from)* = to profit (from) *to benefit (from)* → benefit
decline [dɪ'klaɪn]	Rückgang; Abnahme; Niedergang	The rapid *decline* in sales worried the CEO. *decline* ↔ growth
to **develop** [dɪ'veləp]	(sich) entwickeln	English *developed* from different languages. *to develop* → development
growth [grəʊθ]	Wachstum	This chart shows the population *growth* in the past few years. *growth* → to grow
to **increase** [ɪn'kriːs]	steigen; erhöhen; zunehmen; wachsen	How can we *increase* the motivation of our workers? *to increase* ↔ to decrease *to increase* → increase
industrialisation [ɪnˌdʌstriəlaɪ'zeɪʃn]	Industrialisierung	*Industrialisation* made a lot of people move to the cities in order to find work. *industrialisation* → to industrialise → industry → industrial
infrastructure ['ɪnfrəˌstrʌktʃə]	Infrastruktur	It's a small town, but it has a great *infrastructure*. It's connected to three big cities.
setback ['setbæk]	Rückschlag	The team suffered a major *setback*, but they believe they can improve. ! to experience/to suffer/to receive a *setback*

settler ['setlə]	Siedler/-in	The English *settlers* started colonies in the Northeast. *settler* → to settle → settlement
*to **spread** [spred]	(sich) verbreiten	News *spread* quickly on social media. *to spread* → spread
tie [taɪ]	Beziehung; Bindung	The two countries have developed strong *ties*. *tie* → to tie
trade [treɪd]	Handel	The ivory *trade* is illegal. *trade* → trader → to trade

Social issues and other challenges

affordable [ə'fɔːdəbl]	bezahlbar; erschwinglich	One of the biggest challenges of the city is to create *affordable* housing. *affordable* → to afford
to **aggravate** ['ægrəveɪt]	verschlimmern; verschärfen	Growing carbon emissions *have been aggravating* global warming.
climate change ['klaɪmət ˌtʃeɪndʒ]	Klimawandel	*Climate change* has a huge impact on life on earth. ! to cause/to contribute to/to mitigate/to combat/to adapt to *climate change*
crime rate ['kraɪm ˌreɪt]	Kriminalitätsrate; Verbrechensrate	The *crime rate* has been increasing for years.
to **deteriorate** [dɪ'tɪəriəreɪt]	sich verschlechtern	Measures have been taken to prevent the situation from *deteriorating*. *to deteriorate* ↔ to improve
discrimination [dɪˌskrɪmɪ'neɪʃn]	Diskriminierung	We must stop *discrimination* against women. ! racial/job/gender/disability *discrimination* *discrimination* → to be discriminated against
disparity [dɪs'pærəti]	Missverhältnis; Ungleichheit	We find great *disparities* of wealth in this region.
gentrification [ˌdʒentrɪfɪ'keɪʃn]	Aufwertung durch Luxussanierung	This neighbourhood has changed a lot due to *gentrification*.
homelessness ['həʊmləsnəs]	Obdachlosigkeit	What can we do to end *homelessness*? ! to address/to deal with/to tackle the problem of *homelessness* *homelessness* → homeless
housing ['haʊzɪŋ]	Unterkunft; Wohnungsbeschaffung	The city is facing an acute *housing* crisis. *housing* → house
inequality [ˌɪnɪ'kwɒləti]	Ungleichheit	I recently read a utopian novel about a classless society without any social *inequality*. ! to overcome/to eliminate *inequality* *inequality* → equal → unequal
injustice [ɪn'dʒʌstɪs]	Ungerechtigkeit	Our organisation tries to end social *injustice*. ! to fight/to combat *injustice*
lack of ['læk‿əv]	Mangel an; Fehlen von	He was often criticised for his *lack of* politeness. *lack of* → to lack

pollution [pəˈluːʃn]	Verschmutzung	*Pollution* has made the river dirty. ! air/coastal/environmental/groundwater/light/marine/noise/oil pollution to cut/to reduce/to limit air *pollution* *pollution* → to pollute
poverty [ˈpɒvəti]	Armut	Almost a fifth of the children in Australia live below the *poverty* line. *poverty* → poor
scarcity [ˈskeəsəti]	Knappheit; Mangel	Due to the *scarcity* of affordable homes, a lot of young people are sharing an apartment with others. *scarcity* → scarce
shelter [ˈʃeltə]	Obdach; Schutz; Schutzhütte	He is currently living in a *shelter* for the homeless.
to skyrocket [ˈskaɪˌrɒkɪt]	emporschnellen; sprunghaft ansteigen	Food prices have *skyrocketed* over the past few months.
traffic jam [ˈtræfɪk ˌdʒæm]	Stau	The beginning of the school holidays has caused huge *traffic jams* all across the country. ! to cause/to produce *traffic jams*
wealth [welθ]	Reichtum; Vermögen	She's working very hard to increase her *wealth*. *wealth* ↔ poverty *wealth* → wealthy

Prepositions

English and German often use different prepositions, so it's important to learn new words together with the prepositions they take.

a) Complete the phrases about city life with the correct prepositions.

1. a lack [1] housing
2. discrimination [2] minorities
3. to deal [3] social issues
4. to benefit [4] a variety [5] marvellous attractions
5. to be located [6] Manhattan
6. a high demand [7] office space
7. to depend [8] immigrant workers
8. to adapt [9] New York's chaotic traffic
9. a magnet [10] tourists
10. to go [11] bus, [12] subway or [13] foot
11. the subway consists [14] 28 routes
12. a dramatic increase [15] violent crimes

Some verbs have a particular meaning when combined with a preposition. Make sure you know the meaning of these phrasal verbs, e.g. *to **take off – to leave the ground and start flying. Our plane **took off** at 7:30 a.m.***

b) Explain the meaning of the following phrasal verbs. Then make sentences with them. Use a dictionary if necessary.

1. to get along (with) • 2. to show up • 3. to pick up • 4. to go out • 5. to fit in • 6. to miss out (on sth) • 7. to catch up (with sb) • 8. to carry on • 9. to be up to • 10. to make sth up • 11. to give in

Word families

Some English texts may seem difficult at first, but you'll often understand more than you think. For example, it's helpful to watch out for words that are related to words you already know.

For each word, add as many members of the word family as possible (you may include combinations and phrases), e.g. *awe → awe-inspiring, awesome, awesomeness, awestruck.*

1. to adapt • 2. attraction • 3. to benefit (from) • 4. to breathe • 5. equality • 6. historic • 7. home • 8. justice • 9. memorial • 10. pollution • 11. population • 12. settler

Topic 2 Colonial legacies

Colonialism and the British Empire

to **abuse** [ə'bju:z]	missbrauchen; misshandeln; beschimpfen	Her children had been taken away from her because she'd repeatedly *abused* them. ! to be emotionally/verbally/physically/sexually *abused* *to abuse* → abuse → abusive → abuser
apartheid [ə'pɑ:taɪt]	Apartheid	The South African *apartheid* system ended in 1994.
to **assimilate** [ə'sɪmɪleɪt]	integrieren; eingliedern; assimilieren	It is controversial whether it is good for minorities to *assimilate* into the dominant culture. *to assimilate* → assimilation
atrocity [ə'trɒsəti]	Gräueltat; Grausamkeit	They protested against the *atrocities* that were being committed against their people. An *atrocity* is a cruel and violent act
battle ['bætl]	Schlacht; Kampf	Armies fight in *battles*. *battle* → to battle
boundary ['baʊndri]	Grenze; Abgrenzung	The valley forms the *boundary* between the two regions. ! to create/to set/to draw up a *boundary* *boundary* = border
colony ['kɒləni]	Kolonie	Britain had a lot of *colonies* all over the world for hundreds of years. ! to establish/to set up/to abandon a *colony* *colony* → colonialism → colonist → to colonise
Commonwealth ['kɒmənwelθ]	Commonwealth	The *Commonwealth*, or more precisely, the *Commonwealth* of Nations has more than 50 member states, most of which are former British colonies.
conflict ['kɒnflɪkt]	Konflikt; Auseinandersetzung	The *conflict* ended in a gunfight. *conflict* = fight
to **conquer** ['kɒŋkə]	erobern	The Normans *conquered* England in 1066. *to conquer* → conqueror → conquest
constitution [ˌkɒnstɪ'tʃu:ʃn]	Verfassung	Britain has no written *constitution*. *constitution* → constitutional
to **dominate** ['dɒmɪneɪt]	dominieren; beherrschen	They work as a group – no one person is allowed to *dominate*. *to dominate* → domination → dominant → dominance
empire ['empaə]	Reich	Caesar ruled over the Roman *Empire*. *empire* → imperialism → imperialist → imperial
era ['ɪərə]	Ära; Zeitalter	The Industrial Revolution was an exciting *era* in British history. An *era* is another word for a historical period. ! the Elizabethan/Victorian *era*
to **evict** [ɪ'vɪkt]	gewaltsam vertreiben; zwangsräumen	The native people were *evicted* from their land. *to evict* → eviction
expansion [ɪk'spænʃn]	Expansion; Ausdehnung; Erweiterung	There was a considerable *expansion* of the British Empire between 1600 and the early 20th century. *expansion* → to expand

to **grant** [grɑ:nt]	zusichern; gewähren	We *are granted* equal rights by our democratic constitution.
human rights [ˌhju:mən 'raɪts]	Menschenrechte	*Human rights* are the basic rights and freedoms which everyone should have. ! *human rights* abuse/violation
ideology [ˌaɪdi'ɒlədʒi]	Ideologie; Weltanschauung	Imperialism is an example of an *ideology*. *ideology* → ideological
immigrant ['ɪmɪgrənt]	Immigrant/-in; Einwanderer/Einwanderin	Her parents came to the UK as *immigrants*. ! Nigerian/Jamaican/first-generation/second-generation *immigrant* *immigrant* → immigration → to immigrate
imperialism [ɪm'pɪəriəlɪzm]	Imperialismus	Political and cultural *imperialism* have left their mark on the world. *imperialism* → imperial → imperialist
Indian subcontinent [ˌɪndiən sʌb'kɒntɪnənt]	indischer Subkontinent	The merchants brought spices from the *Indian subcontinent* with them.
Indigenous *(fml)* [ɪn'dɪdʒɪnəs]	einheimisch; heimisch	In Canada there are different *Indigenous* peoples. *Indigenous* = native
to **invade** [ɪn'veɪd]	einmarschieren (in); eindringen (in); überfallen	The Romans *invaded* the country. *to invade* → invasion → invader
legacy ['legəsi]	Erbe; Vermächtnis	What *legacy* did the British Empire leave?
merchant ['mɜ:tʃənt]	Kaufmann/Kauffrau; Händler/-in	A *merchant* sells and buys things.
to **migrate** [maɪ'greɪt]	wandern; umherziehen	Lots of people *migrate* to urban areas to find work. *to migrate* → migration
monarch ['mɒnək]	Monarch/-in	The Bristish *monarch* is Canada's head of state. *monarchs* = kings and queens *monarch* → monarchy
to **oppress** [ə'pres]	unterdrücken	Back then, the government *oppressed* the people.
province ['prɒvɪns]	Provinz	Which *province* of Canada do you live in? *province* → provincial
reservation *(AE)* [ˌrezə'veɪʃn]	Reservat	His ancestors had to abandon their land and move to a *reservation*. *reservation (AE)* = reserve *(CE)*
to **resist** [rɪ'zɪst]	widerstehen; sich widersetzen	Some Indigenous groups tried to *resist* colonisation. *to resist* = to fight back, or to refuse to accept sth and try to prevent it from happening
to **respond to sth** [rɪ'spɒnd tə]	auf etw. reagieren	Different groups of people *responded to* colonisation in different ways. *to respond to* → response *(n)*
root [ru:t]	Wurzel	I'd like to find out more about my *roots*, e.g. where my family came from.
segregation [ˌsegrɪ'geɪʃn]	Segregation; Trennung; Rassentrennung	Apartheid was a system of racial *segregation*. ! racial/religious/social *segregation* *segregation* → to segregate
slave [sleɪv]	Sklave/Sklavin	In the south of the US, *slaves* worked on the cotton fields. *slave* → slavery

spice [spaɪs]	Gewürz	Let's cook a dish with exotic *spices*! *spice* → spicy
territory ['terɪtri]	Gebiet; Revier; Territorium	They conquered the *territory* in a violent war. *territory* → territorial
trade [treɪd]	Handel	The ivory *trade* is illegal. *trade* → trader → to trade
warfare [wɔː'feə]	Kriegsführung; Krieg	Even a small conflict can lead to *warfare*. ! biological/chemical/nuclear/psychological *warfare*

Apartheid and its aftermath in South Africa

activism ['æktɪvɪzm]	Aktivismus	Greta Thunberg stands for environmental *activism*. *activism* → active → activity → activist
civil disobedience [ˌsɪvl dɪsə'biːdiəns]	ziviler Ungehorsam	The protesters were blocking the street as an act of *civil disobedience*.
to clash ['klæʃ]	aufeinanderprallen; zusammenstoßen	This new law clearly *clashes* with the idea of freedom and equal rights, which our country was built on. *to clash* → clash *(n)*
to confront [kən'frʌnt]	konfrontieren; entgegentreten; sich stellen	During therapy she *confronted* her issues. *to confront* = to face
'Coloured' ['kʌləd]	‚farbig'	*'Coloured'* was a racial classification during apartheid.
cosmopolitan [ˌkɒzmə'pɒlɪtn]	weltoffen; international; kosmopolitisch	London is a *cosmopolitan* city. Lots of different cultures live there together.
curfew ['kɜːfjuː]	Sperrstunde; Ausgangssperre	During the pandemic, a *curfew* was introduced to reduce the number of encounters between people from different households. ! to break/to end/to enforce/to impose a *curfew*
to dare [deə]	wagen	The people didn't *dare* to protest because they were scared to be arrested.
diverse [daɪ'vɜːs]	divers; verschieden	Our society has become quite *diverse*. *diverse* → diversity
to enfranchise [ɪn'frænʃaɪz]	jmdm. das Wahlrecht verleihen; befreien; freilassen	1. Do you think *enfranchising* children is a good idea? 2. All the slaves *were enfranchised*. *to enfranchise* → enfranchisement
expatriate [ɪks'pætriət]	Auswanderer/-in; Exiliant/-in	He went to live and work in South Africa as an *expatriate*. *expatriate* = expat
faction ['fækʃn]	Interessengruppe; Lager; Fraktion	There has been a conflict between opposing *factions*.
ghetto ['getəʊ]	Ghetto; Armenviertel	During apartheid, Black people were forced to live in *ghettos*.
ID [ˌaɪ'dɪː]	Identifikations-	Can I see your *ID* card, please? ! *ID* card/number/papers
inequality [ˌɪnɪ'kwɒləti]	Ungleichheit	I recently read a utopian novel about a classless society without any social *inequality*. ! to overcome/to eliminate *inequality* *inequality* → equal → unequal

to **integrate** ['ɪntɪgreɪt]	(sich) integrieren; (sich) einfügen; einbinden	I've been living in this country for three years, but I still don't feel fully *integrated*. If you *integrate* sth, you make it part of sth else.
liberal ['lɪbrl]	liberal; freiheitlich	Which country has a *liberal* policy on immigration? *liberal* = tolerant
minority rule [maɪˌnɒrəti 'ru:l]	Minderheitenherrschaft	The election of Nelson Mandela as president ended white *minority rule* in South Africa.
'mixed marriage' [ˌmɪkst 'mærɪdʒ]	‚Mischehe'	During apartheid, *'mixed marriages'* between whites and 'non-whites' were prohibited.
'non-white' [non'waɪt]	Person nichteuropäischer Abstammung	During apartheid, *'non-whites'* didn't have the same rights as whites.
to **pave the way for** [ˌpeɪv ðə 'weɪ fə]	den Weg bereiten für	Political change *paved the way* for essential reforms.
police state [pəˌli:s 'steɪt]	Polizeistaat	In a *police state*, nobody can ever really feel free.
policy ['pɒləsi]	Politik; politische Linie	! Careful, don't mix up: 1. The government's *policies* have increased the gap between rich and poor. 2. Young people seem interested in politics these days.
privilege ['prɪvlɪdʒ]	Privileg; Recht; Vorrecht	If you have *privileges*, you have more rights and opportunities than other people. *privilege* → privileged
to **prohibit (sb from doing)** [prə'hɪbɪt]	jmdm. untersagen (etw. zu tun); jmdm. verbieten (etw. zu tun)	The students are *prohibited from* using their phones during lessons.
prosperity [prɒs'perəti]	Wohlstand; Erfolg	The *prosperity* in our country has been growing. *prosperity* = wealth *prosperity* → to prosper → prosperous
race [reɪs]	Volksgruppe; Rasse *(in Bezug auf Menschen im Deutschen nicht zu verwenden)*	*'Race'* is a problematic term that is still in use to divide people into groups. ! Careful: In English, 'race' can mean 'ethnic group', but don't use the German translation 'Rasse' to refer to people. *race* → racial → racism → racist
to **relocate** ['reləkeɪt]	umsiedeln	Black, 'Coloured' and 'Indian' people *were relocated* to designated areas under the apartheid regime in South Africa.
riot [raɪət]	Aufruhr; Aufstand	The lack of clean water caused several *riots*. *riot* → rioter
shack [ʃæk]	Baracke; Bretterbude	The poor people in this area haven't got proper houses. They live in *shacks*.
shantytown ['ʃæntitaʊn]	Elendsviertel; Barackensiedlung	Slums are mostly *shantytowns* made up of shacks.
*to **speak up** [ˌspi:k‿'ʌp]	lauter sprechen; *hier:* den Mund aufmachen	We need to *speak up* and fight for our rights!
status ['steɪtəs]	Status; Stellung	He enjoys a lot of privileges due to his celebrity *status*. Your *status* is your position in society.
token ['təʊkn]	symbolisch; Alibi-	The president's apology was a *token* gesture. *token* = symbolic

township ['taʊnʃɪp]	Township *(von Schwarzen und ‚Farbigen' bewohnte, außerhalb der Städte gelegene Siedlungen in Südafrika)*	South Africa's best-known *township* is Soweto (= South Western Townships) in Johannesburg.
tribe [traɪb]	Stamm; Volksstamm	There were lots of different Celtic *tribes*.
warrior ['wɒriə]	Krieger	The Zulu *warriors* were fighting hard. *warrior* → war

Indigenous peoples in Canada

to **apologise** [ə'pɒlədʒaɪz]	sich entschuldigen	Although she *apologised*, he couldn't forgive her. *to apologise* = to say sorry
to **commit** [kə'mɪt]	begehen	Canada has been accused of *committing* cultural genocide. ! to *commit* a genocide/suicide/crime
community [kə'mju:nəti]	Gemeinde; Gemeinschaft	Are you active in your *community*? ! close-knit/religious/Asian/English-speaking/sense of *community*
to **decimate** ['desɪmeɪt]	dezimieren; mindern	The trees in the park were *decimated* by the storm.
disease [dɪ'zi:z]	Krankheit	He died of an unknown *disease*. ! to catch/to transmit/to pass on/to cure/to prevent/to die of a *disease*
ethnic ['eθnɪk]	ethnisch; Volks-	What's your *ethnic* background? *ethnic* → ethnicity
to **exterminate** [ɪk'stɜ:mɪneɪt]	vernichten; ausrotten	They used poison to *exterminate* the rats in the house. *to exterminate* → extermination
First Nations *(CE)* [ˌfɜ:st 'neɪʃnz]	*Bezeichnung für die indigenen Völker Kanadas (ausgenommen Métis und Inuit)*	*First Nations*, Inuit and Métis are the Indigenous populations of Canada.
to **fund** [fʌnd]	finanzieren; fördern	After World War II, Britain was no longer able to *fund* its involvement in the colonies.
genocide ['dʒenəsaɪd]	Völkermord; Genozid	Thousands were killed in this *genocide*. ! mass/cultural *genocide* *genocide* → genocidal
Indian ['ɪndiən]	Indianer/-in; indianisch	Today, the term *'Indians'*, which was used historically and is still used in legal language to refer to First Nations people, is mostly considered offensive.
to **massacre** ['mæsəkə]	massakrieren	The soldiers got *massacred* in the battle. *to massacre* → massacre
multicultural [ˌmʌlti'kʌltʃrl]	multikulturell	Canada is a *multicultural* society. *multicultural* → multiculturalism
to **persist** [pə'sɪst]	beharren; bleiben	Indigenous cultures *have persisted* for thousands of years.
reconciliation [ˌreknˌsɪli'eɪʃn]	Versöhnung; Aussöhnung	After many years of civil war, *reconciliation* may prove impossible. *reconciliation* → to reconcile → (un)reconcilable

residential school *(CE)* [ˌrezɪ'denʃl ˌsku:l]	*staatliches Internat für Kinder der indigenen Bevölkerung Kanadas*	Indigenous children were sent to *residential schools*. These institutons were designed to assimilate the children into the dominant culture.
sustainable [sə'steɪnəbl]	nachhaltig	We must use more *sustainable* energy.
treaty ['tri:ti]	Vertrag	We signed a *treaty*. ! to make/to sign/to accept/to reject/to violate/to break a *treaty*
unmarked grave [ˌʌnmɑ:kt 'greɪv]	anonymes Grab	We don't know who has been buried in this *unmarked grave*.

Synonyms and definitions

Using synonyms or definitions can be useful if you don't know a certain word – and it will also help you expand your vocabulary.

a) Find words in the thematic vocabulary with the same meaning.

1. age • 2. heritage • 3. (a) fight • 4. trader • 5. ingredient to make a dish tasty • 6. separation (often based on race or sex) • 7. border • 8. cruelty • 9. hut • 10. symbolic • 11. emigrant • 12. uprising; revolt • 13. fighter • 14. deal; agreement

b) Complete the gaps with some of the words you've just found.

1. Both countries agreed on a peace [1].
2. Pepper, oregano, cinnamon and basil are [2].
3. The government's economic policy is only a [3] effort to end inequality.
4. Suspicion of electoral manipulation provoked violent [4] on the streets.
5. The [5] committed by colonial powers are unimaginable.

c) Give short definitions of the following terms.

1. reservation • 2. to evict • 3. apartheid • 4. to conquer • 5. township • 6. curfew • 7. civil disobedience • 8. residential school • 9. genocide • 10. reconciliation

Formal vs informal

It's important to use the correct register and style for different situations. Formal words are commonly used in written English but are less likely to appear in oral communication.

a) Replace the following informal words with more formal ones from the thematic vocabulary and write sentences with them.

1. to adapt; to adjust • 2. to mistreat • 3. to give sb the right to vote • 4. to forbid • 5. to kill • 6. to reduce • 7. to throw out

b) These words all occur in texts in Topic 2. Find less formal alternatives for them.

1. due to • 2. to permit • 3. to quell • 4. to be obliged (to do) • 5. animosity • 6. futility • 7. to persist

Informative texts often contain nouns. This kind of style sounds rather formal in English. So it's usually better to express your own ideas using verbs.

c) Express these ideas in your own sentences. Use verbs instead of nouns, e.g. ***emigration*** *due to war* → *Many people* ***emigrated*** *due to the war.*

1. **conquest** of a new territory • 2. **apology** from the government • 3. **colonisation** of India • 4. **trade** with British colonies • 5. British **domination** of the globe • 6. **assimilation** into a new culture

Visions of the future

Freedom and control

biometrics *(sg)* [ˌbaɪə'metrɪks]	Biometrik	She's doing research in the field of *biometrics*.
CCTV [ˌsi:si:ti:'vi:]	Videoüberwachungsanlage; Videoüberwachung	This building is monitored by *CCTV*. *CCTV* = surveillance cameras set up to film a special area like a bank and connected to monitors ! *CCTV* = closed-circuit television
citizen ['sɪtɪzn]	Bürger/-in	She is a British *citizen*.
to **detect** [dɪ'tekt]	aufspüren; feststellen; entdecken	He has *detected* an error in the system.
dystopia [dɪs'təʊpiə]	Dystopie	Most science-fiction novels create a kind of *dystopia* to draw attention to dangerous developments. *dystopia* = any real or imaginary society, place, state, etc., considered to be dangerously imperfect *dystopia* ↔ utopia
to **eavesdrop (on sb/sth)** ['i:vzdrɒp]	lauschen; jmdn./etw. belauschen	You must have been *eavesdropping* on us. Otherwise you wouldn't know about our secret.
facial recognition [ˌfeɪʃl rekəg'nɪʃn]	Gesichtserkennung	The police used *facial recognition* to detect the terrorist in the crowd.
intrusive [ɪn'tru:sɪv]	aufdringlich; übergriffig; (in die Persönlichkeitsrechte) eingreifend	1. Stop following me. You're being *intrusive*. 2. Surveillance technology is becoming more and more *intrusive*.
to **monitor** ['mɒnɪtə]	überwachen	Although the police were *monitoring* the building 24/7, the suspect was able to escape.
surveillance [sɜ:'veɪləns]	Überwachung; Beaufsichtigung	Due to public cameras, you are under *surveillance* in Britain most of the time. ! *surveillance* footage/drone/camera
totalitarian [təˌtælɪ'teəriən]	totalitär	The citizens were controlled by their *totalitarian* regime. *totalitarian* = relating to a dictatorial one-party state that regulates every aspect of life *totalitarian* → totalitarianism

Science and technology

advanced [əd'vɑ:nst]	fortgeschritten	*Advanced* technology has made many aspects of life easier.
to **clone** [kləʊn]	klonen	In 1996, scientists managed to *clone* a sheep. *to clone* → clone
condition [kən'dɪʃn]	Gesundheitszustand	Her *condition* is bad due to a rare blood disorder.
disease [dɪ'zi:z]	Krankheit	He died of an unknown *disease*. ! to catch/to transmit/to pass on/to cure/to prevent/to die of a *disease*
disorder ['i:tɪŋ dɪˌsɔ:də]	Störung; Erkrankung; Unordnung	Due to a genetic *disorder*, my sister learns more slowly than other children.
DNA [ˌdi:en'eɪ]	DNA; DNS (Desoxyribonukleinsäure)	He agreed to a *DNA* test to find out who his father was. *DNA* is short for deoxyribonucleic acid.

ethical ['eθɪkl]	ethisch; moralisch	Technological progress sometimes raises *ethical* issues.
game-changing ['geɪmˌtʃeɪndʒɪŋ]	wegweisend; bahnbrechend	A *game-changing* technology offers solutions which could not have been imagined before.
gene editing ['dʒiːn‿ˌedɪtɪŋ]	Genom-Editierung	*Gene editing* involves adding, removing or replacing segments of DNA in genes.
genetic engineering [dʒəˌnetɪk‿endʒɪ'nɪərɪŋ]	Gentechnik	Some people object to *genetic engineering* because it might involve unknown safety risks. *genetic engineering* = manipulation of genes by means of cloning and transformation
hereditary [hɪ'redɪtri]	erblich; angeboren	A *hereditary* disease runs in my family.
to **implant** ['ɪmplɑːnt]	implantieren; einsetzen	The operation to *implant* the artificial heart took two hours. *to implant* → implant
laboratory [lə'bɒrətri]	Labor	The scientists spent day and night in the *laboratory* to develop a vaccine.
to **modify** ['mɒdɪfaɪ]	ändern; verändern; modifizieren	I don't want to eat genetically *modified* food.
predisposition to sth [ˌpriːdɪspə'zɪʃn]	Veranlagung; Anfälligkeit; Prädisposition	People who have a genetic *predisposition to* a certain disease should have regular check-ups.
reproductive technology [riːprəˌdʌktɪv tek'nɒlədʒi]	Fortpflanzungstechnologie	In the case of infertility, *reproductive technology* might offer solutions.
resistant [rɪ'sɪstnt]	resistent; widerstandsfähig	Manipulating the genes of plants to make them *reistant* to herbicides is a controversial practice.
scientist ['saɪəntɪst]	Wissenschaftler/-in	*Scientists* often work in laboratories. *scientist* → science
screening ['skriːnɪŋ]	Sichtung; Untersuchung	*Screening* programmes can help to detect diseases at an early stage.
vaccine ['væksiːn]	Impfstoff	Scientists are already working on a *vaccine* against the new virus. *vaccine* = substance given to people, usually by injection, to protect them from a disease

Humans and robots

AI *(artificial intelligence)* [ɑːtɪˌfɪʃl‿ɪn'telɪdʒns]	KI *(künstliche Intelligenz)*	The *AI* in this device is constantly learning. *AI* is short for 'artificial intelligence'.
to **assemble** [ə'sembl]	zusammenbauen; montieren	After they *had assembled* all the parts, the bike was ready to be sold.
*to **be capable of** [ˌbi 'keɪpəbl‿əv]	fähig sein zu	They had not expected them to *be capable of* such violence. *to be capable of* ↔ to be incapable of
cognitive ['kɒgnɪtɪv]	kognitiv; geistig	This game helps children to train their *cognitive* skills.
concern [kən'sɜːn]	Angelegenheit; Belang; Sorge	Our financial situation is our major *concern* right now. ! to raise *concerns*; growing/widespread/deep *concern*
conscious ['kɒnʃəs]	bewusst	The patient was fully *conscious*. *conscious* ↔ unconscious *conscious* → consciousness

data *(pl only)* ['deɪtə]	Daten; Angaben	Some apps and websites collect huge amounts of *data*. **!** to collect/to gather/to analyse/to download/to manipulate *data*
device [dɪ'vaɪs]	Gerät; Vorrichtung	Please switch off all your electronic *devices*.
efficient [ɪ'fɪʃnt]	effizient; leistungsfähig	We need a new dishwasher, one that is more energy-*efficient*. *efficient* → efficiency
to **harm** [hɑ:m]	Schaden anrichten; beschädigen; verletzen	Robots may not *harm* human beings. *to harm* ↔ to protect *to harm* → harm → harmful → harmless
machine learning [mə'ʃi:n ˌlɜ:nɪŋ]	maschinelles Lernen	*Machine learning* is connected with AI.
to **program** *(AE)* ['prəʊgræm]	programmieren	I'm learning how to *program* simple apps.
repetitive [rɪ'petətɪv]	sich wiederholend; monoton	Robots can be used to perform *repetitive* tasks. *repetitive* → to repeat → repetition
to **replace (by/with)** [rɪ'pleɪs]	ersetzen (durch)	We *replaced* our old fridge *with* a new one. *to replace (by/with)* → replacement
robotics *(sg)* [rəʊ'bɒtɪks]	Robotik; Robotertechnik	He is an engineer and works in the field of *robotics*. *robotics* → robot
superior [su:'pɪəriə]	überlegen; gehoben	They regard themselves as *superior* to other people. *superior* ↔ inferior

Saving the planet

biodegradable [ˌbaɪəʊdɪ'greɪdəbl]	biologisch abbaubar	The packaging is made of *biodegradable* material.
carbon footprint [ˌkɑ:bn 'fʊtprɪnt]	CO2-Fußabdruck	What can we do to reduce our *carbon footprint*?
to **compensate for** ['kɒmpənseɪt]	ausgleichen; wettmachen	The company had to pay a large amount of money to *compensate for* the environmental damage they had caused. *to compensate for* → compensation
deforestation [di:ˌfɒrɪ'steɪʃn]	Abholzung; Entwaldung	It is a problem when new farmland is created by means of *deforestation*. *deforestation* → forest
to **demand** [dɪ'mɑ:nd]	fordern; verlangen; fragen; wissen wollen	The protesters *demanded* that the government take action.
desertification [dɪˌzɜ:tɪfɪ'keɪʃn]	Wüstenbildung; Desertifikation	The long drought has led to a *desertification* of the land. *desertification* → desert
diet [daɪət]	Ernährung; Diät	1. His *diet* consists mainly of fruit and vegetables. 2. She has been on a *diet*, but she hasn't lost much weight yet. **!** vegan/vegetarian/healthy/unhealthy *diet*
erosion [ɪ'rəʊʒn]	Erosion; Abtragung	Coastal *erosion* is caused by rising sea levels. It means that land is washed into the water.
to **exploit sb/sth** [ɪk'splɔɪt]	jmdn./etw. ausbeuten; jmdn./etw. ausnutzen	They're *exploiting* the country's natural resources. *to exploit sb/sth* → exploitation

farming *(no pl)* ['fɑːmɪŋ]	Landwirtschaft	The region's economy depends on *farming*. ! vertical *farming* (= vertikale Landwirtschaft)/organic *farming* (= biologische Landwirtschaft)/factory *farming* (= Massentierhaltung)
global warming [ˌgləʊbl 'wɔːmɪŋ]	globale Erwärmung	If we want to stop *global warming*, everyone must change their behaviour.
greenhouse gas [ˌgriːnhaʊz 'gæs]	Treibhausgas	To stop climate change, we must try to reduce *greenhouse gases*. *greenhouse gas* = a gas that causes the greenhouse effect, especially carbon dioxide
habit ['hæbɪt]	Gewohnheit	It isn't always easy to give up bad *habits*. ! to develop/to change/to give up a *habit* *habit* → habitual
to **limit (to)** ['lɪmɪt tə]	limitieren (auf); begrenzen (auf); beschränken (auf)	We're trying to *limit* the use of our car. *to limit* → limit
mass migration [ˌmæs maɪ'greɪʃn]	Massenwanderung	If whole areas become uninhabitable, it will lead to *mass migration*. *mass migration* → to migrate
measure ['meʒə]	Maßnahme	Environmental activists have called for more drastic *measures* to fight global warming. ! to take (harsh/tough/effective) *measures*
to **melt** [melt]	schmelzen	Global warming causes the glaciers to *melt*.
natural disaster [ˌnætʃrl dɪ'zɑːstə]	Naturkatastrophe; Umweltkatastrophe	It is often difficult to predict *natural disasters* such as floods, hurricanes and earthquakes.
natural habitat [ˌnætʃrl 'hæbɪtæt]	natürlicher Lebensraum	A lot of animals have lost their *natural habitat* due to deforestation.
to **preserve** [prɪ'zɜːv]	bewahren; erhalten	Our organisation is fighting to *preserve* the natural habitat of the orangutan. *to preserve* → preservation
to **raise awareness for** [ˌreɪz‿ə'weənəs]	das Bewusstsein schärfen für; sensibilisieren für	We're trying to *raise awareness for* people who are already suffering from the effects of climate change.
to **recycle** [ˌriː'saɪkl]	recyceln; wiederverwenden	We separate our trash so that it can be *recycled*. *to recycle* → recycling → recyclable → non-recyclable
resource [rɪ'zɔːs]	Ressource	We shouldn't waste the world's natural *resources*.
sea level ['siː ˌlevl]	Meeresspiegel	*Sea levels* are rising due to global warming.
to **suffer (from)** ['sʌfə frəm]	leiden (unter)	The whole country was *suffering from* the extreme heat.
to **survive** [sə'vaɪv]	überleben	Three people didn't *survive* the earthquake. *to survive* → survival
to **volunteer** [ˌvɒlən'tɪə]	sich freiwillig melden; eine ehrenamtliche Tätigkeit übernehmen	He *volunteered* to reconstruct buildings that were damaged by the flood.
wildlife ['waɪldlaɪf]	Tierwelt *(in freier Wildbahn)*	I'm very interested in nature and *wildlife*.

Word fields

Working with (thematic) word fields can help you expand your vocabulary.

Collect words and phrases that are connected with the following terms and organise them in a suitable way, e.g. in a mind map, chart or list.

1. farming • 2. genetic engineering • 3. artificial intelligence (AI) • 4. surveillance • 5. natural disasters • 6. environmental protection

Start like this: 1. **farming:**
- **types:** organic farming, factory farming, …
- **products:** corn, livestock, milk products, …
- **problems:** fertilisers, antibiotics, erosion, …
- …

Working with adjectives and verbs

You already know several ways of forming words. For example, some verbs and nouns can be turned into adjectives by adding suffixes:

- **-able/-ible:** to drink – drink**able**, to reverse – revers**ible**
- **-ful/-less:** hope – hope**ful**/hope**less**
- **-ive:** to create – creat**ive**
- **-ic/-ical:** strategy – strateg**ic**, logic – log**ical**
- **-al:** industry – industri**al**

Note: **-ful** and **-less** often express opposite meanings, but not all adjectives take both suffixes, e.g. *flawless – ~~flawful~~; beautiful – ~~beautiless~~*

In a similar way, verbs can be derived from adjectives or nouns with certain suffixes:
- **-en:** strength – to strength**en**
- **-ise:** legal – to legal**ise**
- **-ify:** simple – to simpl**ify**

a) Form adjectives by adding suitable suffixes. (You may need to change the word form slightly too.)

1. to harm • 2. to repeat • 3. to desire • 4. nature • 5. to end • 6. technology • 7. gene • 8. education • 9. profit • 10. science • 11. to intrude • 12. power • 13. access • 14. economy • 15. to reproduce • 16. to recycle • 17. politics • 18. success

b) Form verbs by using suitable suffixes.

1. global • 2. just (adj) • 3. weak • 4. digital • 5. modern • 6. diverse • 7. threat • 8. clear • 9. special • 10. intense • 11. short • 12. electric • 13. individual • 14. mode / modus

c) Fill in the gaps by using some of the words from a) and b).

1. Is the Wi-Fi [1] for guests?
2. Is [2] progress really the solution for our problems?
3. AI will help to reduce boring and [3] work.
4. I'd never eat [4] [5] food. That's creepy.
5. Pesticides can have [6] effects on people's health.
6. We need to [7] old and ineffective factories.

Topic 3 Structural change

Talking about economic developments

to **accelerate** [əkˈseləreɪt]	beschleunigen; schneller werden	The new machine significantly *accelerates* the production process. *to accelerate* = to make faster
automation [ˌɔːtəˈmeɪʃn]	Automatisierung	We're working towards complete factory *automation*. ! *automation* software/machinery/solution/technology

to **boost** [bu:st]	antreiben; steigern; fördern	The company has *boosted* sales with their new campaign. ! *to boost* the economy/the industry/sales/production/prices/inflation
business ['bɪznɪs]	Geschäft; Business	What started as a small *business* has now become a huge company.
competitor [kəm'petɪtə]	Mitbewerber/-in; Teilnehmer/-in	Our company has six strong *competitors* on the European market. *competitor* → competition → to compete
to **consume** [kən'sju:m]	konsumieren; verbrauchen	1. For more sustainability we need to *consume* less. 2. My old washing machine *consumes* too much energy. *to consume* → consumer → consumption
decline [dɪ'klaɪn]	Rückgang; Abnahme; Niedergang	The rapid *decline* in sales worried the CEO. *decline* ↔ growth *decline* → to decline
economic [ˌi:kə'nɒmɪk]	ökonomisch; wirtschaftlich	This country has experienced strong *economic* growth. ! Don't confuse: *economic* ≠ economical = (kosten-) günstig; sparsam *economic* → economy
factory ['fæktri]	Fabrik; Werk	Cars, washing machines and cookers are all made in *factories*. *factory* = plant, mill
goods *(pl)* [gʊdz]	Güter; Waren	All kinds of *goods* are sold at this market.
growth [grəʊθ]	Wachstum	This chart shows the population *growth* in the past years. *growth* → to grow
to **increase** [ɪn'kri:s]	steigen; erhöhen; zunehmen; wachsen	How can we *increase* the motivation of our workers? *to increase* ↔ to decrease *to increase* → increase
industry ['ɪndəstri]	Industrie; Branche; Gewerbe	Hollywood is the centre of the US film *industry*. ! heavy/service/textile/advertising *industry* *industry* → industrialisation → industrial
to **invest** [ɪn'vest]	investieren	He has *invested* a large amount of money in his business. *to invest* = to put money in sth or to buy sth because you hope to make a profit *to invest* → investment
manufacturing [ˌmænjə'fæktʃərɪŋ]	Herstellung; Fertigung; produzierendes Gewerbe	This company is known for furniture *manufacturing*.
natural resources *(pl)* [ˌnætʃrl rɪ'zɔ:sɪz]	Ressourcen; Rohstoffe; Bodenschätze	It is important not to waste the world's *natural resources*.
to **produce** [prə'dju:s]	herstellen; produzieren	Our company *produces* cars. *to produce* = to manufacture *to produce* → production → product → producer
raw materials *(pl)* [ˌrɔ: mə'tɪəriəlz]	Rohstoffe; Rohmaterialien	The production will take longer due to a shortage of *raw materials*.
retail ['ri:teɪl]	Einzelhandel	This company makes money in online *retail*.
venture capital [ˌventʃə 'kæpɪtl]	Risikokapital; Wagniskapital	To increase our business, we need to raise €250,000 in *venture capital*.

Industrialisation

age [eɪdʒ]	Alter; Zeitalter	James Watt's steam engine started a new *age* in textile production.
agricultural [ˌægrɪ'kʌltʃrl]	landwirtschaftlich	If you have a farm, you work in the *agricultural* sector. *agricultural* → agriculture
change [tʃeɪndʒ]	Änderung; Veränderung; Wechsel	They started a revolution because they wanted *change*. ! to bring about/to adapt to/to oppose *change* *change* → to change
child labour ['tʃaɪld ˌleɪbə]	Kinderarbeit	In the 19th century, *child labour* was common in Britain.
coal [kəʊl]	Kohle	In the past, people used *coal* to keep their homes warm.
craft [krɑ:ft]	Handwerk; Geschick; Fertigkeit	My *craft* can't be compared to work done by a machine. It's unique.
discovery [dɪ'skʌvri]	Entdeckung	New *discoveries* and inventions accelerated technological progress. *discovery* → to discover
industrial [ɪn'dʌstriəl]	industriell; Industrie-	The *Industrial* Revolution brought about major changes in society. *industrial* → industry
innovation [ˌɪnə'veɪʃn]	Innovation; Neuerung	There have been lots of technical *innovations* recently. *innovation* → innovative
mass production [ˌmæs prə'dʌkʃn]	Massenproduktion	Due to mechanisation, *mass production* became possible.
mechanisation [ˌmekənaɪ'zeɪʃn]	Mechanisierung	The production involves a high degree of *mechanisation*.
to **migrate** [maɪ'greɪt]	wandern; umherziehen	Lots of people *migrate* to urban areas to find work. *to migrate* → migration
miner ['maɪnə]	Bergarbeiter/-in	The *miner* explained everything about the coal mine. *miner* = sb who works in a mine *miner* → mine → mining
pit [pɪt]	Grube; Bergwerk	The miners were down in the *pit*. *pit* = a place where you dig for coal or other materials
to **power** [paʊə]	antreiben; mit Energie versorgen	This machine is *powered* by solar energy. *to power* → power → powerful
progress ['prəʊgres]	Fortschritt	The students have made rapid *progress*.
revolution [ˌrevl'u:ʃn]	Revolution	Their research led to a *revolution* in medicine. ! agricultural/industrial/cultural *revolution*
smoke [sməʊk]	Rauch	There was a lot of *smoke* in the cities due to the factories. *smoke* → smoky
steam engine ['sti:m‿ˌendʒɪn]	Dampfmaschine	The *steam engine* was the most important invention of the 18th century.
to **transform** [træns'fɔ:m]	transformieren; umwandeln; verwandeln	He has *transformed* his garage into an office to start his business. *to transform* → transformation
wealth [welθ]	Reichtum; Vermögen	She's working very hard to increase her *wealth*. *wealth* ↔ poverty *wealth* → wealthy

The changing workplace

challenge ['tʃælɪndʒ]	Herausforderung	One of the biggest *challenges* facing people in the 21st century is global warming.
closure ['kləʊʒə]	Schließung; Stilllegung	Factory *closures* are the last option for the company. ! factory/pit/library *closure* *closure* → to close
condition [kən'dɪʃn]	Kondition; Bedingung	The working *conditions* in textile factories in Bangladesh are often horrible.
contract ['kɒntrækt]	Vertrag	He signed the *contract* for his new job.
to **dismiss** [dɪs'mɪs]	entlassen	Due to budget shortages, we'll have to *dismiss* three employees.
economically underdeveloped [iːkəˌnɒmɪkli_ˈʌndədɪveləpt]	strukturschwach	The unemployment rate is high in this *economically underdeveloped* region.
to **employ** [ɪm'plɔɪ]	einstellen; anstellen; beschäftigen	Our company has *employed* a new IT specialist. If you *employ* people, you pay them to work for you. *to employ* → employment → employer → employee
freelance ['friːlɑːns]	freiberuflich	He's his own boss – he works as a *freelance* journalist.
gig economy [ˌgɪg_ɪ'kɒnəmi]	*auf zeitlich befristeten Verträgen und Freiberuflern basierendes Wirtschaftsmodell*	The *gig economy* has made it hard for some people to find a permanent job.
opportunity [ˌɒpə'tʃuːnəti]	Gelegenheit	He took the *opportunity* to apply for his dream job. ! a missed/lost/golden *opportunity*
part-time [ˌpɑːt'taɪm]	Teilzeit-; Halbtags-	My new job is a *part-time* job. I only work half days.
to **revive** [rɪ'vaɪv]	wieder beleben	This old factory area has been *revived* and is now a popular tourist attraction. ! *to revive* customs/memories/a language/a friendship/a conversation
strike [straɪk]	Streik	The city's bus drivers have been on *strike* for weeks.
trade union ['treɪd ˌjuːnjən]	Gewerkschaft	The *trade unions* threatened to go on strike if the working conditions didn't improve and the wages weren't raised.
transition ['trænzɪʃn]	Übergang; Wende	How has your company dealt with the energy *transition*? A *transition* is the process of change from one stage to another.
unemployment [ˌʌnɪm'plɔɪmənt]	Arbeitslosigkeit	*Unemployment* among young people is a big problem. ! adult/high/increasing/mass/seasonal *unemployment*
workforce ['wɜːkfɔːs]	Arbeitskräfte; Belegschaft	Our company is hiring more people to increase the *workforce*. *Workforce* can mean the total number of people in a region that can be employed or the total number of people who are employed by a particular company.
working from home [ˌwɜːkɪŋ frəm 'həʊm]	Homeoffice	In our company, *working from home* is possible on Tuesdays and Thursdays.
working hours *(pl)* ['wɜːkɪŋ_ˌaʊəz]	Arbeitszeit	I'd prefer a job with regular *working hours*.

Digitalisation

access *(no pl)* ['ækses]	Zugang; Zutritt	Someone must have gained *access* to my personal data. ! *access* → to access → accessible
AI *(artificial intelligence)* [ɑːtɪˌfɪʃl̮ ɪn'telɪdʒns]	KI *(künstliche Intelligenz)*	The *AI* in this device is constantly learning. *AI* is short for artificial intelligence.
algorithm ['ælgrɪðm]	Algorithmus	This app uses *algorithms* to show its users ads that might interest them.
cloud [klaʊd]	*dezentraler Datenspeicherort im Internet*; Wolke	I'm going to upload my photos into the *cloud* to share them with other people.
data *(pl only)* ['deɪtə]	Daten; Angaben	Some apps and websites collect huge amounts of *data*. ! to collect/to gather/to analyse/to download/to manipulate *data*
device [dɪ'vaɪs]	Gerät; Vorrichtung	Please switch off all your electronic *devices*.
digitalisation [ˌdɪdʒɪtlaɪ'zeɪʃn]	Digitalisierung	*Digitalisation* has changed the way we exchange information. *digitalisation* → to digitalise → digital
to **engage (with)** [ɪn'geɪdʒ]	interagieren	Many IT companies try to *engage with* a young audience online. *to engage with* = to interact with, to build a relationship with *to engage* → engagement
hub [hʌb]	Zentrum; Mittelpunkt	Lots of people want to work in Silicon Valley, the technological *hub* of the US.
internet ['ɪntənet]	Internet	You can spend hours surfing the *internet* because you always find something interesting there. ! *internet* access/connection/addiction/banking/café
to **launch** [lɔːnʃ]	einführen; starten; in Gang setzen	A new dating app was *launched* in May.
to **manipulate** [mə'nɪpjəleɪt]	manipulieren; beeinflussen	Algorithms have the power to *manipulate* people's opinions.
network ['netwɜːk]	Netzwerk	In some jobs it's very important to have a good *network* to be successful.
privacy ['prɪvəsi]	Privatsphäre	I've changed my *privacy* settings so that only my best friends can see my pictures. ! *privacy* policy/regulations/settings *privacy* → private
remote [rɪ'məʊt]	Fern-; abgelegen; weit entfernt	1. He fixed my computer using *remote* access. 2. My family lives in a *remote* part of the Scottish Highlands.
security [sɪ'kjʊərəti]	Sicherheit; Schutz	Our company cares a lot about data *security*. ! data/employment/banking/airport *security*
setting ['setɪŋ]	Einstellung	Check your account *settings* for your social network carefully.
start-up ['stɑːtʌp]	Jungunternehmen; Start-up-Unternehmen	This *start-up* produces an innovative device.
tool [tuːl]	Werkzeug; Gerät	A web designer works with different digital *tools*.
to **track** [træk]	verfolgen; aufspüren	This app *tracks* your user behaviour.

24/7 *(twenty-four-seven) (infml)* [ˌtwenti fɔː ˈsevn]	rund um die Uhr, sieben Tage die Woche; immerzu	Some people are online *24/7*. *24/7* = twenty-four-seven
user behaviour [ˈjuːzə bɪˌheɪvjə]	Benutzerverhalten	Your *user behaviour* on social media can reveal a lot about yourself.
work ethic [ˈwɜːkˌeθɪk]	Arbeitsethik; Arbeitsauffassung	Some tech companies in Silicon Valley are known for their particular *work ethic*.

Collocations

Using collocations, i.e. two or more words that frequently appear together, will make your English sound more natural. Typical combinations are:

- noun + noun, e.g. ***app** store*
- verb + noun, e.g. *to launch an **app***
- adjective + noun, e.g. *a user-friendly **app***

Make at least five collocations with the following nouns, using the combinations mentioned above. You can use a dictionary if necessary.

1. internet • 2. data • 3. security • 4. privacy • 5. network

Word building: Nouns and conversion

Knowing how words are formed, e.g. by adding suffixes, will help you expand your vocabulary and understand the meaning of new words. Common suffixes in nouns are:

- **-(at)ion:** combin**ation**, act**ion**
- **-ance/-ence:** dist**ance**, independ**ence**
- **-er/-or:** teach**er**, act**or**
- **-ment:** move**ment**
- **-ness:** happi**ness**
- **-(i)ty:** abil**ity**, cruel**ty**
- **-th:** tru**th**
- **-al:** arriv**al**
- **-ing:** begin**ning**

Careful: Although English and German words may look very similar, the stress is often different, e.g. *pro**duc**tion* – Produ**kt**ion.

a) Form nouns by adding the correct suffixes (more than one may be correct). Use a dictionary if necessary.

1. to manufacture • 2. to consume • 3. busy • 4. dominant • 5. to employ • 6. to approve • 7. to grow • 8. to secure • 9. to transform • 10. competent • 11. to revive • 12. to engage • 13. to be aware • 14. to dismiss • 15. to set • 16. necessary • 17. to work

Sometimes nouns and verbs (or adjectives) can have the same form – through a process called conversion, e.g. *I **visited** Lisa yesterday. – Did you enjoy your **visit** to the US?*

b) Find at least ten words that can be used in this way in the thematic vocabulary. Make sentences with them as shown in the example.

Sometimes a figurative meaning results from conversion, e.g. *a mushroom – to mushroom: Informal settlements **mushroomed** around the city.*

c) Find out how the following nouns can be used as verbs. Write down example sentences with them.

1. a bottle • 2. an eye • 3. a dwarf • 4. a chair • 5. a ship • 6. a tower

Topic 4 Postcolonial developments

Society

to **alienate** ['eɪlɪəneɪt]	entfremden; vor den Kopf stoßen	1. After 30 years of living abroad, he feels *alienated* from his home country. 2. By *alienating* minorities, the government is increasing the risk of social unrest. *to alienate* → alienation
ancient ['eɪnʃnt]	alt; altertümlich; antik	They still practise some of their *ancient* traditions. *ancient* ↔ modern
belief [bɪ'li:f]	Glaube; Überzeugung	He didn't talk a lot about his religious *beliefs*. *belief* → to believe → believable
caste system ['kɑ:st ˌsɪstəm]	Kastensystem	India's *caste system* divides Hindus into four hierarchical groups.
to **contemplate** ['kɒntəmpleɪt]	nachdenken über; erwägen	He *had been contemplating* the issue for hours before he finally made a decision.
contemporary [kən'temprəri]	zeitgenössisch; zeitgemäß	In the city you can find a mix of historic and *contemporary* buildings. *contemporary* ↔ old-fashioned, traditional
cultural heritage [ˌkʌltʃrl 'herɪtɪʤ]	kulturelles Erbe	The organisation's main goal is to protect our *cultural heritage*.
disillusionment [ˌdɪsɪ'lu:ʒnmənt]	Desillusionierung; Ernüchterung	Unfortunately, his high hopes were followed by *disillusionment*. *disillusionment* = a feeling of disappointment at finding out that sth is not as good as expected *disillusionment* → to disillusion
to **displace** [dɪ'spleɪs]	vertreiben	These refugees were *displaced* from their home country.
ethnicity [eθ'nɪsəti]	ethnische Zugehörigkeit; Volkszugehörigkeit	People of different *ethnicities* live in my town. *Ethnicity* means belonging to group that has common national or cultural traditions. *ethnicity* → ethnic
to **grant** [grɑ:nt]	zusichern; gewähren	The teacher *granted* his students permission to leave the class at any time. ! *to grant* civil rights/equal rights/independence
illiteracy *(no pl)* [ɪ'lɪtrəsi]	Analphabetismus	*Illiteracy* among adults is a problem in this country. There are still a lot of people who can't read and write properly.
to **inspire** [ɪn'spaɪə]	inspirieren; anregen	His speech *inspired* protests throughout the country. *to inspire* = to give the idea for sth (e.g. a poem) *to inspire* → inspiration
nation state ['neɪʃn ˌsteɪt]	Nationalstaat	They turned their back on colonialism and created a *nation state*. *nation state* = a state inhabited by the population that belongs to one nation
partition [pɑ:'tɪʃn]	Teilung	The *Partition* of Germany ended in 1990.
pilgrim ['pɪlgrɪm]	Pilger/-in	This place attracts thousands of *pilgrims* each year who come here to worship.

population density [pɒpjəˌleɪʃn 'densɪti]	Bevölkerungsdichte	The *population density* in urban areas is higher than in rural areas.
postcolonial [ˌpəʊstkə'ləʊniəl]	postkolonial *(auf die Kolonialzeit zurückzuführen)*	I studied *postcolonial* literature at college. ! *postcolonial* era/literature/guilt
sanitation *(no pl)* [ˌsænɪ'teɪʃn]	sanitäre Anlagen	The people in this area live with poor or no *sanitation*.
secular ['sekjələ]	weltlich	In a *secular* society, religion isn't very important. *secular* = not connected with religion or the church
to **succeed (in)** [sək'siːd‿ɪn]	Erfolg haben (in/bei/mit) ; gelingen	Britain *succeeded in* expanding its overseas territories. *to succeed* → success
to **uproot** [ʌp'ruːt]	entwurzeln	The announcement of the Partition of India *uprooted* the people and led to violence and mass migration. *to uproot* → root
value ['væljuː]	Wert	Friendship has a high *value*.
to **worship** ['wɜːʃɪp]	verehren; anbeten	Some people regularly go to church to *worship* God.

Politics and the Commonwealth

to **aspire** [ə'spaɪə]	streben; anstreben	This young actor is *aspiring* to fame.
campaign [kæm'peɪn]	Kampagne; Aktion	The candidate made lots of promises during his election *campaign*.
candidate ['kændɪdət]	Kandidat/-in; Bewerber/-in	The ideal *candidate* should be able to take on responsibility.
community [kə'mjuːnəti]	Gemeinde; Gemeinschaft	Are you active in your *community*? ! a close-knit/religious/Asian/English-speaking/sense of *community*
compensation [ˌkɒmpən'seɪʃn]	Entschädigung; Ausgleich	The company had to pay *compensation* for the environmental damage they had caused.
constitution [ˌkɒnstɪ'tʃuːʃn]	Verfassung	Britain has no written *constitution*. *constitution* → constitutional
corruption [kə'rʌpʃn]	Korruption; Bestechung	The politician was found guilty of *corruption* in five cases. *corruption* → corrupt
decolonisation [ˌdiːˌkɒlənaɪ'zeɪʃn]	Entkoloniserung; Dekolonisierung	The process of *decolonisation* was very slow.
dedication [ˌdedɪ'keɪʃn]	Einsatz; Hingabe	I admire the *dedication* with which you're working on your career.
domination [ˌdɒmɪ'neɪʃn]	Herrschaft; Vorherrschaft	The British colonies found themselves under the *domination* of the crown. *domination* → to dominate
electorate [ɪ'lektrət]	Wählerschaft	The candidate is trying to win over the *electorate* by promising lower taxes. *electorate* = the people who have the right to vote *electorate* → to elect → election
to **empower** [ɪm'paʊə]	stärken; fördern; bevollmächtigen	They're launching a campaign to *empower* young people. *to empower* ↔ to weaken

to **fracture** ['fræktʃə]	zerbrechen	She fell off her bike and *fractured* her elbow. *to fracture* → fracture
head of state [ˌhed‿əv 'steɪt]	Staatsoberhaupt	The British monarch is the *head of state* of Australia.
link [lɪŋk]	Verbindung; Beziehung	The two countries have established close *links*. ! to maintain/to strengthen *links*
loyalty *(no pl)* ['lɔəlti]	Treue; Loyalität	On July 4th, a lot of people show their *loyalty* to the US.
member ['membə]	Mitglied	A country has to fulfil a lot of criteria to become a *member* of the EU. ! *member* state/country
monarchy ['mɒnəki]	Monarchie	A lot of people want to abolish *monarchy*. *monarchy* → monarch
to **owe allegiance to sb** [ˌəʊ‿ə'li:dʒns]	jmdm. Loyalität schuldig sein	The people *owe allegiance to* the king.
policy ['pɒləsi]	Politik; politische Linie	Careful, don't mix up: 1. The government's *policies* have increased the gap between rich and poor. 2. Young people seem interested in <u>politics</u> these days.
reparation [ˌrepr'eɪʃn]	Entschädigung; Wiedergutmachung	The minorities demanded *reparations* for their unjust treatment. ! to demand/to pay *reparations*
republic [rɪ'pʌblɪk]	Republik	After declaring their independence, a lot of former colonies chose to become *republics*.
to **safeguard** ['seɪfgɑ:d]	schützen; gewährleisten; sicherstellen	The company promised to *safeguard* adequate working conditions in the factories.
sovereign state [ˌsɒvrɪn 'steɪt]	souveräner Staat	The former colony has now become a *sovereign state*.
*to **stand for** *(BE)* ['stænd fə]	kandidieren; sich zur Wahl stellen	Two strong candidates *are standing for* election. ! *to stand for (BE)* = to run for *(AE)* *to stand for* election/mayor/parliament/prime minister
victory ['vɪktri]	Sieg	When you have beaten another team, you can celebrate your *victory*.
voluntary association [ˌvɒləntri‿əsəʊʃi'eɪʃn]	freiwilliger Zusammenschluss	A *voluntary association* is a group or organisation in which members freely choose to work together to achieve a common goal.
voter turnout [ˌvəʊtə 'tɜ:naʊt]	Wahlbeteiligung	The *voter turnout* in the last election was below 70%.

Economy

advanced [əd'vɑ:nst]	fortgeschritten	*Advanced* technology has made many aspects of life easier.
agriculture ['ægrɪkʌltʃə]	Landwirtschaft	Climate change is already affecting *agriculture*. *agriculture* → agricultural
consumption [kən'sʌmpʃn]	Konsum; Verbrauch	High energy *consumption* is a problem. *consumption* → to consume
crop [krɒp]	Nutzpflanze; Getreide; Ernte	Some *crops* are better suited to dry conditions than others. *Crops* are plants that are grown for consumption in large quantities (e.g. rice, wheat, carrots etc.)

economic growth [ˌi:kənɒmɪk ˈgrəʊθ]	Wirtschaftswachstum	The current energy crisis is inhibiting *economic growth.* ! to drive/to stimulate/to inhibit *economic growth*
to **estimate** [ˈestɪmeɪt]	schätzen	I *estimate* her stay in hospital to take a week.
export [ˈekspɔ:t]	Export; Ausfuhr	The economy of this country is based on *export*. *export* ↔ import
famine [ˈfæmɪn]	Hungersnot	A *famine* is a period of serious shortage of food.
GDP [ˌdʒi:di:ˈpi:]	BIP *(= Bruttoinlandsprodukt)*	The country's *GDP* has been rising. The *GDP (= gross domestic product)* refers to the total value of goods and services produced by a country within a year.
to **generate revenue** [ˌdʒenreɪt ˈrevənju:]	Einkommen generieren	The company has *generated revenue* this year.
infrastructure [ˈɪnfrəˌstrʌktʃə]	Infrastruktur	It's a small town, but it has a good *infrastructure*. It's connected to three big cities.
international relations *(pl)* [ɪntəˌnæʃnl rɪˈleɪʃnz]	internationale Beziehungen	We're improving our *international relations*.
to **invest** [ɪnˈvest]	investieren	He has *invested* a large amount of money in his business. *to invest* = to put money in sth or to buy sth because you hope to make a profit *to invest* → investment
lack of [ˈlæk‿əv]	Mangel an; Fehlen von	He was often criticised for his *lack of* politeness. *lack of* → to lack
manufacturing [ˌmænjəˈfæktʃərɪŋ]	Herstellung; Fertigung; produzierendes Gewerbe	This company is known for furniture *manufacturing*.
profitable [ˈprɒfɪtəbl]	profitabel; gewinnbringend	The café closed because it wasn't *profitable* any more. *profitable* → to profit → profit
to **promote** [prəˈməʊt]	fördern; befördern; voranbringen	The tax reduction *promoted* trade with other countries. ! to *promote* trade/an idea/a person in a job *to promote* → promotion
prosperity [prɒsˈperəti]	Wohlstand; Erfolg	The *prosperity* in our country has been growing. *prosperity* = wealth *prosperity* → to prosper → prosperous
rural development *(no pl)* [ˌru:rəl dɪˈveləpmənt]	ländliche Entwicklung	We need to focus on *rural development* to make living in rural areas more attractive. *rural development* ↔ urban development
service sector [ˈsɜ:vɪs ˌsektə]	Dienstleistungssektor	I'm looking for a job in the *service sector*.
*to **set up** [ˌset‿ˈʌp]	gründen; aufbauen	After ten years of working as an employee, she decided to *set up* a business and be her own boss.
to **sign a contract** [ˌsaɪn‿ə ˈkɒntrækt]	einen Vertrag unterzeichnen	He signed the *contract* for his new job.
silk [sɪlk]	Seide	*Silk* is a shiny and expensive natural fabric.
to **starve** [stɑ:v]	hungern; verhungern	1. In many countries people *starve* because they can't afford to buy any food. 2. Are we going to the restaurant now? I'm *starving*!
unemployment [ˌʌnɪmˈplɔɪmənt]	Arbeitslosigkeit	*Unemployment* among young people is a big problem. ! adult/high/increasing/mass/seasonal *unemployment*

Fighting for justice

to **acquire sth** [ə'kwaɪə]	etw. erwerben; sich etw. aneignen	The British *acquired* countries and declared them colonies. *to acquire* → acquisition
acquittal [ə'kwɪtl]	Freispruch	The trial ended with an *acquittal*. *acquittal* → to acquit
apology [ə'pɒlədʒi]	Entschuldigung	I'm sorry. Please accept my *apology*. *apology* → to apologise
civil rights movement [ˌsɪvl ˌraɪts 'mu:vmənt]	Bürgerrechtsbewegung	A *civil rights movement* has organised a protest march through the city centre.
to **discriminate against sb** [dɪˌskrɪmɪneɪt ə'genst]	jmdn. diskriminieren	Unfortunately, minorities *are* often *discriminated against*. *to discriminate against sb* → discrimination
to **exploit sb/sth** [ɪk'splɔɪt]	jmdn./etw. ausbeuten; jmdn./etw. ausnutzen	They're *exploiting* the country's natural resources. *to exploit sb/sth* → exploitation
impact ['ɪmpækt]	Auswirkung; Einfluss	My middle school teacher had a great *impact* on me. I studied biology because of him. ! usually singular *impact* = effect
to **impose sth on sb/sth** [ɪm'pəʊz ɒn]	etw. über jmdn. verhängen; jmdm. etw. auferlegen	The government *imposed* a curfew *on* the citizens. ! to *impose* a language/punishment/fine/sanction/ban *on* sb
injustice [ɪn'dʒʌstɪs]	Ungerechtigkeit	In my opinion, capitalism creates rather than resolves *injustice*. ! to fight/to combat *injustice*
intolerance [ɪn'tɒlrns]	Intoleranz; Unverträglichkeit	Being a minority, they're often faced with *intolerance*. *intolerance* ↔ tolerance *intolerance* → intolerant
judiciary [dʒu:'dɪʃri]	Gerichtswesen; Rechtssystem; Justiz; Judikative	The minority group is treated unfairly by the *judiciary*. *judiciary* → judge → to judge
police brutality [pəˌli:s bru:'tæləti]	Polizeibrutalität	Black activists are protesting against *police brutality*.
race relations *(pl)* [ˌreɪs rɪ'leɪʃnz]	ethnische Beziehungen	*Race relations* are problematic in this country, resulting in a lot of tension.
to **restore** [rɪ'stɔ:]	wiederherstellen; restaurieren; zurückgeben	It will take years to *restore* this place.
to **spark** [spɑ:k]	zünden; auslösen	The incident has *sparked* a nationwide protest. *to spark* = to trigger
to **struggle for sth** ['strʌgl]	für etw. kämpfen	We'll keep *struggling for* better working conditions. ! *to struggle for* breath/freedom/independence/survival *to struggle for* → struggle
systemic racism *(no pl)* [sɪˌstemɪk 'reɪsɪzm]	institutioneller Rassismus	George Floyd's murder raised awareness of *systemic racism* in the US and other countries.
to **topple** ['tɒpl]	stürzen	The statue was *toppled* by activists. *to topple* = to drag down, to pull down
unarmed [ʌn'ɑ:md]	unbewaffnet	*unarmed* = not carrying weapons *unarmed* ↔ armed

Opposites

By adding certain prefixes, words can be turned into their opposites:

- **un-**: **un**certain
- **dis-**: **dis**honest
- **in-** / **im-** (before b, p, m) / **il-** (before l) / **ir-** (before r): **in**dependent, **im**possible, **il**logical, **ir**regular
- **de-**: **de**motivating

Careful: The prefixes are not stressed in English whereas in German they are, e.g. *inde**pen**dent* – **un**abhängig.

In some cases you need a completely different word to express the opposite, e.g. *growth* ↔ *decline*.

a) Decide which of these words are opposites (formed with prefixes) and which ones aren't.

1. democracy • 2. inequality • 3. disobedience • 4. imperialism • 5. illusion • 6. unprofitable • 7. irreversible • 8. discrimination • 9. deglobalisation • 10. irritating • 11. illegal • 12. understand • 13. inspire • 14. immortal • 15. dedication • 16. involuntary • 17. unconstitutional

b) Find the opposites of these words by adding the correct prefixes or by using another word. Then choose five words and make sentences containing both the word and its opposite.

1. tolerance • 2. acceptable • 3. advantage • 4. colonisation • 5. partition • 6. justice (n), just (adj) • 7. to preserve • 8. majority • 9. equal • 10. prosperity • 11. acquittal • 12. capable • 13. rural

Learning in context

It is always helpful to learn new words or phrases together with related ones you already know, e.g. with **synonyms** (=), **opposites** (↔) or **context-related** (→) words or phrases.

Examples: ***to spark*** = *to trigger*; ***export*** ↔ *import*; ***agriculture*** *(→): crop, livestock, organic farming, to harvest.*

This way, you can revise words you already know and improve your ability to think in context.

Work with the following words using the tips given in brackets.

1. to grant (=, ↔) • 2. ancient (=, ↔) • 3. caste system (→) • 4. to contemplate (=) • 5. to displace (=) • 6. illiteracy (↔, →) • 7. secular (↔) • 8. corruption (→) • 9. to fracture (=) • 10. judiciary (→) • 11. to struggle for (=) • 12. international relations (→) • 13. police brutality (→) • 14. electorate (→) • 15. impact (=)

Topic 5 Global matters

Economic aspects of globalisation

barrier ['bæriə]	Barriere; Sperre	We need to overcome this *barrier*.
*to **be interconnected (with)** [ˌbi ɪntəkə'nektɪd]	zusammenhängen (mit); vernetzt sein (mit)	The two countries *are interconnected* on different levels.
capital ['kæpɪtl]	Kapital-	The company mainly invests in *capital* projects.
to **compete (with/against)** [kəm'pi:t]	konkurrieren (mit); sich messen (mit); in Wettbewerb treten (mit); antreten (gegen)	You're stronger than me. I can't *compete with* you. *to compete (with/against)* → competition → competitive → competitiveness
corporation [ˌkɔ:pr'eɪʃn]	Konzern; Unternehmen	Many product brands actually belong to a few powerful multi-national *corporations*.
crisis, *crises (pl)* ['kraɪsɪs; 'kraɪsi:z]	Krise	A financial *crisis* creates lots of economic problems.

deglobalisation [ˌdiːɡləʊblaɪˈzeɪʃn]	Deglobalisierung	Do you think the world could enter a process of *deglobalisation*? *deglobalisation* ↔ globalisation *deglobalisation* → to deglobalise
economy [ɪˈkɒnəmi]	Ökonomie; Wirtschaft	Today's global *economy* depends on supply chains. *economy* → economic
global player [ˌɡləʊbl ˈpleɪə]	weltweit agierender Konzern	What started as a small company is now a *global player*.
goods *(pl)* [ɡʊdz]	Güter; Waren	All kinds of *goods* are sold at this market.
to **import** [ɪmˈpɔːt]	importieren; einführen	This country needs to *import* most goods because it doesn't produce a lot. *to import* ↔ to export
industry [ˈɪndəstri]	Industrie; Branche; Gewerbe	Hollywood is the centre of the US film *industry*. ! heavy/service/textile/advertising *industry* *industry* → industrialisation → industrial
infrastructure [ˈɪnfrəˌstrʌktʃə]	Infrastruktur	It's a small town, but it has a great *infrastructure*. It's connected to three big cities.
to **invest** [ɪnˈvest]	investieren	He has *invested* a large amount of money in his business. *to invest* = to put money in sth or to buy sth because you hope to make a profit *to invest* → investment
labour [ˈleɪbə]	Arbeit; Arbeitskräfte	1. Working in a mine involves hard *labour*. 2. There's a high demand for skilled *labour*. ! *labour*-intensive/*labour*-saving *labour* = work
logistical [ləˈdʒɪstɪkl]	logistisch	We are out of stock due to *logistical* issues.
to **manufacture** [mænjəˈfæktʃə]	fertigen; herstellen	These tiles were *manufactured* in the new factory. *to manufacture* = to produce *to manufacture* → manufacturing
opportunity [ˌɒpəˈtʃuːnəti]	Gelegenheit	He took the *opportunity* to apply for his dream job. ! a missed/lost/golden *opportunity*
to **outsource** [ˈaʊtsɔːs]	ausgliedern; auslagern	We're going to *outsource* some of our services. *to outsource* → outsourcing
profit [ˈprɒfɪt]	Profit; Gewinn	Our company has made a lot of *profit* this year. *profit* = money you make through selling goods (or services) for more than they cost to produce (or provide) *profit* → to profit → profitability
raw materials *(pl)* [ˌrɔː məˈtɪəriəlz]	Rohstoffe; Rohmaterialien	The production will take longer due to a shortage of *raw materials*.
to **remove** [rɪˈmuːv]	entfernen	During the summit, the UK government finally removed trade barriers. *to remove* = to take away (sth that you don't want) ! *to remove* barriers/problems/doubts
risk [rɪsk]	Risiko; Gefahr	This sport is dangerous. There are high *risks*.
shipping [ˈʃɪpɪŋ]	Versand; Transport *(von Gütern)*	I have to pay for *shipping* when I order something from the US. *shipping* = transportation of goods

supply and demand [səˌplaɪ‿ən dɪ'mɑ:nd]	Angebot und Nachfrage	Prices are determined by *supply and demand*.
supply chain [sə'plaɪ ˌtʃeɪn]	Lieferkette; Versorgungskette	Our *supply chain* was interrupted by logistical issues.
trade [treɪd]	Handel	The ivory *trade* is illegal. *trade* → trader → to trade
to **transport** [træn'spɔ:t]	transportieren; befördern	The goods were *transported* by ship. *to transport* = to take from one place to another *to transport* → transport → transportation
worldwide [ˌwɜ:ld'waɪd]	weltweit	This company sells their products *worldwide*. *worldwide* = global

Environment

*to **become extinct** [bɪˌkʌm‿ɪk'stɪŋkt]	aussterben	There is a danger that rhinos will soon *become extinct*. *to become extinct* → extinction
biodiversity [ˌbaɪədaɪ'vɜ:səti]	Artenreichtum; Artenvielfalt	Global warming is threatening *biodiversity* because the living conditions of many species are changing too quickly for them to adapt. ! a decline in/loss of/policy on *biodiversity*
carbon (dioxide) ['kɑ:bn]	Kohlenstoff; Kohlenstoffdioxid	There is a *carbon* tax on air travel. *Carbon* is short for carbon dioxide.
climate change ['klaɪmət ˌtʃeɪndʒ]	Klimawandel	*Climate change* has had a huge impact on life on earth. ! to cause/to contribute to/to mitigate/to combat/to adapt to *climate change*
drought [draʊt]	Dürre; Trockenheit	The farmers in this area are affected by *drought*.
dump [dʌmp]	Deponie; Halde	Toxic waste *dumps* pose a health hazard to those living near them.
ecological collapse [i:kəˌlɒdʒɪkl kə'læps]	ökologischer Zusammenbruch	If our forests are destroyed, it will lead to an *ecological collapse*.
electronic waste [ˌelektrɒnɪk 'weɪst]	Elektroschrott; Elektronikabfälle	The amount of *electronic waste* is constantly growing as people want to keep their devices up to date. ! *electronic waste* = e-waste
emission [ɪ'mɪʃn]	Ausstoß; Emission	The *emissions* from cars should be reduced. *emission* → to emit
environmental activist [ɪnˌvaɪrnˌmentl‿'æktɪvɪst]	Umweltaktivist/-in	This group of *environmental activists* regularly organises protest marchs.
flooding ['flʌdɪŋ]	Überflutung; Überschwemmung	Severe *flooding* has destroyed lots of houses in the valley.
fossil fuel ['fɒsl ˌfju:əl]	fossiler Brennstoff	Typical *fossil fuels* are coal, mineral oil and natural gas.
non-recyclable [ˌnɒn rɪ'saɪkləbl]	nicht wiederverwertbar	This packaging consists of *non-recyclable* materials. *non-recyclable* → to recycle → recycling
off-shore [ˌɒf'ʃɔ:]	vor der Küste	He works on an *off-shore* oil platform. *off-shore* ↔ on-shore
pollution [pə'lu:ʃn]	Verschmutzung	*Pollution* has made the river dirty. ! air/coastal/environmental/groundwater/light/marine/noise/oil *pollution* *pollution* → to pollute

power grid ['paʊə ˌgrɪd]	Stromnetz	Our little cabin isn't connected to the *power grid*.
renewable [rɪ'nju:əbl]	erneuerbar; verlängerbar	Wind and water are *renewable* energies. *renewable* → new
scarce [skeəs]	knapp; selten; rar	Companies are destroying whole landscapes in an effort to find *scarce* raw materials.
sustainable [sə'steɪnəbl]	nachhaltig	Our company produces *sustainable* fashion.
toxic ['tɒksɪk]	giftig; toxisch	You need to wear a mask when you work with *toxic* substances. ! *toxic* waste/chemicals/gas

Politics and society

armed conflict [ˌɑ:md 'kɒnflɪkt]	bewaffneter Konflikt; bewaffnete Auseinandersetzung	Both sides want to avoid an *armed conflict*.
autonomy [ɔ:'tɒnəmi]	Autonomie; Selbstständigkeit	Gaining *autonomy* means becoming less dependent on others.
border ['bɔ:də]	Grenze	We live close to the French *border*.
commitment [kə'mɪtmənt]	Bindung; Verpflichtung; Engagement	Showing social *commitment* not only helps, but also makes your life meaningful. *commitment* = a plan to do sth or to support sb
democracy [dɪ'mɒkrəsi]	Demokratie	In a *democracy*, people have the power to change things. *democracy* → democratic
domestic [də'mestɪk]	Inlands-	*Domestic* activities are activities that take place within one particular country.
to **endorse** [ɪn'dɔ:s]	unterstützen; befürworten	The Labour Party traditionally *endorses* the rights of workers.
Global South [ˌgləʊbl 'saʊθ]	Globaler Süden *(Sammelbegriff für Entwicklungs- und Schwellenländer)*	Our organisation supports sustainability development projects in the *Global South*. *Global South* ↔ Global North
government ['gʌvnmənt]	Regierung	The main British *government* buildings are in London. *government* → to govern
immigration [ˌɪmɪ'greɪʃn]	Immigration; Einwanderung; Einreise	The USA is a popular country for *immigration*. *immigration* → immigrant → to immigrate
impact ['ɪmpækt]	Einfluss	The decision will have a high socioeconomic *impact*.
lobbyist ['lɒbiɪst]	Lobbyist/-in; Interessenvertreter/-in	*Lobbyists* try to influence politicians to make them act in their lobbies' interests.
malnutrition *(no pl)* [ˌmælnju:'trɪʃn]	Unterernährung; Mangelernährung	The children were so skinny you could see they were suffering from *malnutrition*.
policy ['pɒləsi]	Grundsatz; Richtlinie; Politik; politische Linie	! Careful, don't mix up: 1. The government's *policies* have increased the gap between rich and poor. 2. Young people seem interested in politics these days.
protectionism [prə'tekʃənɪzm]	Protektionismus	*Protectionism* is characterised by policies which restrict imports from other countries by imposing large taxes on them.

public sector [ˌpʌblɪk 'sektə]	öffentlicher Bereich; Staatssektor	The government agreed to spend more money on the *public sector*. *public sector* ↔ private sector
refugee [ˌrefjʊ'dʒiː]	Geflüchtete/-r	In 2015, a lot of *refugees* came to live in our town.
representative [ˌreprɪ'zentətɪv]	Repräsentant/-in; Stellvertreter/-in	Our *representatives* in parliament are elected in a democratic way. *representative* → to represent
self-reliant [ˌselfrɪ'laɪənt]	selbstständig	If you are *self-reliant*, you don't need other people to help you to do things.
standard ['stændəd]	Standard	Environmental *standards* are not the same all over the world. ! to adopt/to lower/to maintain/to raise a standard
*to **stand for** *(BE)* ['stænd fə]	kandidieren; sich zur Wahl stellen	Two strong candidates *are standing for* election. ! *to stand for (BE)* = to run for *(AE)* *to stand for* election/mayor/parliament/prime minister
*to **take action** [teɪk‿'ækʃn]	handeln; eingreifen	Stop talking about the problem. It's time to *take action*!
trade agreement ['treɪd‿əˌgriːmənt]	Handelsabkommen	The two countries have successfully negotiated a *trade agreement*.
tension ['tenʃn]	Spannung	Geopolitical *tensions* have resulted in a war.
to **vote for** ['vəʊt fə]	für jmdn. stimmen; jmdn. wählen	Who did you *vote for* in the election? *to vote for* = to elect *to vote for* ↔ to vote against

Culture

alienation [ˌeɪliə'neɪʃn]	Entfremdung	It's normal to feel a sense of *alienation* when you return to your home country after twenty years abroad. *alienation* → alienated
to **cultivate** ['kʌltɪveɪt]	pflegen	They have *cultivated* their friendship over many years. ! *to cultivate* contacts/a friendship/a relationship
cultural appropriation [ˌkʌltʃrl‿əˌprəʊpri'eɪʃn]	kulturelle Aneignung	You could speak of *cultural appropriation* if somebody uses parts of a different culture (e.g. hairstyles or dance moves) in a disrespectful way.
dialect ['daɪəlekt]	Dialekt	Do people speak a *dialect* where you live?
first language [ˌfɜːst 'læŋgwɪdʒ]	Muttersprache	My *first language* is German, but I also speak French and Spanish. *first language* = native language, mother tongue
heritage ['herɪtɪdʒ]	Erbe	We shouldn't forget our cultural *heritage*. ! cultural/biological/architectural *heritage* *heritage* = (cultural) tradition
lingua franca [ˌlɪŋgwə 'fræŋkə]	Verkehrssprache	English is often used as a *lingua franca*. *lingua franca* = language used for communication between groups who speak different languages
multicultural [ˌmʌlti'kʌltʃrl]	multikulturell	We need to look at the issue from a *multicultural* perspective.

nuclear family [ˌnjuːkliə ˈfæmli]	Kernfamilie; Kleinfamilie	In Germany, usually just members of the *nuclear family* share one household. *nuclear family* ↔ extended family
to **pass down** [ˌpɑːs ˈdaʊn]	überliefern; weitergeben	They're *passing down* their traditions to the next generation. ! *to pass down* (tribal) history/arts/literature/traditions
patriarchal [ˌpeɪtriˈɑːkl]	patriarchalisch	In a *patriarchal* society, men are in control. *patriarchal* ↔ matriarchal
religious belief [rɪˌlɪdʒəs bɪˈliːf]	Glaubensüberzeugung	The writer's *religious belief* is obvious in all his works.
to **share** [ʃeə]	teilen	It helped a lot that you *shared* the information with us. ! *to share* expenses/characteristics/ideas/information/knowledge/one's sorrows
to **tolerate** [ˈtɒlreɪt]	tolerieren; dulden	I can *tolerate* a lot, but I've really had enough of his insults. *to tolerate* → tolerance

'Word partners' (collocations)

Some words often appear together. Learn such combinations to improve your English and get more fluent.

a) Find adjectives that can go with these nouns. Then add at least one more noun for each phrase.

1. [1] player / warming / network / [2]
2. [3] damage / protection / activist / [4]
3. [5] heritage / awareness / appropriation / [6]
4. [7] development / energy / farming / [8]

b) Match the words to make useful phrases.

carbon • climate • financial • fossil • immigration • power • raw • supply

+

chain • change • emissions • fuel • grid • laws • market • materials

c) Note down as many 'partners' as possible that can go before or after these nouns.

1. trade • 2. policy • 3. growth • 4. waste • 5. pollution • 6. labour • 7. energy

Dealing with difficult words

You already know a number of English words you have to pay special attention to, especially:

- false friends, e.g. ***actual*** = tatsächlich (≠ aktuell = *current*)
  *The **actual** results were better than expected.* (tatsächlich)
  *The **current** economic situation is very concerning.* (aktuell)
- words that have several meanings, e.g. ***power*** (Kraft; Macht; Stärke; Strom; Elektrizität; Energie)
  *Most modern monarchs have no real **power** – they rule only formally. / China's economic **power** is still growing. / There was a **power** cut after the storm.*

Look at these words from different topics. Make sure you know their correct meaning(s) and note down example sentences with them as shown above (you can use a dictionary if necessary).

1. sight (Topic 1) • 2. concrete (noun/adj.) (Topic 1) • 3. crime (Topic 1) • 4. reservation (Topic 2) • 5. to abuse (Topic 2) • 6. diet (Visions …) • 7. to consume (Topic 3) • 8. craft (Topic 3) • 9. economical (Topic 3) • 10. capital (Topic 5) • 11. labour (Topic 5) • 12. to stand for (Topic 4, 5)

List of irregular verbs

infinitive	simple past	past participle	German
be [bi:]	was [wɒz]/were [wɜ:]	been [bi:n]	sein
bear [beə]	bore [bɔ:]	borne / AE: born [bɔ:n]	tragen
beat [bi:t]	beat [bi:t]	beaten ['bi:tn] / AE: beat [bi:t]	schlagen
become [bɪ'kʌm]	became [bɪ'keɪm]	become [bɪ'kʌm]	werden
begin [bɪ'gɪn]	began [bɪ'gæn]	begun [bɪ'gʌn]	beginnen, anfangen
bend [bend]	bent [bent]	bent [bent]	biegen, beugen
bet [bet]	bet [bet]/betted ['betɪd]	bet [bet]/betted ['betɪd]	wetten
bite [baɪt]	bit [bɪt]	bitten ['bɪtn]	beißen
blow [bləʊ]	blew [blu:]	blown [bləʊn]	blasen, pusten
break [breɪk]	broke [brəʊk]	broken ['brəʊkn]	(zer-)brechen, kaputt machen
breed [bri:d]	bred [bred]	bred [bred]	züchten, sich vermehren
bring [brɪŋ]	brought [brɔ:t]	brought [brɔ:t]	(mit-)bringen
build [bɪld]	built [bɪlt]	built [bɪlt]	bauen
burn [bɜ:n]	burnt [bɜ:nt]/burned [bɜ:nd]	burnt [bɜ:nt]/burned [bɜ:nd]	brennen
burst [bɜ:st]	burst [bɜ:st]	burst [bɜ:st]	bersten, platzen
buy [baɪ]	bought [bɔ:t]	bought [bɔ:t]	kaufen
cast [kɑ:st]	cast [kɑ:st]	cast [kɑ:st]	werfen
catch [kætʃ]	caught [kɔ:t]	caught [kɔ:t]	fangen
choose [tʃu:z]	chose [tʃəʊz]	chosen ['tʃəʊzn]	(aus-)wählen
come [kʌm]	came [keɪm]	come [kʌm]	kommen
cost [kɒst]	cost [kɒst]	cost [kɒst]	kosten
cling [klɪŋ]	clung [klʌŋ]	clung [klʌŋ]	kleben, klammern
creep [kri:p]	crept [krept]	crept [krept]	schleichen
cut [kʌt]	cut [kʌt]	cut [kʌt]	schneiden
deal [di:l]	dealt [delt]	dealt [delt]	(be-)handeln
dig [dɪg]	dug [dʌg]	dug [dʌg]	graben
do [du:]	did [dɪd]	done [dʌn]	machen, tun
draw [drɔ:]	drew [dru:]	drawn [drɔ:n]	zeichnen, ziehen
dream [dri:m]	dreamt [dremt]/dreamed [dri:md]	dreamt [dremt]/dreamed [dri:md]	träumen
drink [drɪŋk]	drank [dræŋk]	drunk [drʌŋk]	trinken
drive [draɪv]	drove [drəʊv]	driven ['drɪvn]	fahren, treiben
eat [i:t]	ate [et/eɪt]	eaten ['i:tn]	essen
fall [fɔ:l]	fell [fel]	fallen ['fɔ:lən]	fallen
feed [fi:d]	fed [fed]	fed [fed]	füttern, ernähren
feel [fi:l]	felt [felt]	felt [felt]	fühlen
fight [faɪt]	fought [fɔ:t]	fought [fɔ:t]	kämpfen, (sich) streiten
find [faɪnd]	found [faʊnd]	found [faʊnd]	finden
fit [fɪt]	fit [fɪt]/fitted ['fɪtɪd]	fit [fɪt]/fitted ['fɪtɪd]	passen
fly [flaɪ]	flew [flu:]	flown [fləʊn]	fliegen
forbid [fə'bɪd]	forbade [fə'bæd]	forbidden [fə'bɪdn]	verbieten
forget [fə'get]	forgot [fə'gɒt]	forgotten [fə'gɒtn]	vergessen

infinitive	simple past	past participle	German
forgive [fə'gɪv]	forgave [fə'geɪv]	forgiven [fə'gɪvn]	vergeben, verzeihen
freeze [fri:z]	froze [frəʊz]	frozen ['frəʊzn]	gefrieren, erstarren
get [get]	got [gɒt]	got [gɒt]/AE: gotten ['gɒtn]	bekommen, erhalten
give [gɪv]	gave [geɪv]	given ['gɪvn]	geben
go [gəʊ]	went [went]	gone [gɒn]	gehen, fahren
grow [grəʊ]	grew [gru:]	grown [grəʊn]	wachsen, anbauen, züchten
hang [hæŋ]	hung [hʌŋ]	hung [hʌŋ]	hängen
have [hæv]	had [hæd]	had [hæd]	haben
hear [hɪə]	heard [hɜ:d]	heard [hɜ:d]	hören
hide [haɪd]	hid [hɪd]	hidden ['hɪdn]	(sich) verstecken
hit [hɪt]	hit [hɪt]	hit [hɪt]	schlagen, treffen
hold [həʊld]	held [held]	held [held]	halten
hurt [hɜ:t]	hurt [hɜ:t]	hurt [hɜ:t]	verletzen, sich weh tun
keep [ki:p]	kept [kept]	kept [kept]	(auf-)bewahren, behalten
know [nəʊ]	knew [nju:]	known [nəʊn]	kennen, wissen
lay [leɪ]	laid [leɪd]	laid [leɪd]	legen
lead [li:d]	led [led]	led [led]	führen
lean [li:n]	leant [lent]/leaned [li:nd]	leant [lent]/leaned [li:nd]	lehnen, beugen
leap [li:p]	leapt [lept]/leaped [li:pt]	leapt [lept]/leaped [li:pt]	springen
learn [lɜ:n]	learnt [lɜ:nt]/learned [lɜ:nd]	learnt [lɜ:nt]/learned [lɜ:nd]	lernen
leave [li:v]	left [left]	left [left]	(ver-)lassen
lend [lend]	lent [lent]	lent [lent]	leihen
let [let]	let [let]	let [let]	lassen
lie [laɪ]	lay [leɪ]	lain [leɪn]	liegen
lose [lu:z]	lost [lɒst]	lost [lɒst]	verlieren
make [meɪk]	made [meɪd]	made [meɪd]	machen, tun
mean [mi:n]	meant [ment]	meant [ment]	bedeuten, meinen
meet [mi:t]	met [met]	met [met]	treffen
pay [peɪ]	paid [peɪd]	paid [peɪd]	(be-)zahlen
put [pʊt]	put [pʊt]	put [pʊt]	legen, setzen, stellen
read [ri:d]	read [red]	read [red]	lesen
ride [raɪd]	rode [rəʊd]	ridden ['rɪdn]	fahren, reiten
ring [rɪŋ]	rang [ræŋ]	rung [rʌŋ]	klingeln, läuten
rise [raɪz]	rose [rəʊz]	risen ['rɪzn]	aufsteigen, sich erheben
run [rʌn]	ran [ræn]	run [rʌn]	laufen, rennen
say [seɪ]	said [sed]	said [sed]	sagen
see [si:]	saw [sɔ:]	seen [si:n]	sehen
seek [si:k]	sought [sɔ:t]	sought [sɔ:t]	suchen
sell [sel]	sold [səʊld]	sold [səʊld]	verkaufen
send [send]	sent [sent]	sent [sent]	senden, verschicken
set [set]	set [set]	set [set]	setzen, einrichten
sew [səʊ]	sewed [səʊd]	sewn [səʊn]/sewed [səʊd]	nähen
shake [ʃeɪk]	shook [ʃʊk]	shaken ['ʃeɪkn]	schütteln
shine [ʃaɪn]	shone [ʃɒn]	shone [ʃɒn]	scheinen

infinitive	simple past	past participle	German
shoot [ʃu:t]	shot [ʃɒt]	shot [ʃɒt]	schießen
show [ʃəʊ]	showed [ʃəʊd]	shown [ʃəʊn]	zeigen
shrink [ʃrɪŋk]	shrank [ʃræŋk]	shrunk [ʃræŋk]	schrumpfen, weichen
sing [sɪŋ]	sang [sæŋ]	sung [sʌŋ]	singen
sink [sɪŋk]	sank [sæŋk]	sunk [sʌŋk]	sinken
sit [sɪt]	sat [sæt]	sat [sæt]	sitzen
sleep [sli:p]	slept [slept]	slept [slept]	schlafen
slide [slaɪd]	slid [slɪd]	slid [slɪd]	rutschen
smell [smel]	smelt [smelt]/smelled [smeld]	smelt [smelt]/smelled [smeld]	riechen, duften
sow [səʊ]	sowed [səʊd]	sown [səʊn]/sowed [səʊd]	säen
speak [spi:k]	spoke [spəʊk]	spoken ['spəʊkn]	sprechen
speed [spi:d]	sped [sped]/speeded ['spi:dɪd]	sped [sped]/speeded ['spi:dɪd]	sausen, rasen
spell [spel]	spelt [spelt]/spelled [speld]	spelt [spelt]/spelled [speld]	buchstabieren
spend [spend]	spent [spent]	spent [spent]	ausgeben, verbringen
spin [spɪn]	span [spæn]/spun [spʌn]	spun [spʌn]	drehen, spinnen
spit [spɪt]	spat [spæt]	spat [spæt]	spucken
split [splɪt]	split [splɪt]	split [splɪt]	spalten, teilen
spread [spred]	spread [spred]	spread [spred]	(sich) verbreiten
stand [stænd]	stood [stʊd]	stood [stʊd]	stehen
steal [sti:l]	stole [stəʊl]	stolen ['stəʊlən]	stehlen
stick [stɪk]	stuck [stʌk]	stuck [stʌk]	kleben, stecken
sting [stɪŋ]	stung [stʌŋ]	stung [stʌŋ]	stechen
strike [straɪk]	struck [strʌk]	struck [strʌk]	schlagen, zuschlagen
strive [straɪv]	strove [strəʊv]/strived [straɪvd]	striven [strɪvn]/strived [straɪvd]	streben, sich bemühen
swear [sweə]	swore [swɔ:]	sworn [swɔ:n]	schwören, fluchen
sweep [swi:p]	swept [swept]	swept [swept]	fegen
swell [swel]	swelled [sweld]	swollen ['swəʊlən]/swelled [sweld]	anschwellen, anwachsen
swim [swɪm]	swam [swæm]	swum [swʌm]	schwimmen
swing [swɪŋ]	swung [swʌŋ]	swung [swʌŋ]	schwingen
take [teɪk]	took [tʊk]	taken ['teɪkn]	nehmen
teach [ti:tʃ]	taught [tɔ:t]	taught [tɔ:t]	unterrichten, lehren, beibringen
tear [teə]	tore [tɔ:]	torn [tɔ:n]	reißen
tell [tel]	told [təʊld]	told [təʊld]	erzählen
think [θɪŋk]	thought [θɔ:t]	thought [θɔ:t]	(nach-)denken, glauben
throw [θrəʊ]	threw [θru:]	thrown [θrəʊn]	werfen
understand [ˌʌndə'stænd]	understood [ˌʌndə'stʊd]	understood [ˌʌndə'stʊd]	verstehen
upset [ʌp'set]	upset [ʌp'set]	upset [ʌp'set]	aufregen
wake [weɪk]	woke [wəʊk]	woken ['wəʊkn]	wecken, aufwachen
wear [weə]	wore [wɔ:]	worn [wɔ:n]	anhaben, tragen
weep [wi:p]	wept [wept]	wept [wept]	weinen
win [wɪn]	won [wʌn]	won [wʌn]	gewinnen, siegen
write [raɪt]	wrote [rəʊt]	written ['rɪtn]	schreiben

Selected colonial history dates

The British Empire

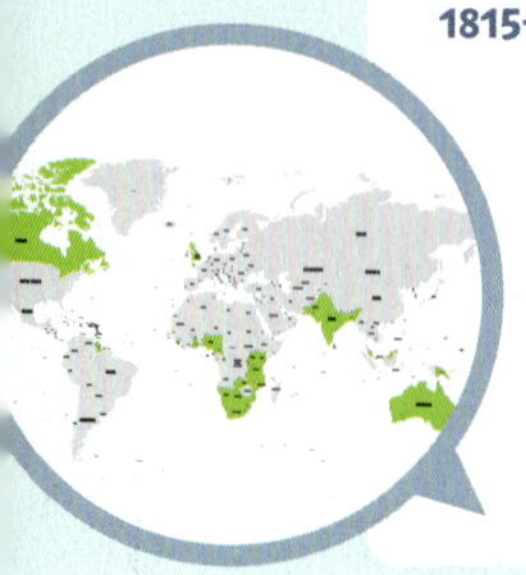

late 1500s Beginnings of the 'First' British Empire with the establishment of permanent colonies on the east coast of North America.

1500s–1800s Transatlantic slave trade

1600 Founding of the British East India Company to trade goods (e.g. spices, cotton, tea) with India. The company eventually controlled substantial parts of India.

1783 The 'Second' British Empire began, with Britain focusing on Asia, Africa and the Pacific after losing its 13 American colonies in the American War of Independence.

1788 The British colonisation of Australia started when the first ships arrived with convicts from Britain.

1815–1914 Britain became the world's predominant colonial power.

1922 The British Empire included a quarter of the world's land area and a quarter of the world's population (ca. 458 million people). It was the "empire on which the sun never sets".

1931 The Statute of Westminster granted the British dominions of Australia, Canada, New Zealand and South Africa full legislative independence.

1945 Decolonisation began after 1945, partly due to increased protest against British rule.

1949 The Commonwealth of Nations in its current form was established.

1997 The British Empire ended when Hong Kong was handed over to China.

2022 The Commonwealth of Nations has 56 members, with a population of 2.4 billion.

Canada

1763 After wars against First Nations and the French, most of what is now Canada came under British rule.

1830s–1996 The Canadian government systematically tried to assimilate Indigenous peoples into European culture, by removing about 170,000 children from their families and forcing them to live in 'residential schools' or with white foster parents.

1931 The Statute of Westminster recognised Canada as a self-governing dominion.

1982 Canada became fully independent from Britain with the Canada Act.

2008 Official apology by the Canadian Prime Minister to residential school children.

2021 Mary Simon was the first Indigenous person to be appointed governor general.

South Africa

1487 The Portuguese were the first Europeans to start exploring southern Africa.

1652 The Dutch established a supply station which later became Cape Town.

1779–1879 The Dutch colonists' attempts to expand their territory resulted in a series of wars against the Xhosa.

1800s Britain occupied the Cape region and expanded beyond. To escape British rule, descendants of the Dutch Cape Town settlers (the Boers) moved into the interior of South Africa and founded two republics of their own.

1880–1902 Britain's attempts to invade Boer territory resulted in the First and Second Boer Wars. Eventually, the Boer republics were integrated into the British Empire.

1910 The white-ruled Union of South Africa became a self-governing dominion of the British Empire.

1912 The African National Congress was founded as a liberation movement advocating the rights of Black people. Today, the ANC is a social democratic political party.

1948 The National Party came into power in South Africa and institutionalised a political system of racial segregation called 'apartheid'. Non-white people were divided into Blacks, 'Coloureds' and Indians and their rights were restricted to different degrees.

1961 Full independence from Britain with the founding of the Republic of South Africa.

1991 Due to international pressure and decades of protests, apartheid officially ended.

1994 Nelson Mandela was elected the first Black president of South Africa.

2000s–now A Black middle class has developed and living conditions have improved for many people. However, South Africa is still the most economically unequal country in the world.

India

1500s–1800s The powerful Muslim Mughal Empire ruled the Indian subcontinent.

1600s The British East India Company successfully collaborated with the Mughal Empire and gained control over large parts of India. French, Dutch, and Portuguese colonists lost their territories to the British.

1852 The first railway was built by the British and ran 33 km from Bombay (today: Mumbai) to Thane. Nowadays, India has the fourth largest rail network in the world.

1857–1858 In India's First War of Independence, Indian soldiers (sepoys) in the East India Company's army rebelled against the rule of the East India Company. Finally, the British government took over their trading company's assets, trading rights, administrative systems and army, gained control over India and made it a British crown colony. The direct British rule over India was known as the British Raj.

1877 Queen Victoria became Empress of India.

1885 Founding of the Indian National Congress, a party promoting independence.

1930 The Salt March led by Mahatma Gandhi was an act of non-violent civil disobedience to protest the British salt monopoly and high taxes on salt in India. It inspired more protest and played an essential part in disestablishing the British Raj.

1947 Independence and Partition of India (installing Pakistan as a separate country).

1947–1964 Jawaharlal Nehru was the first prime minister of the Indian Republic. He promoted a democratic and secular India and is also called the 'Architect of Modern India'.

From 2014 Prime Minister Narendra Modi has been promoting Hindu nationalism and supporting anti-Muslim tendencies, thus shaking people's confidence in democracy.

Kenya

1500s Portuguese explorers arrived on the East African coast and installed naval bases along the coast to gain control over the Indian Ocean.

1698 Arabs from Oman conquered the Portuguese territory.

1884–1885 At the Berlin Conference, seven major European powers divided most of Africa into controlled territories. No Africans were consulted.

1885 A German protectorate was established over the coastal region of Wituland.

1890 Germany handed its protectorate over to Britain.

1895 British East Africa was established as a protectorate of the British Empire comprising roughly the territory of present-day Kenya.

1920 British East Africa became the Colony of Kenya.

1952–1960 A guerrilla army revolted against British rule (the 'Mau Mau rebellion').

1963 Kenya gained independence from Britain and joined the Commonwealth.

1964–1978 Jomo Kenyatta was the first president of the Republic of Kenya. Under him, Kenya installed a one-party system, the economy grew, but there was also a rise in unemployment and social inequality.

1991 Due to pressure from Western governments, Daniel arap Moi, who was Kenya's president from 1978 to 2002, introduced a multiparty system. Corruption thrived under the rule of Moi and the following president Mwai Kibaki (2002–2013).

2004 The Kenyan activist Wangari Maathai was the first African woman to win the Nobel Peace Prize. She advocated social, environmental and political issues, especially women's rights, and was a Member of Parliament from 2003 to 2005.

2007–2008 Mass protests occurred when Mwai Kibaki was announced winner of the presidential election and his opponent claimed that the election had been manipulated. Violent fights between different ethnic groups ensued and about 1,000 people were killed.

2022 William Ruto won the presidential elections against Raila Odinga with only 50.5% of votes. Odinga contested the result, but the Supreme Court declared the election valid. At the announcement of the results, violence erupted in Nairobi and other places. Currently Kenya, the biggest economy in East Africa, is suffering from drought, rising debt and inflation.

Solutions

Spot on language

Topic 1

Exercise 1

l. 2: great – once-in-a-lifetime; l. 4: best – perfect; l. 5: great – awe-inspiring, spectacular; l. 6: great – excellent; l. 7: (a) good – (an) ideal; l. 9: great – spectacular, awe-inspiring; l. 11: good – valuable; l. 12: nice – convenient; l. 14: very good – marvellous

Exercise 2

1. all New Yorkers; any sane New Yorker; thousands of people; herds; droves of people
2. as easy as ABC; as easy as falling off a log; as easy as (apple)pie
3. Chinese, Argentinian, Italian, … restaurants
4. it will be your new home base; I'll have to go there to meet you
5. as safe as any country village; safer than a police station (kindergarten)
6. the Statue of Liberty, Grand Central Station, Times Square, the MoMA, the Met, …
7. quieter than a church at night; so quiet you could hear a pin drop

Exercise 3

1. What really annoys me is the number of cars. (It is the number of cars that …)
2. … But they do enjoy …
3. … The apartment itself is ideal … / … but we would not be able to pay for it ourselves.
4. … but it is the masses of people I cannot stand (but what I cannot stand is …)
5. … do really put me off. / … are what really puts me off.
6. … They would have to do all the work themselves.
7. … What I am worried about is safety. (It is safety that I am worried about.)
8. … but I do see what the move …

Exercise 4

Individual answers. Here are sample statements containing some of the linguistic features trained:

- What matters to me is a clean environment.
- Now that I'm 16 and can drive everywhere on my own they want to get rid of the car. That's just stupid.
- An automobile is such a marvellous invention. What could be more convenient than having a car at one's disposal, for example, if you want to go and see old friends in the countryside?
- Did you know that in a city drivers spend almost a third of their time cruising in seach of parking space? It's the lack of such space that is the biggest problem for car owners in a city.
- Compared to the average speed of cars, New York subway trains are as fast as lightning.
- Well, as it happens, I do care about the environment, but I don't think we can save it by getting rid of our Chevrolet.
- I simply don't get why people worship cars like some modern god. In fact this god is responsible for killing millions of innocent people worldwide.
- Well, if it is air pollution you are worried about, why don't we sell our old banger and exchange it for a slick and small electric car?
- New York has an excellent transit system; you can go anywhere you like in next to no time.
- I'm pretty sure Mom and Dad won't let me ride the subway at night – there are too many tramps, beggars, thieves and psychopaths about.

Topic 2

Exercise 1

- The past perfect simple in line 2 (hadn't colonised) is used in the if-clause, which is part of a mixed conditional sentence. The passive form of the simple past in line 4 (were colonised) is used to show that the focus is on the people affected by colonisation, and not on the colonisers.
- Past perfect progressive (had been living, ll. 5/6): emphasis on duration, before another event.
- Simple past (arrived, l. 7): in the past, over, no emphasis on duration.
- Past perfect simple (had been left alone, ll. 8/9, hadn't been devastated, l. 10, hadn't been stolen, l. 11): part of conditional sentence, condition referring to the past, no emphasis on duration.
- Modal auxiliary in the past (might have developed, l. 9): part of conditional sentence, consequence referring to the past, no emphasis on duration.
- Simple past (were, l. 13): in the past, over, stative verb.
- Simple past perfect (had not developed, l. 13): no emphasis on duration, before another event.
- Simple past (had, l. 15): in the past, over, stative verb.
- Past progressive (were living, l. 16): focus on duration.
- Present perfect simple (has been, l. 17): started in the past, not over yet, stative verb.
- Simple past, passive (was never colonised, l. 20): in the past, over, no focus on duration.
- Present perfect simple (has become, ll. 20/21): happened in the past, focus on result, still relevant at present.
- Present perfect simple (have explored, l. 22): happened in the past, focus on result, may continue.
- Past perfect simple (had killed, l. 24): part of conditional sentence, condition referring to the past, no emphasis on duration.
- Simple past (did, l. 25): in the past, over, no emphasis on duration.
- Modal auxiliary in the past (could have happened, l. 32): part of conditional sentence, consequence referring to the past, no emphasis on duration.
- Past perfect simple (had been, l. 33): part of conditional sentence, condition referring to the past, stative verb.
- Modal auxiliary in the past (might have happened, l. 35): part of conditional sentence, consequence referring to the past, no emphasis on duration.
- Past perfect simple (had won, l. 36, had gone on, l. 37): part of conditional sentence, condition referring to the past, no emphasis on duration.
- Simple past (weren't, l. 43): part of conditional sentence, consequence referring to the present, stative verb.

- Conditional perfect (would have achieved, l. 44): part of conditional sentence, condition referring to the past, focus on the result.

Exercise 2

ll. 1–3: condition referring to the past, consequence referring to the present | **ll. 7–9:** condition referring to the past, consequence referring to the present | **ll. 22–25:** conditions referring to the past, consequence referring to the present | **ll. 42–46:** condition referring to the present, consequence referring to the past (but focus on result)

Exercise 3

1. If Europe's coastal nations **hadn't been** good at building ships, they **couldn't have travelled / wouldn't have travelled** to faraway places.
2. If the Chinese **hadn't invented** gunpowder, Europeans **wouldn't have been able to develop** guns.
3. If Indigenous peoples **hadn't welcomed** the visitors at first, it **wouldn't have been / may not have been** so easy to start new colonies.
4. If other European powers **hadn't been expanding** their territories in Africa from the 1870s, Germany **may not have joined / wouldn't have joined** the competition and **started** its own colonies there.

Exercise 4

1. If explorers **hadn't reached** America, we possibly **wouldn't know** potatoes.
2. If the British **hadn't colonised** India, English **wouldn't be** widely **used** as lingua franca there.
3. If the climate **wasn't tropical** in India, pepper **wouldn't grow** so well there.
4. *(Lösungsvorschlag)* If North America **hadn't been colonised**, many more Indigenous people **would live** there today.
5. *(Lösungsvorschlag)* If it **was / were** possible to travel back in time, many mistakes **could / may / might be** undone.
6. If there **had been** no imperialism, our world **would be** completely different today.

Topic 3

Exercise 1

1. A developer explained that Birmingham had achieved a remarkable transformation in the city centre.
2. The mayor advised not to give up even though there was still a lot of work to be done in some areas. / The mayor stated that they mustn't give up even though …
3. An inhabitant warned that if they didn't act now, some areas of Birmingham might be left behind soon.
4. A former factory worker complained that he / she had been unemployed for five years. He / She wanted to know if there were any measures the City Council was going to take to improve the situation. He / She demanded that politicians (should) do a better job. / He / She added that in his / her opinion, politicians had to do …
5. A member of the City Council mentioned that the City Council would meet there the next day and discuss what could be done to support disadvantaged neighbourhoods.

Exercise 2

Text type: article; **audience**: readers of a local newspaper; **style / register:** formal.
Content:
Headline: Exciting plans for the transformation of Digbeth / …
Include the following information using the passive voice:

- A lot of money has been invested by the government to regenerate disadvantaged neighbourhoods.
- Plans to transform Digbeth have been submitted (by developers).
- Old industrial buildings are to be converted into new residential homes. / It is intended to convert old …
- It is planned to bring the River Rea back into the city centre, running in a channel below street level. / The River Rea is planned to be brought back …
- An important aim is that buildings should be constructed with less carbon emissions.
- If planning permission is granted (by the council), new riverside neighbourhoods including new homes, restaurants, shops, flexible workspace and parks will be built.
- Several events to help answer the community's questions will be held by the council.
- The plans can be viewed and comments can be made by members of the public.
- A similar change to the district's face has never been experienced (before) (by the people of Digbeth).

Exercise 3

Individual answers.

Topic 4

Exercise 1

1. Giving extra information, non-defining: The most important Hindu gods are Brahma, Vishnu and Shiva, **each of whom has** a specific role. / The most important Hindu gods are Brahma, Vishnu and Shiva. **They each have** a specific role.
2. Giving extra information, non-defining: Brahma, **who is usually depicted** with four faces and four arms, is the creator of all things and beings. / Brahma **is usually depicted** with four faces and four arms **and** is the creator of all things and beings.
3. Giving extra information, defining: One says he was born in a lotus flower **which was growing** out of Vishnu's navel.
4. Shortening adverbial clause of time: Another says when **he was creating** the cosmic waters, Brahma planted a seed in them which turned into a golden egg.
5. Shortening adverbial clause of time: **When it had emerged** from it, the egg expanded and became the universe.
6. Shortening adverbial clause of reason: **As he is** responsible for returning to earth to restore the balance between good and evil whenever necessary, he has been reincarnated nine different times.
7. Explaining the implication / consequence of sth: It is believed that he will return a tenth and final time, **and in this way will indicate** the end of the world.
8. Giving extra information, non-defining: Like Brahma, he has four arms, **each of which holds** a different symbol of power: a discus, a lotus flower, a shell trumpet and a club. / Like Brahma, he has four arms, **which each hold** a

different symbol of power: a discus, a lotus flower, a shell trumpet and a club. / Like Like Brahma, he has four arms. **Each of them holds** a different symbol of power: a discus, a lotus flower, a shell trumpet and a club.

9. Shortening adverbial clause of concession; giving extra information, non-defining: **Although it is sometimes viewed** negatively, destruction is seen as an essential part of creation, **which enables** positive change.
10. Giving extra information, defining: He is often shown **as a man who is carrying** a trident and **wearing** a cobra around his neck.
11. Explaining the way sth is done: According to legend, Shiva was once meditating when his wife Parvati covered his eyes. **She did not think** of the consequences.
12. Shortening adverbial clause of reason: **As it did not have** the light from Shiva's eyes, the universe was plunged into darkness. / The universe was plunged into darkness **because it did not have** the light from Shiva's eyes.

Exercise 2

1. The elephant-headed god Ganesh, **said** to remove obstacles and bring happiness, is a very popular Indian god. / **Said** to remove obstacles and bring happiness, the elephant-headed god Ganesh is a very popular Indian god.
2. **Before beginning** a new project, **moving** into a new house or **going** on a journey, people often ask for Ganesh's blessing.
3. According to a legend, Parvati, **not wanting** anyone to disturb her bath, made a boy out of some paste.
4. **After breathing / Having breathed** life into it, she told the boy to guard the door to the bathroom.
5. **Having been told** not to let anyone pass, the boy did not even let Shiva go inside.
6. Shiva became very angry and cut off the boy's head, **(thus) killing** him immediately.
7. **Parvati being** extremely sad, Shiva promised to cut the head off the next living creature he saw **(in order) to replace** the boy's head.
8. Shiva saw an elephant and **after putting** its head on the boy's body, Shiva said that the boy would be the leader of his ganas and called him Ganesh.

Exercise 3

Lösungsvorschlag: Diwali, a special festival for Hindus, is called the Festival of Light. Coming from the Sanskrit *dipwali*, the word means "row of lights". The festival takes place every autumn, marking the start of the Hindu New Year. People all around the world celebrate the holiday representing the triumph of light over darkness and good over evil. They often decorate their homes with oil lamps called *diyas*. They light them for the goddess Lakshmi to find her way into their homes. She is the goddess of wealth and fortune, believed to bring prosperity for the coming year. It is a time for people to exchange gifts, wear new clothes, eat together and enjoy fireworks. Going back to ancient times, the festival is not just celebrated by Hindus but also by Sikhs, Jains and Buddhists.

Topic 5

Exercise 1

- The sentences are very short.
- The grammar is too repetitive and lacks variety.
- The sentences are not connected with pronouns, linking words or relative clauses.
- Some of the vocabulary is very basic and repetitive.

Exercise 2

Lösungsvorschlag: Globalisation 4.0 is a recent concept, which suggests that we are at the start of a new era of globalisation. It proposes that some established thinking about economics will be replaced by newer ideas and there will be significant improvements in technology resulting in the world becoming more globalised. This will result in improved lives for all people and in a reduced impact on the environment.

However, there is a problem with this concept. Global supply chain problems have led to price increases and this, in turn, has brought about food shortages and energy price increases. Some reasons for this include the COVID-19 pandemic and the war in Ukraine. It has been suggested by some people (including business and political leaders) that these issues will lead to 'deglobalisation' of the world economy.

Many businesses have 'just-in-time' supply chains, transporting essential goods between countries just before they are needed. This could change to a 'just-in-case' system, which means keeping a lot of things that may be needed in case there are problems with supply chains. Some businesses which currently use factories in faraway countries to save money could switch to using factories that are more expensive but much nearer. This would be less risky for both economic and political reasons, but it would also result in a less globalised economy.

Exercise 3

a)

1. something previously seen / experienced (French); alternative: I feel I've seen it all before.
2. gung-ho: over-confident, reckless (Chinese); tsunami: sudden huge amount / number (Japanese); alternative: … a reckless attitude … by a huge number of bad debts.
3. marketplace (Persian); alternative: global marketplace
4. high status, prestige (Greek); alternative: … still holds high status in many parts of the world.
5. photographer of celebrities, especially for sensational newspapers / magazines (Italian); alternative: Some celebrities avoid press photographers…
6. leader specialising in one area, especially in politics (Russian); alternative: The government has appointed a new leader for its climate policy.
7. digital graphic which represents a person (Hindi); alternative: Look, this is how I appear in the game.
8. minor technical problem (Yiddish); alternative: There have been some minor technical problems with our supply chain recently.

b) How the words have come to be used / Reasons:

- Sometimes one language has a word for something that another language lacks.
- The import word may have a subtle difference in meaning to the equivalent native word.

- The word may describe an item which is specific to the culture of another country (e.g. 'pizza'/Italy).
- The word may have been popularised in a literary work (e.g. 'bourgeoisie'/French for the middle class in the writings of Karl Marx).

Effect:
- Loanwords in some cases evoke the culture they are borrowed from, and that can be used to create a certain impression. For example, bazaar sounds more exotic in a Western context than marketplace.
- A loanword may allow a concept to be expressed more precisely / effectively / elegantly / briefly than would be possible otherwise.

c) Individual answers. Examples from German:
- skateboard, baby, stress, jeans, container, laptop, online, team: same meaning
- public viewing: In German this means to watch a game in a public space with a large audience; the English meaning is to go see a corpse or to give the public the chance to see an artwork or something not usually on public display.
- handy: In German this is your mobile phone; in English it means to have something readily available or that something is practical

Exercise 4

a) **Examples of indicators of not moving towards deglobalisation:** continued economic growth | continuing global expansion of the internet and communications technology | widespread political and business desire for ever-increasing globalisation | obvious benefits, such as making travel, studying abroad etc. easier
Examples of indicators of moving towards deglobalisation: global supply chain problems | increasing nationalism | regional conflicts | negative public opinion on the effects of globalisation

b) Individual answers.

Grammar

G1

1. **focused**: in the past, over; **had become**: took place before the event in the main clause
2. **didn't focus / became**: past tense with "not until", no past perfect needed although the event in the main clause took place before the one in the subordinate clause
3. **claimed**: in the past, over; **had to shift**: past tense form of modal auxiliary needed because of indirect speech
4. **were industrialised**: in the past, over, passive (not important / possible to tell who exactly did it); **were built**: in the past, over, passive (not important / possible to tell who exactly did it); **came**: in the past, over, event in the main clause took place at the same time or shortly after events in the subordinate clause
5. **have ... been**: in the past, over, but not important when exactly; **have visited**: in the past, over, repeated several times, but not important when exactly
6. **has lost**: in the past, over, but not long ago and the effect is still relevant, visible
7. **have been living**: started in the past, still going on

G2

1. **rains**: always true
2. **was raining**: emphasis on duration (dynamic verb); **were walking**: emphasis on duration (dynamic verb), two events taking place at the same time
3. **was waiting**: emphasis on duration (dynamic verb); **rang**: sth happened in the middle of something else
4. **are talking**: emphasis on sth that is going on at the moment
5. **meet**: regular event; **talk**: regular event
6. **had been training**: emphasis on duration (dynamic verb) of sth that is over; **arrived**: sth put an end to what was going on
7. **joined**: in the past, over, emphasis on the result rather than the process of sth; **had heard**: took place before, emphasis on the result rather than the process of sth
8. **have been rising**: emphasis on the ongoing process that isn't over yet
9. **had known**: stative verb; **was**: indirect speech

G3

1. type 3; 2. type 2; 3. mixed, past perfect / conditional;
4. mixed, past tense / conditional perfect; 5. type 2; 6. type 1;
7. mixed, past tense / conditional perfect

G4

1. We flew to New York **because we wanted** to get to know the city.
2. We flew to New York **because we had always wanted** to get to know the city.
3. **After / When we had checked in**, we had a coffee in the airport lounge.
4. He answered the police officer's questions **while he was** still in shock.
5. **As his things were** in total disorder, it took him some time to find out what had been stolen. / It took him some time to find out what had been stolen because his things were in total disorder.
6. My mother, **who had returned** from work, was surprised to find me at home. / **When my mother had returned** from work, she was surprised to find me at home.
7. The boss appreciated the job **that / which had been done** by her team.
8. **As I was confused** by the way the questions were asked, I wasn't able to answer them immediately. / I wasn't able to answer the questions immediately **because I was confused** by the way they were asked.
9. He tried to walk away quickly **and / while his dog was following him** and **barking** loudly.

G5

1. gerund construction referring to the way something is done, German "*Modalsatz: indem ...*"
2. infinitive construction referring to intention / purpose, German "*Finalsatz: damit ... / um ... zu ...*"
3. infinitive construction (Latin: ACI), same construction as "to want / like / hate sb to do sth", German: "*dass ...*")
4. gerund construction referring to opposites, German "*Adversativsatz: anstatt, dass ... / anstatt ... zu ...*"
5. gerund after certain phrases, similar to "It's no use ..., "There's no point in ...", German: "*dass ... / zu ...*"

G6

1. defining; 2. non-defining; 3. defining, contact clause possible; 4. defining; 5. sentential (commenting), non-defining; 6. defining, contact clause possible

G7

1. To emphasise that they do it without help
2. To emphasise that she has done it without help;
3. To emphasise that he spoke to us in person
4. To emphasise the house as such
5. To emphasise the verb phrase
6. cleft sentence (splitting one sentence into a main clause and a relative clause to emphasise the subject)
7. cleft sentence (splitting one sentence into a main clause and a relative clause to emphasise the adverbial of place)
8. cleft sentence (splitting one sentence into a main clause and a relative clause to emphasise the adverbial of time)
9. cleft sentence (splitting one sentence into a main clause and a what-clause to emphasise the object)

Thematic vocabulary

Topic 1

Prepositions

a) 1 of; 2. against; 3. with; 4. from; 5. of; 6. in; 7. for; 8. on; 9. to; 10. for; 11. by; 12. by; 13. on; 14. of; 15. in

b)

1. to get along (with) = to like each other / to have a friendly relationship with sb: **I get along** really well with people in New York. They're all so polite.
2. to show up = to arrive somewhere (possibly late or unexpected): Jane finally **showed up** at the party.
3. to pick up = to collect sb / sth: You can order a taxi to **pick** you **up** anywhere you want.
4. to go out = to leave your home (esp. to do sth entertaining) / to go to a bar, club etc.: Yesterday, I **went out** with my friends in London.
5. to fit in = to be accepted by / to belong to a particular group: I feel like I **don't fit in** at school.
6. to miss out (on sth) = to fail to use an opportunity / to miss an opportunity or event: You shouldn't **miss out on** the chance to go abroad just because you might feel homesick.
7. to catch up with sb = to go faster to reach sb: You can go to the mall right now, **I'll catch up with** you there.
8. to carry on = to go on / to continue to do sth: If you want to make it on Broadway, you can't give up now – you have to **carry on**.
9. to be up to = to plan / to scheme to do sth: What do you think Josh **is up to**?
10. to make sth up = to invent sth: Lisa **made up** a ridiculous excuse for her missing homework.
11. to give in = to finally agree to sth / to accept sth: They refused to **give in** and stuck to the original plan.

Word families

1. to adapt: adaptation, adapter, adapted, adaptive, adaptable, …
2. attraction: to attract, attractive, attractiveness, …
3. to benefit (from): benefit, beneficial, beneficent, …
4. to breathe: to breathe in / out, breath, breathable, breath-taking, breathless, …
5. equality: equal / unequal, to equalise, inequality, …
6. historic: history, historian, historical, …
7. home: homeless, homelessness, homesick, homey, hometown, homeland, homegrown, home-made, homeward, homeboy, …
8. justice: injustice, just / unjust, to justify, justified / unjustified, justification, …
9. memorial: memory, to memorise, memorable, memorandum, memoir, …
10. pollution: to pollute, polluter, polluted, polluting, non-polluting, low-polluting, pollutant, …
11. population: (densely / sparsely) populated, to populate, populous, the populace, …
12. settler: to settle, to settle down, settled, settlement, to settle an argument, …

Topic 2

Synonyms and definitions

a) 1. era; 2. legacy; 3. battle; 4. merchant; 5. spice; 6. segregation; 7. boundary; 8. atrocity; 9. shack; 10. token; 11. expatriate; 12. riot; 13. warrior; 14. treaty

b) 1. treaty; 2. spices; 3. token; 4. riots; 5. atrocities

c)

1. reservation *(AE)*: a territory where Native Americans were forced to live
2. to evict: to remove sb from their territory / home by force
3. apartheid: a political system of racial segregation in South Africa in the 20th century
4. to conquer: to take control of a place (or a group of people) with (military) force
5. township: an area / a sector of South African towns where the Non-white population was relocated to during apartheid.
6. curfew: a rule / law prohibiting people from leaving their house during a certain time period (usually at night)
7. civil disobedience: a peaceful form of political protest carried out by civilians
8. residential school: a governmental boarding school for Indigenous children (First Nations, Inuit and Métis) in Canada run by churches and religious organisations where the children were mostly treated cruelly and many died from diseases
9. genocide: the systematic killing of a national, political, religious or ethnic group
10. reconciliation: when former opponents / enemies agree on peace or settle their argument

Formal vs informal

a)

1. to assimilate: My parents **assimilated** to the German culture very well after they immigrated from Vietnam.
2. to abuse: Politicians who **abuse** their position of power should be instantly removed from office.
3. to enfranchise: In Germany, women **were enfranchised** in 1918.
4. to prohibit: Did you know that alcohol **was prohibited** in the USA during the 1920s?
5. to exterminate: Due to the eruption of Mount Vesuvius, all of Pompeii **was exterminated**.

6. to decimate: Intensive farming **has decimated** many species.
7. to evict: They **were evicted** from their apartment because they hadn't paid rent on time.

b) 1. because of; 2. to allow; 3. to suppress / to put down; 4. to be forced (to do) / to have to (do); 5. hostility; 6. senselessness / meaninglessness; 7. to continue

c)
1. European countries mostly **conquered** new territories by force.
2. The government finally **apologised** for the atrocities that took place in residential schools.
3. The British began to **colonise** India during the 1600s.
4. Britain's power was based on **trading** with its colonies.
5. At its peak, the British Empire **dominated** around a quarter of the globe.
6. It can be difficult to **assimilate** into a new culture.

Visions of the future

Word fields

2. **genetic engineering:**
- **fields of application / technologies:** medicine, agriculture, reproduction, gene editing, IVF, ...
- **chances:** to eradicate diseases, cloning, to make plants more resistant, ...
- **fears:** 'designer babies', abortion of disabled embryos, selection, unknown long-term consequences, ...

3. **artificial intelligence (AI):**
- **general terms:** machine learning, algorithm, software, robots, ...
- **chances:** robots carrying out undesirable work, driverless vehicles, eliminating human error, ...
- **fears:** job losses, privacy violations, (political) manipulation, deep fakes, ...

4. **surveillance:**
- **means of surveillance:** CCTV, cookies, drones, to listen in to conversations, to control messages, ...
- **reasons:** to increase safety, to prevent crimes, more efficient policing, ...
- **fears:** constant surveillance, invasion of privacy, restriction of personal freedom, police state, ...

5. **natural disasters:**
- **types:** flood, drought, earthquake, hurricane, wildfire, tsunami, ...
- **causes:** global warming, greenhouse gas, melting glaciers, rising sea levels, monocultures, use of pesticides, arson, ...
- **consequences:** casualties, famines, economic damage, (mass) migration, extinction of species, ...

6. **environmental protection:**
- **areas:** climate, water, soil, air, flora and fauna, ...
- **participants:** environmental activists, politicians, civilians, companies, ...
- **activities:** using renewable energies, sustainable / organic farming, not wasting natural resources, creating more natural reserves, using public transport, ...

Working with adjectives and verbs

a) 1. harmful / harmless; 2. repetitive; 3. desirable; 4. natural; 5. endless; 6. technological; 7. genetic; 8. educational; 9. profitable; 10. scientific; 11. intrusive; 12. powerful / powerless; 12. accessible; 14. economic / economical; 15. reproductive; 16. recyclable; 17. political; 18. successful

b) 1. to globalise; 2. to justify; 3. to weaken; 4. to digitalise; 5. to modernise; 6. to diversify; 7. to threaten; 8. to clarify; 9. to specialise; 10. to intensify; 11. to shorten; 12. to electrify; 13. to individualise; 14. to modify

c) 1. accessible; 2. technological / endless; 3. repetitive; 4. genetically; 5. modified; 6. harmful; 7. modernise

Topic 3

Collocations

1. e.g. **internet** access / connection / user / site / traffic / link; to go on / to shop on / to use / to connect to / to access / to surf **the internet**; wireless / high-speed / (un)stable **internet**
2. e.g. **data** management / storage / security / set; to collect / to store / to process / to exchange / to transfer / to analyse / to manipulate **data**; accurate / reliable / empirical / raw / sensitive **data**
3. e.g. **security** system / check / services / camera / staff / arrangements / risk; to give / to provide / to improve / to ensure **security**; economic / financial / maximum / strict / lax / national **security**
4. e.g. **privacy** invasion / policy / regulations / protection / settings / violation / issues / concerns; to respect / to protect / to violate / to invade / to disturb (sb's) **privacy**; complete / individual / strict **privacy**
5. e.g. phone / distribution / road / rail / terrorist / computer **network**; to establish / to operate / to maintain / to modernise a **network**; large / complex / supportive / global / local / social **network**

Word building: Nouns and conversion

a) 1. manufacturing / manufacturer; 2. consumption / consumer; 3. business; 4. domination / dominance; 5. employment / employer; 6. approval; 7. growth; 8. security; 9. transformation / transformer; 10. competence; 11. revival; 12. engagement; 13. awareness; 14. dismissal; 15. setting; 16. necessity; 17. worker

b) e.g. (to) boost, (to) decline, (to) increase, (to) change, (to) age, (to) craft, (to) power, (to) progress, (to) smoke, (to) challenge, (to) strike, (to) transition, (to) access, (to) launch, (to) track
Example sentences: Individual answers.

c)
1. to bottle (= to pour liquid into bottles and seal them): Grandma and I **bottled** our self-made juice in August.
2. to eye (= to look at sb / sth with interest): She constantly **eyed** his food because she was hungry.
3. to dwarf (= to be a lot taller than sb / sth): My son already **dwarfs** me by around three inches.
4. to chair (= to be in charge of a meeting / event / organisation): My mom **chaired** the assembly yesterday.
5. to ship (= to transport sth / sb by sea, air, train, road): **Shipping** our piano from L.A. to New York by truck was very expensive.
6. to tower (= to be very tall or large): The Empire State building **towered** directly in front of us.

Topic 4

Opposites

a) **no opposites:** 1./4./5./8./10./12./13./15.
opposites: 2. (in)equality; 3. (dis)obedience; 6. (un)profitable; 7. (ir)reversible; 9. (de)globalisation; 11. (il)legal; 14. (im)mortal; 16. (in)voluntary; 17. (un)constitutional

b) 1. intolerance; 2. unacceptable; 3. disadvantage; 4. decolonisation; 5. unification; 6. injustice, unjust; 7. to destroy; 8. minority; 9. unequal; 10. poverty / failure; 11. conviction / judgement / sentence; 12. incapable; 13. urban
Example sentences: Individual answers.

Learning in context

a)

1. to grant = to give, to allow; ↔ to take away, to withdraw, to refuse
2. ancient = old; ↔ modern
3. caste system → discrimination, social segregation, injustice, hierarchical order, karma, ...
4. to contemplate = to think (carefully) about, to consider
5. to displace = to evict, to throw out
6. illiteracy ↔ literacy; → education, unable to read and write, problems at school / with finding a job / in everyday life, to feel ashamed, ...
7. secular ↔ religious
8. corruption → money (laundering), to bribe, politicians, civil servants, crime, illegal, (inter)national networks, ...
9. to fracture = to break
10. judiciary → trial, verdict / judgement, acquittal, judge, defendant / the accused, lawyer, law, crime, victim, (un)fair treatment, (in)justice, witness, ...
11. to struggle for = to fight for
12. international relations → trade (in sth / with sb), export, import, to establish / improve / break off relations (with), relations can deteriorate / worsen, (geopolitical) tensions, global player, ...
13. police brutality → racism, discrimination (against), white supremacy, to shoot, killing, prejudice, arbitrary, abuse of power, ...
14. electorate → election, electoral system, electoral manipulation, to vote, voter turnout, candidate, campaign, politicians, to stand for / to run for, democracy, ...
15. impact = effect, influence

Topic 5

'Word partners' (collocations)

a) 1. global; 2. trade / village / economy / ...; 3. environmental; 4. issues / regulation / pollution / ...; 5. cultural; 6. venue / identity / diversity / ...; 7. sustainable; 8. transport / way of living / fashion / ...

b) carbon emissions, climate change, financial market, fossil fuel, immigration laws, power grid, raw materials, supply chain

c)

1. e.g. free / fair / illegal / international / slave / drug **trade**; **trade** agreement / barrier / union / route; to conduct / to develop / to expand / to restrict / to promote **trade**
2. e.g. **policy** decision / making / maker; government / company / trade / controversial / environmental / economic **policy**; to carry out / to follow / to change **a policy**
3. e.g. (socio)economic / significant / sustainable / population / income / GDP **growth**; **growth** rate / area / potential; to accelerate / to boost / to measure **growth**
4. e.g. e-(electronic) / toxic / harmful / industrial / general **waste**; **waste** dump / disposal; to produce / to reduce / to recycle / to dump **waste**
5. e.g. environmental / industrial / air / water / noise / light **pollution**; to cause / to avoid / to reduce / to cut **pollution**; **pollution** level / prevention
6. e.g. (un)skilled / child / slave / risky / hard / arduous **labour**; **labour** market / movement; **labour**-intensive / -saving
7. e.g. nuclear / sustainable / green / clean / renewable / solar / wind / low-cost **energy**; **energy** production / consumption / supply / prices / sources; to waste / to save / to consume **energy**; **energy**-efficient / -saving

Dealing with difficult words

1. sight *(Sehkraft; Anblick; Sehenswürdigkeit)*: The eye specialist said that my **sight** has decreased. / The **sight** of the mountains is marvellous. / Paris has countless **sights**.
2. concrete *(Beton; konkret)*: The grey building over there is made of **concrete**, isn't it? / What's the **concrete** aim of this project?
3. crime *(Kriminalität; Verbrechen)*: We hope this measure will lead to decreasing **crime** rates. / She claimed that she hadn't committed the **crime**.
4. reservation *(Reservat; Reservierung)*: Even on their **reservations**, Indigenous peoples were abused and exploited by white people. / I made a **reservation** for 7pm.
5. to abuse *(missbrauchen; misshandeln; beschimpfen)*: The judge **abused** his power to send him to prison. / People who **abuse** their pets should be punished more severely. / Having received a red card, the footballer started **abusing** the referee.
6. diet *(Ernährung; Diät)*: A well-balanced **diet** is important for our health. / You know that most **diets** don't lead to long-term benefits, right?
7. to consume *(konsumieren; verbrauchen)*: People should **consume** meat more consciously. / Our fridge **consumes** too much energy.
8. craft = *Handwerk, Fertigkeit* (≠ *Kraft* = power; strength): She knows the **craft** of watchmaking. / I can't lift the box – I haven't got enough **power** in my arms.
9. economical = *sparsam* (≠ *ökonomisch* = economic): We need to live more **economical**. The prices are skyrocketing. / **Economic** growth can't last forever.
10. capital *(Kapital; Hauptstadt)*: Starting a company usually requires lots of **capital**. / Berlin is the **capital** of Germany.
11. labour *(Arbeit; Arbeitskräfte; Wehen)*: Child **labour** still exists in many places of the world. / Skilled **labour** is in high demand on the job market. / She went into **labour** in the middle of the night.
12. to stand for *(kandidieren; für etw. stehen)*: My uncle plans **to stand for** mayor. / The company **stands for** producing sustainable fashion.

Bildquellenverzeichnis Action Press GmbH, Hamburg (SOPA Images/SIPA), **104.1**; akg-images, Berlin (GandhiServe India), **221.1**; Alamy stock photo, Abingdon (FineArt [Portrait of a Young Man Bronzino, 1530]), **178.2**; Alamy stock photo, Abingdon (Jacob King/PA Images), **72.2**; Alamy stock photo, Abingdon (Joerg Boethling), **145.1**; Alamy stock photo, Abingdon (Lebrecht Music & Arts), **49.1**; Alamy stock photo, Abingdon (North Wind Picture Archives), **98.1**; Alamy stock photo, Abingdon (RGB Ventures/SuperStock), **122.1**; Alamy stock photo, Abingdon (Tetra Images/Jasmine Hartsook), **56.2**; Alamy stock photo, Abingdon (Tim Gainey), **96.1**; Bridgemanimages.com, Berlin, **52.1**; **180.1**; **180.2**; Bridgemanimages.com, Berlin (Patrice Normand/Leextra), **129.1**; CartoonStock Ltd, Bath (Bill Whitehead), **67.1**; CartoonStock Ltd, Bath (Bob Mankoff), **51.2**; CartoonStock Ltd, Bath (Gahan Wilson), **9.1**; CartoonStock Ltd, Bath (Gustavo Rodriguez), **9.2**; CartoonStock Ltd, Bath (Len Hawkins), **115.1**; CartoonStock Ltd, Bath (McGinn, Steve), **78.1**; CartoonStock Ltd, Bath (Patrick Forde), **51.1**; CartoonStock Ltd, Bath (Tom Toro), **89.1**; ddp media GmbH, Hamburg, **110.2**; Dekelver, Christian Illustration, Weinstadt, **232.1**; **233.1**; Dekelver, Christian, Weinstadt, **73.1**; **231.1**; Dekelver, Christian, Weinstadt ; U.S. Census Bureau release, the 2020 American Community Survey; (Means of transport), **20.1**; Ernst Klett Verlag GmbH, Stuttgart, **166.1**; **167.1**; **177.2**; **177.3**; **177.4**; Ernst Klett Verlag GmbH, Stuttgart ; IMF; (Ranking der 20 Länder mit dem größten Bruttoinlandsprodukt (BIP) im Jahr 2021), **114.3**; Ernst Klett Verlag GmbH, Stuttgart ; nach: Statista/Öko-Institut e.V. 2020/ CC-BY-ND-4.0; (Vorlagegrafik: CO2-Fußabdruck), **83.1**; Ernst Klett Verlag GmbH, Stuttgart ; Pew Reserach Center/Survey conducted Nov. 1–7, 2021; (Majority says brain chip implants for improved cognitive abilities would be bad idea for society; public more open to other applications of human enhancement and AI), **80.1**; Ernst Klett Verlag GmbH, Stuttgart ; Source: CIA WorldFactbook, 2021, **103.2**; Ernst Klett Verlag GmbH, Stuttgart ; Source: U.S. Census Bureau, International Database, 2021, **103.1**; Ernst Klett Verlag GmbH, Stuttgart ; Wikipedia, 2022; (Vorlagegrafik: Birmingham population 1650–1950), **68.1**; Ernst Klett Verlag GmbH, Stuttgart (Klett-Archiv), **234–235.1**; Ernst Klett Verlag GmbH, Stuttgart; nach: (1) CollegeFactual.com; (2–3) United States Census Bureau. American Community Survey 2014–2018 5-Year Estimates., **11.1**; Ernst Klett Verlag GmbH, Stuttgart; Source: Umwelt: https://datenplattform.darmstadt.de (Screenshots vom 26.07.2022, 16:00 Uhr); (Umwelt); Verkehr: https://datenplattform.darmstadt.de (Screenshots vom 26.07.2022, 16:00 Uhr); (Verkehr); Veranstaltungen: https://datenplattform.darmstadt.de (Screenshots vom 26.07.2022, 16:00 Uhr); (Veranstaltungen), **87.1**; Getty Images Plus, München (AVTG), **173.1**; Getty Images Plus, München (blowbackphoto), **18.1**; Getty Images Plus, München (Christy Strever/EyeEm), **124.1**; Getty Images Plus, München (Digital Vision/Klaus Vedfelt), **149.1**; Getty Images Plus, München (DigitalVision/Plume Creative), **31.1**; Getty Images Plus, München (E+/ChrisHepburn), **97.2**; Getty Images Plus, München (E+/Delmaine Donson), **103.4**; Getty Images Plus, München (fizkes), **170.2**; Getty Images Plus, München (iStock/Jennifer Watson), **101.2**; Getty Images Plus, München (iStock/Brasil2), **79.1**; Getty Images Plus, München (kutaytanir/E+), **62.1**; Getty Images Plus, München (metamorworks), **56.1**; Getty Images Plus, München (Mike Powles), **94.1**; Getty Images Plus, München (Moment/john images), **103.3**; Getty Images Plus, München (Moment/Smartshots International), **30.3**; Getty Images Plus, München (Motortion), **177.1**; Getty Images Plus, München (Orbon Alija), **Cover.2**; Getty Images Plus, München (philips), **165.1**; Getty Images Plus, München (SDI Productions), **64.1**; Getty Images Plus, München (vgajic), **156.1**; Getty Images, München (Anadolu Agency), **118.2**; Getty Images, München (Cavan Images), **58.1**; Getty Images, München (GUY TILLIM/AFP), **37.1**; Getty Images, München (JACQUES DEMARTHON), **106.2**; Getty Images, München (Joan Adlen Photography), **14.1**; Getty Images, München (Priya Ramrakha), **127.1**; Getty Images, München (Quinn Harris/Kontributor), **112.1**; Getty Images, München (SEAN KILPATRICK/Kontributor), **220.2**; Getty Images, München (Sergione Infuso – Corbis), **14.3**; Getty Images, München (SIMON MAINA/Freier Fotograf), **50.1**; Getty Images, München (Susan Winters Cook), **38.1**; Getty Images, München (TONY KARUMBA), **106.1**; IMAGO, Berlin (i Images), **107.1**; IMAGO, Berlin (IPON), **125.1**; IMAGO, Berlin (Leemage), **99.1**; IMAGO, Berlin (ZUMA Press), **47.1**; **108.1**; IMAGO, Berlin (ZUMA Wire), **108.2**; Interfoto, München (Writer Pictures Ltd/NMG), **126.1**; iStockphoto, Calgary, Alberta (E+/track5), **111.1**; iStockphoto, Calgary, Alberta (Matt Jeacock), **172.1**; Kate Raworth and Christian Guthier. CC-BY-SA 4.0 https://creativecommons.org/licenses/by-sa/4.0/deed.de, Mountain View ; CC-BY-SA-4.0 Lizenzbestimmungen: https://creativecommons.org/licenses/by-sa/4.0/legalcode; (The Doughnut of social and planetary boundaries (2017) vom Artikel "Doughnut Economic" model arrives in California), **134.1**; laif, Köln (Fernando Moleres), **123.2**; laif, Köln (Sandra Hoyn), **123.1**; Library of Congress, Prints & Photographs Division, C. M. Bell Studio Collection, [Reproduction number LC-DIG-bellcm-10974 (digital file from original)]., **49.2**; Mauritius Images, Mittenwald (Alamy Stock Photos), **25.1**; Mauritius Images, Mittenwald (Andy Barton/Alamy), **88.4**; Mauritius Images, Mittenwald (Arthur Greenberg/Alamy), **114.1**; Mauritius Images, Mittenwald (CPA Media Pte Ltd/Alamy), **99.2**; Mauritius Images, Mittenwald (Francis Vachon/Alamy), **41.2**; Mauritius Images, Mittenwald (Gordon Shoosmith/Alamy), **92.4**; Mauritius Images, Mittenwald (Jeff Gilbert/Alamy), **56.4**; Mauritius Images, Mittenwald (Jeff Morgan 16/Alamy), **72.1**; Mauritius Images, Mittenwald (John Gaffen/Alamy/Alamy Stock Photos), **105.1**; Mauritius Images, Mittenwald (Jonny White/Alamy/Alamy Stock Photos), **41.1**; Mauritius Images, Mittenwald (Keystone Press/Alamy), **35.1**; Mauritius Images, Mittenwald (KGPA Ltd/Alamy), **66.1**; Mauritius Images, Mittenwald (Marmaduke St. John/Alamy), **128.1**; Mauritius Images, Mittenwald (Mikhail Rudenko/Alamy), **63.1**; Mauritius Images, Mittenwald (Paula french/Alamy), **90.1**; Mauritius Images, Mittenwald (Peter Titmuss/Alamy), **140.1**; Mauritius Images, Mittenwald (Richard Levine/Alamy), **17.1**; Mauritius Images, Mittenwald (Science Source), **70.1**; Mauritius Images, Mittenwald (Thomas Cockrem/Alamy), **88.2**; Mauritius Images, Mittenwald (Universal Images Group North America LLC/DeAgostini), **35.2**; Mauritius Images, Mittenwald (ZUMA Press, Inc./Alamy), **95.2**; Picture-Alliance, Frankfurt/M. (AP Photo/Jae C. Hong), **36.1**; Picture-Alliance, Frankfurt/M. (AP Photo/The Canadian Press, Paul Chiasson), **30.4**; Picture-Alliance, Frankfurt/M. (ASSOCIATED PRESS), **88.3**; Picture-Alliance, Frankfurt/M. (dpa/EPA/Stefan Zaklin), **80.2**; Picture-Alliance, Frankfurt/M. (EPA), **104.2**; Picture-Alliance, Frankfurt/M. (Keir Gravil), **110.1**; Picture-Alliance, Frankfurt/M. (Roscosmos/Handout), **118.1**; Romo, Virginia, Stuttgart, **179.1**; ShutterStock.com RF, New York, **82.1**; ShutterStock.com RF, New York (Alfmaler), **54.2**; **54.3**; **54.4**; **54.5**; **54.6**; **54.7**; **54.9**; **54.10**; **54.11**; **159.2**; **159.3**; **159.4**; **159.6**; **159.7**; **159.8**; **159.9**; **159.10**; **159.11**; ShutterStock.com RF, New York (Alla Khananashvili), **143.1**; ShutterStock.com RF, New York (Anton Shahrai), **140.2**; ShutterStock.com RF, New York (Antonello Marangi), **56.3**; ShutterStock.com RF, New York (Beach Media), **76.1**; ShutterStock.com RF, New York (Brian Friedman), **14.2**; **14.4**; ShutterStock.com RF, New York (Charoen Krung Photography), **61.4**; ShutterStock.com RF, New York (Christian Bertrand), **113.1**; ShutterStock.com RF, New York (Christina Kohnen), **85.1**; ShutterStock.com RF, New York (chuyuss), **26.2**; ShutterStock.com RF, New York (CRS PHOTO), **96.2**; ShutterStock.com RF, New York (Curioso.Photography), **79.2**; ShutterStock.com RF, New York (Dan Jardine), **12.1**; ShutterStock.com RF, New York (Delpixel), **27.1**; ShutterStock.com RF, New York (Dijise), **220.3**; ShutterStock.com RF, New York (Dmitry Rukhlenko), **97.1**; ShutterStock.com RF, New York (Don Mammoser), **88.1**; ShutterStock.com RF, New York (Drop of Light), **13.1**; ShutterStock.com RF, New York (EkaterinaN), **147.2**; ShutterStock.com RF, New York (elenabsl), **65.1**; ShutterStock.com RF, New York (emin kuliyev), **21.2**; ShutterStock.com RF, New York (Fabian Strauch), **75.1**; ShutterStock.com RF, New York (Fascinadora), **133.1**; ShutterStock.com RF, New York (Feng Yu), **120.1**; ShutterStock.com RF, New York (fivepointsix), **30.1**; ShutterStock.com RF, New York (fizkes), **164.1**; ShutterStock.com RF, New York (f11photo), **29.1**; ShutterStock.com RF, New York (Gary A Corcoran Arts), **44.1**; ShutterStock.com RF, New York (Gorodenkoff), **61.3**; ShutterStock.com RF, New York (Grey82), **30.2**; ShutterStock.com RF, New York (Ground Picture), **61.2**; ShutterStock.com RF, New York (Hannamariah), **41.3**; ShutterStock.com RF, New York (Ingus Kruklitis), **8.2**; ShutterStock.com RF, New York (Irina Strelnikova), **147.1**; ShutterStock.com RF, New York (Jacques Durocher Photo), **57.2**; ShutterStock.com RF, New York (Jennie Book), **58.2**; ShutterStock.com RF, New York (Joyseulay), **55.1**; ShutterStock.com RF, New York (Juergen_Wallstabe), **34.3**; ShutterStock.com RF, New York (Kit Leong), **66.2**; ShutterStock.com RF, New York (Krikkiat), **48.1**; ShutterStock.com RF, New York (Matt Ragen), **92.1**; ShutterStock.com RF, New York (Menara Grafis), **118.3**; ShutterStock.com RF, New York (metamorworks), **143.2**; ShutterStock.com RF, New York (meunierd), **34.4**; ShutterStock.com RF, New York (Miaron Billy), **101.1**; ShutterStock.com RF, New York (MicroOne), **54.1**; **54.8**; **159.1**; **159.5**; ShutterStock.com RF, New York (Moobatto), **141.1**; ShutterStock.com RF, New York (NareshSharma), **93.1**; ShutterStock.com RF, New York (Nick Starichenko), **12.2**; **139.1**; ShutterStock.com RF, New York (Odua Images), **146.1**; ShutterStock.com RF, New York (Okrasiuk), **60.2**; ShutterStock.com RF, New York (Pereslavtseva Katerina), **182.1**; ShutterStock.com RF, New York (petch one), **33.1**; ShutterStock.com RF, New York (Peter Rhys Williams), **38.2**; ShutterStock.com RF, New York (Petr Pohudka), **75.2**; ShutterStock.com RF, New York (PradeepGaurs), **94.2**; ShutterStock.com RF, New York (PrzemoleC), **221.2**; ShutterStock.com RF, New York (Pyty), **220.1**; ShutterStock.com RF, New York (p-jitti), **85.2**; ShutterStock.com RF, New York (Rainer Lesniewski), **121.1**; ShutterStock.com RF, New York (Rawpixel.com), **114.2**; ShutterStock.com RF, New York (RomanSlavik.com), **82.2**; ShutterStock.com RF, New York (Ronnie Chua), **41.4**; ShutterStock.com RF, New York (Scharfsinn), **136.1**; ShutterStock.com RF, New York (Sean Pavone), **26.1**; **29.3**; ShutterStock.com RF, New York (Seventy-Four), **153.1**; ShutterStock.com RF, New York (SNEHIT PHOTO), **144.1**; ShutterStock.com RF, New York (Songquan Deng), **19.1**; ShutterStock.com RF, New York (Sopotnicki), **102.1**; ShutterStock.com RF, New York (Stefan Schug), **45.1**; ShutterStock.com RF, New York (Stefano Ember), **92.3**; ShutterStock.com RF, New York (Steidi), **138.1**; ShutterStock.com RF, New York (Stephen Finn), **117.2**; ShutterStock.com RF, New York (SvetaZi), **60.1**; ShutterStock.com RF, New York

(Taras Vyshnya), **26.3**; ShutterStock.com RF, New York (The Mumus), **142.1**; ShutterStock.com RF, New York (TILT Photography), **29.2**; ShutterStock.com RF, New York (trabantos), **81.1**; ShutterStock.com RF, New York (travelview), **8.3**; ShutterStock.com RF, New York (UNIKYLUCKK), **182.2**; ShutterStock.com RF, New York (Villiers Steyn), **34.1**; ShutterStock.com RF, New York (warunee singlee), **90.2**; ShutterStock.com RF, New York (wavebreakmedia), **153.2**; ShutterStock.com RF, New York (Wirestock Creators), **34.2**; ShutterStock.com RF, New York (YashSD), **95.1**; ShutterStock.com RF, New York (1000 Words), **57.1**; Standbild aus video supplied by BBC Worldwide Learning, London,, **74.1**; stock.adobe.com, Dublin (alexhitrov), **21.3**; stock.adobe.com, Dublin (Brooke Becker), **125.2**; stock.adobe.com, Dublin (CandyRetriever), **178.1**; stock.adobe.com, Dublin (chayakorn), **122.2**; stock.adobe.com, Dublin (deberarr), **21.1**; stock.adobe.com, Dublin (dell), **14.5**; stock.adobe.com, Dublin (Dmitry Rukhlenko), **92.2**; stock.adobe.com, Dublin (drubig-photo), **170.1**; stock.adobe.com, Dublin (FrankBoston), **64.2**; stock.adobe.com, Dublin (jorisvo), **8.1**; stock.adobe.com, Dublin (LIGHTFIELD STUDIOS), **158.1**; stock.adobe.com, Dublin (Monkey Business), **174.1**; stock.adobe.com, Dublin (Nicola), **64.3**; stock.adobe.com, Dublin (oneinchpunch), **Cover.1**; stock.adobe.com, Dublin (pict rider), **71.1**; stock.adobe.com, Dublin (pressmaster), **175.1**; stock.adobe.com, Dublin (ryanking999), **61.1**; stock.adobe.com, Dublin (SvetlanaSF), **141.2**; stock.adobe.com, Dublin (vospalej), **33.2**; stock.adobe.com, Dublin (Wayhome Studio), **158.3**; stock.adobe.com, Dublin (william87), **16.1**; Thinkstock, München (Hemera), **91.1**; Thinkstock, München (iStockphoto), **117.1**; Thinkstock, München (Peter Hansen), **117.3**; Thinkstock, München (Thomas Northcut), **158.2**; This Place, 2019, HighWater Press S. 183, R. van Camp/S. B. Henderson & S. A. Ford, Like a razor slash, **43.1**; 2014, Boclips/AFPTV, **39.1**; **39.2**; 2017, Boclips/AFPTV, **41.5**; 2020, BoClips/SciShow, **119.1**

Textquellenverzeichnis **14.A** Song: Theme from New York, New York. Texter: Ebb, Fred, Verlag/Subverlag: by EMI Unart Catalog Inc. D/A/CH/Osteuropäische Länder: EMI Partnership Musikverlag GmbH, Hamburg; **14.B** Song: Empire State of Mind. Texter: Carter, Shawn/Hunte, Angela/Keyes, Bert/Keys, Alicia/Robinson, Sylvia/Sewell, Janet Andrea/Shuckburgh, Alexander William, Verlag/Subverlag: Carter Boys Music/EMI April Music/Foray Music/Gambi Music Inc/Global Talent Publishing/J Sewell Publishing/Lellow Productions Inc/Masani El Shabazz EMI Music Publishing Germany GmbH, Berlin/Rolf Budde Musikverlag GmbH, Berlin/Neue Welt Musikverlag GmbH, Hamburg/ Universal Music Publishing GmbH, Berlin; **14.C** Song: The Message. Texter: Chase, Clifton Nathaniel/Fletcher, Edward G./Glover, Melvin/Robinson, Sylvia, Verlag/Subverlag: 1985 Sugar Hill Music Publishing Ltd./Rolf Budde Musikverlag GmbH,Berlin; **14.D** Song: Welcome to New York, Text: Swift, Taylor/Tedder, Ryan B., Verlag: Taylor Swift Music/Universal/MCA Music Publishing GmbH, Berlin, Sony/ATV Music Publishing (Germany) GmbH, Berlin/Write me a song Publishing/Downtown Music GmbH/Concord Music GmbH, Berlin/Budde Music Publishing GmbH; **21** Annette Schimanski, 06.02.2018, https://www.travelbook.de; **23** Data from BCG Henderson Institute: Cities of choice, 2021; **24** © Arjun Neil Alim/Evening Standard; **30** UNDP Human Development Report, 2021; **31.1** Peace 1949, Lord Boyd Orr of Brechin. p. 420 Nobel Lectures in Peace, (1926–1950), Nobel Foundation, 1999; **31.2** Anon; **31.3** Sadiq Khan in The Guardian, 4th July 2006. https://www.theguardian.com/commentisfree/2006/jul/04/post193; **31.4** Ambalavaner Sivanandan quoted by Dr Ian Sanjay Patel in the title of his book We're Here Because You Were There: Immigration and the End of Empire. https://blogs.lse.ac.uk/lsereviewofbooks/2021/04/16/author-interview-q-and-a-with-dr-ian-sanjay-patel-on-were-here-because-you-were-there-immigration-and-the-end-of-empire/; **31.5** Kwasi Kwarteng, 23rd October 2011 in The Guardian. https://www.theguardian.com/books/2011/oct/23/paxman-british-empire-review-kwarteng; **37** Nelson Mandela, 20 April 1964, Statement from the dock at the opening of the defence case in the Rivonia Trial; Zur besseren altersgemäßen Verständlichkeit wurde der Originaltext verändert, ohne den Inhalt und/oder Sinn zu verändern.; **39** From: Born a Crime © 2016 Trevor Noah; **42** Leyland Cecco © 2021 Guardian News & Media Ltd.; **43.1** Quote from „Submission to the Joint Review Panel investigating the proposed McKenzie Valley Pipeline," written by David J. Parker on behalf of the Edmonton Friends of the North Environemtal Society, 01.02.2007 published in This Place, 2019, HighWater Press S. 183, R. van Camp/S. B. Henderson & S. A. Ford, Like a razor slash; **43.Sprechblasen** Frank T'seleie quoted in: This Place, 2019, HighWater Press S. 183, R. van Camp/S. B. Henderson & S. A. Ford, Like a razor slash; **44** Leyland Cecco © 2021 Guardian News & Media Ltd.; **49.1** Rudyard Kipling, † 1936; **49.2** H. T. Johnson, published 1899; **50** From: How to Write About Africa © 2005 Binyavanga Wainaina.; **51.1** Attributed to Carolyn See; **51.2** From: 1066 and all that © 1930 Walter Carruthers Sellar and Robert Julian Yeatman; **51.3** From: What Is History? © 1961 Edward Hallett Carr; **52. Task 1** From: Homegoing © 2017, Yaa Gyasi; **56** Henri-Frédéric Amiel † 1881; **57** From: 1984, George Orwell † 1950; **59.Task 2** attributed to Ray Bradbury; **60** Ian Sample, Hannah Devlin © 2023 Guardian News & Media Ltd.; **61** Warren G. Bennis quoted in The 4-Hour Workweek: Escape 9-5, Live Anywhere, and Join the New Rich © 2009 Timothy Ferriss; **67.1** Karl Heinrich Marx, † 1883; **67.2** Napoleon Bonaparte, † 1821; **67.3** Attributed to Richard Buckminster Fuller; **67.4** From: Disrupt Yourself Or Be Disrupted: Escape CONFORMITY, Reinvent Your Thinking and Thrive in an Era of Emerging Technologies and Economic Anxiety © 2019 Nicky Verd; **70** Thomas Carlyle, Edinburgh Review, 1829; **71** From: Hard Times, Charles Dickens † 1870; **72** Harriet Sherwood © 2021 Guardian News & Media Ltd.; Zur besseren altersgemäßen Verständlichkeit wurde der Originaltext verändert, ohne den Inhalt und/oder Sinn zu verändern.; **75** Carsten Grün, 21.12.2018, www.dw.com/; **79** From HuffPost. © 2020 BuzzFeed. All rights reserved. Used under license.; **80** Stephen Hawking, 2nd December 2014, www.bbc.com; **82.1** Robert Shore © 2014 Guardian News & Media Ltd.; **82.2** West Midlands Combined Authority, www.wmca.org.uk; **88.1** Anita Desai quoted on p. 204 of Anita Desai and Her Fictional World by Neeru Tandon, 2008; **88.2** Attributed to Jomo Kenyatta; **88.3** 2022 Commonwealth Day Message by Her Majesty The Queen, 14 March 2022; **88.4** Barack Obama, 2016. https://abcnews.go.com/; **92** Shashi Tharoor, sports.ndtv.com, 14th November 2012; **95** Suketu Mehta, in India at 75, 2022. https://pen.org/india-at-75/; **96** Bhavya Dore, 3rd March 2021, www.bbc.com; **97** 2023, https://www.bbc.co.uk/bitesize/topics/z7kvf82/articles/zx8sf82#zj4hn9q2; **103** 2018, British Council, https://www.britishcouncil.org/sites/default/files/h198_next_generation_kenya_a4_final_web.pdf; **104** From The Washington Post. © 2022 The Washington Post. All rights reserved. Used under license. https://www.washingtonpost.com; **107** Oren Gruenbaum, 5th April 2022 in The Round Table; The Commonwealth Journal of International Affairs, https://www.commonwealthroundtable.co.uk; **108** Jason Silverstein © 2021 CBS Interactive Inc.; **110** © 2022 Vanessa Kisuule; **111.1** 2013, Crown Copyright. https://www.gov.uk/government/publications/national-curriculum-in-england-history-programmes-of-study/national-curriculum-in-england-history-programmes-of-study; **111.2** © King's Printer for Ontario, 2012–to 23; **115.1** Katty Kay, www.bbc.com, 24th June 2016; **115.2** Kofi Annan in "Sustainable Development: Humanity's biggest challenge in the new century" in Dhaka, Bangladesh, 15 March 2001.; **115.3** attributed to Rene Girard; **115.4** Javier Yanes, 22nd August 2019, https://gdc.unicef.org/resource/mobile-technologies-third-world-development; **115.5** attributed to Nouriel Roubini; **120** From: Is globalisation really doomed? Author: André Sapir, 03/11/2022, https://www.bruegel.org/blog-post/globalisation-really-doomed, Bruegel AISBL, Brüssel; **121** Prof. Dr. Julia Püschel: Deindustrialisierung und High-Tech in den USA, Bundeszentrale für politische Bildung, Bonn, 13.09.2021, unter: https://www.bpb.de/themen/nordamerika/usa/340178/deindustrialisierung-und-high-tech-in-den-usa/ (Zugriff: 12.04.23, gek.); **122** Nick Dearden © 2023 Guardian News & Media Ltd.; **123** Peter Yeung, 29th May 2019, www.bloomberg.com; **124** Charné Hollands, 11th January 20222, https://energycapitalpower.com; **125** Dr. Gerd Müller, 27. November 2018, www.bmz.de; **128** Robin Lustig, www.bbc.com, 23rd May 2018; **142** A miner's life (traditional); **148** decline: Cambridge Advanced Learner's Dictionary, Fourth Edition, Cambridge University Press; **157** From: A Tale of Two Cities, Charles Dickens † 1870; **160.1** Excerpt from ‚Poem in October' by Dylan Thomas, from „Collected poems" 1934–1952, J. M. Dent & Sons, London, 1952; **160.2** Excerpt from „Making cocoa for Kingsley Amis" by Wendy Cope, from Making cocoa for Kingsley Amis, Faber & Faber, London, 1986; **165.1** Ben Smee, Luke Henriques-Gomes, Guardian News & Media Ltd., 2020; **165.2** Felix Allen; The Sun/News Group Newspapers Limited, London, 2020; **101–102** From: I swear by Apollo © 2002 Margaret Ogola; **105–106** From: Running with the Kenyans: Discovering the secrets of the fastest people on earth © 2012 Adharanand Finn; **118–119** Anna Nagurney, 05.04.2021, theconversation.com; **12–13** From New Yorkers © 2021 Craig Taylor; **126–127** From Decolonizing the Mind: The Politics of Language in African Literature © 1986 Ngugi wa Thiong'o; **129–131** From NATIVE SPEAKER © 1995 by Chang-rae Lee.; **133–134** Robert Raymond, 26.01.2021, www.shareable.net; **136–137** John Naughton, © 2022 Guardian News & Media Ltd.; **14–16** From: It's kind of a funny story © 2007 Ned Vizzini; **17–18** From: Insomniac City © 2017 Bill Hayes; **19–20** From The New York Times. © 2020 The New York Times Company. All rights reserved. Used under license. www.nytimes.com; **25–26** Mark Herlihy, 14.05.2021, https://www.schroders.com; **35–36** From: Born a Crime © 2016 Trevor Noah; **45–47** From: Five Little Indians © 2020 Michelle Good; **52–53** From: Homegoing © 2017, Yaa Gyasi; **54–55.Tasks 5+9** From: Homegoing © 2017, Yaa Gyasi; **58–59** © 1951 Ray Bradbury; **62–63** From: Machines like me © 2019 Ian McEwan; Zur besseren altersgemäßen Verständlichkeit wurde der Originaltext verändert, ohne den Inhalt und/oder Sinn zu verändern.; **64–65** Last Chance by Tyler Young. From: Sunvault Stories of Solarpunk and Eco-Speculation, 2017; **73–74** Jasper Jolly © 2021 Guardian News & Media Ltd.; **76–77** From: Uncanny Valley. A memoir © 2020 Anna Wiener; **83–84** Source: Henry Mance, 2019, Silicon Valley is falling short on climate change. Used under licence from the Financial Times. All Rights Reserved.; **86–87** dpa, 2021; Zur besseren altersgemäßen Verständlichkeit wurde der Originaltext verändert, ohne den Inhalt und/oder Sinn zu verändern.; **93–94** From: How to kidnap the rich © 2021 Rahul Raina; **99–100** From: The Parted Earth © 2021 Anjali Enjeti

NEW YORK
THE BRONX
W 155th St.
Harlem River Dr.
W 145th St.
HARLEM
W 125th St.
Frederick Douglas Blvd.
Adam Clayton Powell Jr. Blvd.
Malcom X Blvd.
National Jazz Museum
Henry Hudson Pkwy.
Broadway
MANHATTAN
Park Avenue
2nd Avenue
1st Avenue
Amsterdam Ave.
Central Park
E 106th St.
Randalls and Wards Island
Hudson River
UPPER WEST SIDE
E 96th St.
5th Avenue
W 81st St.
The Metropolitan Museum of Art
E 84th St.
UPPER EAST SIDE
Lincoln Center
Broadway
E 79th St.
Park Avenue
3rd Avenue
2nd Avenue
1st Avenue
E 66th St.
10th Avenue
9th Avenue
Central Park S.
Steinway Tower
Avenue of the Americas
Lincoln Tunnel
Museum of Modern Art
QUEENS
12th Avenue
W 42nd St.
Rockefeller Center
Queensboro Bridge
Times Square
5th Avenue
W 34th St.
Grand Central Station
Chrysler Building
The High Line
E 42nd St.
MIDTOWN
United Nations
9th Avenue
8th Avenue
7th Avenue
Broadway
Empire State Building
Queens Midtown Tunnel
NEW JERSEY
W 14th St.
E 23rd St.
West Side Highway
Jefferson Market Library
Christopher St.
Greenwich Village
E 14th St.
Hudson St.
Bleecker St.
Holland Tunnel
Soho
Avenue D
Broome St.
Broadway
LOWER WEST SIDE
Canal St.
Little Italy
E Houston St.
East River
LOWER EAST SIDE
Chinatown
Museum at Eldridge Street
Bowery
City Hall
Williamsburg Bridge
One World Trade Center
9/11 Memorial
Wall Street
FDR Drive
Brooklyn Bridge
Manhattan Bridge
ELLIS ISLAND
Brooklyn Battery Tunnel
LIBERTY ISLAND
Statue of Liberty
BROOKLYN
MANHATTAN
THE BRONX
NEW JERSEY
QUEENS
BROOKLYN
STATEN ISLAND

INDIA
TAJIKISTAN
KASHMIR
CHINA
AFGHANISTAN
IRAN
TERRITORIAL
CONFLICT
BORDER
BRITISH INDIA
BEFORE PARTITION
ARUNACHAL
PRADESH
PAKISTAN
Delhi
New Delhi
NEPAL
Jaipur
BHUTAN
Lucknow
Varanasi
Ganges
Ahmedabad
Indore
BANGLADESH
Arabian Sea
Surat
INDIA
Kolkata
MYANMAR
Nagpur
Mumbai
Pune
Hyderabad
Goa
Bengaluru
Chennai
Bay of Bengal
SRI LANKA
Indian Ocean
0
500 km
1000 km

KENYA & SOUTH AFRICA
CENTRAL AFRICAN REPUBLIC
SOUTH SUDAN
ETHIOPIA
CAMEROON
SOMALI
UGANDA
Great
Rift
Valley
KENYA
Iten
Eldoret
Nairobi
GABON
CONGO
RWANDA
BURUNDI
D. R. CONGO
Mombasa
TANZANIA
ANGOLA
ZAMBIA
MALAWI
MOZAMBIQUE
ZIMBABWE
Mozambique
Channel
BOTSWANA
NAMIBIA
Kruger
National
Park
Pretoria
Johannesburg
Soweto
ESWATINI
Atlantic
Ocean
SOUTH AFRICA
LESOTHO
Durban
Cape Town
Gqeberha
0
500 km
1000 km
AFRICA
KENYA
SOUTH AFRICA

Alaska
(U.S.)
Aleutian Is.
(U.S.)
CANADA
UNITED KINGDOM
IRELAND
Channel Is.
(U.K.)
UNITED STATES OF AMERICA
Gibraltar (U.K.)
MALTA
Bermuda
(U.K.)
Hawaiian Islands
(U.S.)
BAHAMAS
Turks and Caicos Is. (U.K.)
Virgin Is. (U.K./U.S.)
Cayman Is.
(U.K.)
Anguilla (U.K.)
ANTIGUA AND BARBUDA
BELIZE
JAMAICA
Puerto Rico (U.S.)
DOMINICA
ST. LUCIA
ST. KITTS AND NEVIS
Montserrat (U.K.)
BARBADOS
GRENADA
ST. VINCENT AND GRENADINES
TRINIDAD AND TOBAGO
GUYANA
THE GAMBIA
NIGERIA
SIERRA LEONE
GHANA
LIBERIA
TOGO
CAMEROON
Palmyra Is.
(U.S.)
Howland Is.
(U.S.)
Jarvis Is.
(U.S.)
KIRIBATI
GABON
Ascension
(U.K.)
UVALU
Tokelau Is. (N.Z.)
SAMOA
American Samoa
(U.S.)
Cook Is.
(N.Z.)
Saint Helena
(U.K.)
NAMIBI
TONGA
Pitcairn Is
(U.K.)
Tristan da Cunha
(U.K.)
Gough Is.
(U.K.)
Falkland Is./
Malvinas (U.K.)
Countries in which English is the / an official language
NAME
Independent Commonwealth stat